THE SOUTH AFRICAN BOOK OF Candlewick Embroidery

THE SOUTH AFRICAN BOOK OF Candlewick Embroidery

SUE MILLARD

Photography by Alain Proust

STRUIK

ACKNOWLEDGEMENTS

I am indebted to many people for their enthusiastic support and encouragement.

My sincere thanks to my husband, Phil, for his help with the illustrations and his patience and support; my daughters, Alexandra and Belinda, for the many meals they cooked; Alexandra for candlewicking the picture frame and the tablecloth for the bedroom; Belinda for candlewicking the hearts for the mobile; my son Garrick for helping with the illustrations; Nicholas, my youngest son, for making endless cups of coffee.

My friend, Anne Finnegan, for transporting me all over the countryside to look for venues and helping in many other ways; my friends, Shelagh Allen, Yvonne Mostert, Joan Huisamen and Lindy Harrison, who all worked so hard to produce many of the beautiful projects featured in the book.

Jeanette Hawkins, who designed all but one of the quilt designs; Marianne Ries for the loan of the cot; Andrea van Niekerk of Martha's Vineyard for the loan of the rocking horse; Margie Cloete for the quilt design on page 79; Moya Black for allowing me to use her pattern for the toilet roll holder.

Dr Peter Koepf of *Rustenburg,* and David and Shelagh Miller for graciously allowing us to photograph in their beautiful homes; Mr and Mrs Pieterse for their kind permission to photograph the bathroom in the Stellenbosch Hotel; Daphne Dean of the *Biggie Best* shop in Somerset West for the loan of props; Ulla van der Merwe of *Dainty Daisy* in Somerset West for supplying some of the fabrics for the nursery.

Marje Hemp and Linda de Villiers of Struik Publishers for their infinite patience, encouragement and guidance; Elaine Levitte for styling each room for photography; Jennie Hoare for designing the book and Etienne van Duyker for the cover; Anneke Lipsanen for the pretty illustrations; Sue Thompson for the black and white line drawings; Lellyn Creamer for the layout; Wendy Greig for valiantly typing the manuscript; Alain Proust for the beautiful photographs; and the Monday evening Bible Study Group for their support and prayers.

And finally, to our seven cats and Judy, our dog, who often kept me company in the small hours of the morning.

Struik Publishers
(a member of The Struik Group (Pty) Ltd)
Struik House, Oswald Pirow Street, Foreshore, Cape Town.

Reg. No. 63/00203/07

First published 1989
Second impression 1990
Third impression 1990
Fourth impression 1991

Edited by Linda de Villiers
Layout by Lellyn Creamer
Cover design by Etienne van Duyker
Photography by Alain Proust
Illustrations by Anneke Lipsanen
Line drawings by Sue Thompson

Typeset and reproduced by Sparhams (Pty) Ltd, Cape Town
Printed and bound by Leefung-Asco (Pty) Ltd, Hong Kong

ISBN 0 86977 468 9

Candlewick/quilting hoops and additional sets of designs are available from: Willowtree Products cc
P O Box 103, Somerset West 7130

PUBLISHER'S NOTE Imperial measurements have been adjusted or rounded up or down as appropriate to help the reader.

CONTENTS

SINGER

THE BASICS

Candlewicking is a most fascinating and beautiful form of embroidery that is easy to learn and quick to master. The basic stitches comprise French and colonial knots with finer details embroidered in satin stitch, stem stitch and back stitch. Candlewick embroidery is closely associated with quilting so this technique has also been fully explained.

Throughout the book I have given very detailed step-by-step instructions for each project. Please read through them carefully as the extra time spent in understanding each step will be well worth the effort. Prepare the fabric and cotton lace according to the directions given to prevent any subsequent shrinkage. Remember that accuracy at each stage is very important as it will save you a great deal of time when assembling each item.

I have included projects for both the beginner and the experienced needlewoman, but none is really difficult to do – some just take longer than others. All the items are completely washable and, therefore, practical and pleasurable to use. An added advantage of calico is that it tones in with all colour schemes so that you can move the candlewicked accessories from one room to another and never grow tired of looking at them.

Whatever projects you decide to make, I hope they give you as much joy and happiness as they have given me. I trust that this book will inspire you to make lovely accessories for your own home as well as beautiful gifts you will be proud to give away.

MATERIALS

FABRIC

Originally traditional candlewick embroidery was done on unshrunk 100 per cent cotton calico or muslin. Once the embroidery was complete the fabric was washed in very hot water to shrink the fabric and hold the embroidery stitches firmly in place. Each damp square was then stretched on a blocking board until quite dry before being made into the chosen article. The fabric was never ironed, giving the candlewicked fabric that traditional puckered look.

Today we have lovely fabrics on the market including very good quality 100 per cent cotton calico that is available both preshrunk and unshrunk. Although the unshrunk fabric is usually very stiff, it does wash very well.

NOTE *Many people use a polyester and cotton blend curtain lining, but as it often shrinks it should be prepared in the same way as unshrunk cotton calico. With this particular fabric, the warp thread is made from cotton while the weft thread is made from polyester; it is the cotton that shrinks.*

PREPARATION OF FABRIC

UNSHRUNK CALICO Place the entire piece of fabric in a bath of *plain, cold water* overnight. Hot water will 'cook' the starch into the fabric. You will then not be able to remove the starch and as a result the fabric will not be nearly as soft. It is important not to add any washing powder or fabric softener. (The fabric lying below the surface of the water will be bleached by the washing powder, whereas the fabric lying above the water line because of the air pockets that form, will not be bleached.)

The following day wash the fabric in the washing machine on the hot cycle, using washing powder and fabric softener. Press while still damp.

PRESHRUNK CALICO Wash in the washing machine on a hot washing cycle, using washing powder and fabric softener. Press while still damp.

COTTON LACE

Cotton lace, however good the quality, always shrinks a little.

PREPARATION OF LACE

Wash all cotton lace in very hot water or boil it in plain water for 15-20 minutes. Place the lace in a towel and wring dry.

Iron one end of the lace dry, then measure the width. On an old piece of fabric, draw two parallel lines the width you have measured, to make a template. Iron the lace lengthways, using the template as a guide to ensure an even width throughout.

THE HOOP

It is essential to use a hoop for candlewick embroidery. Buy a 30 cm (12 in) or 35 cm (14 in) quilting hoop as this can be used for embroidery as well as for quilting. Having the hoop mounted on a base will leave both hands free to do the embroidery.

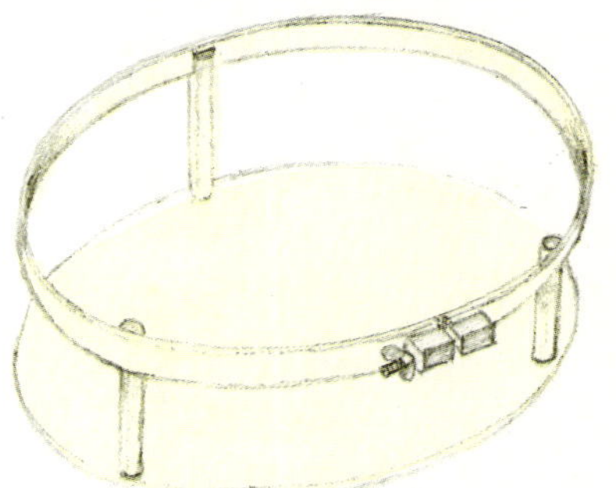

THE NEEDLES

You will need a sharp, large-eyed, sturdy needle such as a No. 22 Chenille needle or a No. 7 crewel embroidery needle. A tapestry needle is unsuitable as it tends to snag the fabric.

TO THREAD A NEEDLE Once a length of thread is cut, it tends to unravel rapidly and there is nothing more frustrating than trying to thread a needle with a badly unravelled thread. To avoid this happening, only cut the thread once the needle has been threaded. Hold the loose end of the thread in your left hand between your thumb and forefinger. Place the needle in your right hand and press the eye of the needle over the loose end of the thread. Now cut the thread.

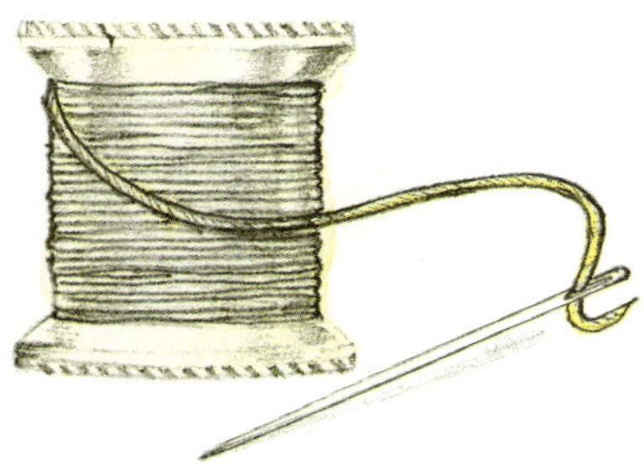

TO MAKE A KNOT Hold the loose end of the thread and the threaded needle between your left thumb and forefinger as shown. Now wrap the thread round the needle once and pull the needle through the loop. A good secure knot will be formed.

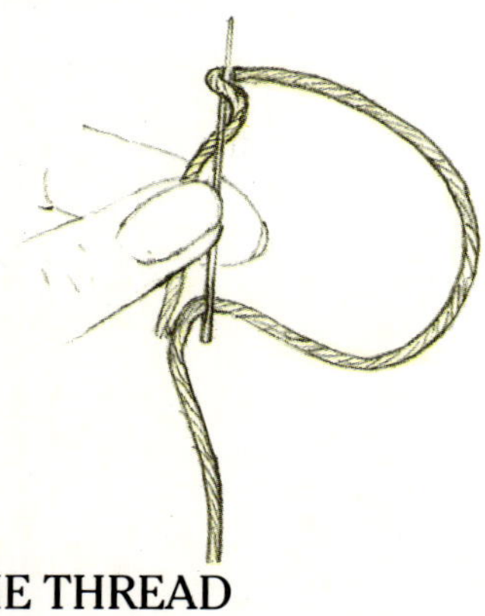

THE THREAD

Although specially manufactured candlewicking thread is not always available, there are many suitable substitutes available. Various types of 100 per cent mercerized cotton and embroidery floss are most suitable and any of the embroidery stitches worked in these threads look beautiful. I prefer a matt, four-ply 100 per cent knitting cotton to work the knots, but try experimenting with a combination of shiny and matt cottons to give an interesting texture to the finished article.

NOTE *Before using coloured thread, test it for colour-fastness by washing it in very hot water.*

Cut an old piece of calico or any plain fabric about 40 cm (16 in) square, place it securely in the hoop and pull it taut. First practise doing the three different knots (French, bullion and colonial) in single threads of different types. Then try using a double thread; that is, thread a single thread approximately 80 cm (32 in) long through the eye of the needle. Bring the ends together and form a knot.

I suggest you experiment with different threads. Try using two or three strands of silky embroidery floss combined with a matt knitting cotton, or perhaps two or three different shades of embroidery floss together. These two combinations of threads add great interest and depth to your work. I often use two or three different types of thread to candlewick the designs for a quilt, using the thicker matt knitting cotton double to accentuate the most important sections of the design.

For the more delicate embroidery stitches, it is best to use No. 5, No. 8 or any cotton thread of a similar thickness. Although it is not traditional, I have, on occasion, also used a No. 5 acrylic crochet thread. It washes extremely well and looks very pretty. On the other hand, you might like to candlewick your quilt traditionally, using only one type of matt thread throughout.

Check the tension of your work to ensure that the knots are lying flat and secure on the fabric. The knots must not be floppy or loose as this will make the work look untidy.

By practising beforehand you will be able to ascertain which type and thickness of thread best suits you.

TRACING MEDIUM

Use a water-soluble marking pen. This is the only pen that works really efficiently as the ink only remains on the fabric until the square is washed. Marks made by other felt-tip or ballpoint pens are impossible to remove.

TRACING THE DESIGN ONTO THE FABRIC

NOTE *Before tracing the design, it is very important to find the centre of the fabric and the design in order to position the design accurately on the fabric.*

To find the centre of a square of fabric, fold it in half vertically and then in half horizontally. Draw your thumbnail across the folds to make a crease. Measure the design at its widest point from the extreme left to the extreme right. Draw a vertical line at the halfway mark. Turn the design round and do the same top-to-bottom. The point where the lines cross is your centre point.

Place the centre point of the fabric square over the centre point of the design and pin them together.

If the design is dark enough you will be able to see it right through the fabric. Trace the design onto the fabric in a solid line as shown in the designs at the back of the book.

NOTE *You may come across designs where the dots are unevenly spaced. This inaccuracy is clearly visible once the embroidery is complete. If the dots on the design you are using are inaccurately spaced, use dressmaker's carbon and a tracing wheel to trace the design onto the fabric, then work the knots (French, bullion and colonial) on every second mark made by the tracing wheel. However, this does depend on the thickness of the thread; with very fine thread you would work a knot on each dot.*

Another method is to stick the design and fabric square onto a windowpane with masking tape before tracing the design.

A third method is to rest a piece of glass on top of two blocks (one block beneath either side of the glass) and to place a torch or bedside light underneath the glass. Place the design and then the fabric square on top of the glass and trace the design onto the fabric. The design shows up very clearly with the light shining beneath it. (A glass-topped coffee table works very well.) If you intend doing a great deal of candlewicking, it would be a good idea to invest in a piece of perspex as it is unbreakable.

TO ENLARGE OR REDUCE A DESIGN

The easiest way to enlarge or reduce a design is on a photocopying machine but for those who don't have access to one, it is preferable to use the grid method. Make an evenly squared grid over the design, then draw another grid the size you would like the design to be. This second grid must have the same number of squares as the first. Now draw the design square by square.

original design

enlarged design

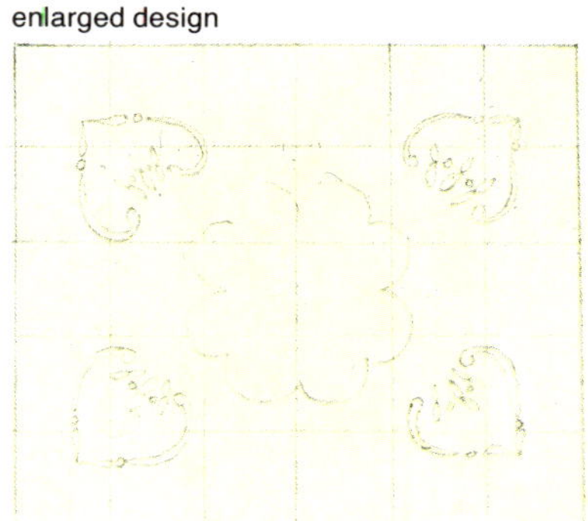

STITCHES

Antique candlewick quilts seen in American museums reveal that the stitches used most frequently by early American candlewickers were large French knots, satin stitch and back stitch. Several other stitches were added later, for example colonial knots, chain stitch and stem stitch.

Today many different stitches can be incorporated most successfully into your designs.

FRENCH KNOT Working from left to right, bring the needle through from the back to the front of the fabric. *Hold the thread towards you* between the left thumb and forefinger. Hold the needle between the right thumb and forefinger. Wrap the thread around the needle once and insert it just to the right of where the thread first emerged. Let the loop formed rest over your left forefinger or thumb and move your finger or thumb about to adjust the shape of the knot. Slip the loop off your finger at the last moment. Pull the needle and thread through to the back until the knot rests quite firmly on the fabric, then come up through the fabric again to execute the next knot. The thread may be used double to produce larger knots. To finish off, run the needle under several stitches at the back of the work.

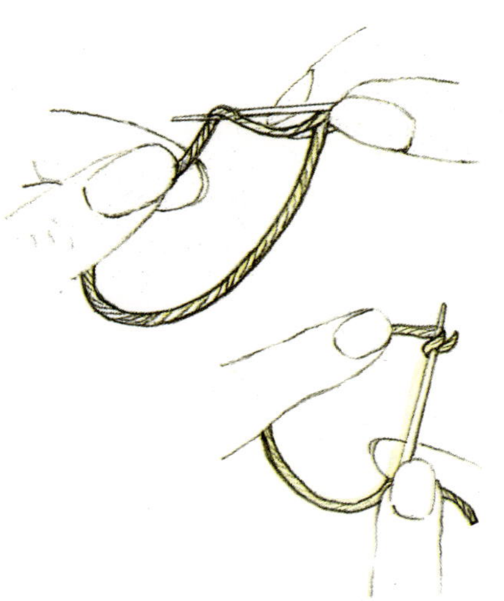

When the thread is wrapped around the needle twice, the stitch is called a bullion knot and shouldn't be confused with the bullion stitch.

SATIN STITCH Satin stitches are straight stitches worked close together, evenly and neatly. Begin across the centre and work towards the end of the design. Turn the work around and complete the other half. Try not to overlap any of the stitches. To finish off, run the needle through the stitches at the back of the work.

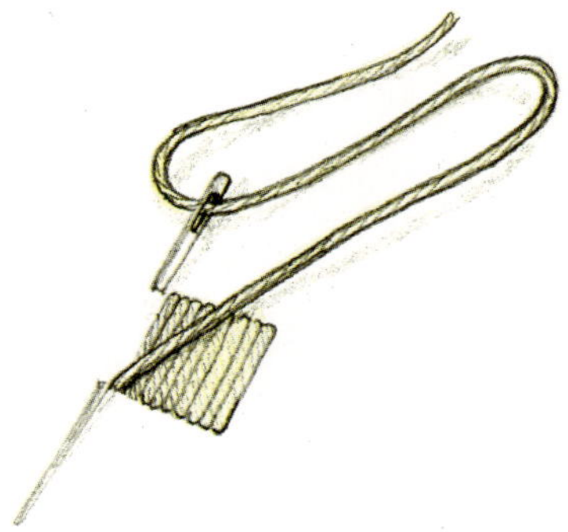

BACK STITCH Working from right to left, bring the needle up at A. Go down at B and come back up at C. Go down at A and come up at D. Continue in this manner making all the stitches equal in length. To finish off, run the needle under several stitches at the back of the work.

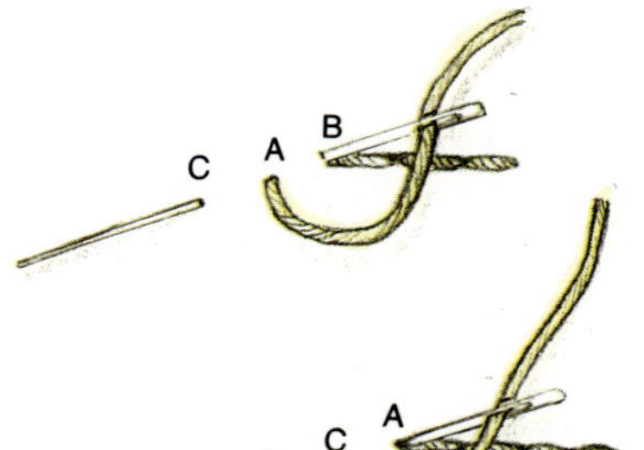

EXTRA EMBROIDERY STITCHES

BULLION STITCH is best worked on fabric which is stretched in a hoop, thus leaving both hands free to work the stitch. Bring the thread to the front at B and insert the needle a short distance away at A. Allow the needle to re-emerge at B. Do not pull the needle through completely. Wrap the thread round the needle six or seven times, gently place the left thumb on the coil and pull the needle through carefully. Insert the needle at A to secure the stitch.

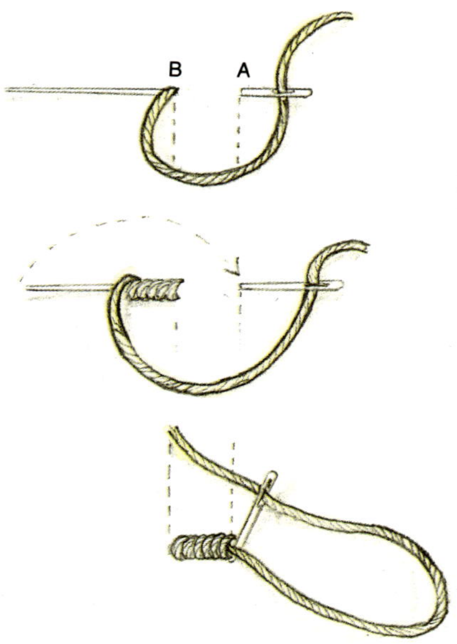

STEM STITCH Stem stitch is worked from left to right. Come up at A. Hold the thread below the stitching line, go down at B and come up at C. Go down at D and come up at E.

Continue in this manner, keeping the stitches equal in length. On a sharp curve, make your stitches smaller to accommodate the curve.

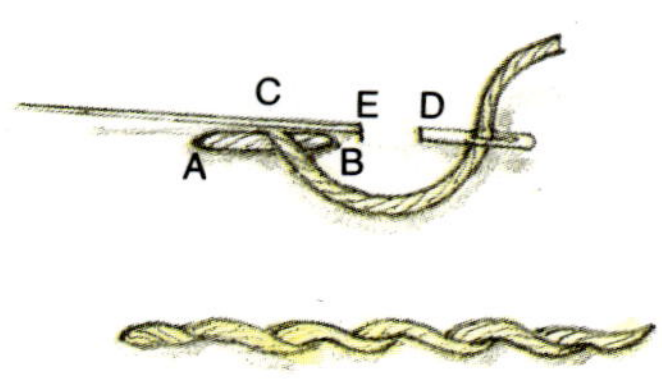

CHAIN STITCH is ideal to use on heavy outlines. Working from right to left, bring the needle up through the surface of the fabric at A. Form a loop with the thread and re-insert the needle at A, coming up at B inside the loop. Pull the thread through, keeping the looped thread below the point of the needle. Re-insert the needle at B leaving a loop. Come up at C which is inside the loop and pull the thread through as before, keeping the looped thread below the point of the needle.

To finish off, secure the last loop by bringing the thread over the loop and pulling the needle through to the back of the work. Run the needle under several stitches.

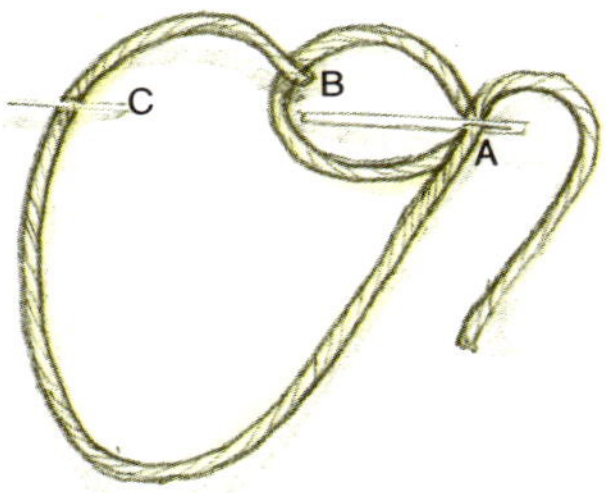

CORAL STITCH is worked from right to left. Bring the thread through the fabric at A, lay the thread along the line of the design and hold it down with your left thumb. Make a small stitch (through the fabric) underneath the line and thread. Keeping the circle of thread below the point of the needle, pull the thread through to form a small knot. I use this stitch to embroider butterflies' feelers and the stamens of flowers.

FISHBONE STITCH is used to embroider leaves and the bodies of butterflies. Work from top to bottom along the centre line of the design. Bring the thread through at A. Insert the needle at B. Pull the needle and thread through at C. Re-insert the needle just below B and pull the needle and thread through at D. Continue working from the centre to the right and then from the centre to the left until you have completed the design. Work the stitches evenly and close together so that no ground fabric is visible.

To finish off, run the needle under several stitches at the back of the work.

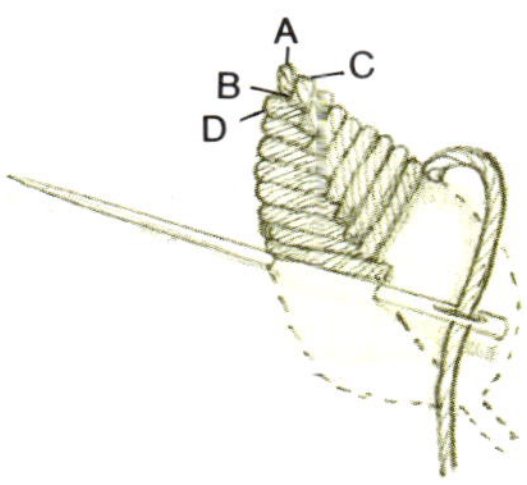

COLONIAL KNOT Working from left to right and holding the thread and needle as you would for a French knot, bring the thread to the front of the cloth at A. Push the needle under the thread, then take the thread over and under the point of the needle to form a figure eight. Re-insert the needle to the right of where the needle first emerged, pulling the needle and thread through to the back of the fabric and tightening the knot exactly the same way as you did for the French knot.

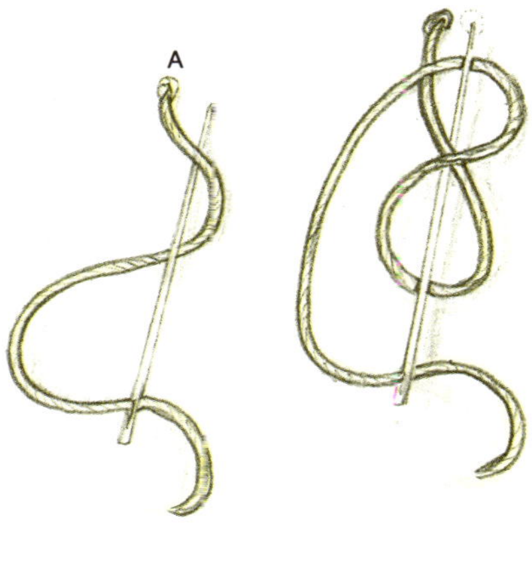

FEATHER STITCH This decorative and quick stitch is easy to perfect and makes an attractive feathery line, whether worked on straight lines or along curves. I often use this stitch to embroider hearts and the veins of leaves.

Working from top to bottom along a centre line, bring the thread up at A. Hold the thread down with the left thumb. On the right-hand side of the centre line, with the thread forming a circle to the right, make a small slanted stitch towards the centre line, keeping the thread below the needle point. Pull the needle and thread through. With the thread forming a circle to the left and on the left-hand side of the centre line, again hold the thread down with the thumb. Make a small slanted stitch towards the centre line, keeping the thread below the needle point. Pull the needle and thread through. Continue in this manner making small slanted stitches (towards the centre line) first to the right and then to the left.

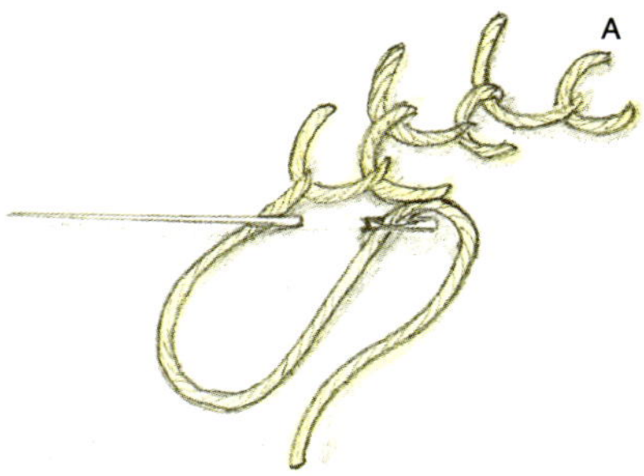

QUILTING

Quilting adds dimension and depth to any project, whether it is used on a candlewicked design or on the border of your quilt.

MATERIALS

A THIMBLE is absolutely essential if you want to prevent raw, punctured fingers. A thimble is used to push the needle through one or more layers of fabric. You will need to wear one on the middle finger of your right hand if you are right-handed (or the middle finger of your left hand if you are left-handed). It is also sensible to wear a rubber fingerguard (turned inside out) on the index or middle finger of your left hand.

NEEDLES used for quilting should be short, sharp and strong, preferably No. 9 or 10 'between' needles. Thread several needles at once, as very often a quilting design has several rows of stitching that need to be worked on simultaneously, and it will save you having to stop and re-thread a single needle too many times.

THREAD   Strong 100 per cent pure cotton quilting thread or specially waxed quilting thread is needed. If the thread has not already been waxed, run it through a piece of beeswax to make it easier to pull through the fabric. Use 40-45 cm (16-18 in) lengths and make a knot at one end.

A QUILTING HOOP with a diameter of 30-35 cm (12-14 in), preferably mounted on a base, makes the quilting of the squares much easier. Large free-standing quilting frames are available and are most useful for quilting very large projects. Unfortunately they take up rather a lot of space, so for the average quilter they are a little impractical. Many people quilt sections of a project, such as the borders of a quilt, with the work resting on a table or their lap.

WADDING/BATTING is available in various thicknesses; for instance 68-100 g wadding/batting is available in most countries. Be sure to use sheet wadding/batting and not polyester stuffing, which is only intended for stuffing pillows and so on. For most quilted projects a thin wadding/batting is the easiest and most suitable to use.

BACKING FABRIC   Use the same calico or fabric that you used for the front of the project. It is preferable not to use a cheaper grade of calico or fabric for the backing as the results may be disappointing.

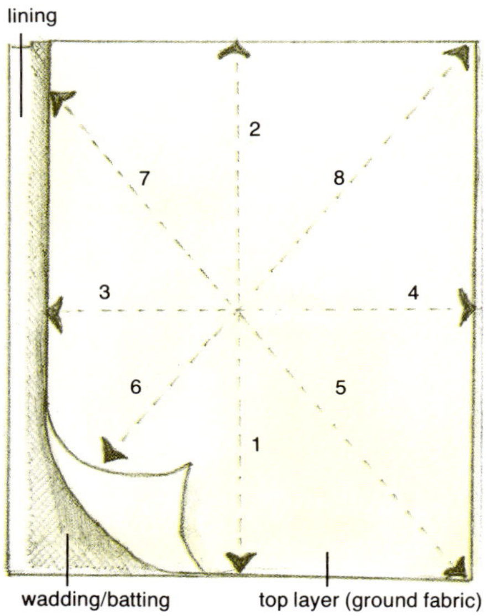

PREPARING TO QUILT

To prepare for quilting, it is essential to tack the three layers (the backing, wadding/batting and the front) of the project together.

Place the backing fabric, wrong side up, on the floor or a flat surface. Place the wadding/batting on top of this, making sure that you smooth out any creases in the backing or wadding/batting. Centre the quilt top (or whatever project you are doing) on top of the wadding/batting.

Pin the three layers together, starting from the centre and working towards the centre point of the outside edges. Then pin from the centre to the corners.

Tack along these rows of pins. Continue to tack until you have done at least 32 rows of tacking for a large project and at least eight for a small project such as a cushion. The quilting will be easier and neater the more you tack. The extra effort is definitely worthwhile.

QUILTING STITCHES

Two basic stitches are used for hand quilting. I use back stitch for quilting the designs on the candlewicked squares and short running stitches for quilting the borders.

The secret of beautiful quilting is small, straight, evenly-spaced stitches worked as close together as you can. With practise you can achieve eight to twelve stitches per 2.5 cm (1 in).

Longer stitches are perfectly acceptable but to look their best, they must be neatly and evenly spaced both back and front.

RUNNING STITCH Thread the needle and make a knot at one end. Work a large stitch through the top fabric and wadding/batting and give a little tug so that the knot becomes buried in the wadding/batting. Come out at the starting point.

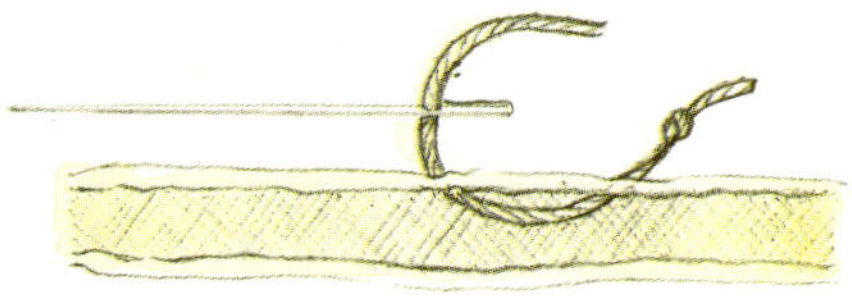

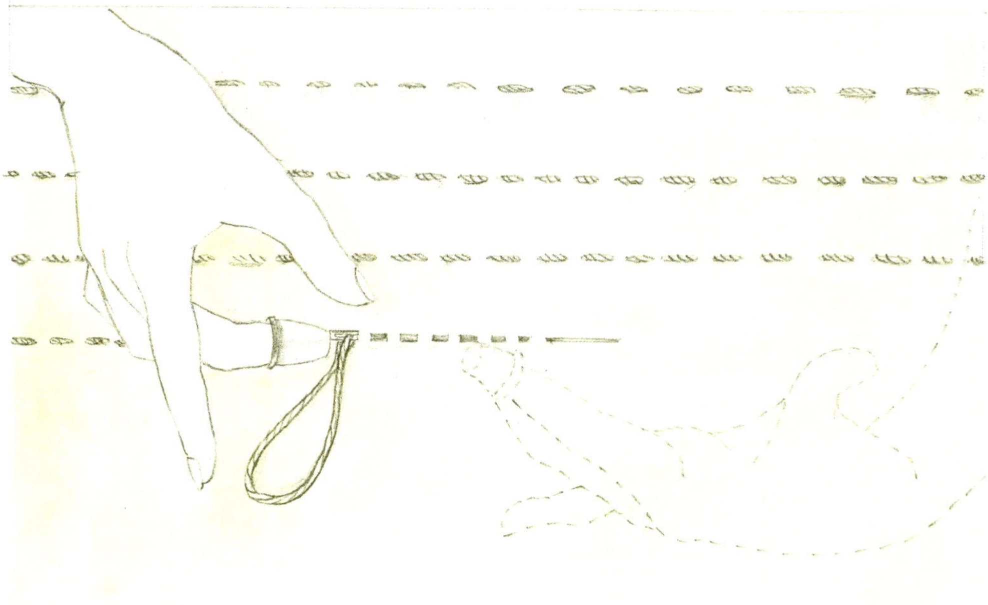

With the thimble on the middle finger of the right hand, push the needle vertically through all three layers until it touches the middle finger of the left hand (which you have placed underneath the project). Tilt the needle quickly so that it makes a small stitch at the back and continue to push the needle up through to the front again. Hold the work in place with the left thumb. Your right wrist must be quite relaxed as you will see that the movement is rather like that of a see-saw as the needle is pushed in and out of the fabric. Try to put several stitches on the needle before pulling it right through the fabric.

BACK STITCH I like to use this stitch when quilting the designs on all my candlewicked projects. I work a back stitch beneath each French or colonial knot so that the quilting stitches are not visible but the effect is still the same.

For this method of quilting you will need to place the fabric in a quilting hoop. Remove the outer hoop, place the project to be quilted straight down over the inner hoop, then replace and tighten the outer hoop. (The outer hoop should not be very tight and the fabric must have a little slack.) Turn the hoop upside down and check that there are no creases underneath. If there are, ease the creases away by pulling the fabric very gently. Now you are ready to quilt.

Make a knot at the end of the thread and push the needle and thread through the top fabric and wadding/batting, coming up again under a French or colonial knot. Give the thread a little tug so that the knot becomes buried in the wadding/batting (see opposite).

Place the left index or middle finger under the first French or colonial knot, pushing it up slightly. Insert the needle into the fabric just behind where the thread first emerged and push it vertically through all three layers until the needle touches the finger underneath. Tilt the needle quickly and push it diagonally through the wadding/batting, coming up under the next French or colonial knot. The quicker you tilt the needle, the smaller the stitch at the back will be. Continue in this manner, working a back stitch under each knot.

To end the row of quilting, tie a knot in the thread about 1 cm (½ in) from the fabric and do a back stitch coming up through the wadding/batting and top fabric a little distance away. Tug gently and the knot will disappear into the wadding/batting. Cut off the remaining thread.

Once the whole project has been quilted, remove the tacking threads.

THE KITCHEN

So many hours are spent in the kitchen every day that it is worthwhile making it an attractive room in which to work. Autumn sunshine, gleaming copper and just-picked roses in this farmhouse kitchen set the scene for these pretty candlewick embroidered creations. Ruffled cottage curtains, apron and oven gloves are charming additions to any kitchen, while the white on white embroidered tray cloth and tea cosy add an air of elegance to this rustic setting.

Towels, a wall-hanging, tablecloth and lampshade are but a few of the other beautifully embroidered projects featured in this book that can be made for this very important room.

TEA COSY

Two different methods of making a tea cosy are described here: in the first method the tea cosy is quilted while in the second the cover is removable and, therefore, cannot be quilted.

Materials for quilted tea cosy

38 cm x 26 cm-wide (15 in x 10 ¼ in-wide) tracing paper

52 cm x 70 cm-wide (20 ½ in x 27 ½ in-wide) fabric

52 cm x 35 cm-wide (20 ½ in x 13 ¾ in-wide) medium-weight polyester wadding/batting

1.4 m x 3 cm-wide (1 ½ yds x 1 ¼ in) cotton lace or broderie anglaise for the frill

1. Fold the tracing paper in half vertically and trace the tea cosy pattern and design on page 76, completing the pattern and design by tracing first one half and then the other.

2. Fold the fabric in half horizontally so that it measures 26 cm x 70 cm (10 ¼ in x 27 ½ in) wide and press the fold firmly. This horizontal line will become the base line of the tea cosy. Open out the fabric and place it on top of the pattern, matching the base line of the pattern with the fold of the fabric.

3. Trace the outline and designs onto the fabric. Trace off a second outline and designs alongside the first one. Do not cut out. (See fig 1.)

4. Place the fabric in a hoop, pull taut and candlewick all four designs.

5. Refold the fabric horizontally and cut out the two sections of the tea cosy along the traced outlines, but not along the fold.

6. Following the instructions on page 8, wash and iron both pieces of candlewicked fabric, then refold horizontally.

7. Fold the wadding/batting in half horizontally and trace the outline of the tea cosy pattern onto the wadding/batting. Cut out along the outlines, then along the fold line. You will now have two pieces of wadding/batting the shape of a tea cosy.

8. Sandwich one piece of wadding/batting between each of the folded tea cosy shapes. (See fig 2.)

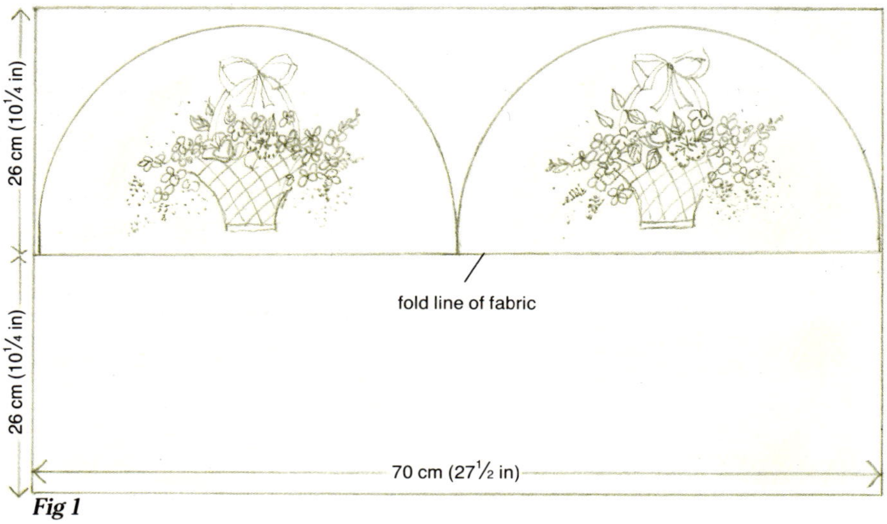

Fig 1

9. Following the instructions on page 12, quilt each of the two sections separately. Quilt only those parts of the designs that you wish to accentuate.

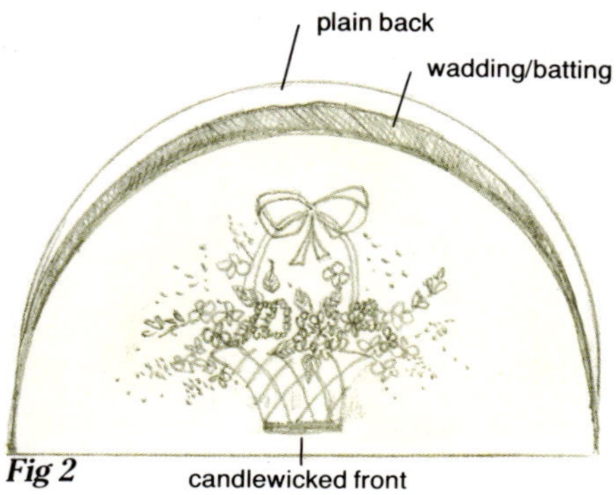

Fig 2

10. Pin, tack and machine stitch around the dome-shaped outline of one half of the tea cosy. Complete the second half in exactly the same way.

11. Gather the lace or broderie anglaise for the frill. Place the frill (with the scalloped edge facing inwards) on the embroidered side of one half of the tea cosy. Pin and tack.

12. Place the second half of the tea cosy on top of the first half, embroidered sides together. Pin the corners together *accurately* and continue to pin towards the dome. Tack, then machine stitch using an overlock stitch or a straight and then a zigzag stitch.

13. Remove tacking threads and trim away any ragged threads. Turn the completed tea cosy right side out.

Materials for removable cover

26 cm x 38 cm-wide (10 ¼ in x 15 in-wide) tracing paper
54 cm x 40 cm-wide (21 in x 16 in-wide) fabric for the cover
1.4 m x 3 cm-wide (1 ½ yds x 1 ¼ in-wide) broderie anglaise or lace edging
52 cm x 70 cm-wide (20 ½ in x 27 ½ in-wide) fabric for the lining
52 cm x 35 cm-wide (20 ½ in x 13 ¾ in-wide) medium-weight polyester wadding/batting

1. Fold the tracing paper in half vertically and trace the tea cosy pattern and design on page 76, tracing first one half and then the other to complete the outline and design.

2. Fold the piece of fabric for the cover in half horizontally so that it measures 27 cm x 40 cm (10 ½ in x 16 in) and press. Using the fold as the base line, position the fabric over the tracing and trace the outline and designs onto one half and then onto the other half of the fabric. Do not cut out. (See page 18, fig 3.)

3. Place the fabric in a hoop, positioning the designs in the centre. Stretch the fabric taut and candlewick the designs.

4. When you have completed the candlewicking, remove the fabric from the hoop and refold it. Cut along the outline and fold line. Following the instructions on page 8, wash and iron the candlewicked fabric very well.

5. Make a hem (to the wrong side) along the straight edges of both halves of the tea cosy cover by turning back 5 mm (¼ in) and then another 5 mm (¼ in). Pin, tack and machine stitch.

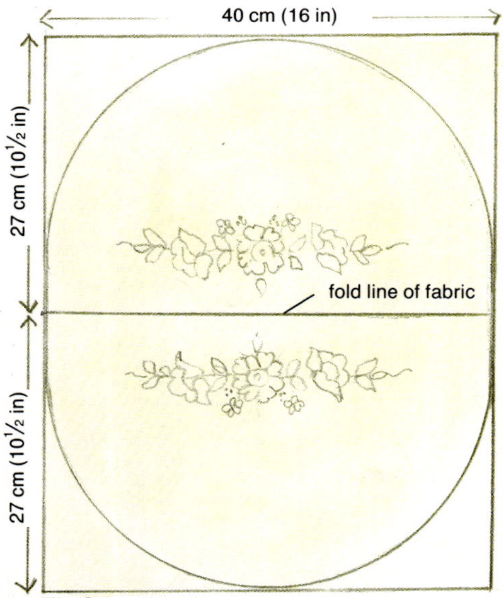

Fig 3

6. Gather the lace and pin the lace frill (with the scalloped edge facing towards the inside of the tea cosy) to the embroidered side of one half of the tea cosy. Tack the lace into place.

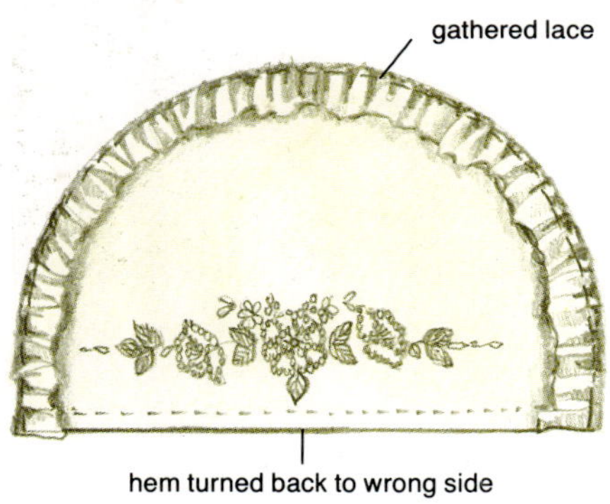

7. With right sides together, pin the second half of the tea cosy to the first, beginning at the corners and continuing towards the centre of the dome. Tack, then machine stitch using an overlock stitch or a straight and then a zigzag stitch. Remove the tacking threads and trim away any ragged threads. Turn the tea cosy cover right side out.

8. For the lining, fold the fabric in half horizontally so that it measures 26 cm x 70 cm (10¼ in x 27½ in) and press. This horizontal line becomes the base line of the tea cosy. Open out the fabric and place it on top of the pattern. Matching the base line of the pattern with the fold of the fabric, trace the tea cosy pattern (but not the designs) onto the fabric. Trace a second outline alongside the first as shown in fig 1. Refold the fabric and cut out the two sections of the tea cosy along the outlines, but not along the fold line.

9. Fold the wadding/batting in half horizontally and trace the tea cosy pattern onto it. Cut along both the outline and the fold line.

10. Sandwich a piece of wadding/batting between each of the folded tea cosy shapes. Pin, tack and machine stitch around the dome-shaped outline of each shape.

11. With right sides together, pin the two tea cosy shapes together, beginning at the corners and continuing towards the dome. Tack and machine stitch using an overlock stitch or a straight and then a zigzag stitch. Trim away any ragged threads, remove the tacking and turn the lining right side out. Fit the lining into the embroidered tea cosy cover.

TRAY CLOTH

Materials

46 cm x 35 cm (18 in x 13¾ in) fabric
45.5 cm x 35 cm (18 in x 13¾ in) polyester wadding/batting (optional)
46 cm x 35 cm (18 in x 13¾ in) backing fabric
1.8 m x 3 cm-wide (2 yds x 1¼ in-wide) cotton lace

1. Select a suitable design for each end, one of the corners or all four corners and trace it onto one of the pieces of fabric.

2. Place the fabric in the hoop and candlewick the designs. Wash and iron the candlewicked fabric, following the instructions on page 8.

3. If you wish to quilt the design/designs, tack the wadding/batting to the wrong side of the backing fabric.

4. Turn back (to the wrong side) a 5 mm (¼ in) seam allowance along one short side of both pieces of fabric and press.

5. With right sides together, pin, tack and machine stitch the candlewicked fabric to the backing fabric along the remaining three sides.

6. Clip the corners, remove the tacking threads and turn the tray cloth right side out. Neatly slipstitch the opening closed.

7. If you wish to quilt the tray cloth, follow the instructions for quilting on page 12. Remove the tacking.

8. Machine stitch the lace to the right side of the tray cloth as near to the edge as possible and mitre (page 60) the corners.

APRON

Materials

Tracing paper
48 cm x 47 cm (19 in x 18 ½ in) calico for the apron bib and pocket
1.5 m x 3 cm-wide (1 ¾ yds x 1 ¼ in-wide) lace for bib (optional)
70 cm x 2.5 cm-wide (31 in x 1 in-wide) satin ribbon for the neck string
24 cm x 27 cm (9 ½ in x 10 ½ in) polyester wadding/batting
50 cm x 80 cm (19 ½ in x 31 in) calico for the skirt
2.6 m (2 ⅞ yds) lace for skirt (optional)
Two 60 cm x 5 cm-wide (23 ½ in x 2 in-wide) pieces of calico for the waistband
Two 48 cm x 2.5 cm-wide (19 in x 1 in-wide) satin ribbons for the apron strings

1. Fold a 24 cm x 27 cm-wide (9 ½ in x 10 ½ in) piece of tracing paper in half vertically to measure 24 cm x 13.5 cm (9 ½ in x 5 ⅜ in). Trace the apron bib pattern and design on page 82 onto the tracing paper, completing the pattern and design by tracing first one half and then the other.

2. Trace a 20 cm (8 in) square on tracing paper for the pocket pattern.

3. Fold the fabric for the bib and pocket in half horizontally so that it measures 24 cm x 47 cm (9 ½ in x 18 ½ in) and press. Open out the fabric and place it on top of the bib pattern as shown. Matching the bottom line of the pattern with the fold line of the fabric, trace the outline and design onto the fabric. Do not cut out.

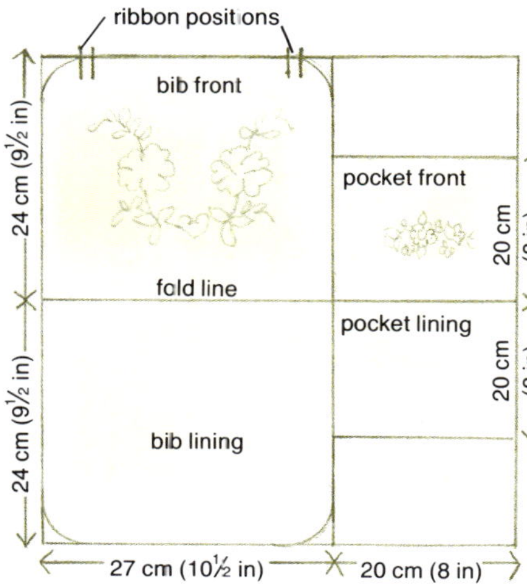

4. Trace the pocket pattern onto the same piece of fabric as shown.

5. Place the fabric in the hoop and pull taut. Candlewick the design on the bib. Once the candlewicking is complete, remove the fabric from the hoop and refold. Cut along the outline of the bib and the pocket. Now cut along the fold line of the bib but not the fold line of the pocket. Set the pocket fabric aside.

6. Wash and iron the candlewicked section of the bib, following the instructions on page 8.

7. If you wish to add a lace ruffle to the bib, gather the lace and, with right sides together and matching the raw edge of the bib with the straight edge of the lace, pin the lace into position along three sides as shown below. Tack and machine stitch close to the raw edges.

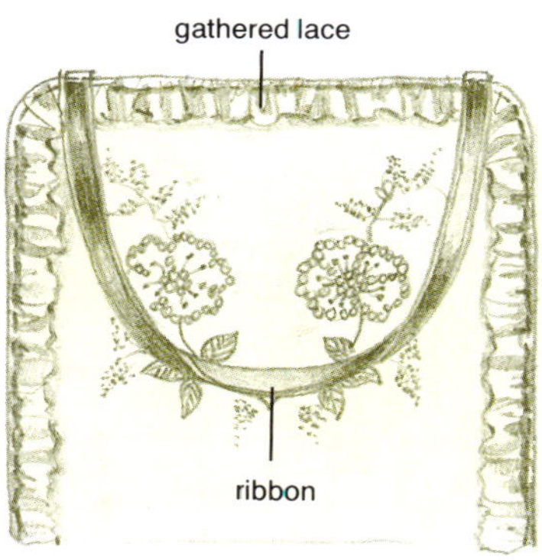

8. Position a loop of 2.5 cm-wide (1 in-wide) ribbon (that goes round the neck) on the bib as shown on page 19 and pin and tack it in place.

9. Tack the wadding/batting to the wrong side of the bib lining. With right sides together, pin the lining and the candlewicked section of the bib together along three sides, leaving the bottom edge open. Tack and machine stitch using an overlock stitch or a straight and then a zigzag stitch. Clip the curves, remove the tacking threads and turn right side out.

10. Prepare the bib for quilting and quilt as described on page 12. Quilt whichever sections of the design you want to accentuate.

11. Tack the open bottom edges together. Remove the tacking done in preparation for quilting.

12. Fold the pocket panel in half and press. This fold line will become the top of the pocket. Turn under (to the wrong side) a 5 mm (¼ in) seam allowance all the way round the other three sides and press.

13. Position the pocket on the right-hand side of the apron skirt fabric and pin, tack and machine stitch it into position.

14. Sew a 1 cm (½ in) hem along both side edges of the skirt fabric and then along the bottom edge.

15. If desired, pin, tack and machine stitch the lace along the sides and bottom of the skirt.

16. Gather the top edge of the skirt until it measures 59 cm (23 ¼ in).

17. With right sides together, pin and tack the raw edge of the bib to the top edge of one of the strips of waistband.

18. Pin and tack the two satin ribbon apron strings in place as shown in the illustration.

19. With right sides together, pin and tack the second strip of waistband to the first strip along the same edge (the bib will be upside down and sandwiched between the two sections of waistband). (See fig 1.)

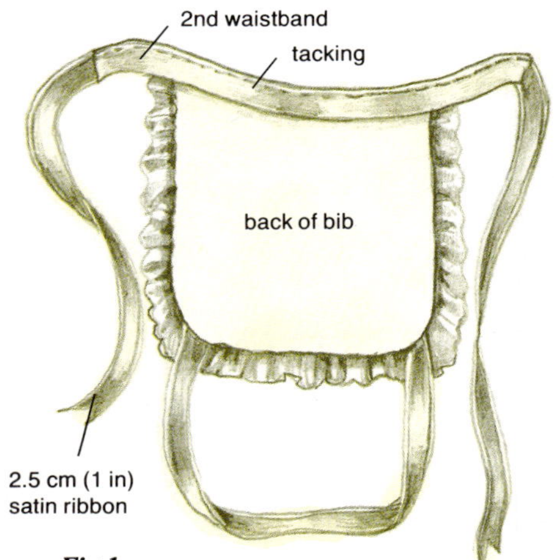

Fig 1

20. With right sides together, pin the gathered edge of the skirt to the bottom edge of the first waistband, leaving 5 mm (¼ in) as a seam allowance at each end of the waistband. Tack and machine stitch into position.

21. Along the bottom edge of the second strip of waistband turn under (to the wrong side) a 5 mm (¼ in) seam allowance and press.

22. With right sides together, pin the two strips of waistband together along both short sides and tack. Machine stitch along first one short side, then along the tacked long side and finally along the remaining short side. Remove the tacking threads and turn the waistband right side out. (See fig 2.)

23. Pin, tack and slipstitch the opening closed.

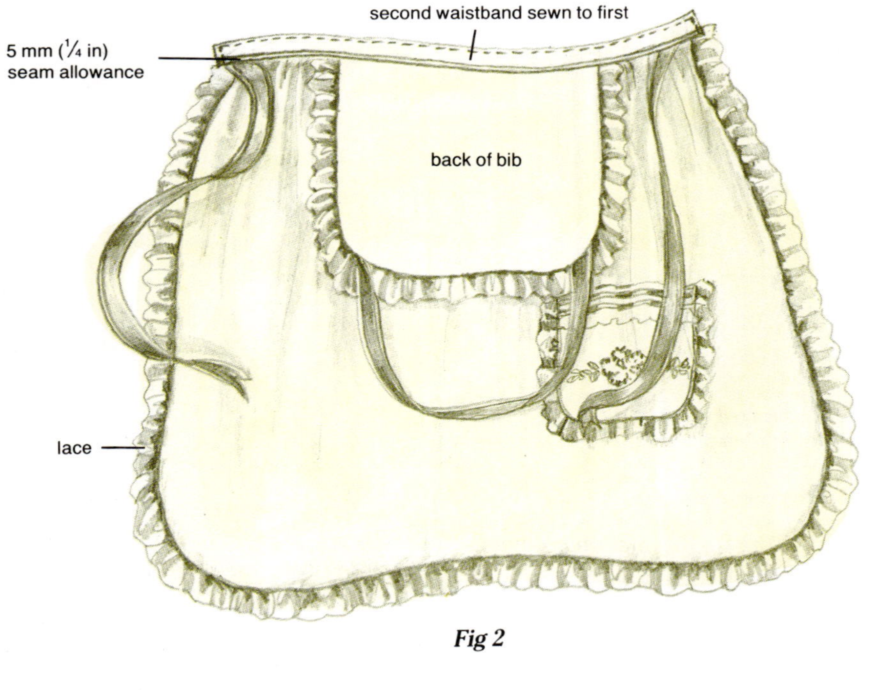

Fig 2

OVEN GLOVES

Make fully-quilted oven gloves or ones with unquilted pockets and removable pads.

Materials for fully-quilted oven gloves
Tracing paper
18 cm x 88 cm-wide (7 in x 34½ in-wide) reversible ready-quilted fabric
50 cm x 40 cm-wide (19½ in x 16 in-wide) plain fabric
50 cm x 20 cm-wide (19½ in x 8 in-wide) polyester wadding/batting
About 2.2 m (2½ yds) bias binding

1. Trace the oven glove pattern on pages 92-93 onto a long piece of tracing paper and cut out the pattern.

2. Fold the quilted fabric in half vertically and pin the long pattern piece to the fabric. Trace the outline onto the fabric.

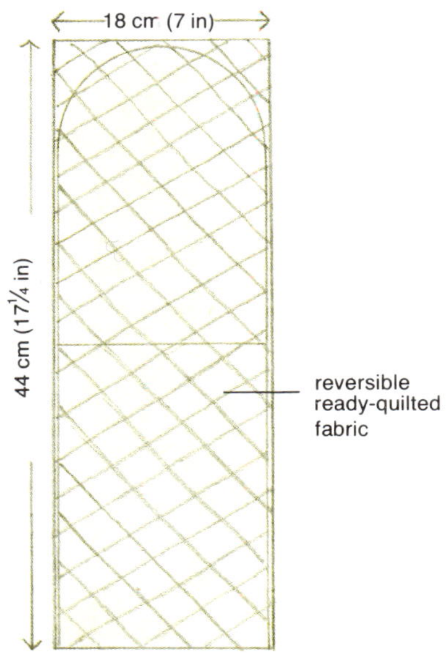

3. Open out the fabric and machine zigzag all the way around the outline. Trim away the excess fabric.

4. Fold the plain fabric in half horizontally so that it measures 25 cm x 40 cm (9¾ in x 16 in) and press. Open out the folded fabric and match the base line of the pocket pattern on page 93 with the fold line of the fabric. Trace the outline and design onto the fabric. Trace another outline and design alongside the first one. Do not cut out.

5. Place the whole piece of fabric in the hoop and pull taut. Candlewick the designs.

6. Refold the fabric and cut along the outlines of the pockets but not along the fold line. Following the instructions on page 8, wash and iron the fabric well.

7. Fold the wadding/batting in half horizontally so that it measures 25 cm x 20 cm (9¾ in x 8 in) and pin the pocket pattern to the wadding/batting. Cut along the outline and then along the fold line.

8. Sandwich a piece of wadding/batting between each of the folded sections of candlewicked fabric. Prepare each pocket for quilting and then quilt the designs as described on page 12.

9. Pin, tack and machine stitch the bias binding to the straight edge of each pocket.

10. Match the rounded ends of the long section of the oven gloves with those of the pockets. Pin and tack the pockets into position.

11. Pin, tack and machine stitch the bias binding to the entire outer edge of the oven gloves, making sure that you secure the corners of the pockets properly. Remove the tacking threads.

Materials for oven gloves with removable pads

Tracing paper
18 cm x 88 cm-wide (7 in x 34 ½ in-wide) reversible ready-quilted fabric
50 cm x 40 cm-wide (19 ½ in x 16 in-wide) plain fabric
About 2.2 m (2 ½ yds) bias binding
46 cm x 36 cm-wide (18 in x 14 in-wide) calico for the pads
46 cm x 18 cm-wide (18 in x 7 in-wide) polyester wadding/batting

1. Trace the pattern on pages 92-93 onto a long piece of paper and cut out the pattern. Fold the quilted fabric in half vertically so that it measures 18 cm x 44 cm (7 in x 17 ½ in). Pin the pattern piece to the fabric. Trace the outline.

2. Open out the fabric, machine zigzag all round the marked outline, then trim away the excess fabric.

3. Fold the plain fabric in half horizontally so that it measures 25 cm x 40 cm (9 ¾ in x 16 in) and press. Open out the fabric and position the straight edge of the pocket pattern on the fold line of the fabric. Trace the outline and design onto the fabric. Trace another outline and design alongside the first. Do not cut out.

4. Place the fabric in a hoop and pull taut. Now candlewick the designs.

5. Refold the fabric and cut along the outlines of the pocket, but not along the fold. Wash and iron the candlewicked fabric well, following the instructions on page 8.

6. Refold the pockets and pin the bias binding to the straight edge of each pocket. Tack and machine stitch.

7. Match the rounded ends of the long section of the oven gloves with those of the pockets and pin and tack the pockets into position.

8. Pin, tack and machine stitch the bias binding to the entire outer edge of the oven gloves, making sure that the corners of the pockets are secure.

9. To make the separate pads, fold the calico in half horizontally so that it measures 23 cm x 36 cm (9 in x 14 in) and press.

10. Pin the pocket pattern to the fabric, matching the straight edge of the pattern with the fold line of the fabric. Trace the outline, then trace a second outline alongside the first.

11. Cut along the outline, then along the fold of each pocket.

12. Turn back (to the wrong side) and press a 1 cm (½ in) seam allowance along all four straight bottom edges.

13. With right sides together, pin and tack two pieces of fabric together. Machine stitch around the raw edges, leaving the straight bottom edge open. Sew the other two pieces together in the same way. Clip the curves, remove the tacking and turn the fabric right side out.

14. Fold the wadding/batting in half horizontally and pin the pocket pattern to the folded wadding/batting. Cut along the outline and then along the fold of the wadding/batting.

15. Slip one piece of wadding/batting into each pad and slipstitch the opening closed.

16. Slip the pads into the pockets of the oven gloves.

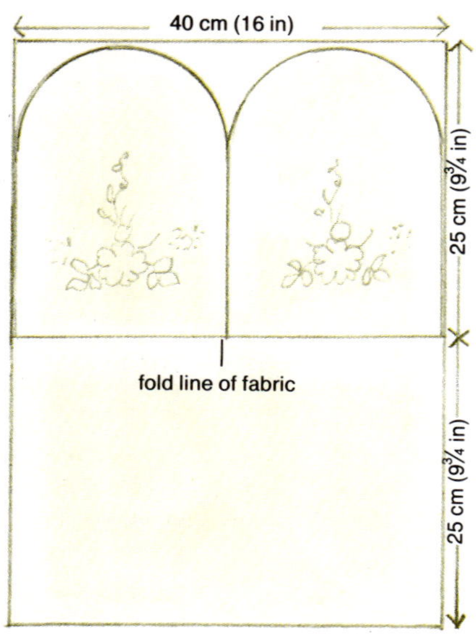

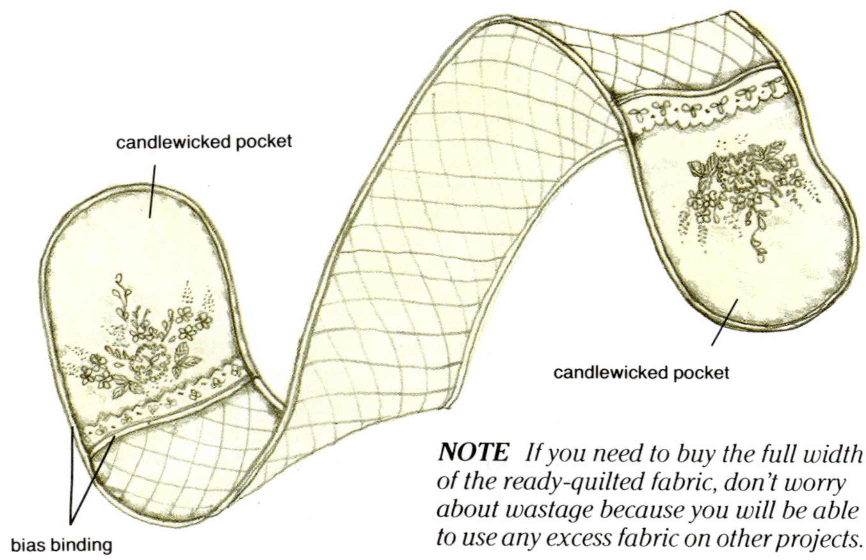

NOTE *If you need to buy the full width of the ready-quilted fabric, don't worry about wastage because you will be able to use any excess fabric on other projects.*

RUFFLED COTTAGE CURTAINS

As windows come in many shapes and sizes, it is impossible to include a list of requirements, but remember that cottage curtains need to be gathered very full and to hang just below sill length to look their best.

TO CALCULATE THE WIDTH AND THE LENGTH OF THE CURTAINS
To calculate the length, measure from the curtain rail (rod) or track to the windowsill and add on 15 cm (6 in) [which will include a 3 cm (1¼ in) turnback at the top of the curtain and a 2 cm (⅞ in) bottom seam allowance]. A 9 cm (3½ in) or 10 cm (4 in) fabric or lace ruffle will be added to this measurement and the curtains will hang approximately 20 cm (8 in) below the windowsill when finished. If the window is positioned just above the kitchen sink, adjust the length accordingly so that the curtain and ruffle do not hang near the taps.

To calculate the width, measure the length of the rail (rod) and at the very least double the measurement. When using preshrunk calico as curtain fabric (unlined), it is preferable to triple the measurement. Divide the double (or triple) measurement in half to give the width measurement for each of the two curtains.

OTHER MATERIALS NEEDED

HEADING (RUFFLETTE) TAPE If you use standard heading (rufflette) tape you will need the same width as the curtains plus about 2 cm (⅞ in) extra *per* curtain for the turnbacks.

LACE OR FABRIC RUFFLE To calculate how much lace or fabric ruffle you will need *per curtain,* measure the length plus the width of the curtain and double the measurement. (Refer to the Box on page 62 for hints on how to make ruffles.)

TIE-BACKS Loop the tape measure around the curtain as if it were a tie-back. The measurement of the loop is the length of the finished tie-back. Add a 2 cm (⅞ in) seam allowance and cut a piece of fabric the required length by 48 cm (19 in) wide. You will also need two pieces of iron-on vilene interfacing measuring the finished length of each panel with a width of 11 cm (4¼ in).

VALANCE You will need triple the measurement of the rail (rod) by 42 cm (16½ in) for the valance. Cut as many widths as required, each with a depth of 42 cm (16½ in) and join the widths using French seams (see steps 11-13).

1. *To make the curtains,* begin by pulling a thread across the width of the material to act as a guide when cutting the edge of the curtains straight. This is very important, otherwise the curtains will not hang correctly.

2. Cut the number of drops (widths) that you need and cut off the selvedges to prevent puckering.

3. If you need to join widths, do so as neatly as possible because with the light shining through the curtains from behind, untidy seams will be very noticeable. (I always use French seams - see steps 11-13 below.)

4. Choose a design to candlewick in one corner of each curtain or perhaps as a border and trace the design onto the fabric.

5. Place the fabric into a hoop and stretch taut. Candlewick the designs, then wash and iron the fabric well as directed on page 8.

6. Trim away ragged threads, as once again, any untidiness will show up with the light shining through the curtains from behind.

7. Once the candlewicking is complete, make the curtains. Make a hem on one side edge only (the side furthest away from the candlewicking) of the curtain by turning under first 1 cm (½ in) and then 2 cm (⅞ in). Pin, tack and machine stitch using a straight stitch.

8. Turn back 3 cm (1¼ in), to the wrong side, along the top edge of the curtain, then press and tack.

9. Gather the preboiled and ironed lace (see preparation of cotton lace, page 8) or fabric ruffle (page 62) and pull up the gathers until it measures the same as the combined length and width measurement of one curtain.

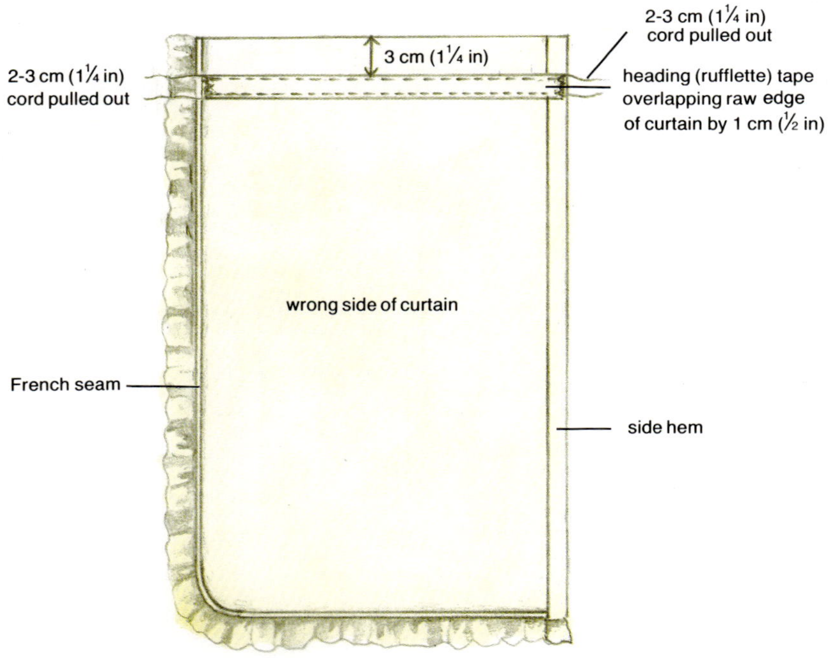

10. Make a hem (to the wrong side) along both short ends of the lace or ruffle and machine stitch.

11. With *wrong sides* together, pin together the straight edge of the gathered lace and the raw edge of the curtain, starting at the top of the curtain.

12. Tack and machine stitch using an overlock stitch or a straight and then a zigzag stitch.

13. Now with right sides together, and adjusting the gathers so that they lie straight, pin and tack a slightly wider seam than before (French seam). Machine stitch using a straight stitch. Press the seam back towards the curtain.

14. Pull out 2-3 cm (⅞-1¼ in) of cord from both ends of the heading (rufflette) tape and knot the cord ends together at one end.

15. Turn under 1 cm (½ in) to the wrong side at each end of the heading (rufflette) tape. Pin the tape to the curtain, overlapping the raw edge of the curtain by 1 cm (½ in). Tack and machine stitch close to the edges of the tape, using a straight stitch. Remember to sew along the short ends of the tape as well.

16. Pull up the cord until the curtain fits the window, then roll up the long end of the cord so that it looks tidy. Do not cut this long length of cord.

17. Complete the other curtain in exactly the same way.

18. *To make a valance* (which may also be candlewicked if you wish), turn back 5 mm (¼ in) and then 1 cm (½ in) along the bottom edge of the valance to make a hem. Make a hem exactly the same way along both side edges of the fabric. Pin, tack and machine stitch using a straight stitch.

19. If desired, first stitch lace (having first made a small hem on both short ends of the lace) along the bottom edge of the valance, then stitch ribbon just above the inside edge of the lace.

20. Turn back 1 cm (½ in) and then 9 cm (3½ in) to the wrong side along the top of the valance. Press. Pin, tack and machine stitch close to the edge of the seam allowance.

21. Push the wooden rod through the casing you made at the top of the valance and hang the rod on the wooden brackets.

22. *For the tie-backs,* draw four panels, each 12 cm (4¾ in) wide, on the fabric. Two of the panels are to be candle-wicked and two are for the lining.

23. Trace the candlewick designs on page 67 onto two of the panels in the positions indicated in the illustration.

24. Place the fabric in the hoop and pull taut. Candlewick the designs.

25. Cut out the four panels and wash and iron the two candlewicked panels very well, following the directions on page 8.

26. Cut two pieces of iron-on vilene interfacing equal to the finished length of each panel with the width measuring 11 cm (4¼ in). Centre the vilene interfacing on each piece of lining and pin it in place, leaving a 5 mm (¼ in) seam allowance all round the edges. Iron the vilene onto each panel so that the vilene becomes bonded to the fabric.

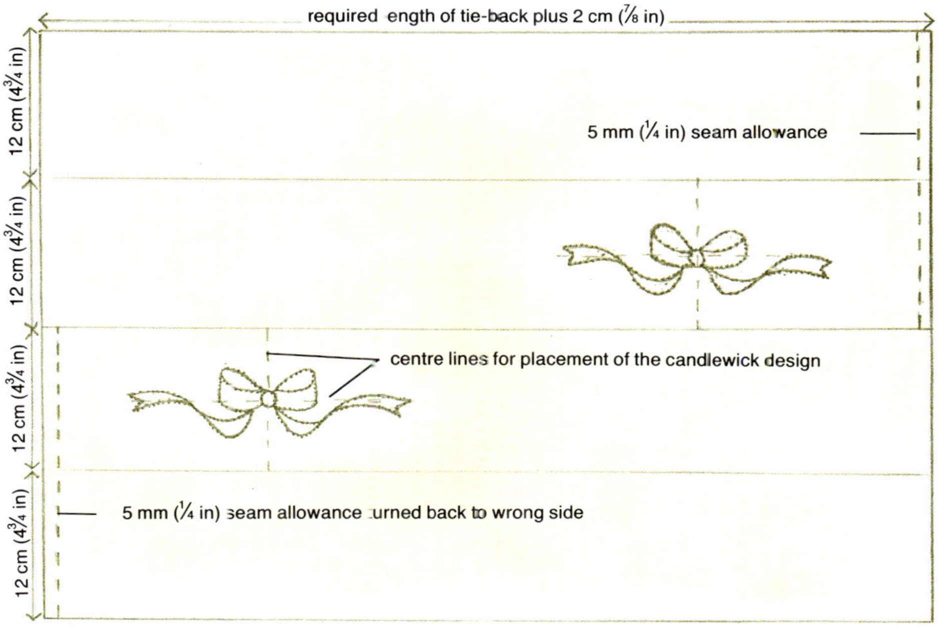

27. Turn back, to the wrong side, a 5 mm (¼ in) seam allowance along one short side of each of the four panels and press.

28. With right sides together (the embroidery to the inside) pin a candlewicked panel to one piece of lining. Tack and machine stitch along the remaining short side and two long sides, clip the corners, then turn the fabric right side out. Slipstitch the opening closed and press.

29. Repeat with remaining candlewicked panel and lining.

30. Sew a small brass ring to the centre of both ends of each strip so that the tie-backs can be hooked onto small hooks screwed into the wall at the side of the curtains.

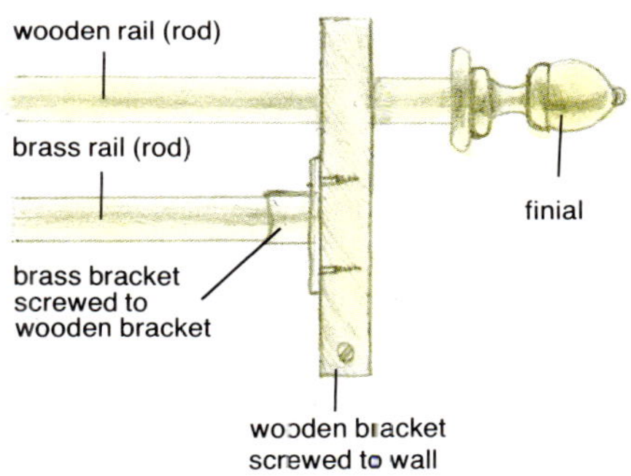

NOTE *You can purchase brass or chrome-plated rods and brackets (from which you will hang the curtains), which should be screwed to the inside edge of the wooden brackets, leaving sufficient space to allow the curtains to be drawn freely.*

THE NURSERY

As a child, I grew up on a smallholding surrounded by open fields and tree-clad mountains. We had a lovely stream running through the bottom of our garden and it was there that I spent many happy hours in a make-believe world. Woodland animals, rocking horses and hearts are but a few of the magical memories of my childhood that I have incorporated into the designs used in this fantasy nursery.

CAROUSEL MOBILE

Materials

Six 40 cm x 40 cm (16 in x 16 in) pieces plain or different coloured felt
Three 40 cm x 1 cm-wide (16 in x ½ in-wide) satin ribbons, each a different colour
Three 45 cm x 1 cm-wide (18 in x ½ in-wide) satin ribbons, each a different colour
Polyester stuffing or potpourri
Wooden or brass curtain ring
Inside hoop of a 30 cm (12 in) embroidery hoop
Glue
2 m (2 ⅛ yds) scalloped cotton lace or broderie anglaise
Seven satin bows
Two small bells

1. Trace the designs on pages 74, 75 and 81 onto the felt, following the directions for tracing a design on page 9. Draw the outline of each design *twice*, remembering that each animal must face to the left and to the right. *Do not cut out.*

2. Place each piece of felt in the hoop and pull taut. Candlewick around the inside outline and any other features, for example faces, manes and tails.

3. Once all the candlewicking is complete, cut out all the animals and hearts along their cutting lines. With *wrong* sides together, pin both sections of each animal and heart together.

4 Insert one end of a length of satin ribbon into each animal and heart and secure. Using the foot of your sewing machine as a guide, stitch around the outline of each shape, leaving a 3 cm (1¼ in) opening along one side.

5. Stuff each shape with polyester stuffing or potpourri. Neatly stitch the opening closed.

6. Tie the other end of each ribbon to the wooden or brass curtain ring.

7. Mark each ribbon 30 cm (12 in) from the curtain ring. Mark the outside of the hoop at 16 cm (6½ in) intervals and apply glue to the wooden hoop at these points. Apply glue to the dull side of each ribbon at the 30 cm (12 in) mark. Allow the glue on both surfaces to become tacky and then press each ribbon very firmly against the outside of the hoop at the points where you applied the glue.

8. Gather the lace or broderie anglaise and sew the two ends together. Pull up the gathers to fit around the outside of the hoop and glue the lace to the hoop.

9. Glue a bow to the hoop between each ribbon. Tie a bow and two bells to the base of the wooden or brass ring.

NURSERY TIDY

Materials

Two 61 cm x 76 cm (24 in x 30 in) pieces calico or other background fabric
Four 20 cm x 2.5 cm-wide (8 in x 1 in-wide) ribbons for hanging the tidy
120 cm x 6 cm-wide (1⅜ yds x 2½ in-wide) contrasting fabric for elastic casing
62 cm x 2 cm-wide (24½ in x ⅞ in-wide) elastic
120 cm x 40 cm (1⅜ yds x 16 in) contrasting fabric for pockets
62 cm (24½ in) narrow elastic
61 cm x 76 cm (24 in x 30 in) polyester wadding/batting
About 2.2 m (2½ yds) bias binding
Satin bow
Curtain rod or dowel

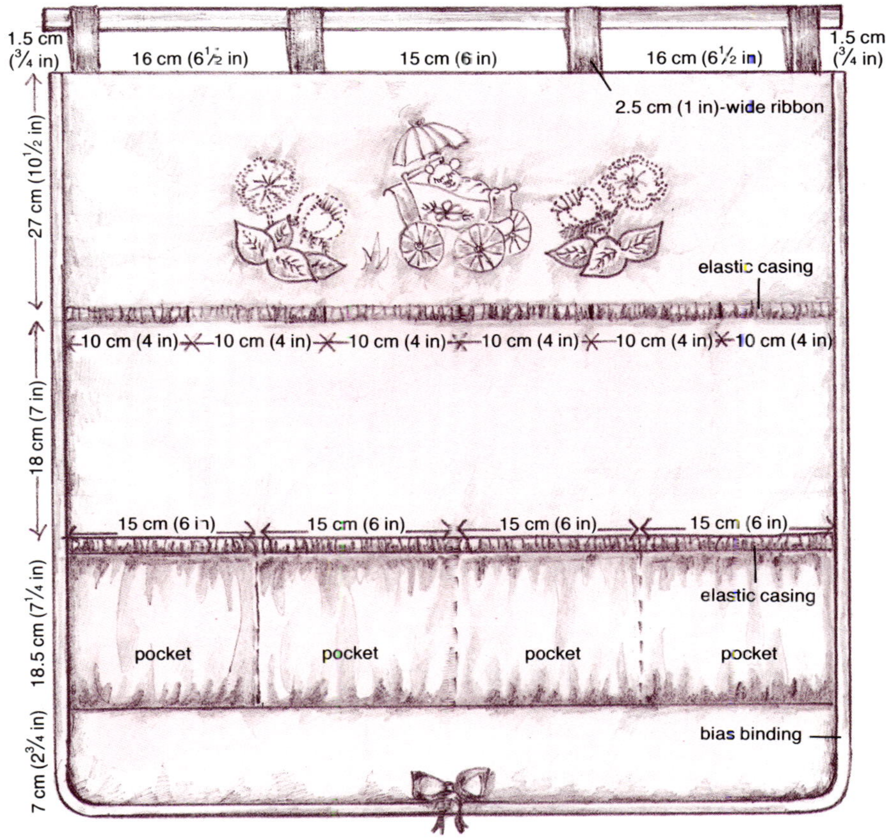

1. Round off the two bottom corners of the two pieces of calico or other plain-coloured fabric.

2. Trace the designs on pages 94-95 to fit the top 27 cm (10½ in) of one piece of calico as shown in the illustration.

3. Candlewick the designs and when complete, wash and iron the fabric well, following the instructions on page 8.

4. Fold the four ribbons in half (wrong sides together) and match their raw edges with that of the fabric. Pin and tack them in position as shown.

5. To make the elastic casing, fold the piece of contrasting fabric in half lengthways. With right sides together, stitch a 5 mm (¼ in) seam along the long raw edge. Turn the fabric right side out.

6. Draw a line across the width of the candlewicked fabric, 27 cm (10½ in) from the top raw edge. Mark the line at 10 cm (4 in) intervals. Mark the elastic casing at 20 cm (8 in) intervals.

7. Thread the wider elastic through the casing and pin both ends to the sides of the tidy at the 27 cm (10½ in) line. Match the marks on the casing with those on the line and machine stitch securely. Sew the loose ends of the elastic and casing to the side edges of the candlewicked fabric.

8. Draw a horizontal line right across the width of the tidy 18 cm (7 in) below the casing. Draw another line 18.5 cm (7¼ in) below that line. Mark both lines vertically at 15 cm (6 in) intervals.

9. Fold the fabric for the pockets in half lengthways so that it measures 120 cm x 20 cm (1⅜ yds x 8 in) and press. Make marks 2.5 cm (1 in) long and 30 cm (12 in) apart along both long edges of the folded pocket fabric.

10. Open out the fabric and gather along the fold line. Pull up the gathers so that the fabric measures 60 cm (24 in) across.

11. Matching the marks on the fold line of the pocket fabric with those on the bottom line on the tidy, pin the gathered fabric to the background fabric. Machine stitch into place.

12. Bring the two raw edges together again and tack. Fold under 5 mm (¼ in) and then 1.5 cm (¾ in) to the wrong side to make a casing for the narrow elastic. Pin, tack and machine stitch. Thread the narrow elastic through the casing.

13. Match the marks along the casing with those on the second line on the background fabric and pin into place.

14. Stitch vertical lines between the marks on the second and third lines.

15. Tack the raw side edges of the pockets to the background fabric. You will now have four separate pockets.

16. Place the backing (lining) fabric and then the wadding/batting on top of the candlewicked side of the tidy. [The four ribbon loops will now be sandwiched between the candlewicked fabric and the backing (lining) fabric.] Matching the raw edges, pin, tack and machine stitch along the top edge, then turn the backing fabric and wadding/batting towards the back. The ribbon loops will now be the right way up.

17. Pin all three layers together around the other three sides and tack. Turn back 5 mm (¼ in) on both ends of the bias binding and pin the binding to the front of the tidy around these three sides. Tack and machine stitch, making sure that you catch the ends of the elastic, casing and pockets. Fold the bias binding (over the raw edge) towards the back of the tidy and pin. Tack and then slipstitch the bias binding in place.

18. If you wish to quilt the candlewick design, prepare to quilt and quilt as described on page 12. Remove tacking stitches.

19. Sew a pretty satin ribbon bow to the bottom of the tidy. Hang the loops of satin ribbon on the curtain rod or dowel.

20. If desired, make four extra felt animals (see Mobile page 28) and hang two from satin loops, on either side of the dowel or rod.

THE COT QUILT

As cot quilts require frequent washing, choose a fabric that launders well. Should you wish to use a pure cotton, wash it well first to prevent shrinkage. A cot quilt candlewicked in colour looks very pretty but you can use a plain, coloured fabric and candlewick the designs using cream or coloured thread.

Materials for a cot quilt with a finished size of 75 cm x 110 cm (29 ¾ in x 43 ½ in)

Two 76 cm x 111 cm (30 in x 43 ¾ in) pieces calico or other fabric
About 3 m (3 ¼ yds) preboiled cotton lace (see page 8)
Two 90 cm (35 in) satin ribbons
Two 126 cm (49 ½ in) satin ribbons
75 cm x 110 cm (29 ¾ in x 43½ in) thin polyester wadding/batting

1. Trace the designs on pages 94-95 and place them together to form the complete design. Use sticky tape at the back of the designs to hold them together.

2. Fold one piece of calico in half vertically and then in half horizontally. Press. Open out the fabric and match the centre lines of the fabric with those of the design. Trace the design onto the fabric.

3. Place the fabric in the hoop and pull taut. As it is rather a large design begin candlewicking in the centre of the design and work your way towards the outside.

4. Once you have finished the candlewicking, wash and iron the fabric very well, following the instructions on page 8. This will be the last time you iron the fabric.

5. Mark off 13 cm (5 ¼ in) from the outside edges all the way round the quilt. Pin the straight edge of the preboiled insertion lace (see page 8 for preparation of lace) along this line all the way round the quilt, mitring the corners (page 60).

6. Tack and machine stitch the lace in place.

7. Pin, tack and machine stitch all the way round the outer edge of the lace.

8. Leaving a 20 cm (8 in) loose length at either end of each of the four satin ribbons, pin the ribbons along the inside edges of the lace as shown in the illustration overleaf. Make sure that the edge of the ribbon slightly overlaps the edge of the lace.

9. Tack and machine stitch along both edges of each of the lengths of ribbon, stopping about 1 cm (½ in) away from each of the corners.

10. Tie bows at each corner of the design.

11. Turn back a 5 mm (¼ in) seam allowance along one short side of both pieces of fabric. Finger-press.

12. Trace the quilting design onto the border of the quilt, beginning the design at the points marked x and working towards the corners.

13. With right sides together and raw edges matching, pin and tack the candlewicked front to the lining along three sides of the quilt. Machine stitch with an overlock stitch or a straight stitch and then zigzag stitch, leaving an opening along the side where you turned back the seam allowance.

14. Clip the corners and turn the quilt right side out.

15. Slip the wadding/batting inside, working the corners of the wadding/batting into the corners of the quilt. Slipstitch the opening closed.

16. Prepare the quilt for quilting by following the instructions on page 12. Quilt all those parts of the design that you wish to accentuate. Quilt the border, as well as along the inside edge of the ribbon and the outside edge of the lace. This will give the border a more quilted effect.

17. Remove the tacking threads.

WALL-HANGING

A colourful, pretty wall-hanging will brighten up any room and is particularly lovely in a child's room. There are several ways of completing a wall-hanging - the simplest being to use an embroidery hoop as a frame.

Materials

40 cm x 40 cm (16 in x 16 in) calico or other plain fabric for background
30 cm (12 in) embroidery hoop for the frame
40 cm x 40 cm (16 in x 16 in) thin polyester wadding/batting
40 cm x 40 cm (16 in x 16 in) muslin
2.5 m (2 ¾ yds) preboiled lace of desired width (page 8)

1. Fold the calico in half vertically and then in half horizontally. Finger-press. Open out the fabric and match the centre lines of the fabric with those of the design on page 81. Trace the design onto the fabric.

2. Place the fabric in the embroidery hoop and pull taut. Candlewick the design.

3. Wash and iron the completed design very well, following the instructions on page 8.

4. Sandwich the wadding/batting between the candlewicked square and the muslin. Prepare for quilting and quilt as described on page 12.

5. Gather the lace (see page 8 for preparation of cotton lace) until it measures 103 cm (1 ⅛ yds). Place the candlewicked and quilted fabric in the hoop and pull fairly taut.

6. Draw a line with a water-erasable pen close to and around the bottom edge of the hoop. Remove the fabric from the hoop and add on an extra 6 mm (¼ in) all round the circumference. Trim away the excess fabric.

7. With right sides together (and the scalloped edge of the lace lying towards the centre of the circle) pin the straight edge of the gathered lace to the raw edge of the circle. Tack, then machine stitch the lace into place using an overlock stitch.

8. Join the two short ends of the lace together by sewing a French seam (page 24, steps 11-13). Trim away any ragged threads and remove the tacking.

9. Centre the candlewicked circle over the inner wooden hoop. Replace the outer wooden hoop and tighten the screw securely. Pull the fabric fairly taut and adjust the lace ruffles so that they will lie flat when the wall-hanging is hung against the wall.

10. Sew a loop of ribbon to the back of the ruffle so that the wall-hanging can hang from a hook or nail.

11. If desired, the back of the wall-hanging can be neatened. Cut a circle of fabric or felt the same size as the inner hoop and zigzag around the outer edge. Glue the fabric to the back of the inner hoop.

THE BATHROOM

Delicate candlewick embroidery enhances guest towels, a toilet seat cover, toilet roll holder and tissue box holder. A cream on cream candlewicked bath mat provides a contrast to the more colourful items. Whether you prefer the neutral look of cream embroidery on calico or the brighter hues of pinks and greens, candlewicked bathroom accessories will harmonize with both contemporary and old-fashioned bathrooms. This often neglected area of your home can be made to look attractive and comfortable with the addition of these eye-catching articles.

TOILET SEAT COVER

Materials

41 cm x 41 cm (16½ in x 16½ in) calico
41 cm x 41 cm (16½ in x 16½ in) calico for lining
41 cm x 41 cm (16½ in x 16½ in) polyester wadding/batting
2-3 m (2¼-3¼ yds) preboiled cotton lace or broderie anglaise
98 cm x 10 cm-wide (1⅛ yds x 4 in-wide) calico for casing
About 30 cm (12 in) bias binding
Narrow elastic
Two 20 cm (8 in) satin ribbons

1. Take a piece of newspaper and place it between the toilet seat and lid. Trace the outline of the lid. Add 1.5 cm (¾ in) all the way round the circumference.

2. Now measure the pattern for the toilet seat lid horizontally and vertically. This will determine how much fabric you will need. For a standard toilet seat lid, the measurements given above under **Materials** should be sufficient.

3. Pin the pattern of the toilet seat lid to the fabric and trace the outline. Do likewise with the lining. Do not cut out as it will not fit into the hoop properly.

4. Find the centre lines of the toilet seat cover by folding the outline in half vertically and then horizontally. Press.

5. Match the centre lines of the fabric with those of the design and trace the design onto one piece of fabric. Place in the hoop and pull taut. Candlewick the design.

6. Once the candlewicking is complete, cut along the outlines on both pieces of fabric and wash and iron the candlewicked fabric.

7. Cut a piece of wadding/batting exactly the same size and sandwich it between the candlewicked fabric and the lining. Prepare for quilting and quilt the design as described on page 12.

8. Measure the circumference of the pattern of the toilet seat lid and double the measurement, adding on a 3 cm (1¼ in) seam allowance. This will determine the length of lace required.

9. Gather the lace to fit around the circumference of the cover. With right sides together, position the lace on the toilet seat cover with the scalloped edge facing towards the centre. Leaving a 3 cm (1¼ in) loose end, pin, tack and machine stitch the lace in place. When you reach the place where you began, make a French seam on the lace as follows: With *wrong* sides of the lace together, pin and machine stitch a 5 mm (¼ in) seam. Turn the lace so that *right* sides are together and stitch a slightly wider seam than before. Stitch the lace to the cover.

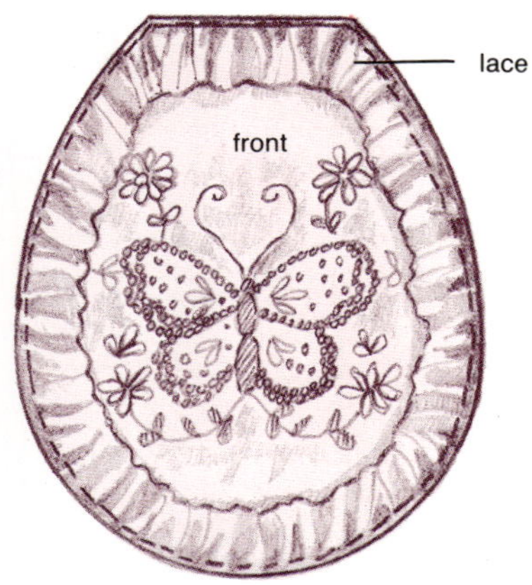

10. Make a seam at either end of the long piece of calico. For the casing for the elastic, turn back 5 mm (¼ in) and then 1.5 cm (¾ in) to the wrong side along one long side. Pin, tack and machine stitch.

11. With right sides together, pin this long strip to the candlewicked side of the toilet seat cover. (The lace or broderie anglaise will be sandwiched between the candlewicked side and the long strip of calico.) Machine stitch in place. Remove tacking threads.

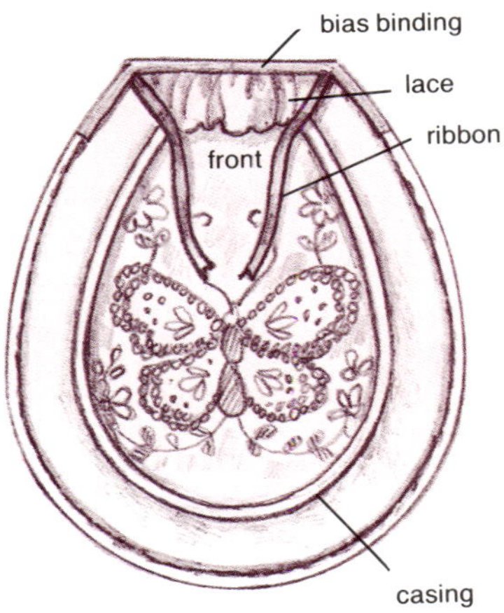

12. Place the bias binding as indicated in the illustration and sew it into position.

13. Turn the seat cover right side out and thread the elastic through the casing, pulling the elastic up until the cover fits the toilet seat lid securely. Secure the ends of the elastic to the casing with several rows of stitching.

14. Stitch the satin ribbon to either end of the casing as shown.

Toilet Roll Holder

For this project, cut a piece of fabric wide enough to be placed in an embroidery or quilting hoop. Once the candlewick embroidery is completed, the excess fabric will be cut away and can be used for another project.

Materials

106 cm x 40 cm-wide (42 in x 16 in-wide) calico

26 cm x 2.5 cm-wide (10¼ in x 1 in-wide) satin ribbon

Brass ring

1. On the left-hand side of the calico, mark off a panel 106 cm x 24 cm (42 in x 9½ in) wide. Ignore the extra fabric on the right-hand side as you will cut it off after you have candlewicked the design.

2. Fold the 24 cm x 106 cm (9½ in x 42 in) panel in half vertically and press along this line.

3. Place the top right-hand section of the panel (G) on top of the design on page 75 and trace the design.

4. Place the fabric in a hoop and pull taut. Candlewick the design, then cut off the 106 cm x 24 cm (42 in x 9½ in) panel. Wash and iron the whole panel

but particularly concentrate on the candlewicked portion (see page 8).

5. Thread the ribbon through a brass ring, bring the ends together and secure.

6. Place the folded satin ribbon in position as shown (AA-BB) and tack in place.

7. Turn back, to the wrong side, a 1 cm (½ in) seam allowance along the bottom edge of the panel.

8. With right sides together, (the candlewicking will be to the inside) refold the panel vertically and pin the raw edges together along the top and side edges. Machine stitch along the top and side seams and clip the corners. Turn the panel right side out and neatly slipstitch the bottom edge closed. Press.

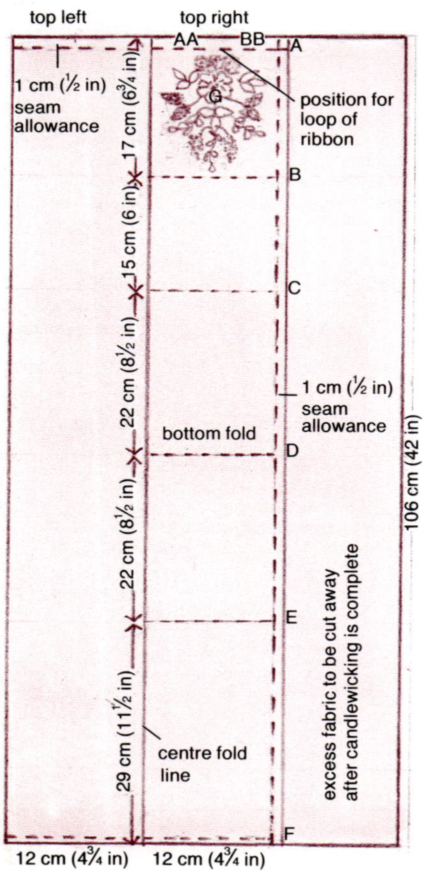

9. From the top edge (A) measure and mark off 17 cm (6¾ in) (B). From (B) measure and mark off 15 cm (6 in) (C). From (C) measure and mark off 22 cm (8½ in) (D) which becomes the bottom fold line. From (D) measure and mark off 22 cm (8½ in) (E). From (E) measure and mark off 29 cm (11½ in) (F).

10. Pin (E) to (C) and (F) to (B) on the front of the toilet roll holder. Tack and sew right across the width of the fabric. You will now have a holder with two loops in which to insert two toilet rolls.

11. If desired, hang two candlewicked hearts stuffed with potpourri from the brass ring and tie a pretty bow to the base of the brass ring.

BATH MAT

Materials

82 cm x 56 cm (32 in x 22 in) fabric
82 cm x 56 cm (32 in x 22 in) fabric for lining
82 cm x 56 cm (32 in x 22 in) polyester wadding/batting
Ribbon and lace

1. Fold one piece of fabric in half horizontally and then vertically to determine the centre point. Match the centre point of the fabric with those of the design and trace the design onto the fabric.

NOTE *It is important to use a central design as the quilting will anchor the three layers (candlewicked top, wadding/batting and lining) and prevent the bath mat bunching in the middle.*

2. Place the fabric in a hoop and pull taut. Candlewick the design and then wash and iron the fabric very well, following the directions on page 8.

3. If you wish to decorate the bath mat with lace and ribbon, do so at this stage. There are many ways in which you can decorate the bath mat but if you wish to make the one featured here, first pin, tack and sew on all the lace as shown in the illustration.

4. Position each length of ribbon so that one edge overlaps the edge of the lace slightly and hides the machine stitching on the lace. Pin, tack and machine stitch the lengths of ribbon in place.

5. Turn back, to the wrong side, a 5 mm (¼ in) seam allowance along one short side of both the front and back sections of the bath mat. Press.

6. Tack the wadding/batting to the wrong side of the lining. With right sides together, pin, tack and machine stitch the candlewicked front of the bath mat to the lining along the other short side and both long sides, using an overlock stitch or a straight and then a zigzag stitch.

7. Clip the corners, remove tacking threads and turn the bath mat right side out. Neatly slipstitch the opening closed.

8. Prepare the mat for quilting and quilt as described on page 12. You may also wish to quilt along the edge of the ribbon (closest to the candlewicking design) and along the edge of the lace. Remove the tacking stitches.

TISSUE BOX HOLDER

Materials

Tracing paper
42 cm x 52 cm-wide (16½ in x 20½ in-wide) calico
42 cm x 26 cm-wide (16½ in x 10¼ in-wide) thin polyester wadding/batting
20 cm x 26 cm-wide (8 in x 10¼ in-wide) calico for the inset
20 cm x 13 cm-wide (8 in x 5¼ in-wide) thin polyester wadding/batting
Four 20 cm (8 in) satin ribbons
1.6 m (1¾ yds) bias binding

1. Fold the tracing paper in half vertically. Align the fold line with the centre fold line of the pattern on page 80. Trace all the details including the design onto the tracing paper. Do the same for the inset (page 81).

2. Cut along the traced outlines, turn the folded pattern pieces over and complete the other half of the design and details. Open out the tracing paper.

3. Fold the 42 cm x 52 cm-wide (16¼ x 20½ in) fabric in half horizontally to measure 21 cm x 52 cm (8¼ in x 20½ in) and finger-press. Place the bottom fold line of the tissue box holder pattern on the fold of the fabric, pin the pattern to the fabric and trace around the outline.

4. Turn the fabric over and hold it up to a windowpane. Trace the outline of the pattern on the back to correspond with the outline on the front.

5. For the lining, trace a second outline on the front of the fabric alongside the first but do not turn the fabric over as you did in Step 4.

6. Open out the fabric and place it on top of the pattern, matching the outline on the fabric with that of the pattern. Trace the design. Turn the fabric around and trace the design onto the other half of the outline. *Do not cut out.*

7. Place the fabric in a hoop and stretch taut. Candlewick the design on the front half, remove the fabric from the hoop and place the second design to be candlewicked in the hoop and pull taut. Candlewick the second design.

8. Refold the fabric and cut along the outlines of both the candlewicked fabric and the lining. Wash and iron the candlewicked section carefully.

9. Fold the 42 cm x 26 cm-wide (16½ in x 10¼ in-wide) wadding/batting in half horizontally to measure 21 cm x 26 cm (8¼ in x 10¼ in). Place the bottom fold line of the pattern on the fold of the wadding/batting. Pin and cut out.

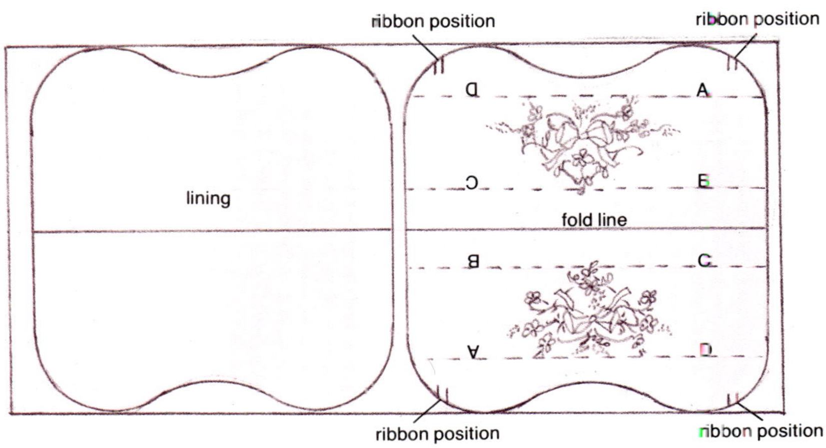

10. Place this wadding/batting between the candlewicked fabric and the lining. Prepare the fabric for quilting and quilt as described on page 12.

11. Fold the second piece of fabric in half horizontally so that it measures 10 cm x 26 cm (4 in x 10¼ in). Pin the inset pattern piece with the curved bottom fold line on the fold of the fabric. Trace around the outline. Trace another outline alongside the first. Cut along first one outline and then the other.

12. Fold the 20 cm x 13 cm-wide (8 in x 5¼ in-wide) wadding/batting in half horizontally to measure 10 cm x 13 cm (4 in x 5¼ in). Place the inset pattern piece on the wadding/batting, pin and then cut out. Cut along the fold line. [You will now have two pieces of wadding/batting 10 cm x 13 cm (4 in x 5¼ in).]

13. Sandwich a piece of wadding/batting between each folded inset piece. Pin, tack and machine stitch close to the raw edges of first one inset and then the other.

14. Pin the bias binding to the long straight edge of each inset. Tack and machine stitch using a straight stitch.

15. *To assemble the tissue box holder:* with wrong sides together pin the left top corner of the inset to the main section of the tissue box holder at (A). Pin the left bottom curved corner to (B), the right curved corner to (C) and the top right corner to (D).

16. Tack from (A) to (D) and machine stitch in place, easing the straight edge of the main section of the holder round the curved corners of the inset.

17. Pin, tack and machine stitch the second inset to the main section of the tissue box holder in the same way.

18. Tack the ribbons in the positions indicated on the illustration.

19. Turn back 5 mm (¼ in) to the wrong side along the short end of the bias binding and finger-press. Beginning in an inconspicuous place, pin the bias binding all around the outer edge of the tissue box holder. When you return to where you began, overlap the turned back beginning of the bias binding by 1 cm (½ in). Machine stitch the bias binding in position.

20. Fold the bias binding over the raw edges and tack in position. Hand sew the binding in position, using a blind hem stitch. Remove tacking.

21. Place the box of tissues in the completed tissue holder and tie the satin ribbons either end into bows.

GUEST TOWELS

Hand-embroidered guest towels are lovely to look at and a pleasure to use in one's own home. They also make wonderful gifts. Should you wish to make a really special gift, use huckaback, Irish or Belgian linen, as these are the traditional fabrics used for fine guest towels. You may, of course, use terry towelling or a purchased guest towel for a less expensive version. Whichever fabric you use, ensure that it is both easily washable and absorbent.

Materials for one guest towel

40 cm x 40 cm (16 in x 16 in) fabric for the candlewicked panel
33 cm x 8 cm (13 in x 3¼ in) very thin polyester wadding/batting (optional)
53 cm x 33 cm (21 in x 13 in) linen, huckaback or towelling
Two 33 cm x 8 mm-wide (13 in x ⅜ in-wide) satin ribbons
33 cm (13 in) cotton lace or broderie anglaise

1. *If you are making your own guest towel,* draw a rectangle 33 cm x 8 cm (13 in x 3¼ in) wide onto the fabric for the candlewicked panel.

2. Find the centre lines of the panel by folding the rectangle in half vertically and then horizontally. Press the folds.

3. Open out the fabric and match these lines with the centre lines of the design on page 91. Trace the design onto the panel.

4. Do not cut out the panel as it will then be too small to fit in the hoop. Place the fabric in a hoop and pull taut. Now candlewick the design.

5. Stitch around the outside edges of the panel using a zigzag stitch and cut it out. Wash and iron the panel carefully, following the instructions on page 8.

6. If you wish to quilt the panel, cut a piece of the thinnest wadding/batting available the same size as the panel.

7. With a water-erasable pen, draw a line 8 cm (3¼ in) from the bottom raw edge of the towel and position the bottom edge of the wadding/batting and the candlewicked panel on this line. Pin both layers to the towel.

8. Tack and machine stitch close to the raw edges of the panel.

9. Prepare the panel for quilting and quilt as described on page 12.

10. Zigzag the short ends of the panel to the towel as close to the raw edges as possible.

11. Pin a strip of satin ribbon to the edge of each long side of the panel, so that the ribbon overlaps the panel and hides the machine stitching.

12. Tack and machine stitch the ribbon into place.

13. Make a hem along both the long sides of the towel by turning under 5 mm (¼ in) and then 1 cm (½ in) to the wrong side. Pin, tack and machine stitch using a straight stitch.

14. Make a hem in the same way along the top and bottom edges of the towel.

15. Machine stitch cotton lace or broderie anglaise to the bottom hem of the towel.

16. Remove the tacking threads.

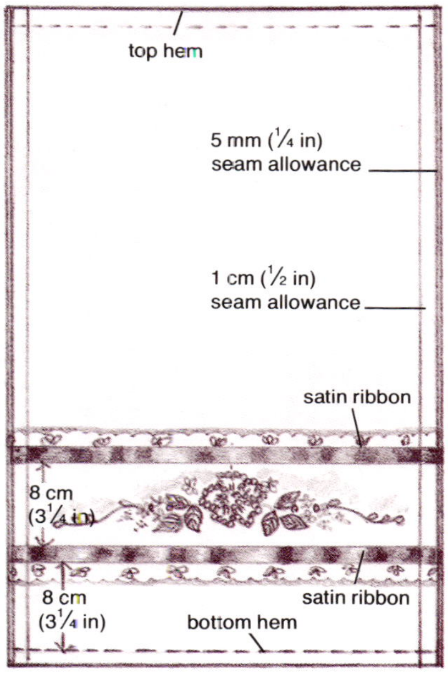

1. *If you are using a purchased guest towel,* measure the width of the towel and draw a rectangle 8 cm (3¼ in) wide x the width of the towel onto the fabric for the candlewicked panel. Add an extra 2 cm (⅞ in) to the length of the panel to allow for the seam allowance.

2. Find the centre lines of the panel by folding the rectangle in half vertically and then horizontally. Press the folds.

3. Open out the fabric and match these lines with the centre lines of the design on page 91. Trace the design onto the panel.

4. Do not cut out the panel as it will then be too small to fit in the hoop. Place the fabric in a hoop and pull taut. Candlewick the design.

5. Stitch around the outside edges of the panel using a zigzag stitch and cut it out. Wash and iron the panel carefully, following the instructions on page 8.

6. Turn back to the wrong side a 1 cm (½ in) seam allowance on both short sides of the panel. Press.

7. If you wish to quilt the panel, cut a piece of the thinnest wadding/batting available the same size as the panel.

8. With a water-erasable pen, draw a line 6 cm (2½ in) from the bottom hem of the towel and position the bottom edge of the wadding/batting and the candlewicked panel on this line. Pin both layers to the towel.

9. Tack and machine stitch along the two long edges close to the raw edges of the panel.

10. Tack, then slipstitch the side edges.

11. Prepare the panel for quilting and quilt as described on page 12.

12. Turn under 1 cm (½ in) at both ends of each satin ribbon.

13. Pin a length of ribbon to the edge of each long side of the panel, so that the ribbon overlaps the panel and hides the machine stitching.

14. Tack and machine stitch the ribbon into place. Slipstitch the short ends in place.

15. Stitch cotton lace or broderie anglaise to the bottom hem of the towel. Remember to make a narrow hem on both short ends of the lace.

16. Remove the tacking threads.

THE BEDROOM

With their neutral tones and simple designs, candlewicked handicrafts blend well with almost any style of décor, but it is in romantic, soft-furnished interiors that they really come into their own. This cottagey bedroom has a delightfully old-fashioned mood that evokes strong feelings of nostalgia. The pale cream colour scheme is offset by the warm tones of wood and thatch, while a juxtaposition of different fabrics – cotton, calico, ribbon, lace and linen – introduces interesting textural contrasts. Precious heirloom quilts, cushions and bed linen, enhanced by decorative candlewick embroidery, add to the tranquil country setting.

QUILTS

Before beginning work on your quilt, read very carefully through the general instructions and the two methods of assembling a quilt. This is essential, as it will help you to determine what size squares are to be cut out.

TRADITIONAL METHOD Should you wish to make a traditional quilt, where each square is framed by lace and the quilt has both horizontal and vertical sashing, the squares will be smaller.

EASIER METHOD However, should you prefer a simpler way of completing the quilt, you can sew all the squares together without any sashing in between. The squares, therefore, must be proportionately larger to make up for the lack of sashing. The lace is then sewn on top of the seams.

To determine the overall dimensions of the quilt
Before you can work out the number and size of the squares, you will need to work out the exact dimensions of the quilt for your particular bed. In order to do this you must first measure the mattress:

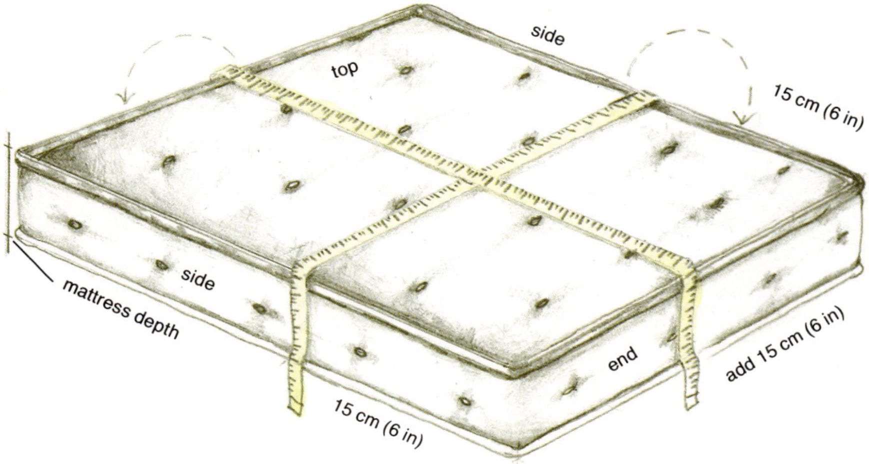

1. Measure the *width* of the mattress and add on twice the depth. Add on an extra 30 cm (12 in) to allow for an overhang of 15 cm (6 in) either side of the mattress.

2. Measure the *length* of the mattress and add on twice the depth. Add an extra 15 cm (6 in) to allow for an overhang at the foot of the bed. As one normally uses a valance (nightfrill) on the base of the bed, the quilt needs to hang 15 cm (6 in) longer than the mattress only on three sides of the bed (not at the top end).

NOTE If your bed has both a footboard and a headboard, it would not be necessary to add an extra 15 cm (6 in) to the length measurement.

CONVENTIONAL BED SIZES

To determine the number and size of the squares for your quilt, consult the tables (pages 56-57) for quilts with sashing (the vertical and horizontal strips between the squares) and for those without. The calculations are based on the measurements of a modern innerspring mattress with a depth of about 18 cm (7 in) and cover many of the popular sizes of mattresses available.

Cutting out squares, borders and sashing

Before cutting out the squares, add on an extra *2 cm (⅞ in)* per square. For example, if the measurement of the square given in the table above is 45 cm (17 ½ in), add on an extra 2 cm (⅞ in). The size of the square you will cut out will be 47 cm x 47 cm (18 ½ in x 18 ½ in). This extra 2 cm (⅞ in) includes a 6 mm (¼ in) seam allowance and allows for shrinking and puckering of the fabric.

At a later stage, once you have completed the candlewicking, the squares will be washed and then blocked (cut exactly square).

Add on an extra *2 cm (⅞ in)* to the width of each piece of sashing and an extra *2 cm (⅞ in)* to the width of each border.

UNCONVENTIONAL BED SIZES

You may find that the measurements of your mattress and, therefore, the size of your quilt, do not conform with those given in the tables on pages 56-57.

If this is the case, refer to the tables and select the quilt size closest to the one you require. It is preferable to choose a quilt that is too large rather than too small for your bed.

However, you may wish to try to calculate the size of the squares yourself, as detailed below.

To calculate the size of the squares for a quilt with sashing

Once you have measured the mattress and determined the overall size of the quilt required for your particular bed, do the following calculation:

From the full width measurement, subtract twice the width of the border [e.g. 2 x 30 cm (2 x 12 in)] plus twice the width of the sashing [e.g. 2 x 10 cm (2 x 4 in)]. (You will see in the illustration on page 44 that there are only two lots of sashing in the width of a quilt made up of twelve squares.) Now divide by three (there are three squares in the width).

Subtract twice the width of the border [e.g. 2 x 30 cm (2 x 12 in)] plus three times the width of the sashing [e.g. 3 x 10 cm (3 x 4 in)] from the full length measurement. (The illustration on page 44 shows three lots of sashing in the length.) Now divide this total by four (there are four squares in the length).

For example, if you have calculated that you require a 200 cm x 250 cm (80 in x 100 in) quilt for your double bed, subtract as follows:

Width measurement		200 cm/80 in
subtract sashing		
(e.g. 2 x 10 cm/4 in)		20 cm/ 8 in
	=	180 cm/72 in
subtract borders		
(e.g. 2 x 30 cm/12 in)		60 cm/24 in
	=	120 cm/48 in
divide by three	=	40 cm/16 in
Length measurement	=	250 cm/100 in
subtract sashing		
(e.g. 3 x 10 cm/4 in)		30 cm/12 in
	=	220 cm/88 in
subtract borders		
(e.g. 2 x 30 cm/12 in)		60 cm/24 in
	=	160 cm/64 in
divide by four	=	40 cm/16 in

You require twelve 40 cm x 40 cm (16 in x 16 in) fabric squares to make this quilt.

These particular measurements happened to work out exactly but very often they do not. Remember that the width of the sashing and borders is fairly flexible and can either be reduced or enlarged or the sashing can be left out altogether.

NOTE *The width measurement of the horizontal sashing must equal that of the vertical sashing. The width of the borders, too, must be uniform throughout.*

To calculate the size of the squares for a quilt without sashing

In order to get the above calculations to work, you will only need to subtract twice the width of the borders from the width measurement and twice the width of the borders from the length measurement.

For example, if the double bed quilt you want to make measures 200 cm x 250 cm (80 in x 100 in), work out the size of the squares as follows:

Width measurement	=	200 cm/80 in
subtract borders		
(e.g. 2 x 25 cm/10 in)		50 cm/20 in
	=	150 cm/60 in
divide by 3	=	50 cm/20 in
Length measurement	=	250 cm/100 in
subtract borders		
(e.g. 2 x 25 cm/10 in)		50 cm/ 20 in
	=	200 cm/80 in
divide by 4	=	50 cm/ 20 in

This quilt will consist of twelve 50 cm x 50 cm (20 in x 20 in) squares with borders 25 cm (10 in) wide.

NOTE *If your calculations to determine the size of the squares (whether for a quilt with sashing or for one without sashing) do not work out, try dividing the length measurement by five instead of four. If this works out, you will then need to make a quilt with fifteen rather than twelve squares.*

Remember to add on the extra 2 cm (⅞ in) to the measurement of each square and an extra 2 cm (⅞ in) to the width measurement of each border before cutting them out.

QUILT WITH SASHING

Materials for 200 cm x 250 cm (80 in x 100 in) double-bed quilt with sashing

10 m x 150 cm-wide (11 yds x 60 in-wide) or 12 m x 120 cm-wide (13 yds x 48 in-wide) calico for the squares, sashing, borders and backing
20-22 m x 7 cm-wide (21½-24 m x 2¾ in-wide) lace
214 cm x 264 cm (84½ in x 104 in) thin polyester wadding/batting
Crochet cotton or embroidery thread

1. Prepare the fabric for the quilt as described on page 8.

2. Follow the instructions on page 44 for measuring the mattress. Refer to the tables of quilt measurements on pages 56-57 and select the size quilt that will fit your particular bed. Remember to add on an extra 2 cm (⅞ in) to all the measurements given to allow for shrinkage and puckering. A 6 mm (¼ in) seam allowance is included.

3. Cut out the number of squares, plus enough fabric for the sashing and borders required for your quilt. Cut the vertical sashing and all the borders a little longer than the finished length and width of the quilt. Cut the horizontal sashing the full width of the fabric but do not cut it into short lengths yet. Always pull a thread, do not tear the material, as this will stretch the edges and make the assembling of the quilt more difficult.

4. Prepare the cotton lace as described on page 8.

5. Trace the designs onto the calico squares, centring them accurately as described on page 9. Any inaccuracy will be apparent once the quilt is complete.

NOTE *Accuracy is most important at all stages of making a quilt, as it will save you a great deal of time when you assemble your quilt.*

6. Place each calico square in turn in the hoop and stretch the fabric taut.

7. Select the threads you enjoyed using on your sampler and candlewick the designs.

> HINT The marks made by the water-erasable pen can be removed at this stage by dipping the squares in plain, lukewarm water and hanging them up to dry.

8. When you have candlewicked *all* the squares, wash them all plus the fabric for the sashing and the borders, in the same soapy water. Wash each square very carefully, making quite sure that you have removed the ring marks that the hoop might have made, as well as any other dirty marks.

NOTE *It is very important that all dirty marks are removed during this wash. If any of the squares need to be washed a second time, they will become a shade lighter than the rest of the squares. This will spoil the overall look of your quilt.*

9. Rinse all the fabric in plain water and then use a fabric softener.

10. Wrap each square individually in a towel and squeeze dry. Do the same for the fabric required for the sashing and borders. Do not hang out to dry.

11. Place a thick towel, (not an embossed one) folded double, on the ironing board. Put each square, candlewicked side down, on the towel and iron it carefully. Do not use too hot an iron as it might scorch the fabric.

12. Always iron the sashing and borders lengthways to ensure an even width throughout.

To block the squares
13. The tension of your work and the ironing will have altered the original size of the squares and it is important that they are all the same size. Measure each square horizontally and vertically to determine which is the smallest. Use graph paper (this is the only reliable way of making a template) to make an accurate template of the measurement of the smallest square. Paste this template onto fairly stiff cardboard or an x-ray plate and cut it out carefully.

14. Find and mark with a water-erasable pen the centre point of the sides of the template and of each fabric square.

15. Place the fabric square on a smooth table surface. *Do not stretch* the edges of the fabric square, even if the thread has shrunk and pulled the square out of alignment. *Smooth* the edges and stick the fabric square to the table with tape. Line up the centre points of the template with those of the square, draw round the edge of the template and cut out. Your fabric square should now be a perfect square.

To assemble the quilt
16. Lay the horizontal sashing on the table and, using the same template as before, mark and cut the sashing to the correct size. These will become the short pieces of sashing to be sewn between the squares. The edges of your sashing and the fabric squares will be exactly the same length.

17. If you wish to frame each square with lace, cut the lace exactly the same width or length as the square (you can use the same template as you used to block the squares and short sashing). Make sure that the pattern of the lace is balanced at both ends (that is, that it doesn't stop halfway through a pattern on one side and not on the other). Cut four pieces of lace for each square.

18. Pin, tack and sew the lace to the top and bottom of each square and then to the sides, stitching about 2-3 mm (⅛ in) from the raw edge of the square and 2-3 mm (⅛ in) from the inner edge of each strip of lace. Tack the raw ends of the lace to the edges of the fabric. Complete all 12 squares in exactly the same way.

19. Lay out the completed squares in the desired positions.

20. Trace the quilting designs onto all the short pieces of horizontal sashing (see page 48, step 28) before you assemble the quilt. Matching the bottom corners of a square with the top corners of a piece of sashing, pin from the centre to the corners. Ease, tack and sew, using the foot of your machine as a guide (in this way, the row of stitching on the lace will not be visible as it will be sewn to the inside of the seam).

21. Sew the top of the next square to the bottom edge of the sashing. Continue in this manner until you have sewn the first panel of four squares. Now assemble the second panel of four squares and then the third. You will now have three panels of four squares.

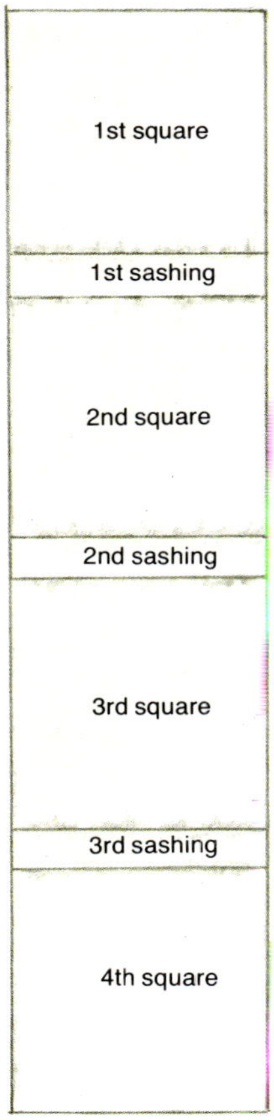

22. To strengthen the seams, overlock them all or use a straight stitch and then a zigzag stitch. Press all the seams towards the squares.

23. Trace the quilting designs onto both pieces of vertical sashing (see step 28).

NOTE *Following the next few instructions carefully will make all the difference as to whether all the corners line up accurately or not.*

24. To assemble, first measure the distance between where the sewing machine needle enters the fabric when using a straight stitch and the raw edge of the square. This measurement will be about 6 mm (¼ in), depending on the make of your machine, and will be the seam allowance for all your seams.

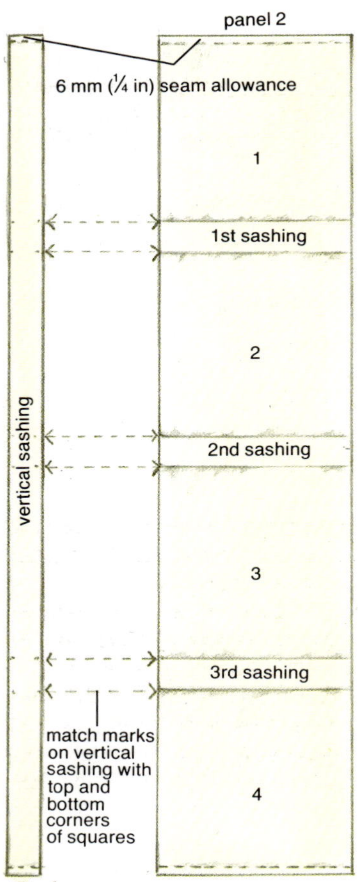

Fig 1

25. Draw this 6 mm (¼ in) seam allowance right across the top end of both pieces of vertical sashing and the first square of each of the three panels. Take the measurement from the 6 mm (¼ in) mark at the top left-hand corner of the first square to the bottom left-hand corner of this same square. Take another measurement from the bottom left-hand corner of the first square to the bottom left-hand corner of the first strip of horizontal sashing. Mark these measurements on a long strip of paper. Now, starting from the 6 mm (¼ in) mark at the top end of the vertical sashing, mark off these two measurements all the way down both sides of both pieces of vertical sashing. (See fig 1)

26. Matching these marks with the corners of the squares, pin the three panels to the two pieces of vertical sashing. Tack and machine stitch using an overlock stitch or a straight and then a zigzag stitch.

27. Measure the front of the quilt across the width and cut out the top and bottom borders slightly longer than this measurement. Measure the length of the quilt and add on the width of the top and bottom borders [that is an extra 60 cm (24 in)]. Cut out the side borders slightly longer than this measurement.

28. Trace the quilting design onto the four border pieces, beginning at the centre point of each border and working out towards the corners. This will prevent having an incomplete design at one end and a complete design at the other end of the border. (See fig 2)

29. Pin, tack and sew the borders to the squares, beginning with the top and bottom borders and then the sides. Overlock these seams and give the completed front of the quilt a final pressing. Do not press the borders with a steam-iron if you have used a water-erasable pen to trace the quilting design as any steam or water will erase it.

To attach the wadding/batting and backing fabric

30. Measure the completed quilt front and cut the wadding/batting and backing fabric approximately 5-7 cm (2-2¾ in) wider on all four sides than the quilt top. [In other words you will add 10-14 cm (4-5½ in) to the length and 10-14 cm (4-5½ in) to the width.]

31. Place the backing fabric on the floor, centre the wadding/batting over it and smooth it out. Now lay the quilt front (candlewicked side uppermost) on top of the wadding/batting. Make quite sure that you straighten out any creases in the backing and wadding/batting before you start to pin (you may need the help of a friend).

32. Pin all three layers together, beginning in the centre and working your way out towards the centre of the outside edges. Then pin from the centre to each corner.

33. Using a strong thread, tack along these pinned lines and between each of these lines. Continue to tack until you have done *at least* 32 rows of tacking. It really is worth the effort. The more you tack, the easier it is to quilt because the wadding/batting does not shift as much (see page 12).

34. Quilt the 12 candlewicked squares, starting from the centre of the quilt and working your way towards the outside edges and corners. (See page 12 on quilting.) Smooth any excess fullness toward the edges as you work.

35. Quilt the horizontal and vertical sashing and finally, the borders.

NOTE *When quilting the sashings and the borders, always start at the centre point of each piece and work towards the corners/edges.*

36. Once you have completed the quilting of the borders, trim the excess wadding/batting and backing so that it is the same width all the way around the

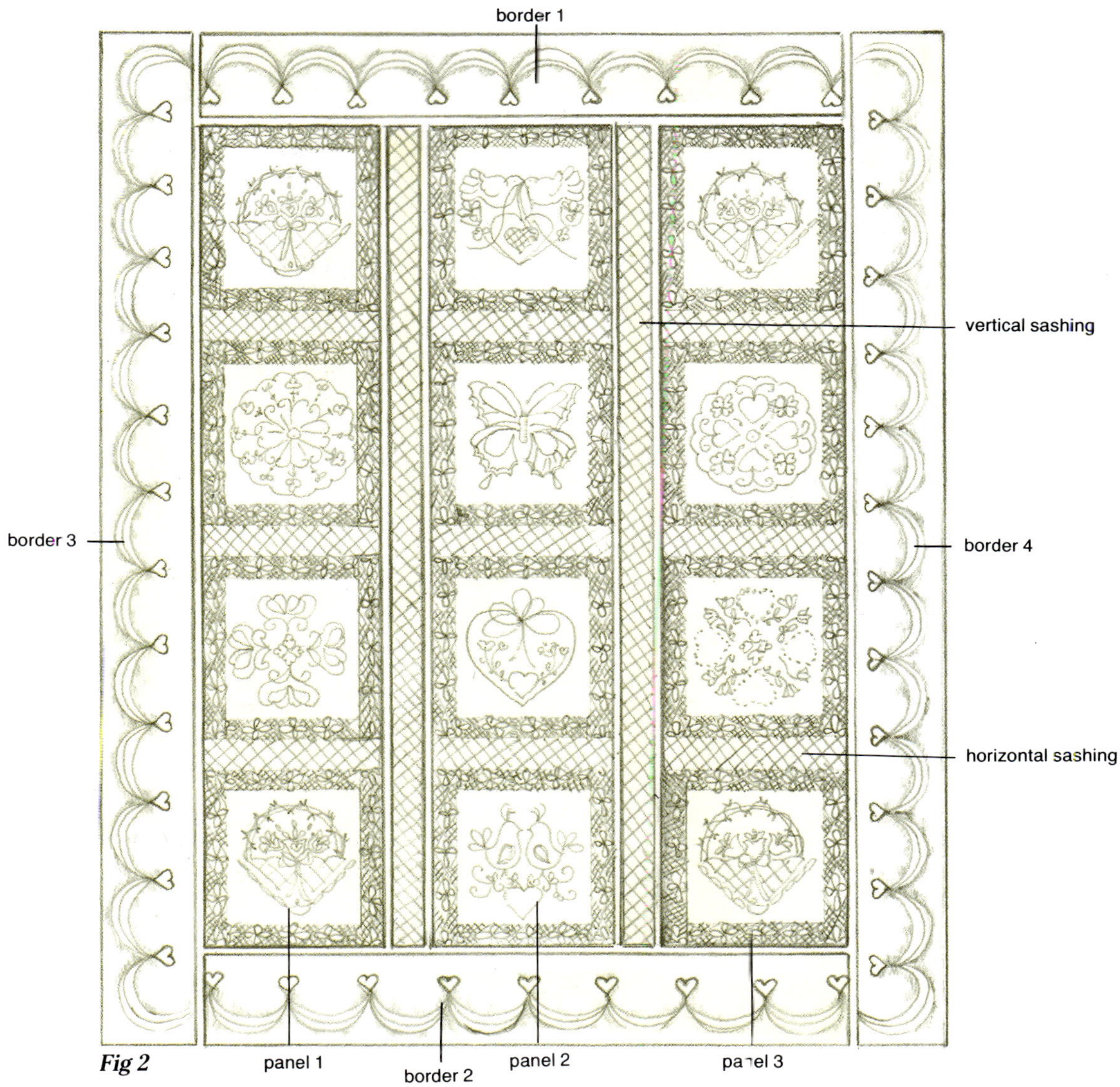

Fig 2

quilt. Turn the raw edges of the backing approximately 2 cm (⅞ in) to the wrong side (towards the wadding/batting) and press.

37. Now fold the backing fabric over the quilt front to create a self-binding. Begin with the top and bottom edges first and then the side edges. Pin, tack and slipstitch into place. To make sure that the wadding/batting is held firmly in place, quilt close to the hem that has just been made. Remove all the tacking threads.

QUILT WITHOUT SASHING

This method is much quicker and easier than the first method and is by far the more suitable for a beginner. Whether you use the first or second method, you are sure to be delighted with the finished quilt. As mentioned before, it will be necessary to make the squares proportionately larger to make up for the lack of sashing.

Materials for 204 cm x 252 cm (80 in x 100 in) double-bed quilt without sashing

10 m x 150 cm-wide (11 yds x 60 cm-wide) or 12 m x 120 cm-wide (13 yds x 48 in-wide) calico for squares, borders and backing

About 16 m x 5-9 cm-wide (18 yds x 2-3½ in-wide) lace

266 cm x 218 cm (104 in x 86 in) polyester wadding/batting

1. Prepare the fabric for the quilt as described on page 8.

2. Follow the instructions on page 44 for measuring the mattress. Refer to the tables of quilt measurements on pages 56-57 and select the size quilt that will fit your particular bed. Add on an extra 2 cm (⅞ in) to all the measurements given to allow for shrinkage and puckering. A 6 mm (¼ in) seam allowance is included.

3. Cut out the number of squares required for your quilt. Cut the borders a little longer than the finished width and length of the quilt [that is 204 cm (80 in) and 252 cm (100 in)]. Always pull a thread, do not tear the material as this will stretch the edges, making it more difficult to assemble the quilt.

4. Prepare the cotton lace as described on page 8.

5. Trace the designs onto the squares, centring them accurately as described on page 9 as any inaccuracy will be apparent once the quilt is complete.

6. Place each calico square in turn in the hoop and stretch the fabric taut.

7. Select the threads you enjoyed using on your sampler and candlewick the designs.

> **HINT** The marks made by the water-erasable pen can be removed at this stage by dipping the squares in *plain* lukewarm water and hanging them up to dry.

8. When you have candlewicked all the squares, wash them all plus the fabric for the borders and backing, in the same soapy water. Wash each square very carefully, making quite sure that you have removed the ringmarks that the hoop might have made, as well as any other dirty marks.

9. Rinse all the fabric in plain water and then use a fabric softener.

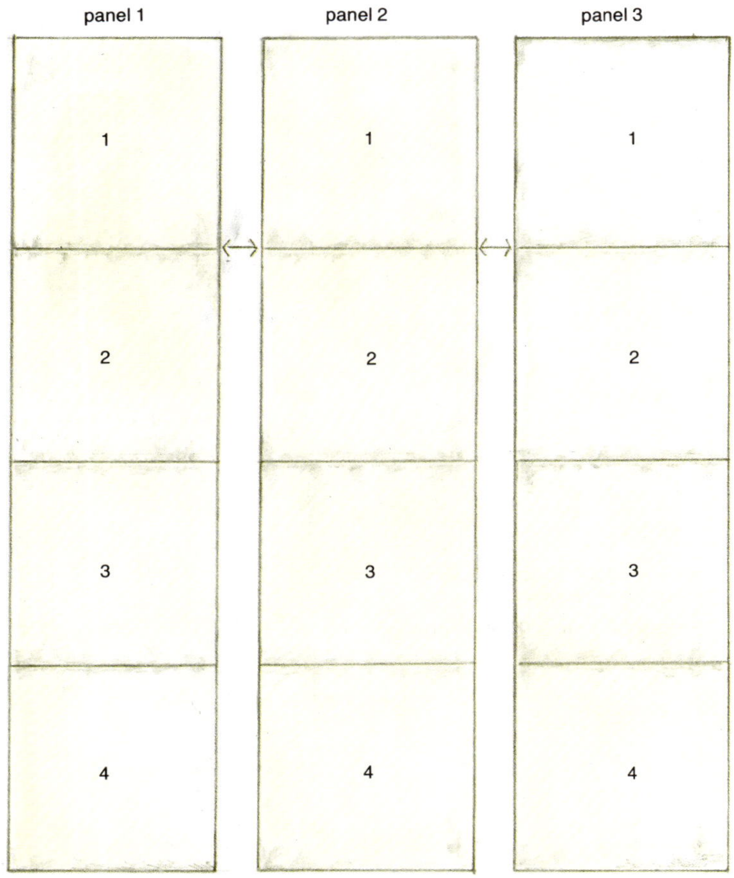

Fig 1

10. Wrap each square individually in a towel and squeeze dry. Do the same for the fabric required for the borders. Do not hang out to dry.

11. Place a thick towel, (not an embossed one) folded double, on the ironing board. Put each square, candlewicked side down, on the towel and iron it carefully. Do not use too hot an iron as it might scorch the fabric.

12. Iron the borders lengthways to ensure an even width throughout.

To block the squares

13. The tension of your work and the ironing will have altered the original size of your squares and it is important that they are all cut the same size. Measure each square horizontally and vertically to determine which is the smallest. Use graph paper to make an accurate template of the measurement of the smallest square. Paste this template onto fairly stiff cardboard or an x-ray plate and cut it out carefully.

14. Find and mark with a water-erasable pen the centre point of the sides of the template and of each fabric square.

15. Place the fabric square on a smooth table surface. *Do not stretch* the edges of the fabric, even if the thread has shrunk and pulled the square out of alignment. *Smooth* the edges and stick the fabric square to the table with sticky tape. Line up the centre points of the template with those of the square, draw around the edge of the template and cut out.

The embroidered fabric should now be a perfect square.

To assemble the quilt
16. Lay out the squares in the desired positions. Now sew the squares together in three panels of four squares as shown in the illustration. Overlock all the seams and press them so that they all lie in the same direction.

17. Placing two panels right sides together, match the corners, pin, tack and sew. Sew panel 1 to panel 2 and panel 2 to panel 3. Overlock the seams and press. (See fig 1.)

18. Measure the front of the quilt across the width and cut out the top and bottom borders slightly longer than this measurement. Measure the length of the quilt and then add on the width of the top and bottom borders [that is an extra 60 cm (24 in)]. Cut out the side borders slightly longer than this measurement.

19. Cut three lengths of lace a little longer than the width of the quilt (before the borders are sewn on), making sure that the pattern is balanced at both ends of the lace. Match the centre lines of the lace with the three horizontal seam lines and pin the lace to the fabric. Tack and sew into place.

20. Cut two lengths of lace a little longer than the length of the quilt (before the borders are sewn on), again making sure that the pattern is balanced at both ends of the lace. Match the centre lines of the lace with the two vertical seam lines and pin the lace to the fabric as shown opposite. Tack and sew the lace into place.

21. Tack the raw ends of the lace to the edges of the fabric.

22. Sew on the top and bottom borders of the quilt and then the two side borders. Press.

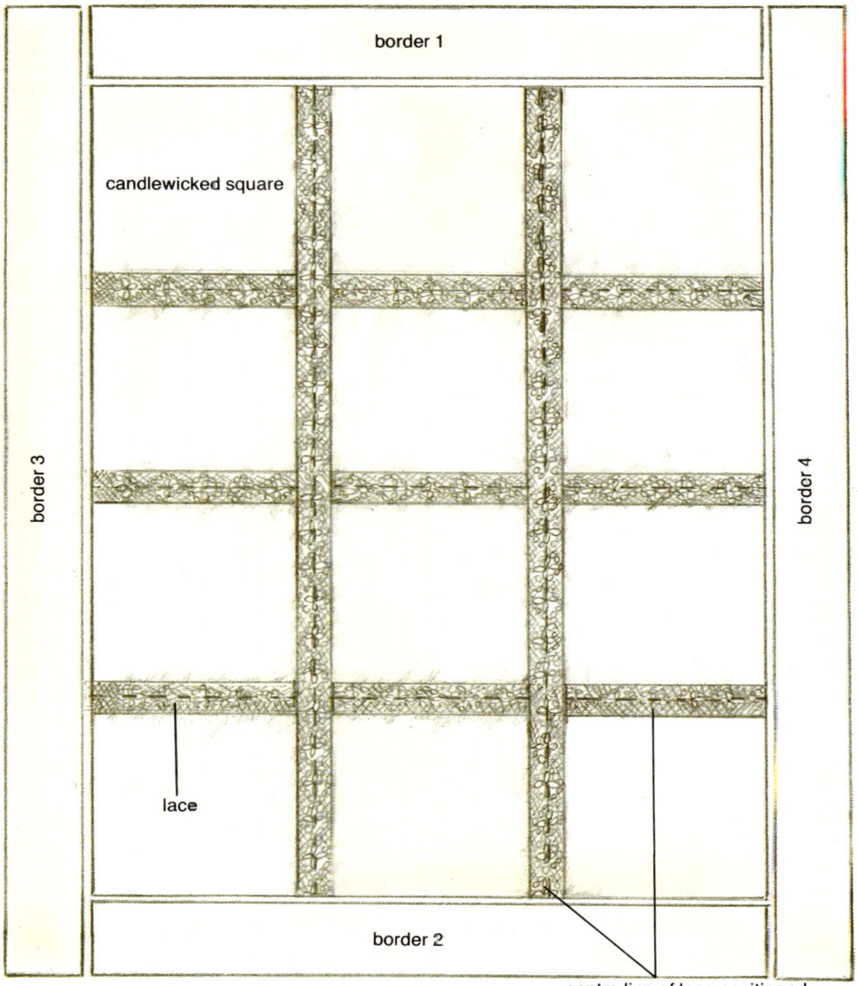

23. Pin on the lace that frames the entire central section of the quilt in the position shown in the illustration. Mitre the corners, tack and sew into place.

24. Trace the quilting designs onto the four borders, beginning in the centre of each and working towards the corners.

To attach the wadding/batting and backing fabric
25. Measure the completed quilt front and cut the wadding/batting and backing fabric approximately 5-7 cm (2-2¾ in) wider on all four sides than the quilt top. [In other words you will add 10-14 cm (4-5½ in) to the length and 10-14 cm (4-5½ in) to the width.]

26. Place the backing fabric on the floor, centre the wadding/batting over it and smooth it out. Now lay the quilt front (candlewicked side uppermost) on top of the wadding/batting. Make quite sure that you straighten out any creases in the backing and wadding/batting before you start to pin (you may need the help of a friend).

27. Pin all three layers together, beginning in the centre and working your way out towards the centre of the outside edges. Pin from the centre to each corner.

28. Using a strong thread, tack along these pinned lines and between each of these lines. Continue to tack until you have done at least 32 rows of tacking. The more you tack, the easier it is to quilt because the wadding/batting does not shift as much (see page 12).

29. Quilt the 12 candlewicked squares, starting from the centre of the quilt and working your way towards the outside edges and corners. (See page 12 on quilting.) Smooth any excess fullness toward the edges as you work.

30. Quilt the borders, beginning the quilting at the centre point of each border and working towards the corners. Once you have completed the quilting of the borders, trim the excess wadding/batting and backing so that it is the same width all the way round the quilt.

31. Turn the raw edges of the backing 2 cm (⅞ in) to the wrong side and press. Now fold the backing fabric over the quilt front to create a self-binding. Begin with the top and bottom edges first and then the side edges. Pin, tack and slipstitch into place. To ensure that the wadding/batting is held firmly in place, quilt close to the hem that has been made. Remove tacking threads.

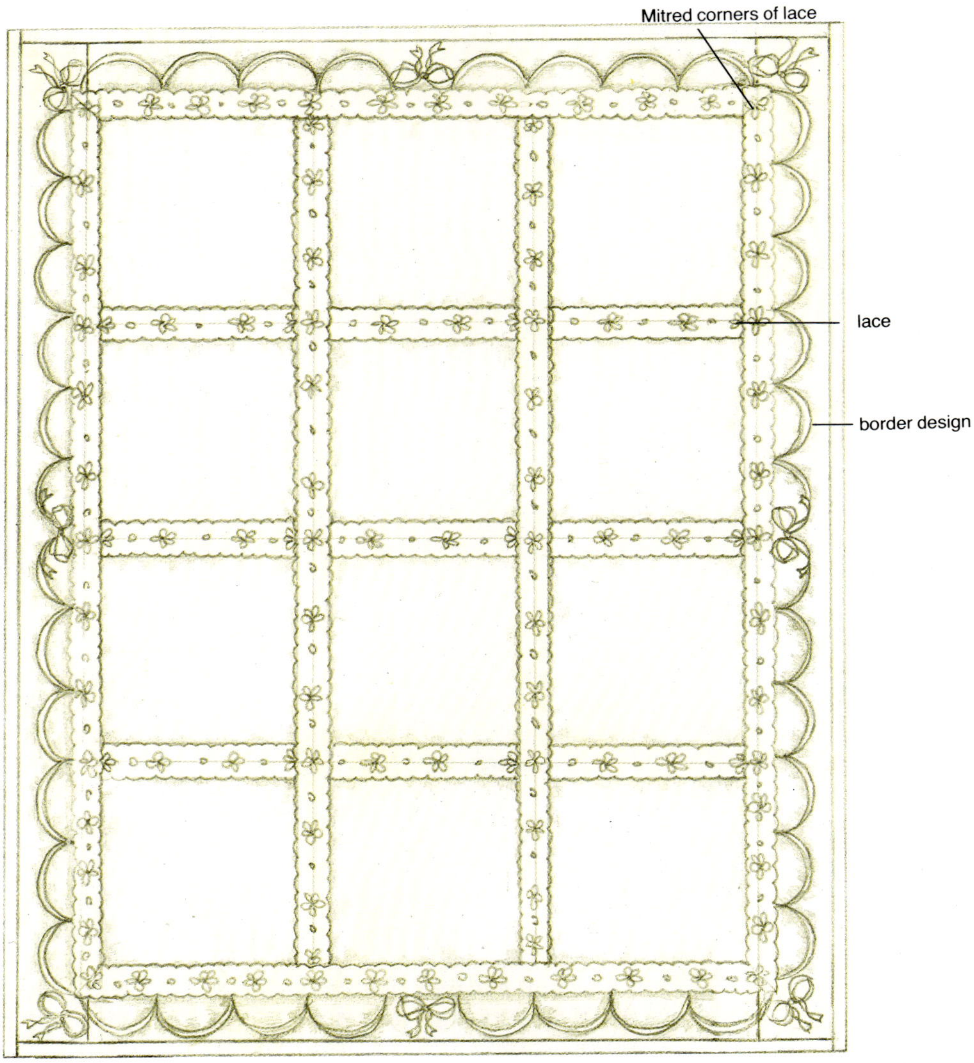

BED LINEN

Making your own candlewicked sheets and pillowcases is a very easy project to begin with, as you can make your own by buying sheeting from a fabric shop. Alternatively, you can buy ready-made sheets and pillowcases that only need to be candlewicked.

SHEETS AND PILLOWCASES

Materials for a sheet

Ready-made sheet or sheeting (see Box on page 55)
Scalloped cotton edging lace or broderie anglaise
Satin ribbon

1. In order to position the candlewick design on page 59 accurately, [or any other design measuring approximately 5 cm (2 in) in depth], it is necessary to find the centre lines of the sheeting. On the right side of the fabric, measure 13 cm (5 in) from the top raw edge and draw a line parallel to the raw edge. Fold the sheet in half lengthways to find the vertical centre line. Finger-press about 20 cm (8 in) along this vertical fold line, starting at the raw edge.

2. Match the centre lines of the design with the centre lines of the sheeting and trace the design onto the right side of the fabric.

3. Stretch the sheeting in an embroidery hoop and candlewick the design.

4. Make a hem along the raw edge by turning under 1 cm (½ in) and press. Now turn under a further 8 cm (3¼ in) to the wrong side. Pin, tack and machine stitch. This wide hem will enclose the wrong side of the candlewicking so that the sheet looks neat.

5. Stitch the edging lace or broderie anglaise to the right side of the edge of the hem to make the sheet look pretty and feminine.

6. To determine the length of each satin ribbon, measure the width of the sheet and add on 2 cm (⅞ in). Stitch the ribbons in position as shown in the photograph.

7. Make the bottom hem by turning under 1 cm (½ in) and then 2 cm (¾ in) to the wrong side. Pin, tack and machine stitch.

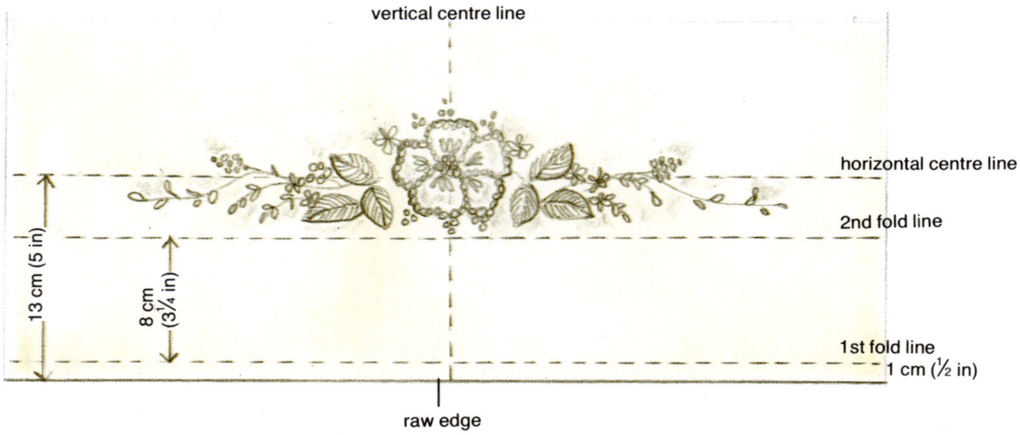

PILLOWCASES

Materials for two pillowcases with lace ruffles

1 m x 200 cm-wide (1⅛ yds x 78 in-wide) sheeting

About 10 m x 9 cm-wide (10¾ yds x 3½ in-wide) cotton lace or broderie anglaise

1. Cut the sheeting into four 50 cm x 72 cm (19½ in x 28 in) pieces for the pillowcases and two 50 cm x 22.5 cm (19½ in x 8¾ in) pieces for the flaps. (See fig 1 opposite.)

2. Trace the designs on page 75 and 77 onto tracing paper. This will make inverting the designs much easier.

3. Match the outside edges of the pattern with those of the fabric and trace the design onto as many of the corners as you wish to candlewick.

4. Place the fabric in the hoop and candlewick the designs. Once you have completed the candlewicking, wash and iron the fabric very well, following the instructions on page 8.

5. Prepare the lace as described on page 8. Cut the lace into two equal lengths and gather by hand or machine. Most machine-made lace has one slightly thicker thread fairly close to the straight edge. Find this thread, pull it gently to gather the lace easily. If you prefer to gather the lace by machine, set the machine on the longest stitch, loosen the top tension slightly and work two rows of stitching fairly close to the straight edge of the lace. Pull both threads carefully at the same time and gather to the required length. Reset your machine to the normal stitch length.

6. Pin the gathered lace, right sides and raw edges together, to the front of the pillowcase. Leaving about 3 cm (1¼ in) of loose gathered lace at each end, machine stitch the lace in place. When you are 2-3 cm (⅞-1¼ in) from the first corner, leave the needle in the fabric, lift the presser foot and push as much of the gathered lace as you can under it. Release the presser foot and stitch until you get to about 6 mm (¼ in) from the corner. Again leave the needle in the fabric and lift the presser foot. Turn the fabric and push as much gathered lace as possible under the foot. Release the presser foot and continue machine stitching. Repeat this process at each corner.

7. When you reach the point where you started, release the presser foot and cut the thread. With *wrong* sides of the lace together, pin and machine stitch a 5 mm (¼ in) seam. Now turn the lace so that *right* sides are together and stitch a slightly wider seam than before. This is called a French seam and is a neat way of finishing off any visible seams. Machine stitch the ruffle to the fabric.

8. Turn under 5 mm (¼ in) and then 1 cm (½ in) along one long side of one of the flaps. Pin, tack and machine stitch.

9. With right sides together, pin and tack the other long side of the flap to one of the short sides of the candlewicked front.

10. Open out the flap so that it lies away from the candlewicked front. Turn under 5 mm (¼ in) and then 1 cm (½ in) along one short side of the fabric for the

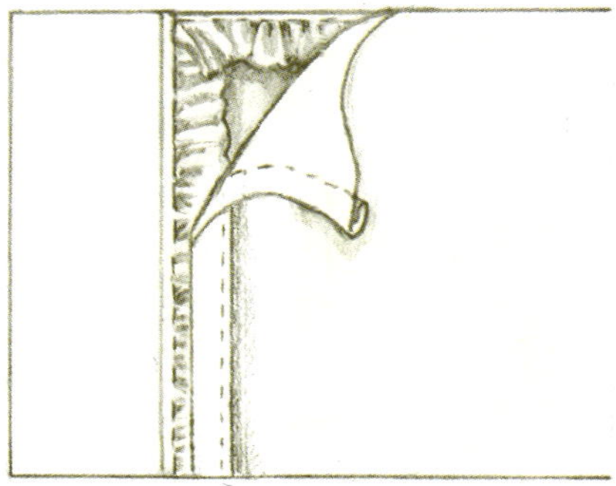

back of the pillowcase. Pin, tack and machine stitch.

11. With right sides together, pin and tack the other three sides of the back to the front (the lace will be sandwiched between the two layers).

12. Return the flap, and pin and tack in place.

13. Machine stitch around all four sides through all thicknesses using a straight and then a zigzag or an overlock stitch.

14. Remove tacking threads and turn the pillowcase right side out.

15. Repeat steps 6-14 for the second pillowcase.

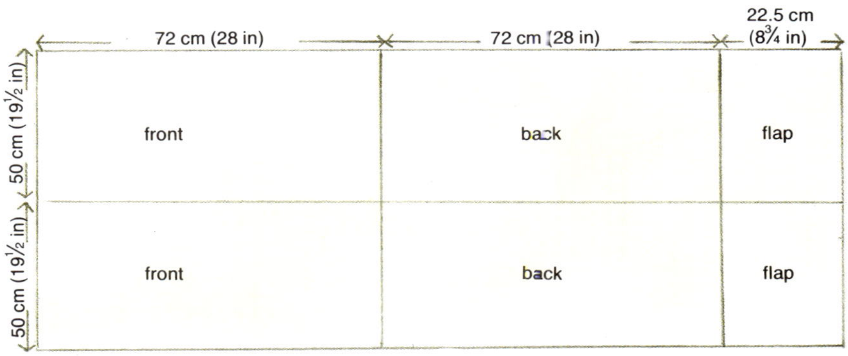

Fig 1

To calculate the amount of fabric needed to make a sheet.
Measure the width of the mattress and add on twice the depth. Add on about 40 cm (16 in) to allow one to tuck in the sheet. Use sheeting that has a width closest to this measurement to avoid having to sew hems on these two sides.

Measure the length and add on twice the depth. Remember to add on the 40 cm (16 in) tuck-in allowance.

To calculate the fabric required for a pillowcase.
Measure the width and length of the pillow and add on a 1 cm (½ in) seam allowance all round. Cut two pieces of fabric this size. Cut another piece of fabric the same width measurement x 20 cm (8 in).

If you are making a plain pillowcase without a ruffle, cut the fabric all in one piece from very wide sheeting.

To calculate the fabric required for the ruffle.
Measure the circumference of the pillow and double the measurement. Add on 1.5 cm (¾ in) for seam allowances. The width of the ruffle is flexible but remember to add 2.5 cm (1 in) to the width measurement for the hem (of a fabric ruffle) and seam allowances.

QUILTS WITH SASHING

QUILT SIZE*	No. of squares	×	Size of squares	+	No. of sashings	×	Width of sashings	+	No. of borders	×	Width of borders
SINGLE-BED QUILT (12 Squares)											
Width 181 cm (71 in)	3	×	37 cm (14½ in)	+	2	×	10 cm (4 in)	+	2	×	25 cm (9¾ in)
Length 228 cm (89½ in)	4	×	37 cm (14½ in)	+	3	×	10 cm (4 in)	+	2	×	25 cm (9¾ in)
Width 190 cm (75½ in)	3	×	40 cm (16 in)	+	2	×	10 cm (4 in)	+	2	×	25 cm (9¾ in)
Length 240 cm (95½ in)	4	×	40 cm (16 in)	+	3	×	10 cm (4 in)	+	2	×	25 cm (9¾ in)
SINGLE-BED QUILT (15 Squares)											
Width 160 cm (63½ in)	3	×	30 cm (12 in)	+	2	×	10 cm (4 in)	+	2	×	25 cm (9¾ in)
Length 240 cm (95½ in)	5	×	30 cm (12 in)	+	4	×	10 cm (4 in)	+	2	×	25 cm (9¾ in)
Width 165 cm (65¼ in)	3	×	35 cm (13¾ in)	+	2	×	10 cm (4 in)	+	2	×	20 cm (8 in)
Length 255 cm (100¾ in)	5	×	35 cm (13¾ in)	+	4	×	10 cm (4 in)	+	2	×	20 cm (8 in)
DOUBLE-BED QUILT (12 Squares)											
Width 195 cm (76½ in)	3	×	45 cm (17½ in)	+	2	×	10 cm (4 in)	+	2	×	20 cm (8 in)
Length 250 cm (98 in)	4	×	45 cm (17½ in)	+	3	×	10 cm (4 in)	+	2	×	20 cm (8 in)
Width 200 cm (80 in)	3	×	40 cm (16 in)	+	2	×	10 cm (4 in)	+	2	×	30 cm (12 in)
Length 250 cm (100 in)	4	×	40 cm (16 in)	+	3	×	10 cm (4 in)	+	2	×	30 cm (12 in)
QUEEN-SIZE BED QUILT (16 Squares)											
Width 250 cm (98 in)	4	×	45 cm (17½ in)	+	3	×	10 cm (4 in)	+	2	×	20 cm (8 in)
Length 250 cm (98 in)	4	×	45 cm (17½ in)	+	3	×	10 cm (4 in)	+	2	×	20 cm (8 in)
Width 250 cm (100 in)	4	×	40 cm (16 in)	+	3	×	10 cm (4 in)	+	2	×	30 cm (12 in)
Length 250 cm (100 in)	4	×	40 cm (16 in)	+	3	×	10 cm (4 in)	+	2	×	30 cm (12 in)

KING-SIZE BED QUILT (16 Squares)

QUILT SIZE*	No. of squares	×	Size of squares	+	No. of sashings	×	Width of sashings	+	No. of borders	×	Width of borders
Width 260 cm (101½ in)	4	×	45 cm (17½ in)	+	3	×	10 cm (4 in)	+	2	×	25 cm (9¾ in)
Length 260 cm (101½ in)	4	×	45 cm (17½ in)	+	3	×	10 cm (4 in)	+	2	×	25 cm (9¾ in)

QUILTS WITHOUT SASHING

SINGLE-BED QUILT (15 Squares)

Width 165 cm (65¼ in)	3	×	35 cm (13¾ in)			+			2	×	30 cm (12 in)
Length 235 cm (93¾ in)	5	×	35 cm (13¾ in)			+			2	×	30 cm (12 in)

Width 170 cm (67½ in)	3	×	40 cm (16 in)			+			2	×	25 cm (9¾ in)
Length 250 cm (99½ in)	5	×	40 cm (16 in)			+			2	×	25 cm (9¾ in)

DOUBLE-BED QUILT (12 Squares)

Width 204 cm (81 in)	3	×	48 cm (19 in)			+			2	×	30 cm (12 in)
Length 252 cm (100 in)	4	×	48 cm (19 in)			+			2	×	30 cm (12 in)

Width 200 cm (78 in)	3	×	50 cm (19½ in)			+			2	×	25 cm (9¾ in)
Length 250 cm (97½ in)	4	×	50 cm (19½ in)			+			2	×	25 cm (9¾ in)

QUEEN-SIZE BED QUILT (20 Squares)

Width 220 cm (86 in)	4	×	40 cm (15½ in)			+			2	×	30 cm (12 in)
Length 260 cm (101½ in)	5	×	40 cm (15½ in)			+			2	×	30 cm (12 in)

Width 220 cm (86 in)	4	×	45 cm (17½ in)			+			2	×	20 cm (8 in)
Length 265 cm (103½ in)	5	×	45 cm (17½ in)			+			2	×	20 cm (8 in)

KING-SIZE BED QUILT (16 Squares)

Width 260 cm (102 in)	4	×	50 cm (19½ in)			+			2	×	30 cm (12 in)
Length 260 cm (102 in)	4	×	50 cm (19½ in)			+			2	×	30 cm (12 in)

*Imperial measurements have been adjusted or rounded up or down as appropriate to help the reader

TELEPHONE BOOK COVER

This would not only make a very practical gift but also an attractive addition to any telephone table. Choose a fabric that launders well. As telephone directories tend to differ in size, measure the book for your area and adjust the measurements accordingly.

Materials

31 cm x 68 cm (12¼ in x 26½ in) calico or desired plain fabric
31 cm x 68 cm (12¼ in x 26½ in) thin polyester wadding/batting
31 cm x 68 cm (12¼ in x 26½ in) fabric for lining

1. Draw a line vertically 21.5 cm (8⅜ in) from the raw edge on the right-hand side of the fabric to be candlewicked and another horizontally 15.5 cm (6¼ in) from the top raw edge (fig 1).

2. Match the centre lines of the fabric with those of the design and trace the design onto the fabric.

3. Place the fabric in the hoop and pull taut. Candlewick the design and when the candlewicking is complete, wash and iron the fabric carefully, following the instructions on page 8.

4. Tack the wadding/batting to the lining around the edges. Turn under a 5 mm (¼ in) seam allowance along one short side of both the candlewicked fabric and the lining. Press.

5. With right sides together, pin and tack the front to the lining along the other three sides. Machine stitch using an overlock stitch or a straight and then a zigzag stitch. Clip the corners and turn right side out. Slipstitch the open end closed.

6. Prepare for quilting and quilt the design (and the rest of the fabric, if desired) as described on page 12.

7. Turn the rectangle of quilted fabric over (with the lining uppermost) and fold over 9 cm (3½ in) towards the lining at both ends as shown. Stitch close to the top and bottom edges of the pockets (fig 2). Remove the tacking threads.

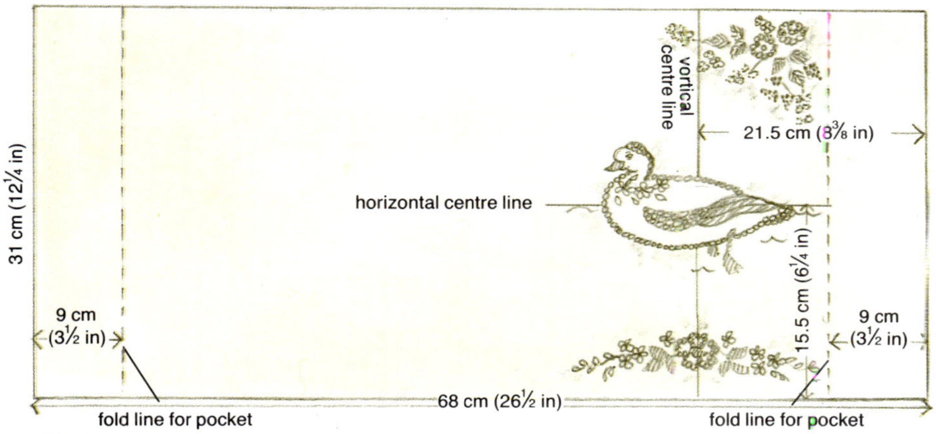

Fig 1

Fig 2

TABLECLOTH

Materials for a square cloth
71 cm x 71 cm (28 in x 28 in) calico or other fabric of desired colour
3 m x 3-7 cm-wide (3¼ yds x 1¼-2¾ in-wide) lace

1. Matching the raw edges of the corner of the fabric with those of the design on page 82, trace the designs onto one or more corners.

2. Place the corners, one at a time, in the hoop and pull taut. Candlewick all the designs, finishing off the back of the work very neatly.

3. Once all the candlewicking is complete, wash and iron the fabric well, following the instructions on page 8.

4. Make a hem along the top and bottom edges first and then along the two side edges by turning under 5 mm (¼ in) and then 1 cm (½ in). Pin, tack and machine stitch. Alternatively the corners can be mitred as shown.

5. Sew the lace to the right side of the tablecloth as near to the edge as possible, mitring the corners.

To calculate the fabric required for a tablecloth.
Measure the length and breadth of the table and add on 10 cm (4 in) all round. For example, if a table measures 50 cm (20 in) square, you will need a piece of fabric 60 cm (24 in) square.

TABLE NAPKINS

Choose a cotton or any other fabric that has enough body to stay crisp and fresh-looking when laundered.

Materials
For a set of six
114 cm x 76 cm (1 ¼ yds x 30 in) fabric
10 m x 3 cm-wide (11 yds x 1 ¼ in-wide) lace (optional)

1. Cut the fabric into six 38 cm x 38 cm (15 in x 15 in) pieces.

2. Trace the design onto one or more corners of each square, matching the corner of the design with those of the napkin.

3. Place them one at a time in the hoop and pull taut. Candlewick the designs and then wash and iron the pieces of fabric, following the instructions on page 8.

4. Make a hem around all four sides of each napkin by turning over 5 mm (¼ in) and then another 5 mm (¼ in), mitring the corners.

5. If you like lacy linen, pin, tack and machine stitch the lace to the edge of each napkin, mitring the corners.

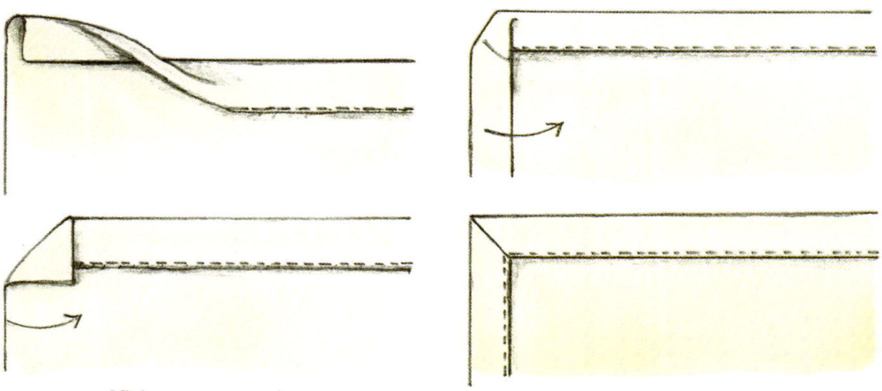

Mitring corners on a hem

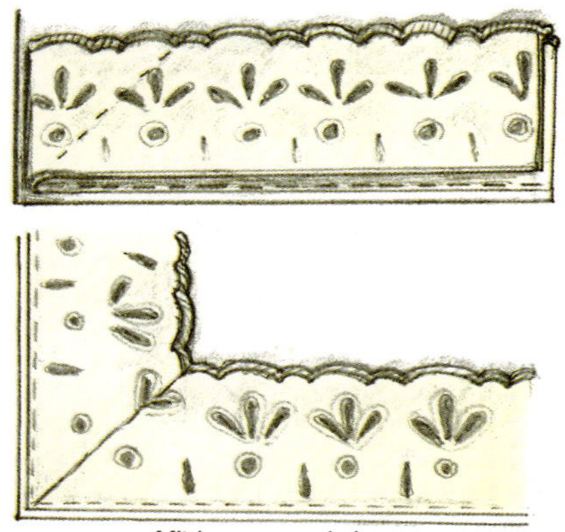

Mitring corners in lace

CUSHIONS

There is nothing more inviting than a comfortable chair, sofa or bed with lots of plump, pretty cushions on it. Add a cup of tea and a book and you'll be all set for a delightful afternoon!

Cushions are really very easy to make once you know how. Whether they are ruffled or plain, elegant cushions, they must be completely washable and practical, so choose fabrics and lace that launder well. Remember to wash enough fabric for the cushion front, back and ruffle.

Bear in mind that the cushion will become much smaller once it is stuffed.

Materials for a plain square cushion

47 cm x 47 cm (18½ in x 18½ in) fabric for front
47 cm x 47 cm (18½ in x 18½ in) polyester wadding/batting
47 cm x 47 cm (18½ in x 18½ in) muslin
50 cm (19½ in) zip
47 cm x 49 cm-wide (18½ in x 19¼ in-wide) fabric for back

1. Fold the fabric for the front in half horizontally and then vertically and finger-press.

2. Match the centre lines of the fabric with those of your design and trace the design onto the fabric.

3. Place in a hoop and pull taut. Candlewick the design and when complete, wash and iron the fabric very carefully, following the instructions on page 8.

4. Sandwich the wadding/batting between the cushion front and the muslin (or old, plain sheeting) and tack from the centre to the edges and then from the centre to the corners.

5. Quilt the fabric as described on page 12.

6. Fold the fabric for the back of the cushion in half vertically and finger-press. Cut along the fold line.

7. Turn under 1 cm (½ in) to the wrong side along one long side of each half and finger-press. Place the zip, right side up, between the two pieces of fabric. Tack and machine stitch using a zipper foot. Remove tacking threads.

8. Open the zip and, with right sides facing, pin and tack the front to the back of the cushion.

9. Machine stitch around the four sides of the cushion using an overlock stitch or a straight and then a zigzag stitch. Clip the corners, remove tacking threads and turn the cushion right side out. Remove the tacking threads made in preparation for the quilting.

Materials for lace and beribboned cushion with lace ruffle

42 cm x 42 cm (16½ in x 16½ in) calico for the front
Four 44 cm (17¼ in) lengths of narrow scalloped lace
Four 44 cm (17¼ in) lengths of satin ribbon
4.25 m (4½ yds) wide cotton lace
42 cm x 42 cm (16½ in x 16½ in) polyester wadding/batting (optional)
42 cm x 42 cm (16½ in x 16½ in) prewashed muslin (optional)
44 cm x 42 cm (17¼ in x 16½ in) calico for the back

1. Fold the fabric for the front of the cushion vertically and horizontally to find the centre lines. Finger-press.

RUFFLES If you are going to make several cushions with ruffles, cut 4.5-5 m (4⅞-5½ yds) of fabric into 10-12 cm-wide (4-5 in-wide) strips. Use a narrow hemming foot, which is available for every type of sewing machine, to sew a neat hem. If using this foot, remember to move the needle slightly to the right so that it does not slip off the edge of the hem.

If you are going to make lots of ruffled items, for instance curtains, cushions, tablecloths and so on, it would be a good idea to buy a special gathering foot called a ruffler. This wonderful gadget will gather metres and metres of frill in a matter of minutes. It is important, however, to have this foot demonstrated to you first.

Double-sided ruffles If you wish to make a double-sided ruffle, cut 20-24 cm-wide (8-9½ in-wide) strips. With wrong sides facing, fold the strips in half lengthways, pin and sew. You will now have a double-sided 10-12 cm (4-5 in) ruffle.

To gather a ruffle, set the machine onto the longest stitch and sew two rows of stitching near the raw edge. Remember that a ruffle around the edge will make the cushion look much bigger.

REMOVABLE COVERS Allow at least 2 cm (⅞ in) extra across the width of the fabric for the back of your cushion if you are using a zip. For an opening like a pillow sham, allow an extra 18-20 cm (7-8 in) for the sections to overlap.

TO MAKE A SEPARATE INSIDE CUSHION, measure the cushion cover and add on 1 cm (½ in) all round. For example, if the cushion cover is 47 cm x 47 cm (18½ in x 18½ in), the inside cushion will be 49 cm x 49 cm (19¼ in x 19¼ in). Remember that the inside cushion becomes smaller once it is stuffed. Pin the two pieces of calico together. Machine stitch with an overlock stitch or a straight and then a zigzag stitch around three sides. Turn right side out and press. Stuff the cushion with polyester stuffing, pushing it right into the corners. Pin and tack the opening closed. Machine stitch using an overlock stitch or a straight and then a zigzag stitch. Trim away any ragged threads. Place the cushion inside the cover.

2. Match the centre lines of the front with those of the design and trace the design onto the fabric. The design should be no larger than 25 cm (9¾ in) square.

3. Place the fabric in a hoop and stretch taut. Candlewick the design and when complete, wash and iron the fabric carefully, following the instructions on page 8.

4. Place the candlewicked square on a flat surface. Measure and mark a line 5 cm (2 in) from the raw edge of each of the four sides.

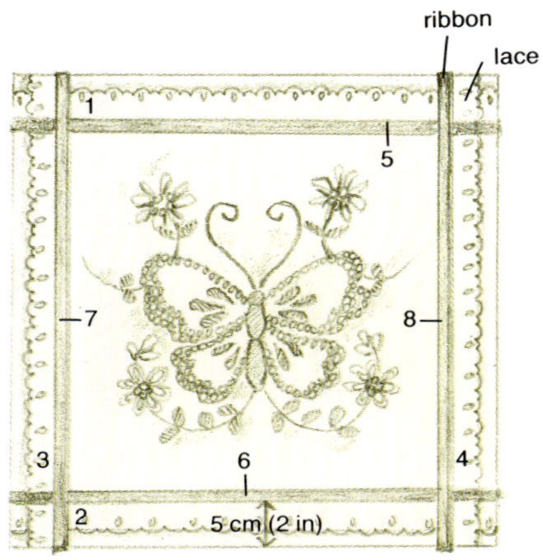

5. With the scalloped edge of the lace facing outwards, place the straight edge of one length of lace along one of the marked lines, leaving 1 cm (½ in) at each end. Pin, tack and machine stitch close to the straight edge of the lace.

6. Repeat with the remaining three lengths of lace, pinning, tacking and machine stitching them in the sequence shown in the illustration.

7. Pin one length of satin ribbon along the straight side of the first piece of lace so that the edge of the ribbon overlaps the lace and hides the stitching. Tack, then slowly machine stitch with a straight stitch along both edges of the ribbon. Repeat with the remaining ribbons as shown.

8. If you wish to quilt the design on the front, prepare the front for quilting and quilt as described on page 12.

9. Gather the cotton lace and pin it, right sides and raw edges together, to the cushion front. Leave 3 cm (1¼ in) of gathered lace loose at either end. Machine stitch the lace to the cushion front, remembering to leave the needle in the fabric and lift the presser foot about 2-3 cm (⅞-1¼ in) from the corners. Push as much lace as possible under the foot, then release the presser foot and stitch to within 6 mm (¼ in) of the corner. Once again leave the needle in the fabric and lift the presser foot. Turn the fabric and push as much lace as possible under the foot. Release the presser foot and continue stitching. Repeat the process at each corner.

10. When you reach the place where you began, sew a French seam on the raw ends of the lace as follows: With wrong sides facing, pin and machine stitch a 5 mm (¼ in) seam. Turn the seam the other way out so that right sides are facing and machine stitch a slightly wider seam than the first one. Machine stitch the lace to the fabric.

11. Complete the cushion by following the instructions on how to make a plain cushion (steps 6-10).

LAMPSHADE

All the measurements given below are for a lampshade cover that fits a 36 cm (14 in)-diameter Tiffany frame.

Materials

36 cm (14 in)-diameter Tiffany lampshade frame
72 cm x 72 cm (28½ in x 28½ in) calico or fabric of desired colour
3 m x 7 cm-wide (3¼ yds x 2¾ in-wide) cotton or acrylic lace
Four 75 cm x 2.5 cm-wide (29½ in x 1 in-wide) satin ribbons

1. Follow the instructions for making the tablecloth on page 60 steps 1-5, including the candlewicking and sewing on the lace. Finish off the embroidery on the wrong side of the cloth very neatly as it will be highlighted once it is placed on the lampshade frame and the light is switched on.

2. Find the centre point of the cloth by folding it in half horizontally and then vertically. Finger-press.

3. Measure the diameter of the top circle of the lampshade frame. Using a compass and placing it on the centre point where the horizontal and vertical lines meet, draw a circle with this diameter.

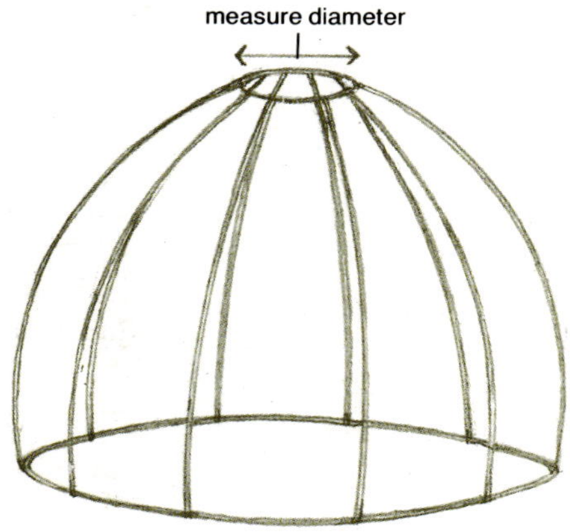

4. Using buttonhole stitch or a machine satin stitch, sew along the outline of the circle.

5. Carefully cut out the fabric within the circle.

6. Tie the satin ribbons into four bows and sew each one to the cloth, positioning them 8 cm (3¼ in) from the edge and 34.5 cm (13½ in) from each corner.

7. Place the lampshade cover over the frame and pass the light fitting (without the bulb) through the central opening. Replace the light bulb.

Quilt and bathmat design

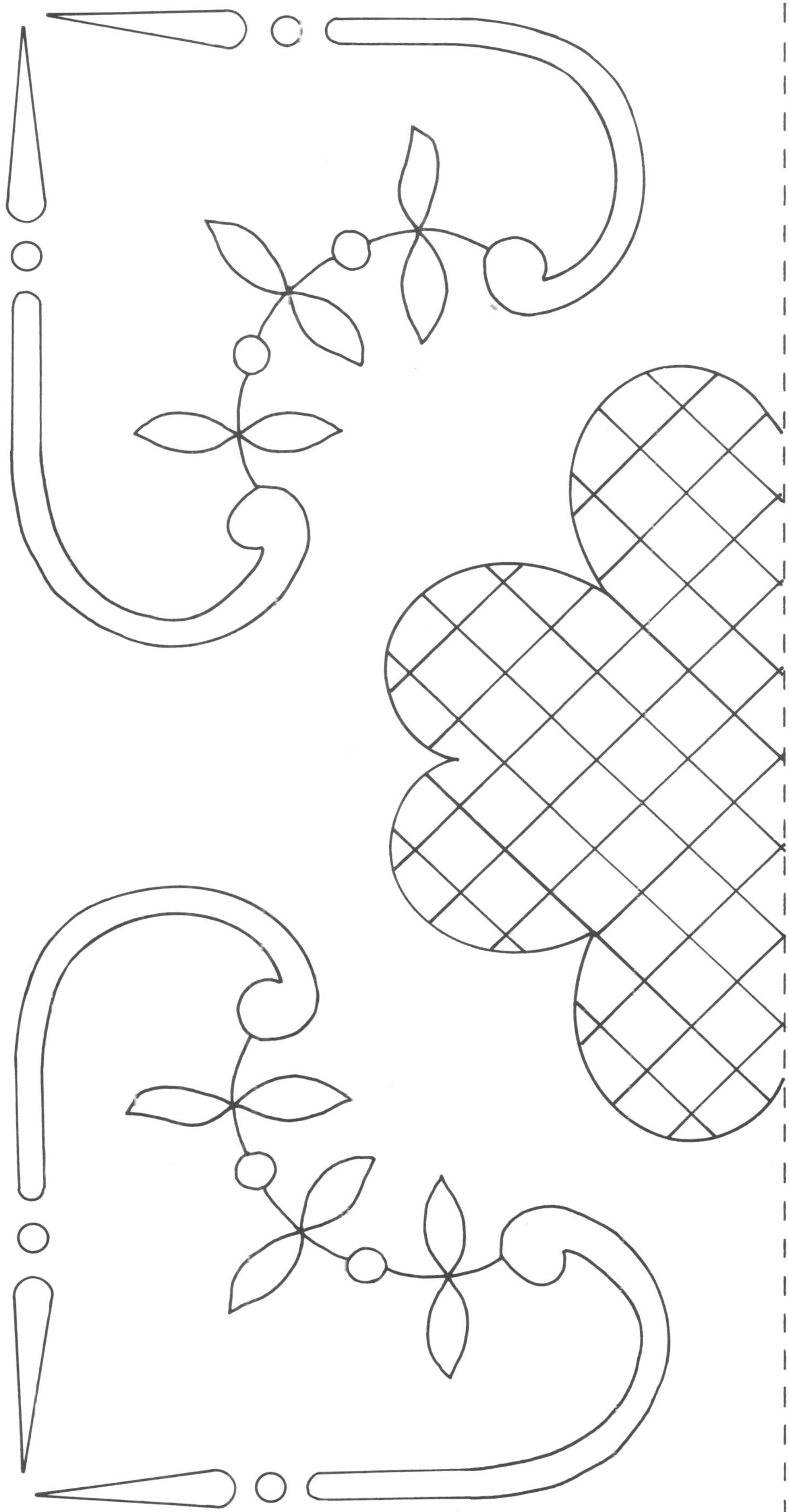

NOTE: In order to fit in as many designs as possible, it has been necessary in some cases to reproduce only half the design. Trace the design onto the tracing paper, tracing first one half and then the other to complete the design.

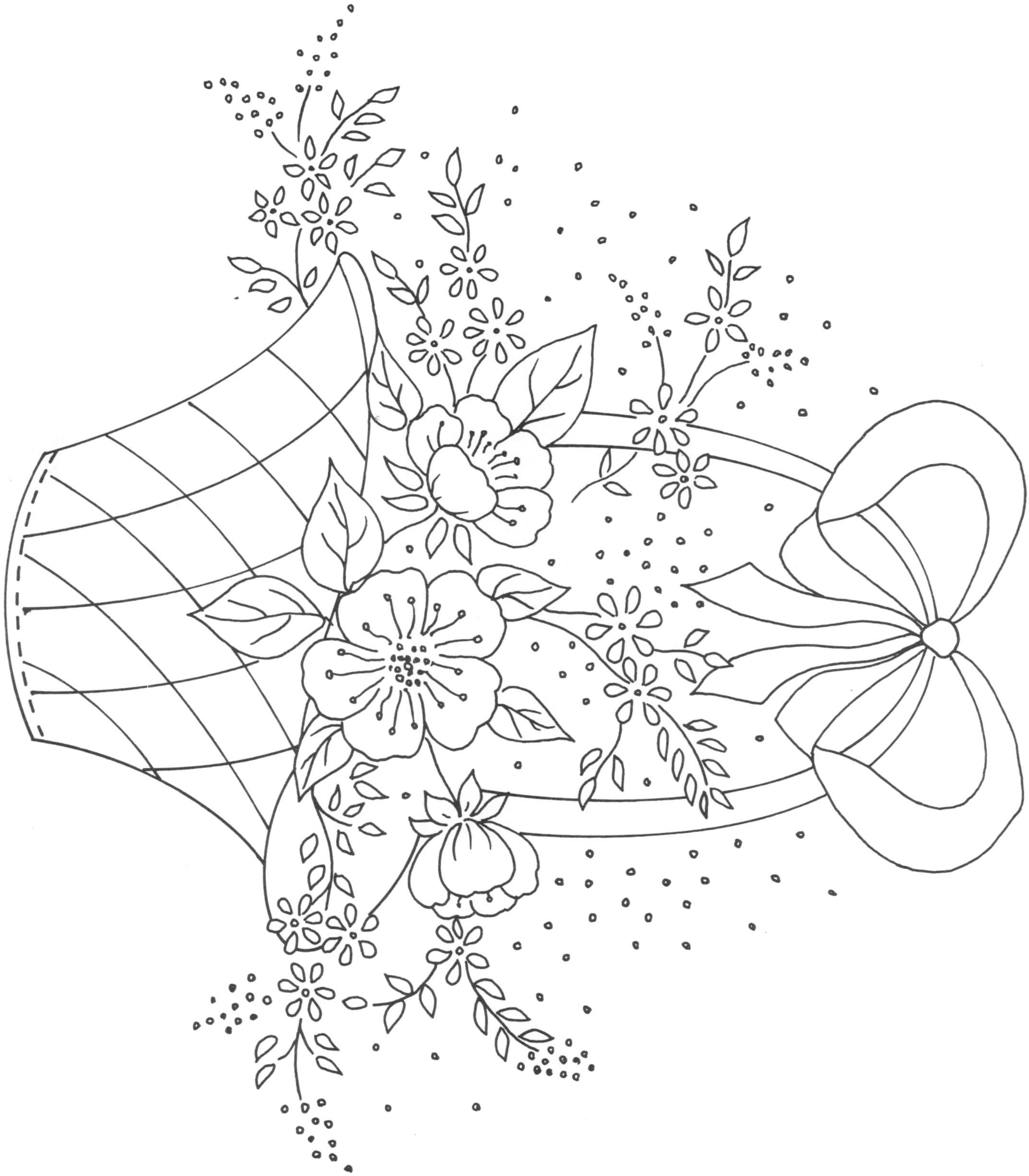

Apron, tea cosy, tray cloth and large tablecloth design

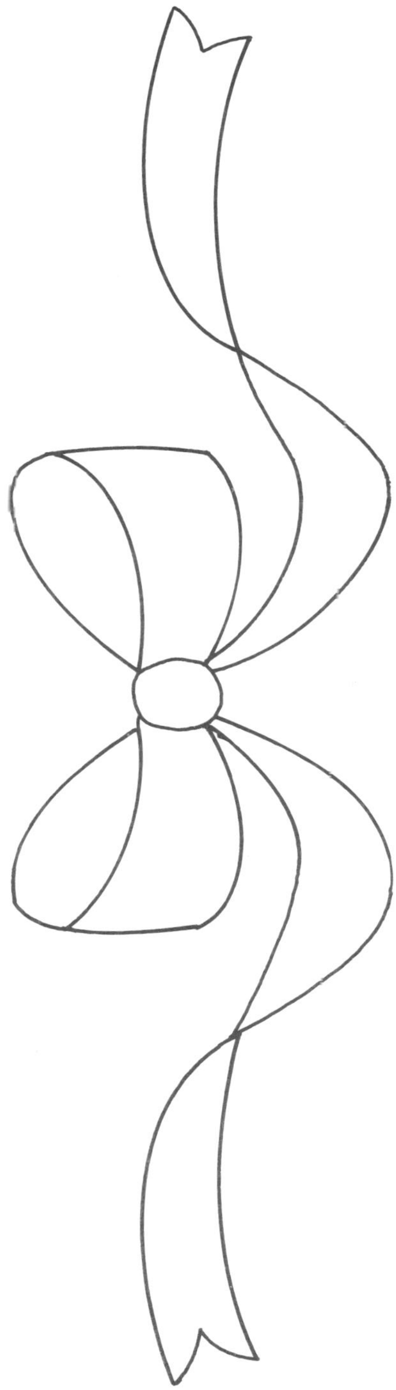

Tie-back quilting design

Curtain design

(Corner design suitable for tea cosy, tablecloth, napkins, lampshade etc)

Sheet design

Quilt and cushion design

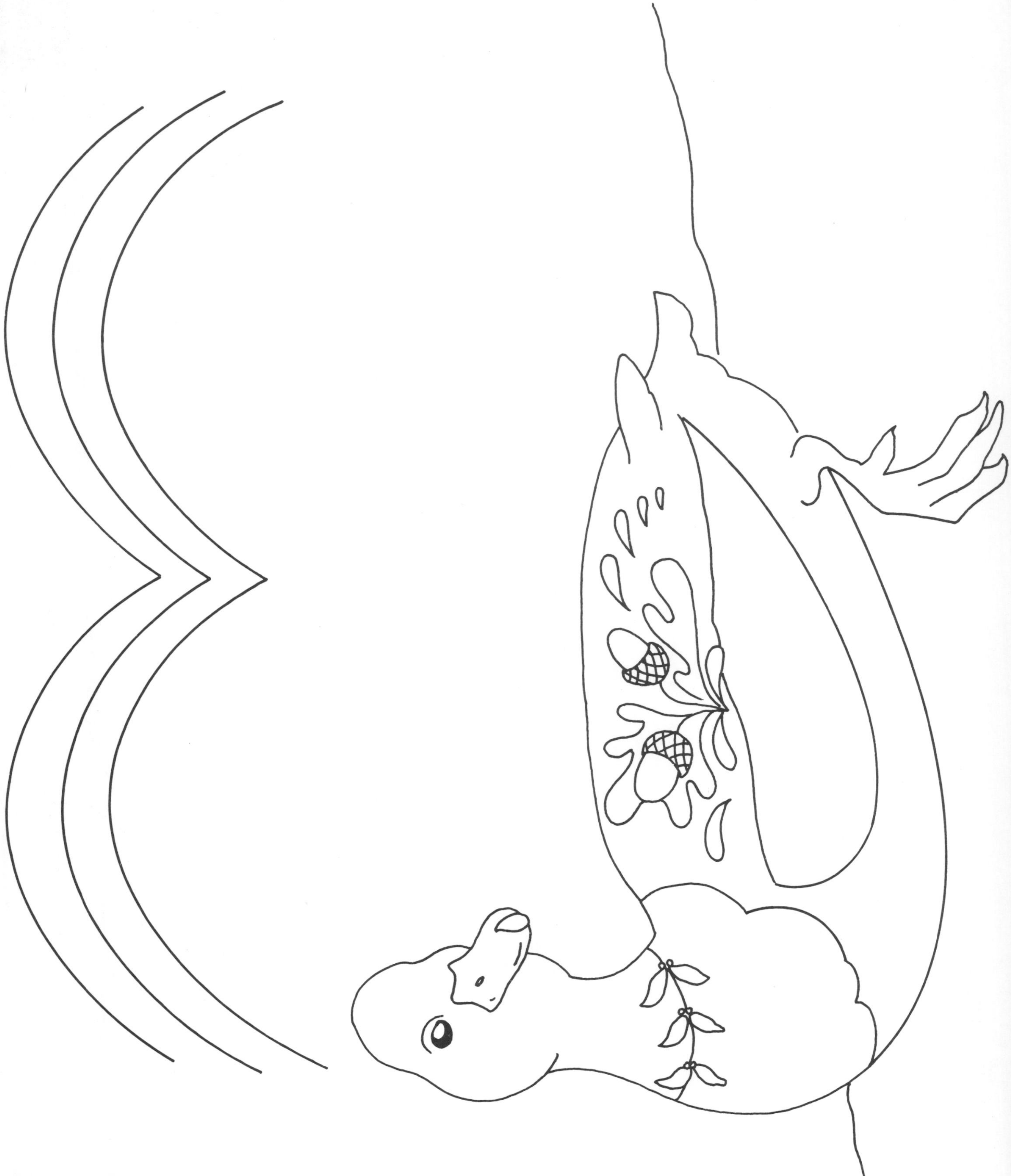

Quilting design for border of a quilt

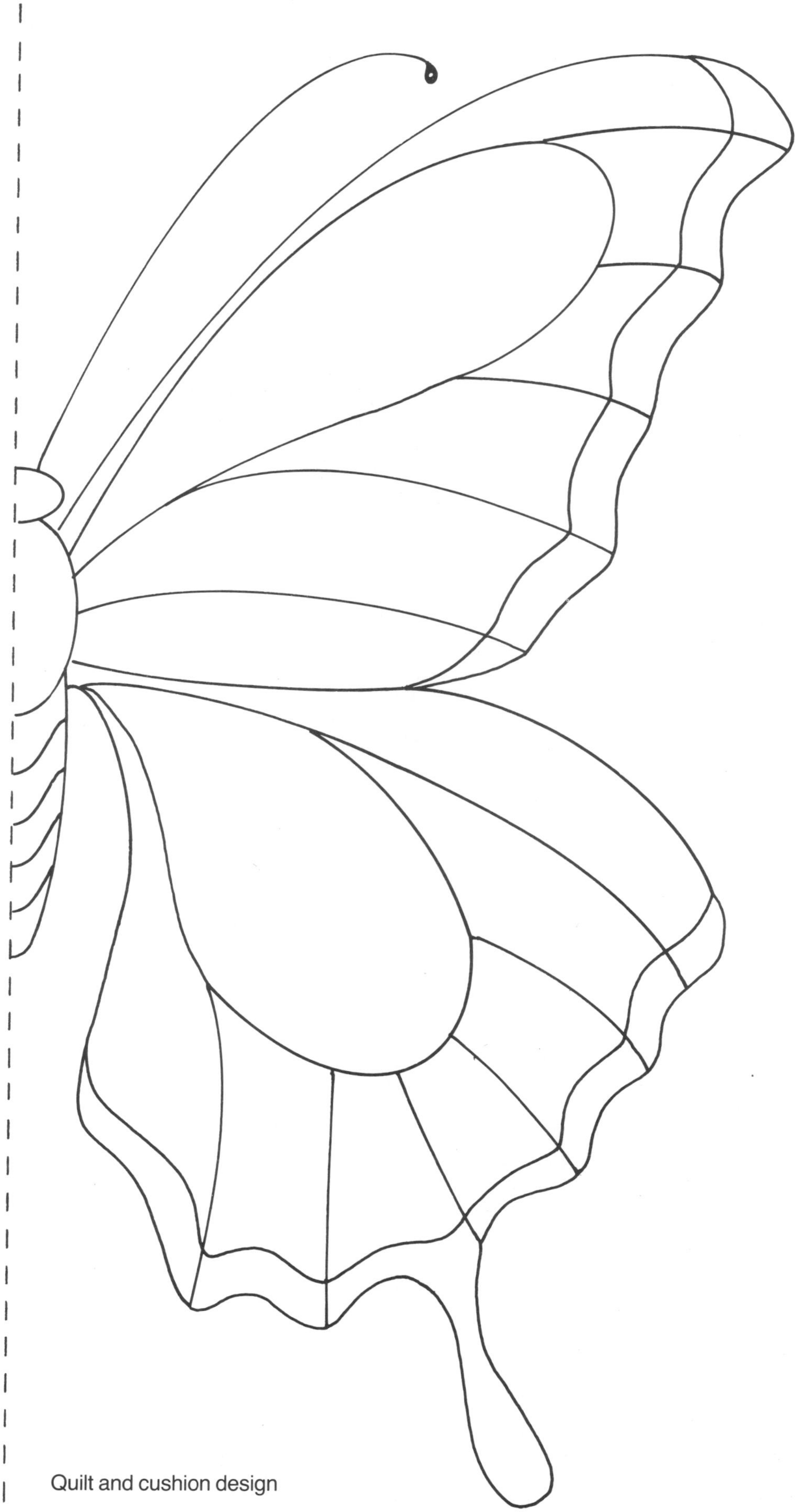

Quilt and cushion design

Quilt and cushion design

Carousel mobile pattern

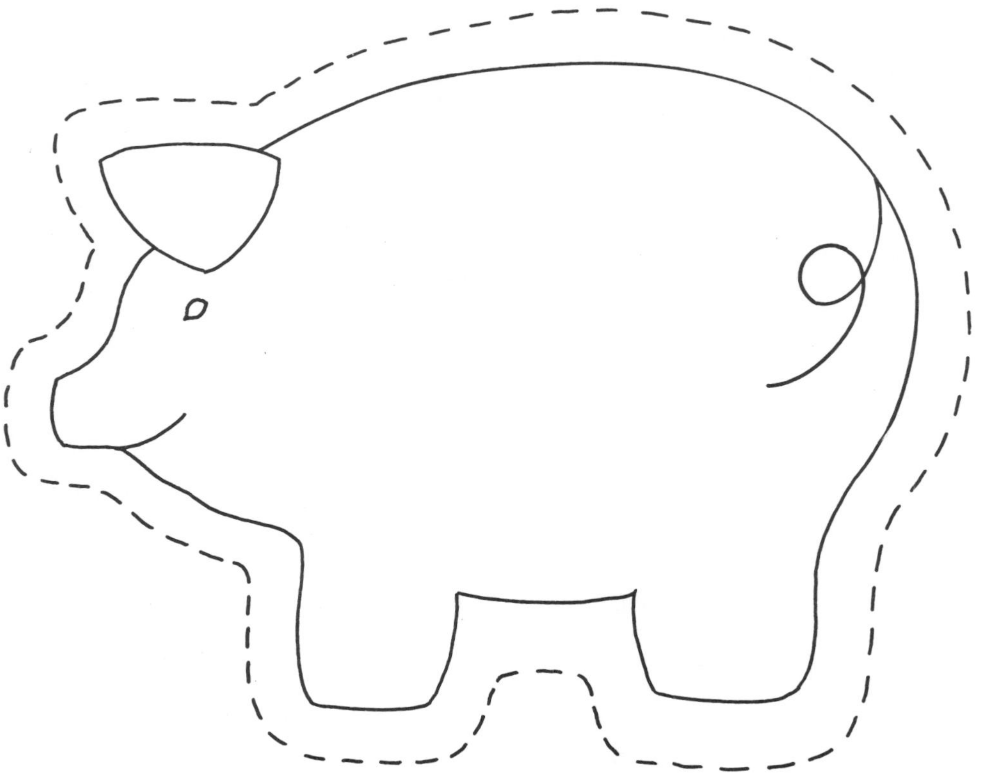

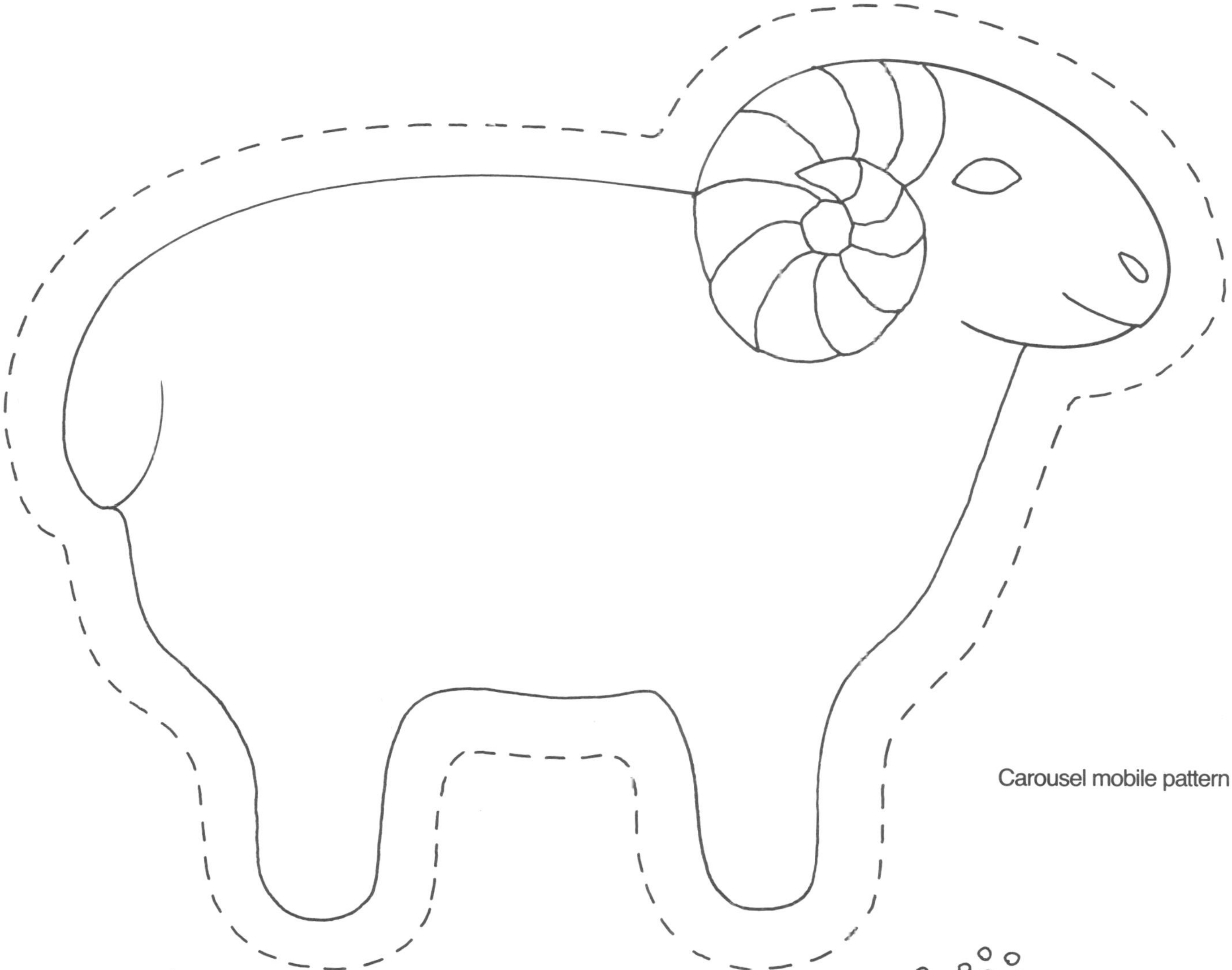

Carousel mobile pattern

Carousel mobile pattern

Tea cosy pattern and design

Pillowcase design

Quilt and cushion design

Quilt and cushion design

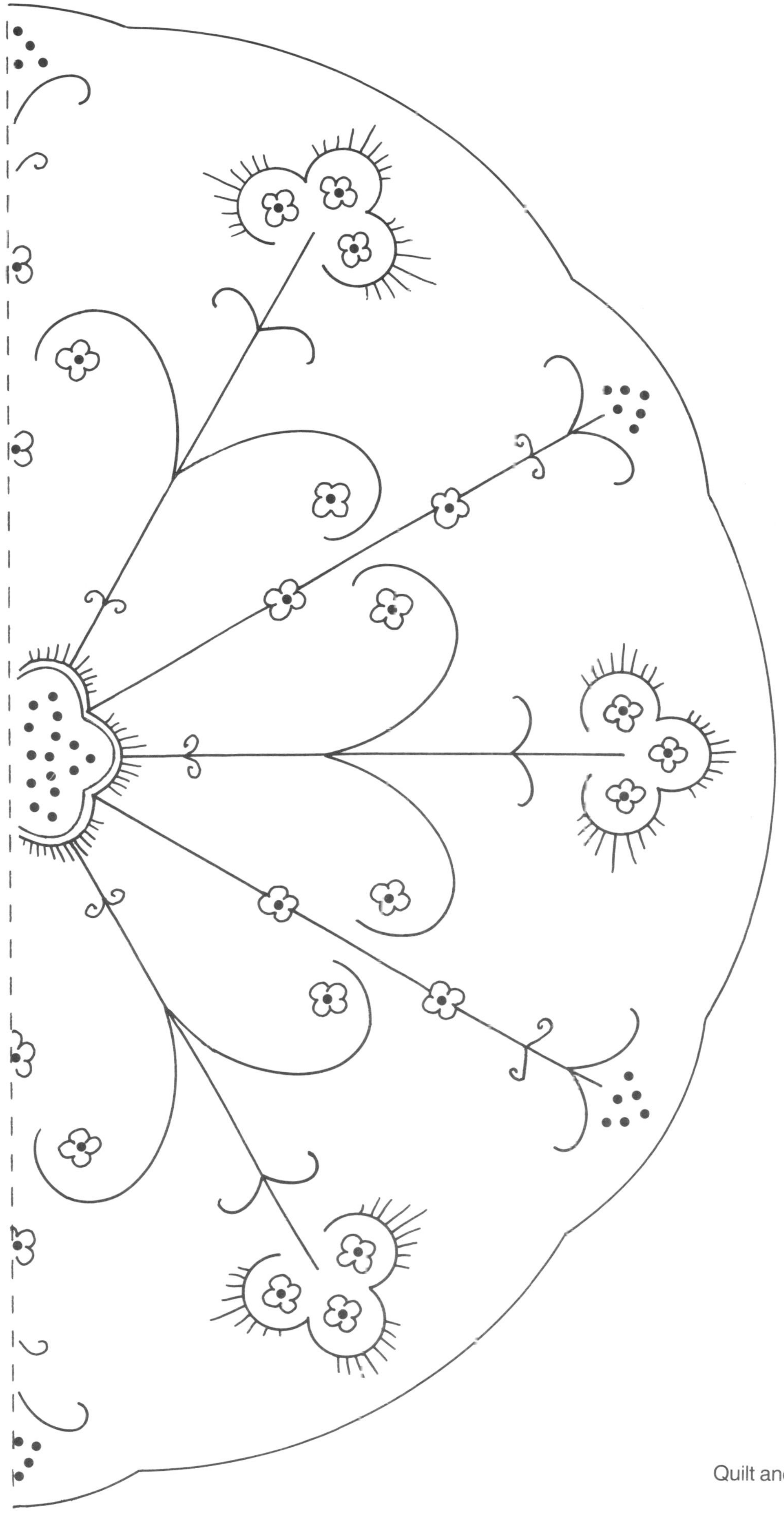

Quilt and cushion design

Tissue box holder pattern

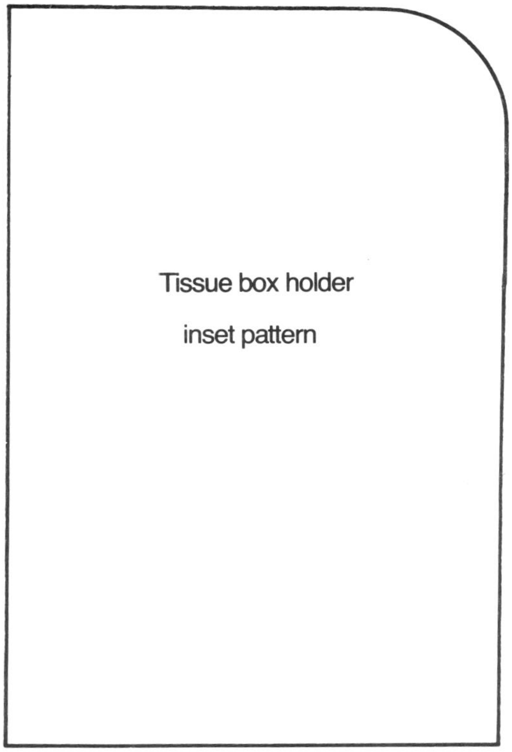

Tissue box holder
inset pattern

Carousel mobile pattern

Apron bib pattern

Quilt and cushion design

Quilt and cushion design

Quilt and cushion design

Quilt and cushion design

Quilt and cushion design

Quilt and cushion design

Guest towel design

Oven gloves pattern

Oven gloves pocket pattern and design

Cot quilt design

Cot quilt design

INDEX

Candlewick/quilting hoops and additional sets of designs are available from:
Willowtree Products cc,
P O Box 103, Somerset West 7130.
Tel: (024) 24914.

DOG PAINTING
1840~1940

A social history of the dog in art

Including an important historical overview
from earliest times to 1840
when pure-bred dogs became popular

WILLIAM SECORD

ANTIQUE COLLECTORS' CLUB

First published 1992
Reprinted 1992, 1993

ISBN 1 85149 139 2

British Library CIP Data
Secord, William
Dog painting 1840-1940: A social history of the dog in art
I. Title
758.3

Printed on Consort Royal Satin from Donside Mills, Aberdeen

Frontispiece. *Charles van den Eycken.*
Willpower, *1891. Oil on canvas, 20 x 14ins. (51 x 35.5cm).*
While van den Eycken was a Flemish artist who specialised in genre and interior scenes, he exhibited in London where he was widely collected. Note how this Pug's muzzle is much longer than that of today's Pug *Private collection; photography Grant Taylor*

Printed in England by the Antique Collectors' Club Ltd., Woodbridge, Suffolk, England

THE ANTIQUE COLLECTORS' CLUB

The Antique Collectors' Club was formed in 1966 and now has a five figure membership spread throughout the world. It publishes the only independently run monthly antiques magazine *Antique Collecting* which caters for those collectors who are interested in widening their knowledge of antiques, both by greater awareness of quality and by discussion of the factors which influence the price that is likely to be asked. The Antique Collectors' Club pioneered the provision of information on prices for collectors and the magazine still leads in the provision of detailed articles on a variety of subjects.

It was in response to the enormous demand for information on 'what to pay' that the price guide series was introduced in 1968 with the first edition of *The Price Guide to Antique Furniture* (completely revised 1978 and 1989), a book which broke new ground by illustrating the more common types of antique furniture, the sort that collectors could buy in shops and at auctions rather than the rare museum pieces which had previously been used (and still to a large extent are used) to make up the limited amount of illustrations in books published by commercial publishers. Many other price guides have followed, all copiously illustrated, and greatly appreciated by collectors for the valuable information they contain, quite apart from prices. The Antique Collectors' Club also publishes other books on antiques, including horology and art reference works, and a free catalogue is available from the address below.

Club membership, which is open to all collectors, costs £19.50 per annum. Members receive free of charge *Antique Collecting,* the Club's magazine (published ten times a year), which contains well-illustrated articles dealing with the practical aspects of collecting not normally dealt with by magazines. Prices, features of value, investment potential, fakes and forgeries are all given prominence in the magazine.

Among other facilities available to members are private buying and selling facilities, the longest list of 'For Sales' of any antiques magazine, an annual ceramics conference and the opportunity to meet other collectors at their local antique collectors' clubs. There are over eighty in Britain and more than a dozen overseas. Members may also buy the Club's publications at special pre-publication prices.

As its motto implies, the Club is an organisation designed to help collectors get the most out of their hobby: it is informal and friendly and gives enormous enjoyment to all concerned.

For Collectors — By Collectors — About Collecting

The Antique Collectors' Club, 5 Church Street, Woodbridge, Suffolk IP12 1DS

This book is dedicated to the late Richard D. Hammond

Contents

Foreword

Mrs. Vincent Astor

It was the greatest pleasure and honor to be asked to write a short foreword to *Dog Painting 1840-1940*, and I accepted readily, even though I had not yet read it. However, when it arrived, I could not put it down. William Secord takes us through the beginning of the different breeds of dogs as they rise to power and the development of their characteristics. He starts with the hunting dog and from there goes on to the beginning of the earliest dog shows, when dogs of all breeds were shown and began to be known. This, of course, created their social standing. Gordon Stables, a respected writer on canine topics, is quoted as saying, in 1877, 'Nobody now who is anybody can afford to be followed about by a mongrel dog.' Queen Victoria not only owned numerous dogs, but started the precedent for the commissioning and collecting of dog paintings. This apparently became the rage and eventually not only pedigree dogs, but also amusing and lovable pets of questionable breeding had their portraits done for the pleasure of their owners, many of which are shown in the book.

This book is not only a delight to read because of its wit and charm, but also for the real information it gives to anyone who really cares for dogs. For a dog lover, it is a MUST.

Brooke Astor

Brooke Astor

Acknowledgements

While many individuals have been of great assistance in the completion of this book, there are a several people who I would like to mention in particular. Special thanks are due to Roberta Vesley, the now retired director of The American Kennel Club Library, who was invaluable in directing me to new and pertinent material. Theresa Slowick, the Librarian at The Kennel Club, was also of invaluable assistance, as was Charles Noble, Assistant to the Surveyor of the Queen's Pictures.

Without the permission of the owners to reproduce their paintings, this book would have been impossible to produce. I am especially pleased to include paintings from the Royal Collection, St. James's Palace (copyright Her Majesty Queen Elizabeth II). My grateful thanks also to The American Kennel Club, The Kennel Club and, of course, to The Dog Museum, St. Louis, which some ten years ago first opened my eyes to the world of pure-bred dogs and dog paintings.

Many private collectors have been most generous in making their collections available to me. I would like to give special thanks to several who have been very supportive: Mrs. Vincent Astor, Mario Buatta, Mrs. Walter M. Jeffords, Mr. and Mrs. Lawrence Kalstone, Ruth Havemeyer Norwood, Frances G. Scaife and Mrs. Eileen Weiler have been especially helpful in New York. Dan Cane, Mrs. Elizabeth C. Clark, Walter F. Goodman, Gilbert Kahn, Mr. and Mrs. William Kendrick, Mrs. Gwynne G. McDevitt, Mrs. Damon Raike, Mr. and Mrs. John H. Remer, Jnr., and Cynthia Wood are among those to whom I am especially grateful. Special thanks go as well to those collectors who prefer to remain anonymous.

Both English and American dealers have been helpful, and I would in particular like to thank Arthur Ackermann & Son, Ltd., The Burlington Gallery, Sara Davenport, Richard Green, Iona Antiques, The MacConnal-Mason Gallery and The Tryon Gallery. In America, Bellechasse Antiques of New York and Red Fox Fine Art of Middleburg, Virginia, have been most helpful. In London, Bonhams as well as Christie's South Kensington provided photographs of many dog paintings.

I would also like to thank my assistant, Michael Vana, for his superior word processing abilities and great stamina, as well as my manager, Robert Mooney, for his understanding during the many days that I left him to run the gallery while I was completing my research. Thanks and my continuing admiration are due to George J. Nowicki, Jnr., who continued to be supportive in the face of what he knew to be an obsession.

Finally, I would like to thank Shirlee Kalstone for her tireless efforts in going over the text. Her suggestions and additions were invaluable.

ABBREVIATIONS

A.	Associate (of R.A., R.W.S., etc.)
A.K.C.	The American Kennel Club
b.	born
c.	circa
Ch.	Champion
exh.	exhibited
fl.	floruit (flourished)
K.C.	The Kennel Club
P.	President (of R.A., etc.)
P.S.	Pastel Society
R.A.	Royal Academy; Royal Academician
R.B.A.	Royal Society of British Artists
R.B.C.	Royal British Colonial Society of Artists
R.E.	Royal Society of Painters and Etchers
R.I.	Royal Institute of Painters in Watercolours
R.O.I.	Royal Institute of Painters in Oil Colours
R.P.	Royal Society of Portrait Painters
R.S.A.	Royal Scottish Academy
R.W.S.	Royal Watercolour Society
S.W.A.	Society of Women Artists

Introduction

> 'Toy Spaniels of the present day have some very grave defects, and breeders should turn their attention seriously to them. Some of the judges are beginning to do so, and I managed to get a clause as to soundness inserted in the Toy Spaniel standard a year or two ago. Up to the present, however, very little attention has been paid to it in practice, unsoundness passing unnoticed to championship honours.'

How many times have we heard this lament, or one similar to it, bemoaning the fact that modern-day breeders have changed the true nature of the breed, focused on beauty rather than function and, in the case of toy dogs (which after all have very little function except to be beautiful companions), have altered the dog to suit their particular preference while ignoring physical soundness?

It does seem surprising, though, to realise that this rather pithy commentary was written in 1911 by the Hon. Mrs. Neville Lytton, the granddaughter of another dog fancier, Lord Byron.

In *Toy Dogs and Their Ancestors,* her fascinating treatise on 'Japanese, Pekingese, Pomeranians, and Toy Spaniels', Mrs. Lytton goes into extensive detail on the history of these four toy breeds. She explains how the true nature of the breeds has been subverted and, commenting on her fellow dog breeders, states:

> Nature ruthlessly destroys the weaklings, the weeds, and the failures. The conditions of life are too uncompromising and they die. The modern man preserves them at infinite trouble and expense, and offers prizes for them on the show bench. He breeds from individuals which would never naturally breed, which are too small, too feeble, or too deformed to propagate their species in a natural condition, and, moreover, often have a violent aversion in doing so. This a grievous mistake.

While for some, Mrs. Lytton's ambitious book may seem a bit acerbic, she does hit upon a concern which is heard over and over again: how should a particular breed actually look?

While it is most tempting to indulge in the historical sleuthing required to determine the 'correct' way the some 142 breeds recognised collectively by The Kennel Club and The American Kennel Club should look, it is not the province of this work. The literature on this topic is vast and fascinating, although inconclusive, and would require a far more specialist knowledge than the author possesses to be fully covered in any one (however large!) volume.

No attempt will be made to promote one type of dog over another. While reference will certainly be made to the development of individual breeds, we shall leave to the many expert cynological historians the study of their exact origins. The primary concern of this book, rather, is to trace the development of pure-bred dogs in Britain and America, and to illustrate it with a selection of paintings, the majority of which were created in the period between 1840 and 1940.

Over the last ten years there has been a tremendous surge of interest in nineteenth century dog paintings, yet little is known about the specialised historical context in which they were created. Rather than look at these pictures from an art historical perspective (although this aspect is not excluded), this volume will explore the specific social and historical milieu from which the paintings came: the evolution of pure-bred dogs, the people who owned them, and the organisations which evolved to promote and monitor the pure-bred dog fancy.

It was only with the nineteenth century that our modern-day concept of breeds developed. Up until the turn of the eighteenth century individual breeds were certainly recognised, but an interest in their history and appearance, and the categorisation of the various breeds was primarily a nineteenth century development.

It was during the early years of the century, for example, that treatises on individual dogs, in particular the Greyhound and the Irish Wolfhound, began to appear. In 1866 George R. Jesse published the then comprehensive work *Researches into the History of the British Dog.* As the eminent cynologist Clifford Hubbard has pointed out, this book was the first of its kind to deal in any comprehensive way with the history of individual breeds.

Arising out of an interest in developing breeds, and in promoting pure-breds over mongrels, one-breed shows were held in England as early as 1840. The first organised multiple-breed dog show took place in June 1859 at Newcastle upon Tyne, when fifty sporting dogs were entered — twenty-three Pointers and twenty-seven Setters. Among the judges was Dr. John Henry Walsh, editor of the influential sporting magazine *The Field.*

Judged by modern standards the Newcastle show would be considered unpretentious, but at the time it was a momentous occasion. So much so that several other dog shows were organised in that same year, the most important of which were at Birmingham and Redcar. Subsequently, the idea of exhibiting dogs became so popular that shows were soon being staged in many parts of the country.

It was during this period too that the first dog clubs were formed with the goal of more accurately defining the breeds to which the members were devoted. These loosely organised groups of amateurs met to ensure the purity of their breed and to set standards, or what is referred to as 'breed type'.

Early dog shows were rather easy-going events and there were no regulations to govern them. As the number of shows increased, however, it became necessary to formulate regulations to standardise their organisation. As more breeds began to be exhibited, there was also a need for breed standards, or written descriptions, so that judges could compare and evaluate the dogs.

One of the first influential people to campaign for breed standards was Dr. Walsh. In 1867, *The Dogs of the British Islands,* a book containing articles

Gustav Muss-Arnolt.
Pointers in the Field. *Oil on canvas, 12 x 16ins. (30.5 x 40.5cm).*
Muss-Arnolt was a master at the sporting dog portrait, where the performance of the dog in the field was much more important than whether it conformed to the breed, as in the pure-bred dog portrait
Photography courtesy The Artis Group

reprinted from *The Field,* and edited by Walsh (under his pseudonym 'Stonehenge'), was published. It focused on the various kinds of dogs found in Great Britain and defined the parts of each breed's conformation. Each written description included a scale of points (which totalled 100) to guide judges in their evaluations. In the preface, Walsh (who was also the work's major contributor) wrote that the work 'embodied the opinions of most good judges on the principal points of several breeds ..At present, exhibitors do not know what points will ensure a prize, and all is confusion; while, if they could depend on any recognised scale, they would know what course to pursue.'

The five editions *The Dogs of the British Islands,* published between 1867 and 1886, enjoyed great success and today they are still considered some of the most authoritative works on dogs ever written During the period from 1880 to 1900 other books on the various breeds proliferated, many of them illustrated with reproductions of fine paintings.

As new breeds were developed and still others were imported into England, shows became more organised, The Kennel Club was formed, and standards were codified.

The primary purpose of the breed standard, or written description of what the ideal specimen of a breed looks like, was to provide breeders with a recognised guide, to aid the dog show judge in his task and to provide some uniformity in the breeds. In a sense, the ideal never actually exists but is more or less embodied in each breed specimen. In order for the judge to make a distinction between one dog and another, however, criteria had to be established and the standard for each breed, however arbitrary, provided these criteria.

With the standards established, individual fanciers could 'breed to the standard', or use the principles of selective breeding to produce an animal which would win in the show ring. Breed standards were of course, open to interpretation, and they were periodically changed.

One fascinating aspect of any study of dog painting is to note when the individual breeds came into existence, and how the breeds physically changed over the years. Many of today's Bulldog fanciers, for instance, would barely recognise a specimen from 1820 as an example of their breed. The old Bulldog was much taller in proportion to his length, and his head smaller. Moreover, the animal was quick and alert, attributes which were necessary when he was pitted against a bull.

In order to illustrate such changes, the black and white illustrations in this book are, whenever possible, organised chronologically by breed. When a painting is not dated, and in particular when little is known about the development of an artist's work, it is placed on the basis of the style of the artist's work. Dating on the basis of style can be an impressionist art at best, and the order should not be viewed as being strictly chronological.

During the mid- to late nineteenth century, great emphasis was placed on the way the pure-bred dog looked and great pride was taken in the showing of dogs, a sport in which there was keen competition.

It seems only logical that an active breeder and/or dog owner would want a portrait of his dog, especially if he were a recorded champion. Add to that the natural pride of ownership involved with an animal which in many cases shared the owner's home and was a friend of the family, and it does not seem surprising that in an era before colour photography, dog portraits proliferated.

The pure-bred dog also played an important social role in the mid- to late nineteenth century. With the rise of the middle class in England, and the attendant increase in leisure time, the dog was no longer needed to ensure the economic livelihood of the family.

Royalty and the landed gentry had kept dogs as pets since at least the time of Charles I, but it was only during the nineteenth century that commoners had the money and leisure to keep dogs as pets. During the nineteenth century the dog went beyond its role as companion and became an animal to be exhibited and presented publicly for the scrutiny of others and for the bestowing of awards.

While in the late twentieth century we take for granted the existence of very separate and well-established breeds, the distinctions between breeds in the mid-nineteenth century were much more blurred. However, as breeds were recognised, it became clear that the ownership of a pure-bred dog, and in particular a prize-winning specimen, improved the social status of the owner.

Mixed breeds, or mongrels, were associated with the lower classes and were to be avoided at all costs. As Harriet Ritvo has pointed out in her book *The Animal Estate:* 'If association with the lower order compromised the standing of even pedigreed animals, dogs without breed standing were unquestionably beyond the pale...But it behooved more elevated members of society to avoid "vulgar" companionship. Manual after manual warned that a careless choice of pet could signal the owners lack of distinction and discrimination.' Or as Gordon Stables, a respected writer on canine topics pointed out in 1877: 'Nobody now who is anybody can afford to be followed about by a mongrel dog.'

Pure-bred dogs, long established in the upper classes, became a way of distinguishing members of a new and active middle class. Dog shows proliferated and the popularity of pure-bred dogs as pets increased dramatically.

Queen Victoria, perhaps the archetypal nineteenth century animal lover, provided an extraordinary precedent for the commissioning and collecting of dog paintings. Her lead, as well as the active involvement of prominent dog fanciers, created and encouraged countless others. One can hardly imagine

Henry Bernard Chalon. Ready to Play, *1819. Oil on panel, 6½ x 10ins. (16.5 x 25.5cm). One occasionally comes across fine pet portraits which pre-date 1840. This happy little dog is more than likely an early Maltese, its soft white coat clipped in the fashion of the day* Private collection

nineteenth century painting, for instance, without the sometimes anthropomorphic paintings of Sir Edwin Landseer, one of Queen Victoria's favourite artists. His work for the Queen and Prince Albert, in England as well as in the Scottish Highlands, provides a fascinating chronicle of the many breeds whose companionship the royal couple enjoyed.

Nor was their patronage limited to Landseer, for Burton Barber, Gourlay Steell, Maud Earl, and Friedrich Wilhelm Keyl to name a few, were also employed to depict royal pets.

This interest in chronicling one's pet, pure-bred or otherwise, was certainly not limited to royalty and in the last quarter of the nineteenth century pet portraits reached a height of popularity.

This was a separate and distinct development from the evolution of hound and sporting dog paintings of the eighteenth century, for such paintings emphasised function, that is to say how well the dog performed in the field. Owners of these earlier dogs were interested in performance, so artists depicted foxhounds running after their prey, and sporting dogs working in the field.

In contrast, in the pure-bred dog portraits of the late nineteenth century, the specific breed and its conformation to the standard for the breed was paramount. As we have seen, pure-bred dog fanciers went to great lengths to establish the separate breeds, as well as to delineate the fine points which distinguished one dog from another within each breed.

This was evident in the visual arts as early as 1855 when R. Marshall painted the earliest known depiction of a dog show, held almost twenty years before the formation of The Kennel Club (Colour Plate 77). The painting, now appropriately in the collection of The Kennel Club, depicts a group of men seated at tables in Jemmy Shaw's public house, the Queen's Head Tavern in London. While we shall return to this painting for closer study, it is important to note that even in 1855 the finer points of Spaniels and Toy Terriers were being debated.

Thus, two important categories of dog painting emerge. The first includes depictions of sporting dogs and hounds, painted to illustrate the superior working abilities of the animals. The second is that of the pure-bred dog, depicted to illustrate the breed characteristics in general and the finer points of one animal in particular.

A third category of dog painting may also be delineated, one which by its nature is more generic — that of the pet portrait. While pure-bred dog fanciers may have celebrated the finer points of their breed, the owner of a beloved pet,

Colour Plate 1. *Maud Earl.* Greyhounds, *c.1900. Oil on canvas, 40½ x 51ins. (103 x 129.5cm).*
This is a majestic portrait of Greyhounds in the field, perhaps shown together because the rules of coursing dictated that they hunt in this way. It is a pure-bred dog portrait, for the dogs are carefully posed to show off their salient breed characteristics

Photograph courtesy Guy Nevill Fine Paintings

whether pure-bred or not, was no less interested in having a lasting portrayal of his dog.

The pet dog might also be pure-bred, but in the pet portrait the intention was to depict the dog more casually in a domestic environment. The pet portrait portrayed the animal engaging in typically canine activities such as resting, sleeping, begging or performing tricks.

These three categories also relate to parallel developments in the United States, although the pure-bred dog portrait did not become as popular there until the early twentieth century. Dog painting in nineteenth century America was dominated by the sporting breeds, which were among the first to be shown in organised American dog shows.

In the nineteenth century, in both England and America, a group of artists evolved who specialised in the depiction of dogs. While in England the names Edwin Landseer, Richard Ansdell and Gourlay Steell remain closely linked with royalty, there emerged many others who became known for their dog paintings. George Earl, John Emms, John Noble, Frank Paton, Briton Riviere, and Arthur Wardle are well known, but they are only a handful among many.

In America, similar, if somewhat later developments created a fascinating chronicle of American dogs. While Arthur Fitzwilliam Tait predominated in the nineteenth century, others such as Percival Rosseau, Edmund Osthaus, Gustav Muss-Arnolt and J.M. Tracy became known for their portraits of sporting dogs in the late nineteenth and early twentieth centuries.

This book is intended to bring together a wide range of dog paintings to illustrate the social history of pure-bred dogs in the British Isles and America. Chapter 1: The Dog in Continental Art looks at the dog in art from prehistoric times up until the eighteenth century, a period in which for the most part the dog in art was portrayed as a secondary subject. It also provides a background to the prolific dog portraiture of the nineteenth and early twentieth centuries.

Colour Plate 2. *Arthur Wardle.*
Working on a Hedgerow. *Oil on canvs, 16 x 20ins. (40.5 x 51cm).*
These early Wire Fox Terriers are working in the field, searching for the vermin that they were expert at extracting. However, as with the Maud Earl portrait of Greyhounds opposite, this must also be considered a pure-bred dog portrait, for Wardle has taken great pains to pose the dogs in order to show off their special breed characteristics Private collection; photography Dave King

Chapter 2 Pre-Victorian England, studies the origins of the various breeds which existed in Great Britain up until 1840, and explores in depth these individual breeds as they appear in nineteenth and early twentieth century art.

In Chapter 3: Victorian England, and Chapter 4: Between Victoria and World War II, the introduction and development of various breeds are discussed in the context of prominent dog owners. The early development of the conformation dog shows and field trials, early prominent judges and dog breeders, including Queen Victoria, are examined with a view to illustrating the various breeds which were popular during the period. In Chapter 5: Dog Painting in America, parallel developments in the United States see the establishment of The American Kennel Club, dog shows and field trials.

The Appendix: Selected Dog Artists fulfils two purposes. In the first place it lists all artists (with their dates and nationalities) whose works appear in this book, and gives the illustration references. Secondly, it provides more detailed biographical and art historical information for those artists who have contributed significantly to the genre. The Selected Bibliography is intended to introduce the reader to the literature of the pure-bred dog as well as make reference to the few books which include information about nineteenth and early twentieth century dog paintings.

This book serves as an introduction to nineteenth and early twentieth century dog paintings, placing them in the little known context of the history of pure-bred dogs. Such an undertaking is by its nature incomplete, but it is hoped that the current volume will provide a starting point for more research.

Plate 1. *Prehistoric cave painting.*
Dogs and dog-like creatures appear in several prehistoric cave paintings, indicating that the dog was indeed one of the first domesticated animals Photograph courtesy The Dog Museum, St. Louis

CHAPTER 1

The Dog in Continental Art

If the visual record of a society is some indication of its values and priorities, then surely the dog has been of great importance to man.

The image of dog-like creatures appears in the prehistoric cave paintings of the palaeolithic period. A Chow-Chow-like breed, a Gazehound, a Terrier and a Mastiff-type breed appear in Egyptian hieroglyphics and wall paintings. The Greeks of classical Athens left behind many depictions of the Greyhound, the Mastiff and the diminutive Maltese Terrier. Equally impressive are the Babylonian wall reliefs, now in the British Museum, depicting the great Mastiff-type dogs of the seventh century B.C. which were used to hunt wild horses and lions as well as to attack the enemy during battle.

The dog, however, was not the primary subject matter. It appeared as part of a hunting scene, a religious, mythological or allegorical story, or accompanying its master in a portrait. While this record by its nature leaves an inadequate impression, herein lies part of its fascination. The ambiguity of an image or a canine symbol taken out of its context of time and place often brings new puzzles. What remains certain, however, is that dogs were of great importance to man as early as the hunter/gatherer societies of prehistory.

For our purpose, it is important at the outset to note that even from the time of recorded history it is difficult to determine the breed depicted in a work of art with any degree of certainty. This is undoubtedly the case when looking at prehistoric cave paintings (Plate 1), but it is also evident when looking at pictures as recent as the seventeenth century. Unless literary records exist which name the breed of dog, one can only surmise.

The modern notion of breeds which are genetically pure for generations is a relatively recent phenomenon. Until the establishment of The Kennel Club in 1873 and its American equivalent in 1884, The American Kennel Club, interbreeding was the rule rather than the exception. Maintaining the purity of a breed was a very rare notion indeed. For this reason we shall refer, for instance, to Mastiff-like creatures rather than Old English Mastiffs.

The origins of the dog as a domesticated animal are shrouded in the veil of prehistory. Most authorities agree, however, that domestication of the dog (probably a member of the wolf family) began in the Middle East or south-west Asia about 12,000 to 10,000 B.C. in the upper palaeolithic period of the late Pleistocene Epoch. This early date makes the dog the first animal to be domesticated by man.

As time passed, the beginnings of selective breeding occurred when early domesticated dogs produced their first litters Man's primitive efforts as a breeder were undoubtedly for ecological reasons — he needed dogs to cope with the problems of day-to-day survival in his environment. Selection played a part in the long process of domestication: only the swiftest dogs were kept to pursue and capture prey. Those that could retrieve well were used for hunting in the forest, and larger and stronger dogs were used for protection and to warn against approaching predators or enemies.

The process of domestication probably occurred simultaneously in many areas of the world over a long period of time and involved a number of different types of canines. By 9000 B.C., the fossilised remains of domestic dogs uncovered from such diverse places as Illinois, Greece, England and Denmark seem to indicate the dog's important role in the life of early man.

Egypt, Assyria and Babylonia

At the dawn of history, the beginnings of organised society were emerging in the Middle East, particularly Egypt. The domesticated dog had developed into a number of different types by this time, some of which were ancestors of present day breeds.

Dogs were treated with great affection in ancient Egypt and their images appear in art from the earliest times. It is difficult to generalise about a period

Plate 2. The Great Lion Hunt, *seventh century B.C. Limestone relief from the North Palace of Assurbanipal, Nineveh.*
Mastiff-like dogs have throughout history been used to hunt and to wage war, their owners taking advantage of the dogs' massive size and strength. Notice the aggressive, growling expressions of these dogs
Collection British Museum, courtesy The Trustees of The British Museum

which spanned thousands of years, but representations of dogs do appear in the Archaic period, approximately 4400 years before Christ. Greyhound- and Mastiff-type dogs appear on slate tablets, of uncertain purpose, and both are shown attacking wild animals.

Two other distinct breed types are seen in Egyptian art by around 3000 B.C.: a smaller version of the Greyhound and a distinctly Spitz-type dog. Other canine types continue to appear, including the Saluki, the Wolfhound, and what appears to be an ancestor of the modern Great Dane. Such speculations, however, are only tentative, as these dogs may have been mixed breeds, and their similarity to pure-breds a happy coincidence.

What we do know, is that by the New Empire, around 1500 B.C., dogs were very much revered, being used in battle, for the chase and for herding, as well as in the home as pets. Wall paintings show them inside homes lying under their masters' chairs.

Herodotus wrote that when a favoured animal died, its owners went into mourning, shaved their bodies and heads, and refused to touch food present in the household at the time of the death. Elaborate plans were made for the embalming of the dog, because the dog's body was preserved by the same method as that used for humans. Each step was governed by religious ritual. Once prepared, the body was wrapped with strips of linen, and when the master passed on to the other world the dog joined him, his carefully embalmed body being put into the sarcophagus beside his master.

The ancient Assyrians and Babylonians used dogs to hunt lions, to herd and guard sheep, to wage war and to protect their homes. Saluki- and Mastiff-type dogs were depicted on carvings and war shields. King Assurbanipal of Assyria, who reigned from 668-626 B.C., was an ardent hunter and maintained large kennels of dogs to hunt lions and wild horses. Clay tablets, now in the British Museum, show Saluki-type hounds and fierce Mastiff-type dogs being held on leash by strong warriors (Plate 2).

Classical Greece and Rome

In classical Greece, the dog also held an important and esteemed role as a pet, as a hunter, and as a guard for livestock as well as the home. Xenophon writes of hunting wild boar with dogs, and legend has it that the fierce dogs of Corinth were renowned for their loyalty. According to one story, some fifty dogs were left to guard a fortress as the soldiers inside slept. During the night, the fortress was attacked and the dogs bravely warded off the enemy. Forty-nine of them lost their lives in the process. Just as the fiftieth was about to be killed, the soldiers awoke and rescued him. The brave dog was subsequently retired from duty and given a life of luxury and great honours.

Aristotle was the first to discuss the anatomy and physiology of the dog. In 350 B.C., he listed the 'most useful' known breeds, among them the Epirotic dog, the Laconian and the Molossian, the ancestor of our present day Mastiffs.

In general, identification of the breeds in Greek art is made more difficult by the tendency of many artists to stylise or idealise their subjects, but several

Plate 3. Actaeon Attacked by Dogs. *Bell krater.*
Dogs abounded in Greek and Roman mythology, the most feared being Cerberus, the three-headed hound which guarded the gates of Hades. The dogs here depicted are ancestors of our present-day Greyhounds, one of the oldest of all breeds

Collection Museum of Fine Arts, Boston, H.L. Pierce Fund

Plate 4. *Attic small red figure vessel. Early third quarter fifth century* B.C.
This small dog, most probably an ancestor of the Maltese, is believed by some to have originated on the island of Malta. The artist's abstracted depiction of the dog, however, makes breed identification difficult

Collection The University Museum, University of Pennsylvania

breed types can be recognised. While the Greyhound (Plates 3 and 5) is certainly the most prevalent, other breeds such as the Mastiff and the Maltese appear (Plate 4). An Afghan-type dog is even depicted on Athenian artefacts. Saluki-type dogs also appear.

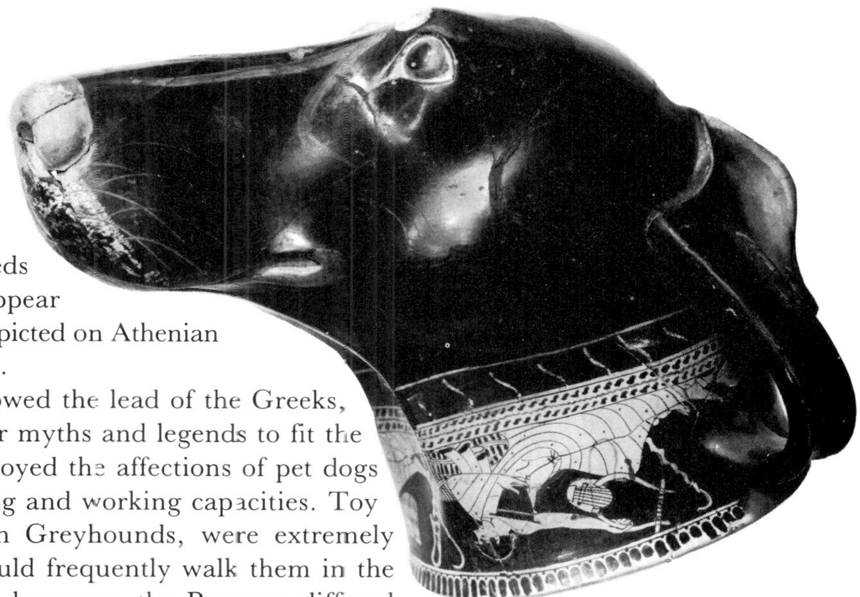

Plate 5. *Rhyton in the form of a hound's head. Sixth century B.C. Greek artists often depicted the dog, and in particular Greyhound- and Maltese-types. The rhyton, an unfooted drinking vessel, is the ancestor of the stirrup cup. Such cups were traditionally offered to a mounted horseman, often before the start of the hunt*

By permission of the Villa Giulia Museum, Rome

As in most things, the Romans followed the lead of the Greeks, emulating their art and reworking their myths and legends to fit the needs of the Empire. The Romans enjoyed the affections of pet dogs and actively employed dogs in guarding and working capacities. Toy dogs, particularly Maltese and Italian Greyhounds, were extremely popular with Roman women, who would frequently walk them in the streets. When it came to waging war, however, the Romans differed from the Greeks in their methods. The Greeks had used their huge Mastiff-like dogs in waging battle, but the Romans clad their dogs in heavy coats embellished with spikes and sharp blades, protecting the dog's neck with spiked iron collars. Some of these ancient war dogs, complete with armour, are depicted on the Column of Marcus Aurelius in Rome.

On a more pleasant note, great sympathy was shown toward the dog at home, and perhaps no images could be more poignant than those of the ash-entombed corpses at Herculaneum, dogs which, with their families, were unable to escape the horrors of the volcano. Here, too, are the beautiful mosaics found on the floor in the entrance halls of houses. At Pompeii, the *cave canum* mosaics are well-known (Plate 6), showing the dog barking or in repose. Were these a warning to guests that they should beware of the household pet? More likely, they simply denoted the presence of a dog. The Romans adored their dogs and the animals depicted, although barking, could hardly be called fierce or alarming enough to scare off a thief.

While dogs were not formally worshipped as the incarnations of Gods, they were very influential in Greek and Roman mythology. Perhaps the most famous Greek mythological dog is the dreaded Cerberus, the three-headed hound who guarded the entrance to the underworld, an image which appears again and again in Greek art. Vulcan (known to the Greeks as Hephaestus), the Roman God of Fire, is said to have forged a dog of bronze, and to have breathed life into it.

The Virgin Goddess of the Chase, Diana (known to the Greeks as Artemis), always appears accompanied by her hunting hounds. Followers of Diana/Artemis believed that she stopped hunting on the Ides of August, and it was forbidden to hunt at that time; hunting dogs were crowned with garlands of flowers and men temporarily put away their hunting weapons.

Both the Greeks and Romans feared the appearance in the sky of the Greater Dog Star, Sirius. To them, the coming of Sirius in the sky each summer signalled the beginning of a period of unbearable heat, increased disease and burned crops. They called the hottest weeks of summer 'dog days' (as we still do), and believed that Sirius's appearance enhanced the sun's heat, caused hydrophobia, and that dogs were most susceptible to madness at this time.

Plate 6. Cave canum *mosaic. From the House of The Poet, Pompeii. The Romans were very fond of their dogs, keeping them as pets. Even though translated literally,* cave canum *means beware of the dog, such inscriptions were undoubtedly intended to denote the presence of the household dog, rather than any particular danger*

There are many examples of the dog in Roman pottery and sculpture, and during the Hellenistic period the dog was depicted with great sympathy and keen observation. The sculpture *Sick Dog,* now in the Louvre, is a masterpiece of this period. It renders with great detail a sympathetic view of a suffering animal, a subject matter which never would have appeared in the art of classical Greece. Indeed, there are many such examples in the Vatican where dogs are depicted with a kindness and devotion which is absent from the idealised figures of classical Greece.

The Middle Ages

The Middle Ages began with the fall of the Roman Empire in the West, and ended with the destruction of the Roman Empire in the East and the capture of Constantinople by the Turks. It was a dismal period for both dog and man, and as we shall see the dog rarely appeared in the visual arts, except in the north where it slowly became important in depictions of the hunt.

The early part of the Middle Ages was a dark period for the dog, for with it came many middle eastern prejudices. Perhaps because it roamed as a scavenger in search of prey, some societies came to hate the dog, an antipathy which has continued to some degree in the Islamic world today. Horrible superstitions about dogs were revived, fuelled by packs of wild dogs which roamed Europe scavenging for their food. This attitude was also reflected in the visual arts. When dogs were depicted in sculpture, for instance, they were shown with their lips drawn back in a snarl, with threatening teeth and glaring eyes. Indeed, the word 'dog' became an insult, and thieves and murderers were commonly called curs.

Furthermore, the urban life which had been enjoyed by the Greeks and the Romans was now replaced by an economy based in the countryside, and there was little room for the pampered pet, except in the rare instance for the very rich.

Around A.D. 500, however, the dog slowly began to regain importance, this time in association with the hunt. Hunting during this period was for most people a source of food, but for the wealthy nobleman, hunting with dogs for sport became a symbol of privilege and wealth.

Large hunting packs were maintained, and noblemen in France at the time of Charlemagne became so fond of their animals that they would take them into church where their barking and general misbehaviour created a great fuss. Despite its dependence on the noblemen for monetary support, the church prohibited the dogs from entering, and went so far as to make the owning of dogs by priests and abbots illegal.

One can only imagine the resistance this must have caused, and the noblemen responded with a great show of devotion for their dogs: they refused to enter the church, and stood outside with their animals in order to listen to the service from afar! It is said that the priests were forced to leave the church to bless the noblemen, in order that they might not incur their rage, and from this evolved the tradition of the blessing of the hounds.

Keeping many dogs was a privilege of the very rich, and for the most part the dog performed three roles: as a pampered pet, as a worker on the farm, and in the hunt. The dog was much loved by royalty, including Louis IX who is said to have imported Gazehounds — hounds which hunt by sight rather than by smell — into France. Stories about royal affection for the canine are legion: Louis XI ordered a ruby-studded collar for his favourite Greyhound, while Charles VII is reputed to have let his most successful hunting dogs sleep in his bed in turn.

By the end of the Middle Ages, hunting was no longer a necessity for the gathering of food, but became the privilege of the very wealthy, associated with the secular control that was exercised by feudal lords. The hunt became much more ceremonial, costly and elaborate and it was with hunting that the iconography of medieval dogs reached its apex, for hunting manuals as well as woodcuts and paintings all depicted them. The other remaining images of the dog from this dark period are seen in illuminated manuscripts and tapestries.

One of the first embroidered pieces to portray dogs is the Bayeux Tapestry, probably produced soon after 1066. The tapestry illustrates the story of the Norman conquest of Britain, and in one of the scenes King Harold is shown setting out on a hawking expedition accompanied by five dogs (Plate 7). Other scenes depict animals which are definitely dogs wearing collars with leash rings. The renderings, although magnificent, are not detailed enough to allow identification of the breeds.

This is not the case, however, with illuminated manuscripts, often miniature gems of realistic painting. *Les Très Riches Heures du Duc de Berry,* for instance, depicts several views of feudal life, brilliantly painted and illuminated with gold leaf. The most powerful is perhaps the hunt for the boar, in which three varieties of hunting dogs bring down their prey.

This view was undoubtedly depicted to record an important event, but also to glorify the power of the king. As we have seen, the right to hunt had gradually become a privilege of the nobility, and the aim of hunting was quite clearly no longer the procurement of food. One can only imagine the excesses perpetrated in the name of the hunt, and by the mid-seventeenth century it had reached an extraordinary position in the life of the French court. At the death of Louis XII, for example, a virtual army of servants was required to assist in the hunt. These included forty lieutenants, four sub-lieutenants, forty noble huntsmen, two hunting pages, four knights of the kennels, seventeen masters of the kennel on foot, eighteen Bloodhound guides, four dog servants, and more.

The Middle Ages were also the time of the crusades, and the knights developed a serious interest in hunting. They learned techniques from one another, and the dog became a valued asset in the hunt. The crusaders undoubtedly exchanged dogs, searching for superior examples; indeed, the dog historian Walter Hutchinson says that Salukis became the fashion among the knights who hunted with them and then brought them back to Europe as proof of their pilgrimage.

As the hunt developed, so did the rules which governed it. When a servant was admitted to the hunt, for instance, he was allowed to wear the hunting livery, but not carry a knife. This apprenticeship lasted three years and new skills were acquired each year: the first year was the performance of purely mechanical tasks, the second for learning how to control the dogs and the third for working on a one-to-one basis with a particular hound, learning the language of the hunt and the various types of game. But throughout, the nobility continued to retain the exclusive right to hunt.

The Renaissance

By the end of the Middle Ages, the dog had again established its role as hunter, but with the Renaissance, the dog emerged as never before in all its many roles. The home of the Renaissance was Italy where a revival of classical values and attitudes saw the re-establishment of the city as the focal point of society. With the emergence of new wealth, the dog once again became a highly prized pet, a guardian, and a worker as well as a hunter. This was reflected in the visual arts with the dog featured in mythological and allegorical scenes as well as in religious ones.

Many of the advances of the Renaissance in Italy, as well as in the north,

Plate 7. *Bayeux Tapestry (detail), c.1073-1083. Wool embroidery on linen, height 20ins. (51cm). While the breed of these dogs is impossible to determine, they were probably hunting hounds. King Harold is seen going off to hunt with his hawk in hand* Courtesy of the town of Bayeux

were based on classical precedents. The Renaissance man also looked to the antique for guidance in artistic endeavours, and he took an active interest in the dog as part of his pursuit of scientific matters. This resulted in the publication of veterinary treatises with carefully rendered diagrams of the dog's anatomy.

In the south the image of the dog in art reappeared in many guises, but always as an adjunct to the principal subject matter of the painting. In the hierarchy of subject matter suitable for the artist's attention, religious art was first, then historical or mythological scenes, and lastly secular art which was represented for the most part by portraits of wealthy businessmen. While some artists maintained what now seems an antipathy toward the dog, each of these categories of painting often included a dog's image.

The great Giotto (c.1266-1337) introduced the dog into his famous fresco in the Arena Chapel in Padua, although it is probably not a portrait of a specific dog. Duccio di Buoninsegna (c.1240-1340) also integrated the dog into his religious paintings.

The artist Antonio Pisano, called Pisanello (c.1380-1455) created a magnificent portrait of animals in *The Vision of St. Eustace* in which two Greyhounds, a Hound, and two small Spaniel-like dogs in the foreground can be seen (Plate 8). Unlike Giotto, there is in Pisanello an accuracy of detail

Plate 8. *Pisanello.*
The Vision of St. Eustace, *c.1440. Oil on panel, 21½ x 25¾ ins. (54.5 x 65.5cm).*
The dogs and other animals in this painting are depicted with a realism which would imply that Pisanello used live animals as his models. Note the pair of small Spaniels in the left foreground, no doubt ancestors of our present-day King Charles Spaniels
Reproduced by courtesy of the Trustees, The National Gallery, London

which makes us think that even in a religious painting such as this he may have used contemporary dogs as models.

As the Italian City States developed and the power of the secular leaders reached new heights, so did their influence on the arts. This was particularly true in Venice where the great merchants were often depicted in portraits accompanied by their favourite dog. Perhaps the greatest of these Venetian artists was Tiziano Vecellio (c.1487-1576), known as Titian, for he represented a new realism as well as a psychological insight which had been absent in portraits up to this time. In his portrait of Giovanni dell'Acquaviva, for instance, the Retriever-type dog stands pensively with his head bowed, perhaps an indication of the true temperament of the sitter (Plate 9).

Titian also liked to portray very large dogs in the presence of little children,

Plate 9. *Titian.*
Giovanni dell'Acquaviva, *c.1552. Oil on canvas, 91 x 60½ins. (231 x 153.5cm).*
While it is tempting to identify the dog in this painting as a yellow Labrador, the breed was unknown when this painting was completed around 1550. Whatever the breed, he seems quite oblivious to all his master's finery
Photograph courtesy Gemäldegalerie, Cassel

almost as if he took delight in exaggerating the size of the dog and the vulnerable qualities of children. He was equally at home painting small dogs, and for their place in the history of the breed his depictions of the small red and white Spaniel dog are particularly interesting. Painted about 1505, the Uffizi *Venus* includes a red and white Spaniel curled up on the bed, just as one appears in his portrait of the Duchess of Urbino. It is clear that the dog was a common inhabitant of the great houses and palaces of the Italian Renaissance.

Second only to Titian for his depictions of the dog is Paolo Veronese (1528-1588), an artist who obviously held the dog in great affection. Dogs appear in his religious, mythological and secular paintings. As the eminent dog historian Brian Vesey-Fitzgerald has pointed out, the paintings of Veronese are especially interesting to the history of the Toy Spaniel. While the Toy Spaniels of Titian and Palma Vecchio have long, pointed noses, slim bodies and straight tails, Veronese painted a dog whose origins appear much more oriental. In his *Hermes, Herse and Aglauros,* for instance, the little red and white dog has a very high domed skull, a short and compact body and a relatively short nose, traits which are associated with the Pekingese and other oriental dogs (Plate 10). Perhaps such dogs were imported from China by the sea-faring Venetians.

Veronese is also recognised as the first artist to introduce a Saluki-type dog into his paintings, and they appear often, as in the work *Christ in the House of Simon the Pharisee.* One can only imagine that the palaces of the Venetian merchant princes must have been filled with dogs!

Plate 10. *Veronese.*
Hermes, Herse and Aglauros *(detail). Oil on canvas, 91⅓ x 68ins. (232 x 172.5cm).*
This charming little pet is undoubtedly the ancestor of our present day King Charles Spaniel — or could it be a Japanese Chin?
Collection Fitzwilliam Museum, Cambridge

Plate 11. *Diego Velázquez.*
Court Dwarf *(Don Antonio el Ingles), c.1630. Oil on canvas, 60 x 42ins. (152.5 x 106.5cm).*
This portrait of a court dwarf with an unknown breed of dog falls squarely in the tradition of Las Meninas, *where a large Mastiff-like dog is portrayed with children. Such a juxtaposition underlined the vulnerable, helpless aspect of the human*
Collection The Prado, Madrid

Plate 12. *Antonio Moro.*
Cardinal de Granville's Dwarf. *Oil on canvas.*
The size and power of this huge dog is accentuated by portraying it with a court dwarf. While the dwarf is well-armed and ornately dressed, he seems vulnerable beside the dog
Collection The Louvre, Paris; photograph courtesy Réunion des Musées Nationaux

Plate 13. *Albrecht Dürer.* The Vision of St. Hubert, *1501. Engraving, 14 x 10ins. (30 x 26cm).*
Hunting in the forest one day, Hubert suddenly saw a magnificent stag with the crucified Christ hovering between its horns. Falling to his knees, he swore never to hunt again. He was eventually named the patron saint of animals
Collection The National Gallery of Canada, Ottawa

During the baroque period in southern Europe and throughout the art of the seventeenth century in general, the dog continued in its two principal roles: as a companion to man in portraits, and as a hunter.

In Spain, the painter most noted for his depiction of the dog was the great Velázquez (1599-1660). Who can forget the image of the massive Mastiff in the right foreground of his *Las Meninas* or the equally impressive *Court Dwarf* of c.1630 (Plate 11)? Other sixteenth century Spanish artists such as Antonio Moro (1517-1575) employed the same convention (Plate 12). The huge dog placed in the company of children or, in the case of the two illustrations shown here, a dwarf, gives a picture added drama and highlights the smallness of the human being.

Plate 14. *Jan Van Eyck.* The Marriage of Giovanni Arnolfini and Giovanna Cenami, *1434. Oil on canvas, 33 x 22½ ins. (84 x 57cm). The little Griffon Terrier at the feet of the bride and groom was evidently a symbol of fidelity, and at the time was a popular breed in northern Europe. The entire scene is reflected in a convex mirror on the back wall*

Reproduced by courtesy of the Trustees, The National Gallery, London

Velázquez was equally adept at painting little dogs, and in his portrait of the Infante Philip Prosper, the son of Philip IV, there is a Toy Spaniel very similar to that painted by Veronese. It is undoubtedly what was to become known in England as the King Charles Spaniel.

Northern Europe

In northern Europe, the dog seems to have enjoyed a position of equal importance, and there, too, it continued to appear in both religious and secular painting. As in the south, the artist began to show the dog in all its anatomical detail. Looking at *The Vision of St. Hubert,* by the great German artist Albrecht Dürer (1471-1528), for instance, one cannot doubt that the Greyhounds and hunting dogs in the foreground were drawn from life (Plate 13). Just as in his famous anatomically correct rendering of a hare, now in the Albertina in Vienna, Dürer imbued his dogs with a new naturalism and vitality. Indeed, they have almost the same individuality as humans.

Other artists of this period also portrayed dogs in their paintings. They include Hans Memling (1430/5-1494) and the Flemish Jan Van Eyck (1390-1441), the latter having painted the famous Arnolfini wedding in which the newly married husband and wife stand boldly facing the spectator, while prominently placed between their feet is one of the most famous little dogs in the history of art, a Griffon Terrier (Plate 14). The breed was not known to the southern painters but was quite common in the north.

While the dog does not appear a great deal in the art of the north of the sixteenth century, it does appear with great regularity during the period in the seventeenth century known as the Northern Baroque. Indeed, in the seventeenth and eighteenth centuries it was not the art of Italy, but that of northern Europe which provided the foundation for much of nineteenth century English animal painting.

A new school of painting grew up which did not rely on historical, mythological or religious subject matter: that of genre painting and landscape. Artists such as the Dutchman Albert Cuyp (1620-1691), Adrian van Ostade (1610-1685), Adrian Brouwer (1605-1638) and Gerard Terborch (1617-1681) all introduced dogs into their compositions (Plate 15), but more importantly they signalled a shift in attitude; because of them, once scorned subject matter was now viewed as appropriate for the painter's attention. Before this, paintings of the common man, of landscapes and of animals were considered beneath the serious attention of the artist.

Landscape, for instance, was thought to be only an adjunct to the principal subject matter — it could not exist on its own. Nor could the poor, no matter how interesting, be depicted unless they were part of a religious, mythological or historic theme.

Another important shift occurred during the seventeenth century in the north, for dogs were no longer to be depicted as the prized pets of the very rich. They were often the companions of the lower classes or the poor and are shown in everyday life, without aggrandisement. They do not pose stiffly with their

Plate 15. *Albert Cuyp.*
Starting For The Hunt. *Oil on canvas, 43¼ x 61½ ins. (110 x 156cm).*
This painting depicts Michiel and Cornelius van Meedervoort, with their tutor and coachman, about to start for the hunt. Notice the Greyhounds running in the background
Collection The Metropolitan Museum of Art, New York, bequest of Michael Friedsam

masters or perform in the hunt, but are found doing what the dog is best at: resting, playing, growling and fighting, and in general doing what dogs do in real life. There can be no doubt that these dogs are not the idealised symbols of earlier Italian art, for they are depicted with a realism that is in some cases startling.

From the point of view of the historian of the dog, works by such artists as Frans Snyders (1579-1657), Paul de Vos (1625-1695) and Abraham Hondius (1625-1695) are of great importance, for they depicted many breeds including the Griffon, Pug, Spaniel, Pomeranian, Greyhound, Retriever, and a dog which closely resembles the Labrador. From the perspective of an art historian, these painters were also crucial to the development of the animal portrait, and in particular that of the dog. They were among the first to recognise that mundane subject matter, such as a landscape or a genre scene, was worthy of the artist's attention. They depicted animals realistically, without idealisation, and they depicted members of the middle class, all important precedents for animal painting in nineteenth century England.

These artists were the first seriously to consider the possibility that the dog was of interest in its own right and, although later artists continued to disagree

Plate 16. *Paul de Vos.*
Spaniels. *Oil on canvas.*
While many of the paintings of de Vos exhibit the violent, aggressive nature of dogs, this intimate portrait portrays their more relaxed side, resting after the hunt
Photograph courtesy The Tryon Gallery

Plate 17. *Peter Paul Rubens.*
The Wolf and Fox Hunt, *c.1617. Oil on canvas, 96 x 148½ ins. (244 x 377cm).*
Rubens, who represented the epitome of the Northern Baroque, created an active composition representing the excitement and danger of the hunt. The Greyhounds create a dynamic outline beneath the horse Collection The Metropolitan Museum of Art, New York, the John Stuart Kennedy Fund

Colour Plate 3. *Abraham Hondius.*
The Dog Market, *1677. Oil on panel, 40 x 50ins. (101.5 x 127cm).*
With the rise of a newly wealthy merchant class in Holland came a craze for collecting, and a new interest in the dog. This painting is a veritable encyclopaedia of the breeds which were available at the time. Curiously, Hondius has also depicted an array of dog collars at the front of the painting
Collection Walter F. Goodman; photography Grant Taylor

with this notion, they in effect made the animal art of eighteenth and nineteenth century England possible.

The work of Frans Snyders and Paul de Vos tended to be rather violent, often depicting the dog in combat with wolves, lions and other wild animals. In Snyders's *Stag Hunt,* for instance, one sees the fallen stag viciously attacked by the hounds, while one of them is crushed by the stag's antlers, his head raised to grasp hopelessly at the stag. The work of Snyders and de Vos was characterised by a realism and sense of drama not seen in the painting of the previous century (Plate 16), and their art was to have an influence on the nineteenth century British artist, Edwin Landseer.

Plate 18. *Gabriel Metsu.*
The Sleeping Sportsman. *Oil on canvas, 16⅝ x 14⅝ ins. (42 x 37cm).*
The dog portrayed is undoubtedly an ancestor of our present day sporting Spaniel, bearing a strong resemblance to the English Springer Spaniel

By permission of the Trustees of the Wallace Collection, London

Another Flemish artist who was to influence Landseer and English art in general was Peter Paul Rubens (1577-1640), who visited England several times. Creating paintings that epitomised the vibrant and dramatic compositions of the baroque, Rubens often integrated the dog into his work. He was a great scholar, and his dogs add a charming and commonplace touch to his large historical and mythological canvases — from his hunting scenes such as *The Wolf and Fox Hunt* (Plate 17) to *The Raising of the Cross* for the Cathedral in Antwerp, into which he incorporated a portrait of his own Spaniel.

Animal painting during the baroque period in the north was not restricted to the Flemish, however, for in Holland a virtual mania for dogs had developed. Holland was a rich trading nation and dogs were actively bought and traded among the newly rich middle class, a member of which can be seen in the painting by Gabriel Metsu (1630-1667) of *The Sleeping Sportsman* (Plate 18).

The work of Abraham Hondius (1625-1695) also reflected this craze, and he created many portraits for the picture-hungry middle class. In *The Dog Market* of 1677, alternatively titled, *The Dogs of the Palatine,* one sees the great attention

Plate 19. *School of Fontainebleau.*
Diana the Huntress, *c.1540.*
Diana the Huntress, accompanied by her Greyhound, has been a recurring theme throughout the history of art Collection The Louvre, Paris; photograph courtesy Reunion des Musées Nationaux

Plate 20. *Jean-Honoré Fragonard.*
The Love Letter. *Oil on canvas, 32¾ x 26⅜ins. (83 x 67cm).*
In France, Fragonard, along with Boucher, perhaps best represented the epitome of the light, frivolous style which became known as the rococo. The little Spaniel seems oblivious to the romantic intrigues of his mistress Collection The Metropolitan Museum of Art, New York, the Jules Bach Collection

which he lavished on his animal portraits, even to the highly specialised collars lined up at the front (Colour Plate 3). In a reversal of the human/dog ratio of previous centuries, the dogs have taken over almost the entire painting, with the human element and the classical architecture merely a backdrop for the canine drama before them.

Hondius painted the work in great detail, and over sixteen distinct breeds are depicted, the large fawn Mastiff taking centre stage. Very little is known about the painting, although when it was sold at auction in London in 1726 the historian George Vertue commented in his diary that 'the celebrated Dog Market was esteemed as Hondius' masterpiece.'

Other Dutch animal painters of the period included Jan Steen (1626-1679) known for his *Dance of the Dog,* and Paul Potter (1625-1654) who depicted animals with a great attention to detail. Potter had a very short life, dying at the age of twenty-nine, but he had an intensity of vision when it came to portraying dogs and other animals which was unrivalled during the period.

Moving to France, one sees very few depictions of the dog in seventeenth century art. The classical, rational art of Nicolas Poussin (1594-1665) and

Colour Plate 4. *Jean-Baptiste Oudry.*
Black Greyhound, *1723. Oil on canvas.*
This double portrait creates a charming interplay between the Greyhound and the diminutive Poodle, and includes many of the rich, colourful details for which Oudry was known. Notice the red parrot in the tree and the beautifully painted collar around the Greyhound's neck Private collection

Claude Lorrain (1600-1682) is considered by most to be the opposite of the colourist Peter Paul Rubens, and their work portrayed different subjects as well. It seems that there was little place for sentiment in these French artists' work, dominated as it was by great classical and religious themes.

By contrast, the eighteenth century in France was to present the dog in all its glory, and the French painters Alexandre-François Desportes (1661-1743) and Jean-Baptiste Oudry (1686-1755) produced some of the great masterpieces of dog painting in the history of art. While such artists as Jean-Baptiste Greuze (1725-1805) painted sentimental scenes in which the dog played an active role, it was the court which created the milieu for the great painters of the day.

Antoine Watteau (1684-1721), François Boucher (1703-1770), and Jean-

Plate 21. *Jean-Baptiste Oudry.* Pointer Pointing at Quail. *Oil on canvas, 41 x 54ins. (104 x 137cm).*
Oudry was a master at depicting the hunting dog, capturing his alert pose and intense expression. Louis XV, for whom Oudry worked, maintained extensive kennels, housing many hundreds of hunting dogs with whom he spent hours
Collection The Dog Museum, St. Louis, gift of Mr. and Mrs. Philip S.P. Fell; photography Grant Taylor

Honoré Fragonard (1732-1802) all had access to the court and all were dog lovers. Watteau, who was to transform the face of French painting, was himself a student of the Flemish school, and his early work was greatly influenced by those painters. His mature work, however, is the epitome of the light, crisp frivolity of the period. François Boucher was to continue in this tradition. A favourite of Madame de Pompadour, for whom he began working in 1746, his paintings could be at once light and frivolous as well as monumental and serious. Of most interest to us are his portraits of court ladies, often painted with their pets, the diminutive ancestors of the Toy Spaniel, or the Chien-de-Lion.

Fragonard studied with Boucher and continued his predecessor's style as well as his penchant for light hearted subject matter. The Toy Spaniel appears repeatedly in such paintings as the *Love Letter* (Plate 20) and *Love Crowned,* but perhaps none is more charming than in *The Souvenir* in which a toy Spaniel looks longingly at his mistress while she inscribes the letter 'S' or 'F' on the stone before her.

The two greatest painters of dog of this period, however, were associated with the hunt: Desportes and Oudry. As we have seen earlier, by the seventeenth century the hunt had become of critical importance to the establishment of a social hierarchy and as a show of power. Desportes and Oudry glorified the King by portraying the hunt in all its splendour.

Desportes started out as a portrait painter in the court of Poland and later moved to France to paint in the court of Louis XIV. At this time the hunt was still a highly ritualised social event and great sums were lavished on its production. The hunt staff alone was immense, and was composed of two equerries, fourteen lieutenants, twenty-four captains, five valets for the Bloodhounds and 780 grooms, while the kennels were said to house as many as 400 dogs!

Designated the official painter of the hunt for Louis XIV, Desportes created many fine and action filled canvases and was the first artist to create carefully observed dog portraits in which the animals filled the entire canvas.

With the reign of Louis XV, Desportes continued in the service of the court, but he was eventually supplanted by the younger Oudry. Starting out as a portrait painter, Oudry apprenticed with the colourist Nicolas de Largillière (1656-1746) and quickly advanced in court circles. In 1723 he was given a studio in the Tuileries where, in 1725, he established lodgings. He was invited to Versailles in 1726, and named painter to the royal tapestry works at Beauvais in the same year. He was later appointed inspector at the Gobelin tapestry works.

Oudry painted a diverse group of pictures early in his life, including many portraits, still-lifes and a few history pictures. But it is with his paintings of animals that he came into his own (Plate 21 and Colour Plate 4). Between 1719 and 1721 he developed his own style, culminating in a command exhibition at Versailles in 1726.

As an animal painter, Oudry was unparalleled, and in his many portraits of the King's dogs one sees a combination of acute observation and an appreciation for lavish decorative effects. In *The Dead Roe* of 1721, now in the Wallace Collection, for example, the hunting dogs are faithfully rendered, their smooth coats and strong physicality brilliantly captured, while Oudry's palette of pinks and blue-greens is offset with white and grey to create a sophisticated decorative counterbalance.

Missi and Turlen, Two Greyhounds Belonging to Louis XV, of 1725, is perhaps one of Oudry's most straightforward portraits, showing two of the King's favourite Greyhounds, their names painted in large gilt letters on the canvas itself. Painted for the young King, they were displayed in Oudry's command exhibition at Versailles in 1726. The painting is extraordinary in its matter-of-fact yet elegant portrayal of two dogs in a landscape. Not a hunt painting *per se,* for it is set in a park rather than a forest, it is a precursor of the British portraits of the late eighteenth and nineteenth centuries. Indeed, one can almost detect a sympathetic or sentimental aspect to this portrait, an attitude which places the work squarely in the tradition of the pet portrait, which we shall see in the work of later artists in England.

The dogs of eighteenth century France enjoyed the favours of the King and his court. Toy dogs frolicked in the rococo style portraits of the important ladies of court and, clearly, they were highly prized and much doted upon. As we have seen with the art of Desportes and Oudry, the hunt was of critical importance to the prestige and stability of the court. And herein lies the essential reason for the nineteenth century break with the great tradition of the eighteenth: the Revolution. The great animal art of the eighteenth century had been almost entirely based on court life, and with its disintegration went the French tradition of animal art.

Curiously, the next great school of animal artists in France looked not to the rational values of eighteenth century France, but, as in England, to the art of the Low Countries, and to dogs realistically depicted in the context of everyday life.

Painters such as Louis-Godefroy Jadin (1805-1882) and Philippe Rousseau

Plate 22. *Antoine-Louis Barye.* King Charles Spaniels, *c.1830. Bronze.*
Barye was the most influential of the animalier *sculptors. While the majority of his work was of other animals, his dogs are among the most popular* Photograph courtesy Walters Art Gallery, Baltimore

(1816-1887) were influenced by the genre and animal painters of the Low Countries, and some think by the work of Edwin Landseer. And while Rosa Bonheur is certainly ranked among the greatest of French animal painters, her work evolved very much from the Flemish and Dutch tradition. In contrast to the very sociable Landseer, in later years Rosa Bonheur went into seclusion to paint her beloved animals. She did so without the narrative context or sentimental associations which had come to characterise the work of Landseer.

The contribution of nineteenth century France to animal art is not to be found in painting, however. In sheer numbers if nothing else, animal painters were overshadowed by the French animal sculptors known as *animaliers.* Perhaps the best known of all the French *animalier* school, Antoine-Louis Barye (1796-1875) first exhibited his bronze animal sculptures at the Paris salon in 1831. His work was at the time somewhat of a shock, for animals on their own had only rarely been depicted in three dimensions, and a somewhat outspoken critic dubbed Bayre an 'animalier: a maker of animals. A species deprived of human nobility.' The name stayed with him and became the general term used to describe what we now see as an entire school of sculptors who depicted the animal (Plate 22). Barye dared to depict animals as they were, fighting with one another, snarling, and struggling to exist in the harsh reality of nature.

Although the majority of Barye's works are of animals other than dogs, he was to have a great influence on a group of sculptors who strove to depict not only the realistic appearance of the animal, but also the spirit within. Artists such as Pierre-Jules Mêne (1810-1879), Jules Moigniez (1835-1894) and Emmanuel Frémiet (1824-1910) created many dog portraits in bronze, and together with dozens of other French artists created a school of art which was to have a lasting influence on animal lovers around the world. While these artists did not have a great influence on painting, the primary subject matter of this study, they were very popular in Britain during the mid- and late nineteenth century. The British enthusiasm for country life and animals ensured that these sculptures were avidly collected and easily found a home along with the dog paintings of nineteenth century Britain.

CHAPTER 2

Pre-Victorian England

While the primary subject matter of this book is the explosion of artistic expression which surrounded pure-bred dogs in the nineteenth and early twentieth centuries in England and America, the history of dogs and the dog in art which predated this development is of particular interest both for its own sake and as the setting for what was to come later.

Dogs had been the companions of man in England for centuries, but up until the end of the seventeenth century, what passed for the pure-bred dog was almost entirely the perquisite of wealthy landowners and the nobility. In the visual arts, the dog continued to be portrayed as a companion, pictured with members of the family (Colour Plate 10).

It was in England during the eighteenth century that the dog first appeared as the primary subject matter of the painting, representing a pride of ownership and an interest in the dog's appearance rather than in its performance. The vast majority of dog paintings completed during this period, however, belong to the sporting dog type, where the performance of the dog is the prime reason for the painting.

Dogs during the eighteenth and early nineteenth century in England may be divided into several breed categories which are helpful in understanding the rich visual history which emerged during this period. They are: Greyhounds, Mastiffs or guard dogs, toy dogs including the King Charles Spaniel and the Pug, Bulldogs, Bull Terriers and Foxhounds.

England was the first of the European countries to develop scientific attitudes about animal husbandry, and the selective breeding of animals to improve stock was widespread among members of the English gentry. The portraits of prize bulls by George Stubbs (1724-1806) or John Boultbee (1742-1812) attest to the pride with which the English kept their animals, and the social prestige which was associated with having the best. This was also true of the breeding of dogs, and certain breeds, notably Foxhounds, Spaniels and Greyhounds, became very much associated with the landed gentry and their interest in a way of life based on the ownership of land.

The origins of the domesticated pet dog in England are lost in history. Distinct breeds of dogs in England were found as early as the Roman period when Julius Caesar found Mastiff-type dogs in Britain in 55 B.C. Certainly dogs in general were fairly widespread by the time Alfred the Great came to the throne in 871.

However, as in the rest of northern Europe, the Middle Ages in England were a dark time for the canine race. The nobility had a vested interest in maintaining the game on their land for the purpose of sport hunting, while the peasantry were more interested in gathering food. Poaching was widespread, not only for the procurement of food, but also to keep such animals as rabbits from eating the garden vegetables. While records do not exist delineating the various breeds popular during the Middle Ages, it is known that Greyhounds, Mastiffs, Scent Hounds, Spaniels and Terriers of some description existed.

In order to protect the interests of the landed gentry, a set of rules and regulations known as the Forest Laws was drawn up. The first such laws, known as the Canute Laws, were enacted at the Parliament held in Winchester in 1016. These dictated the behaviour of all those who lived in or around a forest where hunting was traditionally the perquisite of the king and his court, and they gave the king's representatives great powers. For example, except under a grant from the king, the keeping of Greyhounds and Spaniels in the forest was prohibited entirely, and Mastiffs were allowed to roam only if their feet had first been maimed so they could not run with any speed. Small dogs were allowed in the forest, but only if they could pass through a wire loop of a certain size, evidently indicating that they were of no potential harm to game. Poaching was believed to have a disastrous effect on the morals of the community, but during a period when the gentry hunted for food as well as for sport, it seems likely that such laws were instituted to protect the king's source of game.

William I (reigned 1066-1087) added to these laws saying, amongst other things, that the eyes were to be put out of any person who took a stag or a buck. And John (reigned 1199-1216) was so angered by poaching that he is said to have ordered all the dogs found in forests to be slaughtered.

In stark contrast to their role among the peasantry, dogs held a significant place in the lives of royalty and the landed gentry. By the reign of Henry VIII (reigned 1509-1547) the court had become so overrun that the King was prompted to prohibit all large dogs from entering. Evidently the court was becoming so crowded by dogs that their presence threatened the household's standards of health. The King proscribed 'the said greyhounds and dogs to be kept in kennel and other neat places out of court as is convenient so as the premises duly observed, and the houses abroad, may be sweet, wholesome, clean and well furnished as to a princes house and state appertain.'

Our principal source for dogs in the sixteenth century is Dr. Johannes Caius, founder of Gonville and Caius College at Cambridge, and physician-in-chief to Elizabeth I. In 1570 he wrote a long letter to Conrad Gesner, a Swiss naturalist, telling him about the different kinds of English dogs. The information was to be used in Gesner's monumental work on natural history, *Historia Animalium,* which was to be published later. Caius's treatise was published separately in England in 1570, however, under the title, *De Canibus Britannicus.* The original was written in Latin, but a translation by Abraham Fleming quickly appeared in 1576, entitled *Englishe Dogges.*

Dogs which were included in the book were the sporting breeds then in the British Isles, 'the homely kind [pet dogs]', 'the shepherds dogge' and 'the maastive or Bandogge'. Another group included a miscellaneous assortment, including 'Wapps, Turnespets and Dauncers'.

European books of the period also sometimes referred to English dogs, and in 1576 George Turbervile published *The Noble Arte of Venerie or Hunting.* It is,

Plate 23. *Francis C. Barlow.* The Game Larder, *1672. Oil on canvas, 43 x 54½ ins. (109 x 138.5cm). As the first Englishman to paint purely sporting subjects, Barlow has been called the father of English sporting art. This painting is done in the tradition of the Flemish still-life, although the squawking chicken in the basket on the table is somewhat of a surprise* Photograph courtesy Arthur Ackermann & Son, Ltd.

however, almost a word for word translation of a French work, *La Vénerie,* by Jacques du Fouilloux.

Until the late seventeenth and early eighteenth centuries in England, the principal breeds which we would recognise today were the Greyhound, the Mastiff, and a Spaniel-type. However, the early literature on the subject is, for the modern reader, made confusing because of a nomenclature which does not necessarily correspond to today's.

Several authors, for instance, refer to the 'bandogge', clearly not a breed which we recognise. Indeed, it was not a breed at all, but was named because of its function, simply referring to a dog which was 'banded' or collared and tied up during the day so that it would not roam. At night, when it was meant to protect property, it was let loose to guard against unwanted marauders. While most agree that the bandogge was the ancestor of the Mastiff, there is some discussion as to whether it may well have been an early Bulldog, used for a similar purpose.

Nevertheless, dogs in pre-Victorian England are best studied by their breed development. While we cannot look at each breed in detail, several are representative of dogs during the period.

For this reason, we shall look at Greyhounds, Mastiffs, several toy breeds including the King Charles Spaniel and the Pug, the Bulldog — perhaps the most *English* of all breeds, Terriers, Bull Terriers, and Foxhounds.

The Greyhound

The Greyhound in pre-Victorian England has a well documented and fascinating history, being used predominantly for hunting and coursing the hare. Although the Greyhound's origins in England are somewhat

Plate 24. *Francis C. Barlow.*
Coursing. *Oil on canvas, 43 x 72ins. (109 x 183cm).*
Many of Barlow's compositions have a naïve quality which adds to their appeal. Even though the hare, further away from the viewer than the Greyhound, should by the rules of perspective be quite small, it appears rather large Photograph courtesy The Tryon Gallery

controversial, there can be no doubt that it existed from very early times. Number 31 of the original Canute Laws, for example, given by John Manwood in his *Laws of the Forest* in 1598 and 1615, states:

> No meane person may keep any Greyhounds: but freemen may keep Greyhounds, so that their knees be cut before the Verderors of the forest, and without cutting of their knees also, if they doe abide ten miles from the bounds of the Forest. But if they doe come any nearer to the Forest, they shall pay TWELVE pence for EVERY mile: but if the Greyhounds bee found within the Forest,the master or owner of the dog, shall forfeit the Dog and ten shillings to the King.

Greyhounds were kept in packs, although when hunting the hare the rules of the hunt stated that no more than two Greyhounds, or a brace, should be used at any one time. Indeed, to prevent the slaughtering of hare, and the discouragement of a good day's sport, a set of rules which applied to coursing was drawn up by the Duke of Norfolk (1558-1603), a Greyhound enthusiast.

Pointers or Spaniels were used in the finding of the hare, and upon point the brace of Greyhounds was let loose. In order for the hare not to be killed quickly, the Duke felt it should have a head start of at least twelve score yards; to put an end to the Greyhounds simply tearing the hare apart, and effectively finishing the day's sport, the hare was taken from the dogs by the first person to come upon the death.

Plate 25. *Benjamin Marshall.*
Colonel Thornton's Greyhound. *Oil on canvas, 25 x 32½ins. (63.5 x 82.5cm).*
Coursing, or hunting rabbits with Greyhounds, was a very popular sport in the eighteenth century. Note that the dog's coat has been shaved in a 'T', no doubt to indicate that it was owned by Colonel Thornton Courtesy Arthur Ackermann & Son, Ltd.

The Duke of Norfolk established some eighteen rules for the sport of coursing hare with Greyhounds, and they were generally accepted. Coursing clubs or societies eventually evolved, adding a further note of competition, as well as consistency, to the sport.

In 1776, for instance, the Earl of Orford established the Swaffham Coursing Society whose membership was restricted to twenty-five. Even at this date, long past the time when the Forest Laws were repealed, the composition of the club was composed largely of titled landowners. To an extent this was, of

Right: Colour Plate 5. *John Wootton.*
Two Dogs Attracted to a Squirrel. *Oil on canvas, 44 x 35ins. (111.5 x 89cm).*
While at first glance the squirrel appears too large in proportion to the dogs, they may well have been early Italian Greyhounds, a small breed which was in England at the time, and known to have been crossed with Greyhounds Courtesy Rafael Valls Ltd., London

Plate 26. *Philip Reinagle, R.A.* Lurcher. *Engraving from* The Sportsman's Cabinet, *1803. The Lurcher, often known as a poacher's dog, is considered to be a mixed breed, looking like a course Greyhound with long hair. Note how Reinagle has portrayed the dog at night, the traditional time for poachers to effect their work* Collection The American Kennel Club; photography Dave King

course, a reflection of the leisure time available to them, but coursing hare with Greyhounds also carried a certain social cachet. By 1798 the society consisted of twenty-four members and was very successful.

By today's standards, Lord Orford's passion for Greyhounds may seem extravagant, but he threw himself into the sport and the breeding of Greyhounds with great enthusiasm. At one point he maintained a kennel of fifty brace (one hundred dogs)! Moreover, he took great pains in improving the breed, keeping puppies until they had proven or disproven themselves at the sport, and introducing new blood into the breed.

It is said that in an attempt to improve the breed, Lord Orford cross-bred

Plate 27. *Philip Reinagle, R.A.* Major. *Engraving from* The Sportsman's Cabinet, *1803. Major was a famous Greyhound — the winner of the Thousand Guinea Challenge Cup for Coursing on Epsom Downs. Reinagle has depicted him in the standard pose of the victor, with the rabbit at his feet. Additional interest is provided, however, by the ongoing hunt in the middle-ground of the picture*

Collection The American Kennel Club; photography Dave King

Plate 28. *John Frederick Herring, Snr.*
John Sabine's Greyhounds Spot, Skylark, Nettle and Sly, *1829. Oil on canvas, 20 x 30¼ ins. (51 x 77cm).*
Herring Snr., as he is referred to, was the father of the artist John Frederick, Jnr The father's work, however, is far superior, as seen in the brilliant rendering of the Greyhounds' musculature and coat texture. Even at this date there appears to have been little consistency in the size of Greyhounds
Photograph courtesy Arthur Ackermann & Son, Ltd.

his Greyhounds with almost any animal which resembled it, including a Lurcher (Plate 26) and an Italian Greyhound (Colour Plate 5). His last attempt was a Bulldog which, after seven further generations, is said to have considerably improved the breed, for he obtained Greyhounds with 'small ears, rat tails, and skins almost without hair, together with that innate courage...rather to die than relinquish the chase.'

The fame of the first club encouraged others. Among the most well known was the Ashdown Park meeting, held annually at the Red Lion Inn at Lambourn in Berkshire on the second Monday in November. It had been instituted and established in 1780 by Lord Craven, a friend of the late Lord Orford, in co-operation with Lord Ashbrook and Lord Sefton. Numerous

Colour Plate 6.
John Frederick Herring, Snr. Doctor Fop. *Oil on canvas, 20 x 24ins. (51 x 61cm). Herring Snr. is known primarily as a horse painter, but this brilliant portrait of a Greyhound and King Charles Spaniel proves that he was equally proficient when it came to dogs. Notice the quality of the painting in the sky, and the bravura brushstroke of the landscape* Private collection; photography Grant Taylor

clubs and societies were subsequently established, the most important one being held at Newmarket, which was started in 1805.

It was during the early part of the nineteenth century that the sport of coursing made great strides. The pedigrees of the most celebrated Greyhounds were recorded with as much care as the best bred horses of the turf.

With the industrial revolution of the eighteenth century, many new and wealthy individuals moved to the country, eager to establish themselves and align their names with the older families who had been there for generations, and of course to find appropriate diversions for themselves at their new country homes. The membership of the many coursing clubs increased dramatically during this time, and the sport became extremely popular.

The Waterloo Cup, now recognised as the 'Derby' of the coursing world, was established in 1836 as a result of a meeting at Sefton Altcar, a village near Liverpool, the Waterloo Hotel being the rendezvous. It became the most famous of British coursing events and the Greyhounds who won it are landmarks in the history of the breed (Colour Plate 7).

Famous winners of the Waterloo Cup include Fulerton, a four time winner,

Plate 29. *J.R. Ryott.*
Camarine, *1840. Oil on canvas, 20½ x 24½ins. (52 x 62cm). According to the inscription on this painting, Camarine was the property of J. Story Jnr., winning the Caledonian Gold Cup for coursing in June of 1838. She won the Liverpool stake of one hundred sovereigns during the same year*

Photograph courtesy Iona Antiques

Plate 30. *George Morley.*
Eos with her Puppies, *1841. Oil on canvas, 20 x 24ins. (51 x 61cm). While little known today, George Morley completed a number of commissions for Queen Victoria as well as other members of the royal family. Eos was Prince Albert's favourite Greyhound, and here she poses proudly with her offspring*

Collection Her Majesty the Queen

and Cerito who won three times. None was more famous, however, than Master McGrath, owned by Lord Lurgan of Northern Ireland, a black dog with a few white marks. He was so well known that he was eventually introduced to Queen Victoria, and fêted as a hero.

Plate 31. *O.A. Tompkins.*
Dandy, *1860. Oil on canvas, 12 x 16ins. (30.5 x 41.5cm).*
Little is known about Tompkins, although he was an artist of considerable skill, portraying this brindle dog with great sensitivity. The other Greyhound in the background and the men on horses would indicate that they have been out coursing hare, a sport which became popular in the eighteenth century

Collection Mrs. Vincent Astor; photography Dave King

Colour Plate 7. *Maud Earl.*
Farmdon Fancy, Fairy Footsteps and Fabulous Fortune, *1902. Oil on canvas, 18 x 30ins. (45.5 x 76cm).*
Maud Earl was a great lover of pure-bred dogs and knew all the famous dog breeders of her day, receiving many commissions from them. The above Greyhounds, for instance, were all winners of the famous Waterloo Cup coursing event

Collection Mr. and Mrs. N.J. Reese

By 1858, The National Coursing Club was established and a code of rules drawn up, partly based on the Duke of Norfolk's laws of coursing established in Queen Elizabeth's reign. These fixed the routine of coursing meetings in the British Isles as well as around the world. No dog was allowed to run in any meeting of importance held under the rules of the Coursing Club unless it had been registered with its pedigree in the Stud Book.

The National Coursing Club Committee consisted of men chosen by interested clubs with more than twenty members. In a similar way to The Kennel Club or The Jockey Club, The National Coursing Club became the final arbiter of any controversial matters in respect to coursing.

While the Greyhound had been depicted in art before the advent of coursing events, it was in the eighteenth century that pride of ownership prompted the country gentleman to have portraits of his individual dogs painted. In the same tradition of the racehorse portrait, paintings of Greyhounds served to commemorate an important animal. In this case, it was undoubtedly the dog's performance which was of paramount importance and many Greyhound portraits depict the animal with the dead hare at his feet (Plate 27).

While this dog portrait tradition continued until well into the late nineteenth century, it was eventually supplanted by the tradition of the pure-bred dog portrait in which the animal depicted is important for how he conforms to the standard for the breed, a subject which will be explored in the next chapter.

Colour Plate 8. *Arthur Wardle, R.I., R.B.C., P.S.*
La Joie de Vivre. *Oil on canvas, 28 x 36½ ins. (71 x 92.5cm). Wardle is known for his portraits of dogs, but he occasionally included people in his compositions. The Greyhounds have obviously spied some game, and the little girl is hard pressed to control them* Collection Roger Rechler; photography Dave King

DUCHESS OF DELVIN
TALBOT — SISTER MARY

CROWTHER

Plate 34. *Lucy Kemp-Welch.*
Ben, a Lurcher. *Oil on canvas, 28 x 36ins. (71 x 91.5cm).*
While little known today, Lucy Kemp-Welch was a prominent animal painter who excelled in the depiction of horses. She worked in a loose, painterly style which greatly influenced some of her students at her school for animal painting at Bushey, Hertfordshire

Photograph courtesy The Tryon Gallery

Opposite above: Plate 32. *Wilson Hepple.*
Duchess of Delvin, *1881. Oil on canvas, 11 x 15ins. (28 x 38cm).*
The lineage of this Greyhound was obviously of great importance to the owner, for it has been inscribed lower right

Collection Ronald H. Menaker; photography Dave King

Opposite: Plate 33. *Henry Crowther.*
Greyhounds, *1930. Oil on canvas, 14 x 18ins. (35.5 x 45.5cm).*
Little is known about this artist, although many of his dog paintings continue to come on the market. His work is characterised by a broad brushstroke, with some of his dogs having a rather stiff quality

Photograph courtesy Bonhams

The Mastiff

With the Greyhound, the Mastiff is one of the oldest of all the breeds known to man today. Used by some as a fighting or a baiting dog similar to the Bulldog, the Mastiff is most probably the 'bandogge' to which the sixteenth century writer Dr. Caius referred. Rendered almost extinct because of rationing during the Second World War, the Mastiff had enjoyed a popularity which, if we are to judge by the works of art left behind depicting the breed, reflected its prominent place in English history.

As we have seen, a dog greatly resembling the Mastiff was in England when the Roman legions invaded England in 55 B.C., and it has evidently been in the country ever since. Of uncertain origins, the breed most likely developed

Colour Plate 9. *Abraham Hondius.*
Bear Baiting, *1650. Oil on canvas, 21 x 26ins. (53.5 x 66cm).*
The baiting of animals was not limited to bulls, and in the late seventeenth century, bulls, bears, badgers, and even lame horses were attacked by dogs, let loose by their masters so that they could take wagers on who might be the victor Collection The Dog Museum, St. Louis, gift of Marie A. Moore

Colour Plate 10. *Attributed to Sir Peter Lely.*
Lord Lempster, *1685. Oil on canvas, 49 x 37ins. (124.5 x 94cm).*
By the seventeenth century the portrait tradition of the sitter accompanied by his dog was well established. Lely, who came to England in 1637, became a favourite of the King and the English nobility after the death of Van Dyck Collection The Dog Museum, St. Louis, gift of Marie A. Moore

in the far eastern regions of Assyria, where a Mastiff-type dog was depicted in bas-reliefs as early as 2200 B.C. (Plate 2).

Whatever its origins, the breed figures largely in the pre-Victorian history of England, being used as a fighting dog, but more significantly as a guard dog which protected the estates of the landed gentry. Tied up during the day, the Mastiff was let loose at night to roam vast areas of land. It is said that the dog, once shown the boundaries of the estate, never roamed beyond them.

The Mastiff also figures largely in the Forest Laws of 1066, in which it is specifically mentioned. Farmers and others living on the outskirts of a forest were allowed to keep them to guard their property. Like the Greyhounds, however, they were suspect creatures, for it was feared that they too would be used to chase and kill deer, the hunting of which was the perquisite of the king. As a result, the barbarous task of 'expediating' the dog was instituted: in order that the dog could not run as swiftly as the deer, the claws of one of the front feet of the Mastiff were cut off with a chisel.

Henry VIII was clearly fond of Mastiffs, though, and he used them in battle as well as for the hunt. He is reputed, for instance, to have sent Charles V of Spain four hundred dogs which helped him in his war with the French.

During the reign of James I (1603-1625) bear baiting with Mastiffs and Irish Wolfhounds became a common practice. William Harrison, in his *Description*

Plate 35. *Anthony Van Dyck.* The Children of Charles I, *c.1630. Oil on canvas, 64¼ x 78¼ins. (163 x 199cm). While painted over three hundred years ago, the Mastiff which Van Dyck has made a focal point of his composition is very similar indeed to our present day dogs. Notice how the sheer size of the animal forms a contrast with the vulnerability of the baby who reaches for the dog*

Collection Her Majesty the Queen

of England, 1586, explains that the bandogge was so called:

> Because manie of them are tied up in chaines and strong bonds in the daie time for doing hurt abroad, which is in a huge dog, stubborn, ouglie, eager, burthenouse of bodie (and therefore of little swiftness), terrible and fearful to behold...For although this dog be capable of courage, violent, valiant, and bold, yet will they increase these their stomachs by teaching them to bait the bear, the bull, the lion, and other such like cruell and bludie beasts.

The practice of bear baiting had been popular from the time of Edward the Confessor's reign (1042-1066) and it continued unabated until the time of Oliver Cromwell when Parliament stopped it. A barbaric practice, a dog was let loose on a bear which had been tied up, and sometimes muzzled. Viewed as a sport, the bear was attacked again and again by the dog — usually a Mastiff or a Bulldog — until either one or the other expired or was too exhausted to go on (Colour Plate 9). As in the case of bull baiting, it was an opportunity for people to bet on which dog might win.

Not all Mastiffs were of the fighting, aggressive sort, however, for as we see in Anthony Van Dyck's painting of *The Children of Charles I,* the great Mastiff-like dog appears docile and friendly (Plate 35).

Indeed, the integration of large dogs in a portrait commission, in particular with children, had been an artistic convention since the time of Titian. As we have seen, Antonio Moro had included a huge Mastiff in his portrait, *Cardinal de Granville's Dwarf* (Plate 12), in which the dog's head reaches well above the

Plate 36. James Lambert, Snr. Lion *(detail), 1778. Oil on canvas, 15½ x 19½ins. (39.5 x 49.5cm). James Lambert, Snr., father of the animal artist James Jnr., was born in Sussex and for the most part was a painter of landscapes. Compare this Mastiff with the more modern looking Mastiff by Reinagle, Plate 37* Collection The American Kennel Club; photography Dave King

dwarf's shoulders, and Velázquez was known to have included a Mastiff in paintings more than once (Plate 11). The brindle Mastiff which appears so prominently in the right-hand side of the famous *Las Meninas,* is reputed to be one which Charles II had given to Philip IV, King of Spain.

Indeed, the same dog is reputed to be a direct descendant of the Mastiffs developed by the Legh family at Lyme Hall in Cheshire. It is believed that the breed existed at Lyme Hall as early as 1415, and was one of the three distinct strains of Mastiffs in England that can be traced back for centuries.

According to the story, Sir Piers Legh of Lyme Hall fell mortally wounded on 25 October, 1415, at the Battle of Agincourt. His body was found being guarded by a Mastiff bitch who was brought back to England and Lyme Hall. Evidently, she must have been pregnant, for her puppies are said to have established the Lyme Hall Mastiff which eventually became the most sought after of any of the Mastiff strains.

By the eighteenth century, the Mastiff was well established as a guard dog and the general esteem in which it was held is indicated by what the eminent

Plate 37. *Philip Reinagle, R.A.* Mastiff *(detail), 1803. Engraving. In the seventeenth century, the Mastiff was sometimes called a 'bandogge'. This referred to the fact that it was 'banded up' during the day and let loose at night so that it could guard his owner's property. Depicted on the banks of the Thames, it is likely that this Mastiff was indeed a guard dog* Collection The American Kennel Club; photography Dave King

Colour Plate 11. *Attributed to George Charles Morland.*
Mastiff and a Landseer Newfoundland, *1792. Oil on canvas, 16 x 20ins. (40.5 x 51cm). While the dog on the left does not conform to today's standard for the Old English Mastiff, it is obviously a Mastiff-type. Its tightly cropped ears indicate it was probably kept for bull and animal baiting rather than as a guard dog* Collection The Dog Museum, St. Louis, gift of Marie A. Moore

Left: Colour Plate 12. *Charles Towne.*
Dogs Fighting, *1809. Oil on panel, 8 x 10ins. (20.5 x 25.5cm). Dog fights were a common occurrence during the life of this painter. Here we see a Mastiff being attacked by two mongrels. The small scale and extensive detail of this painting is typical of Towne's work* Collection The Dog Museum, St. Louis, gift of Marie A. Moore

Colour Plate 13. *William Henry Hamilton Trood.*
A Domestic Scene, *1888. Oil on canvas, 26 x 48ins. (66 x 122cm).*
Trood's work is characterised by an academic, highly finished quality, and in this painting he captures the character of each of his subjects; from the noble Bloodhound to the Terrier puppies fighting over a riding crop
Collection The Dog Museum, St. Louis, gift of Marie A. Moore

Opposite, right: Colour Plate 14. *H. Hardy Simpson.*
The Mastiff Lara, *1882. Oil on canvas, 20 x 26ins. (51 x 66cm).*
By 1882, the Mastiff was well established in the show ring, although it was still undoubtedly used as a guard dog. The dog's straightforward pose, in profile, was to become the standard in depicting pure-bred show dogs Collection The Dog Museum, St. Louis, gift of Marie A. Moore

Colour Plate 15. *Arthur Wardle.*
Mastiff, *1930. Oil on panel, 22 x 18ins. (56 x 45.5cm).*
Wardle's sensitive portrayals of eye expression, coat texture and anatomy, made him a favourite painter among dog breeders around the turn of the century. Like Maud Earl, Wardle had the ability to capture the typical expression of a dog without sentimentality
Collection The Dog Museum, St. Louis, gift of Marie A. Moore

Plate 38. *Richard Ansdell, R.A.*
The Poacher, *1865. Oil on canvas, 53 x 83ins. (134.5 x 211cm).*
This large painting depicts the exact moment at which the Mastiff has caught the trespassing poacher, discovered with his illegal bounty spread before him. Intensely loyal, the Old English Mastiff was reputed to have roamed only his master's property, never trespassing its boundaries
Collection The Dog Museum, St. Louis, gift of Marie A. Moore; photography Grant Taylor

Plate 39. *R.S. Moseley.*
Mastiff with Terrier, *1871. Oil on canvas, 24 x 30ins. (61 x 76cm).*
Moseley, whose work is characterised by a rather heavy application of paint, specialised in dog portraiture. The Mastiff's immense size is here effectively contrasted with the small toy Terrier
Collection The Dog Museum, St. Louis, gift of Marie A. Moore

Plate 40. *Edwin Frederick Holt.* In Times of Peace, *1877. Oil on canvas, 20 x 27ins. (51 x 68.5cm). This painting is characteristic of Holt's style for he often romanticised his dogs, giving them a rather sentimental touch. Note how both the mother and one of the puppies seem to embody a look of concerned anticipation*

Collection The Dog Museum, St. Louis, gift of Marie A. Moore

historian of the dog, Sydenham Edwards wrote in his beautifully illustrated *Cynographia Britannica:*

> What the lion is to the cat, the Mastiff is to the dog, the noblest of the family; he stands alone and all others sink before him. His courage does not exceed his temper and generosity, and in attachment he equals the kindest of his race. His docility is perfect: the teasing of the smaller kinds will hardly provoke him to resent, and I have seen him down with his paw the terrier or the cur that has bit him without offering further injury. In a family he will permit the children to play with him, and suffer all their pranks without offence...

The popularity of the breed fell away in the early part of the nineteenth century, however, and it was only in 1835 that T.H.V. Lukey set out to reconstruct the breed into what it had been in earlier times. Purchasing a brindle bitch from the Duke of Devonshire at what was considered the exorbitant price of £40, he bred her to a dog purchased from Lord Waldegrave. Another breeder who was to have a great influence on the modern breed was Captain J.E. Garnier who bought animals from, among others, the famous dog dealer Bill George, one of which came from the Lyme Hall strain.

George had become famous for the quality of the dogs which he sold. During the eighteenth and early nineteenth centuries, there were no pet shops to choose animals from. Rather, certain individuals kept their premises for the sole purpose of breeding dogs, and occasionally providing an arena for the fighting of Terriers and Terrier/Bulldog crosses.

Colour Plate 16. *Henry Bernard Chalon.*
Blenheim King Charles Spaniel in a Landscape, *1816. Oil on canvas, 8½ x 10¼ ins. (21.5 x 26cm).*
Chalon was a well known animal painter during the first half of the nineteenth century, having been appointed animal painter to the Duchess of York in 1795 as well as to William IV. Notice how similar this King Charles is to the larger sporting Spaniels (see Plate 42)

Collection Mrs. Vincent Astor; photography Dave King

Colour Plate 17. *Samuel Raven.*
Tricolour King Charles Spaniel in a Classical Landscape, *c.1830. Oil on canvas, 9 x 12ins. (23 x 30.5cm).*
Samuel Raven was a Birmingham artist who painted dogs and sporting scenes in a small format. The column behind the little dog no doubt indicates that this King Charles Spaniel lived in a large English country house

Collection Mrs. Vincent Astor; photography Dave King

Colour Plate 18. *Samuel Spode.*
Tricolour King Charles Spaniel in a Landscape, *1835. Oil on canvas, 18 x 24ins. (45.5 x 61cm).*
Spode is known to have painted portraits of horses and dogs. Although his work can be somewhat awkward, this painting has a straightforward charm about it, while the dog's expression looks surprisingly like the modern Cavalier King Charles Spaniel

Collection Mrs. Vincent Astor; photography Dave King

The King Charles Spaniel

Not all the breeds in pre-Victorian England were of the larger sort, for as we have seen, the court favoured the keeping of small toy dogs as pets. The monarchs' affections for these dogs is well documented. James I (reigned 1603-1625), for instance, had a great affection for the Italian Greyhound, a breed that is believed to have developed more than two thousand years ago in the Mediterranean basin. Charles I (reigned 1625-1649) and Charles II (reigned 1660-1685) each kept toy dogs, and as is seen in Van Dyck's *The Children of Charles I* (Plate 35), they were beloved members of the family. The huge Mastiff in this painting contrasts not only with the small size of the children, but also with the Spaniel to the right of the composition. This little dog was soon to become very popular indeed, for with the ascension to the

Plate 41. *Studio of Anthony Van Dyck.* The Three Eldest Children of Charles I, *c.1630. Oil on canvas 50⅛ x 58¼ ins. (127.5 x 148cm). This portrait depicts Charles I's daughter Mary and the future Kings Charles II and James II. Charles II was so closely associated with the dogs illustrated that they became known as King Charles Spaniels. While both dogs are the same breed type, they differ a great deal in size*

Collection The Metropolitan Museum of Art, bequest of Collis P. Huntington, 1925

Plate 42. *English School.*
Spaniel and Toy Spaniel with Red Macaw, *c.1770. Oil on canvas.*
Probably dating from the eighteenth century, this painting depicts the two types of Spaniel in England at the time — the sporting Spaniel on the left, and the Toy Spaniel on the right

Photograph courtesy The Tryon Gallery

Colour Plate 19. *English School.*
Tricolour King Charles Spaniel, *c.1840. Oil on canvas, 14 x 18ins. (35.5 x 45.5cm). This painting, indistinctly signed, is characteristic of an English portrait style which flourished in the early to mid-nineteenth century. Situated in a landscape, the dog is seen from the side, looking out sympathetically at the viewer* Collection Mrs. Vincent Astor; photography Dave King

throne of Charles II in 1660, the breed enjoyed an unprecedented place in the royal household; King Charles Spaniels are said to have been allowed free access at all times to Whitehall, Hampton Court and the other royal palaces.

Pepys, after a visit to the Council Chamber of Charles II recorded that: 'All I observed was the stillness of the King, playing with his dogs all the while and not minding his business.' So great was the King's affection for his little dogs, that when one or another was lost or stolen — a relatively common occurrence — he was inconsolable and advertised for their return. Not surprisingly, these small pet Spaniels, as opposed to the sporting variety described in contemporary texts, became known as King Charles Spaniels.

The true origin of the King Charles Spaniel is rather obscure. Dr. Caius describes a Toy Spaniel, most probably an early ancestor of the King Charles, as follows:

> Of the delicate, neate, and pretty kind of dogges called the Spaniel gentle, or the comforter...these dogges are little, pretty, proper, and fyne, and sought for to satisfie the delicatenesse of daintie dames and wonton

Plate 43. *English School.* King Charles Spaniel. *Oil on canvas, 18½ x 26½ins. (47 x 67.5cm).*
This painting is a typical pet portrait, painted with all the charm of a truly naïve work. The small scissors and the spools of thread in the foreground undoubtedly identify it as a lady's pet
Collection Mrs. Damon Raike; photograph courtesy Exclusively Dogs

> women's wills, instrumentes of folly for them to play and dally withall, to tryfle away the treasure of tyme. These puppies, the smaller they be, the more pleasure they provoke, as more meete playfellowes for mincing mistresses to beare in their bosoms, to keepe company withal in their chambers, to succor with sleepe in bed, and nourish with meate at boarde, to lie in their lappes, and licke their lippes as they ride in their waggons.

According to Dr. Caius, the superstitious people of the Middle Ages, even in enlightened England, believed that little Spaniels were able to assuage sickness of the stomach by being worn as plasters or borne in the bosom of diseased people.

Plate 44. *School of Landseer.* King Charles Spaniel on a Cushion, *c.1840. Oil on panel, 17 x 21ins. (43 x 53.5cm).*
While this painting is indistinctly signed, and is in the style of Sir Edwin Landseer, it was probably completed by a follower of the artist. Landseer had a great influence on nineteenth century artists and was often emulated
Private collection; photography Dave King

Plate 45. *Abraham Cooper, R.A.* Fidelia, *1833. Oil on panel, 12 x 15ins. (30.5 x 38cm).*
This portrait, obviously of a favourite pet, was exhibited at The Royal Academy in 1833
Collection K. Mimi Hamann; photography Dave King

The Spaniels depicted in the portrayals of the children of Charles II are the ancestors of what is known in England today as the King Charles Spaniel, and in America as the English Toy Spaniel. What is now known as the Cavalier King Charles Spaniel is a relatively new breed, being developed some seventy years ago.

Early in the twentieth century certain dog fanciers became dissatisfied with the development of the descendants of the King Charles Spaniel, considering them too small and too flat-faced. Indeed, they wanted a dog that looked more like the toy which appeared in the paintings of Van Dyck (Plates 35 and 41).

In the early 1920s Roswell Eldridge of Long Island, New York, a breeder of Blenheim English Toy Spaniels, decided to do something about the way the dog looked. In 1926 he offered cash prizes at the prestigious Crufts Dog Show in London for Blenheim Spaniels 'of the old type', the prizes to continue for five years. Eldridge preferred the type with a more pronounced muzzle and a flat rather than a domed head and he hoped that other breeders would respond by showing this type.

Other people had evidently been thinking along the same lines, for this type did appear at dog shows, and in 1928 fanciers formed a club for the advancement of the 'new breed'. Within just a few years their new breed, to be known as the Cavalier King Charles Spaniel, became established, and while The American Kennel Club does not recognise it, in England it has been recognised by The Kennel Club since 1944.

Colour Plate 20. *Gourlay Steell, R.S.A.*
Jeannie, *1858. Gouache on paper, 24 x 26ins. (61 x 66cm).*
Gourlay Steell's paintings are characterised by a vibrant colour sense and an eye for rich detail, here including a glove to indicate Jeannie's size. This dog, reputed to have been owned by Queen Victoria, was clearly a pampered pet Collection Mrs. Eileen Weiler; photography Dave King

Opposite: Colour Plate 21. *Richard Ansdell, R.A.*
Two King Charles Spaniels in a Landscape. *Oil on canvas, 36 x 28ins. (91.5 x 71cm).*
Attributed to Richard Ansdell, this painting is brilliantly painted, with lavish textural effects. While the green curtain and other domestic surroundings are somewhat incongruous with a landscape setting, it is nevertheless a very pleasing composition Photograph courtesy Richard Green

Plate 46. *John Dalby.*
King Charles Spaniels, *1849. Oil on canvas, 12 x 16ins. (30.5 x 40.5cm).*
Dalby was primarily a painter of hunting scenes. Although this portrait is rather stiff, he nevertheless has succeeded in capturing the expression of these canine subjects
Photograph courtesy Arthur Ackermann & Son, Ltd.

Plate 47. *Edwin Frederick Holt.*
Blenheim Spaniel at Rest, *1871. Oil on canvas, 6½ x 8½ins. (16.5 x 21.5cm).*
Holt's portraits of dogs have an endearing, almost anthropomorphic quality about them. This work, on a small scale, is the picture of a contented pet
Collection Judith H. Green

Plate 48. *William Nedham.* Spaniels. *Oil on canvas, 43 x 54ins. (109 x 137cm).*
Nedham, who painted predominantly horses and hounds, here illustrates the two types of Spaniels: the Sporting Spaniel on the right and the Toy Spaniel on the left Collection Mrs. Vincent Astor; photograph courtesy Arthur Ackermann & Son, Ltd.

Plate 49. *Arthur James Stark.* A King Charles Spaniel seated on a Red Chair. *Oil on canvas, 14 x 18ins. (35.5 x 45.5cm).*
Stark was an animal and landscape painter. This Blenheim Spaniel, recumbent by a cane and gloves, is obviously waiting for his mistress
Photograph courtesy Bonhams

Colour Plate 22. *Frederick Hall.* Recumbent King Charles Spaniel. *Oil on canvas, 18½ x 24ins. (47 x 61cm).*
Like many Victorian artists, Frederick Hall included accessories in his paintings which would imply a story. The gloves, for instance, suggest that the dog is waiting for the absent master, making the dog's faraway look all the more poignant Collection MacConnal-Mason Fine Paintings

Plate 50. *Maud Earl.*
King Charles Spaniels, *c.1890. Oil on canvas.*
Maud Earl was a master at capturing expressions typical of each breed, as well as the dog's individual personality. Here, each of the colour varieties of the breed are depicted: from left to right, the Black and Tan, the Tricolour, the Ruby and the Blenheim
Photograph courtesy The Tryon Gallery

Colour Plate 23. *Mary Lascelles Leesmith.*
Black and Tan King Charles Spaniels, *1882. Oil on canvas, 22 x 36ins. (56 x 91.5cm).*
Mary Leesmith exhibited three portraits at the Royal Academy between 1893 and 1897 and while she was not primarily an animal painter, she has captured the adoring expressions of these King Charles Spaniels
Private collection; photography Grant Taylor

Plate 51. *Philip Eustace Stretton.*
King Charles Spaniels, *1907. Oil on canvas, 18 x 24ins. (45.5 x 61cm).*
While little known until recently, Stretton's work is characterised by a bold brushstroke and a sympathy for his subject matter which gives an endearing, almost human quality. Compare this with his portrait of a German Shepherd, Pekingese and Fox Terrier (Plate 223) Collection Mr. and Mrs. William Kendrick; photography Dave King

The Pug

The popularisation of a specific breed was not restricted only to one monarch, for the Pug is another which gained popularity because of royal sponsorship. The very early history of the Pug has been a matter for conjecture. It is believed that the breed originated in the far east, and although it is not known how it first came to Europe, it is recorded in Holland in the sixteenth century. Some historians say it may have been introduced to Holland by the Portuguese soon after they opened sea trading routes with China around 1550. Another theory is that the Pug was brought to Holland by members of the Dutch East India Trading Company. Still other canine historians have written that Pugs came to Holland via 'Muscovy'.

Plate 52. *William Hogarth.*
The Painter and his Pug, *1745. Oil on canvas, 35½ x 27½ins. (90 x 70cm).*
Hogarth was a painter of portraits, historical and 'conversation' paintings, and one of the most influential of English artists. This painting, with his pet Pug Trump in the foreground, is as much a portrait of the Pug as of the artist Collection The Tate Gallery, London; photograph Art Resources, N.Y.

Plate 53. *Philip Reinagle, R.A.* Pugs. *Engraving* from The Sportsman's Cabinet, *1803. Pugs, which had been popularised in England by William and Mary, were popular pets in the early nineteenth century. Reinagle has typically painted an extensive background, here including a mother and child, no doubt the pets' owners* Collection The American Kennel Club; photography Dave King

Plate 54. *Charles Towne.* Pug. *Oil on board, 8 x 10ins. (20.5 x 25.5cm). Towne, who specialised in small, detailed pictures of animals, often placed his subjects in extensive landscapes. Compare this dog with those in Plate 53, probably completed several years before. Paradoxically, the earlier dogs have a more 'modern' look*

Photograph courtesy Arthur Ackermann & Son, Ltd.

Colour Plate 24. British School.
Pug in a Landscape, *1808. Oil on canvas, 20 x 24ins. (51 x 61cm).*
Although today's Pug is distinguished by an almost flat face, the Pug of 1800 had a distinct muzzle, and in this case cropped ears. The collar with the miniature padlock was very typical of collars of the period The Richard D. Hammond Collection; photography Grant Taylor

When the Pug first appeared in Holland it was called the Dutch Mastiff or Dwarf Mastiff (which it is not) because its body contour and wrinkled head resembled those of the Mastiff. Indeed, Sydenham Edwards noted that the small 'Dutch Mastiff or Pug-dog was much in fashion'. In the early part of the eighteenth century it was commonly called the Dutch Pug. Its name, wrote 'Stonehenge', is derived from the Latin word *pugnus,* or fist, 'because the shadow of a clenched fist was considered to resemble the dog's profile.'

By whatever route it came to Holland, the Pug more or less became the official dog of the House of Orange after one of the breed saved the life of William I ('William the Silent') in 1572 at the battle of Hermigny, when it gave alarm at the approach of the Spaniards.

William III of Orange, great grandson of William the Silent, and his wife, Mary, also adored Pugs and numerous Pug dogs accompanied them when they crossed the English Channel in 1688 to ascend the throne of England. Indeed,

Colour Plate 25. *B.A. Howe.*
Pug, *c.1850. Oil on canvas, 20 x 24ins. (51 x 61cm).*
Except for the fact that he lived in London, little is known about this Victorian artist. The Pug is sensitively painted, although the tightly cropped ears are somewhat of a shock to modern eyes. The cropping of ears continued in England until 1895 when it was outlawed as inhumane
The Richard D. Hammond Collection; photography Grant Taylor

it was the general custom to attach orange-coloured ribbons to Pugs' collars to denote their connection with the House of Orange. As a result of its popularity, the Pug found its way to other parts of the Continent, vying with King Charles Spaniels and Maltese as court favourites and as prized pets of the wealthy and the elite.

The breed was well-established by the time of William Hogarth who introduced the Pug into many of his compositions. Perhaps the most fitting tribute to the breed is Hogarth's self-portrait with his Pug (Plate 52).

Hogarth owned two Pug dogs, the first named Pug and the other Trump. In the self-portrait, Hogarth placed Trump prominently in the right foreground, an indication of his devotion for the animal. His critics, however, did not let the resemblance between the two go unnoticed, and Charles Churchill published a sarcastic pamphlet, entitled 'Epistle to William Hogarth' several years later. Hogarth retaliated by printing a satirical engraving entitled

Plate 55. *Carl Steffeck.*
Papillon with a Playful Pug, *1856. Oil on canvas, 16½ x 22½ ins. (42 x 57cm).*
During the nineteenth century, the British amassed dog paintings — in this case from a German painter. Black and tan Papillons (as here) are very rare indeed Private collection; photography Grant Taylor

Plate 56. *John Paul.*
The Pug Pearl and Manchester Terrier Beauty, *1871. Oil on canvas, 18 x 24ins. (45.5 x 61cm).*
During the mid-nineteenth century the Pug had lost its popularity in favour of some of the other toy breeds. It is here pictured with a Manchester Terrier Photograph courtesy Arthur Ackermann & Son, Ltd.

Plate 57. *Walter Harrowing.*
Pug with a Bell Collar, *1875. Oil on canvas, 14 x 12ins. (35.5 x 30.5cm).*
This portrait by the relatively little known Harrowing, depicts a Pug with a very fine bell collar, often worn by the breed in the nineteenth century. It is interesting to note that even the leather liner along the edge of the collar is clearly delineated

Collection Mr. and Mrs. Michael Svirsky; photography Dave King

Colour Plate 26. *Richard Ramsey Reinagle.*
Pug. *Oil on canvas, 25 x 30ins. (63.5 x 76cm).*
The son of Philip Reinagle, Richard was primarily a landscape painter, though he also did many horse and dog portraits. This Pug, typical of the early nineteenth century, is much taller than present day examples, and has a much more discernible muzzle

Collection The American Kennel Club; photography Dave King

The Bruiser, in which the image of a bear replaced Hogarth's. Trump remained, however, but he was pictured urinating on Churchill's pamphlet!

Hogarth is of further importance to the history of the English dog for the publication of his *Four Stages of Cruelty* series. One particularly grisly scene depicts a group of cheering children egging on two youths as they torture a cat and a dog. Hogarth recognised the cruel treatment of animals during his time and sought to bring it to the public's attention.

The Pug's great popularity continued until the middle of the nineteenth century when it became fashionable to own other new small breeds which appeared on the scene. Indeed Pugs fell on such hard times that many authorities of the day considered them to be nearly extinct. Idstone lamented in 1872 that 'it would be hard to find more than half a dozen specimens equal to what existed a hundred years ago.'

Plate 58. *Charles Burton Barber.*
Rover and Puggy, *1878. Oil on canvas, 25 x 30⅜ ins. (63.5 x 77cm).*
While Barber exhibited over thirty-two works at the Royal Academy from 1866 on, his work only rarely appears on the market today. Many of his dog portraits are in the Royal Collection. The discarded tennis rackets and balls would seem to indicate that it is time for the Collie and Pug to play
Collection Her Majesty the Queen

As the years went on, though, Pugs began to regain their prestige. In 1885 attention was focused on the breed at the Pug Dog Show held at the Aquarium in London. The following report appeared in an issue of the *Stock Keeper* in June that year: 'There is no mistake about Pugs being first favourites with the fair sex. The gallery was full of ladies.' Several of the winning Pugs even wore costly necklaces. Lion, for example, a first-prize winner, was bedecked in a necklace of turquoise. According to the *Stock Keeper* report, the Pug Club had engaged a showman whose powerful voice outside the Aquarium was equal to the occasion. 'Now then! now then! now then! This way! this way! this way for the Puggery. Come and see Puggie, Puggie, Puggie!' Many people who had no knowledge of what a Puggery might have been, paid to gain admission.

Colour Plate 28. *John Emms.* Punch, *c.1890. Oil on canvas, 10 x 14ins. (25.5 x 35.5cm). While John Emms is better known for his portraits of Foxhounds and Fox Terriers, he painted many pets, including this slightly overweight Pug. By this date, around 1890, breeders had developed a dog with much shorter legs*

The Richard D. Hammond Collection; photography Grant Taylor

Plate 59. *Maud Earl.* A Pug in a Garden, *c.1895. Oil on canvas, 18 x 24½ins. (45.5 x 62cm). This portrait, undoubtedly of someone's favourite pet, is typical of Maud Earl's style around 1895. The painting is full of details which contribute to its charm*

Photograph courtesy Bonhams

Opposite: Colour Plate 27. *John Sargent Noble, R.B.A.* Pug and Dachshund, *1875. Oil on canvas, 35 x 27ins. (89 x 68.5cm). Noble is well known for his paintings of Bloodhounds and Otter Hounds, but this painting is typical of his work in that it tells a story. Note the little tin can around the Wire-Haired Dachshund's neck, implying that he is begging for a donation from a dog of higher breeding*

Collection The American Kennel Club; photography Dave King

Plate 60. *British School.*
Pug Puppies. *Oil on canvas, 10 x 14ins. (25.5 x 35.5cm).*
Typical of many pet portraits, this painting accentuates the endearing qualities of the puppies, one with a bow around its neck Private collection; photography Grant Taylor

Plate 61. *Queen Victoria's Black Pug, from* The Ladies' Kennel Journal, *1895.*
The Black Pug was believed to have been introduced to England late in the nineteenth century, but Queen Victoria had Black Pugs in her kennels at Windsor as early as the 1850s. Note the white blaze on the dog's chest, quite common in black Pugs at the time

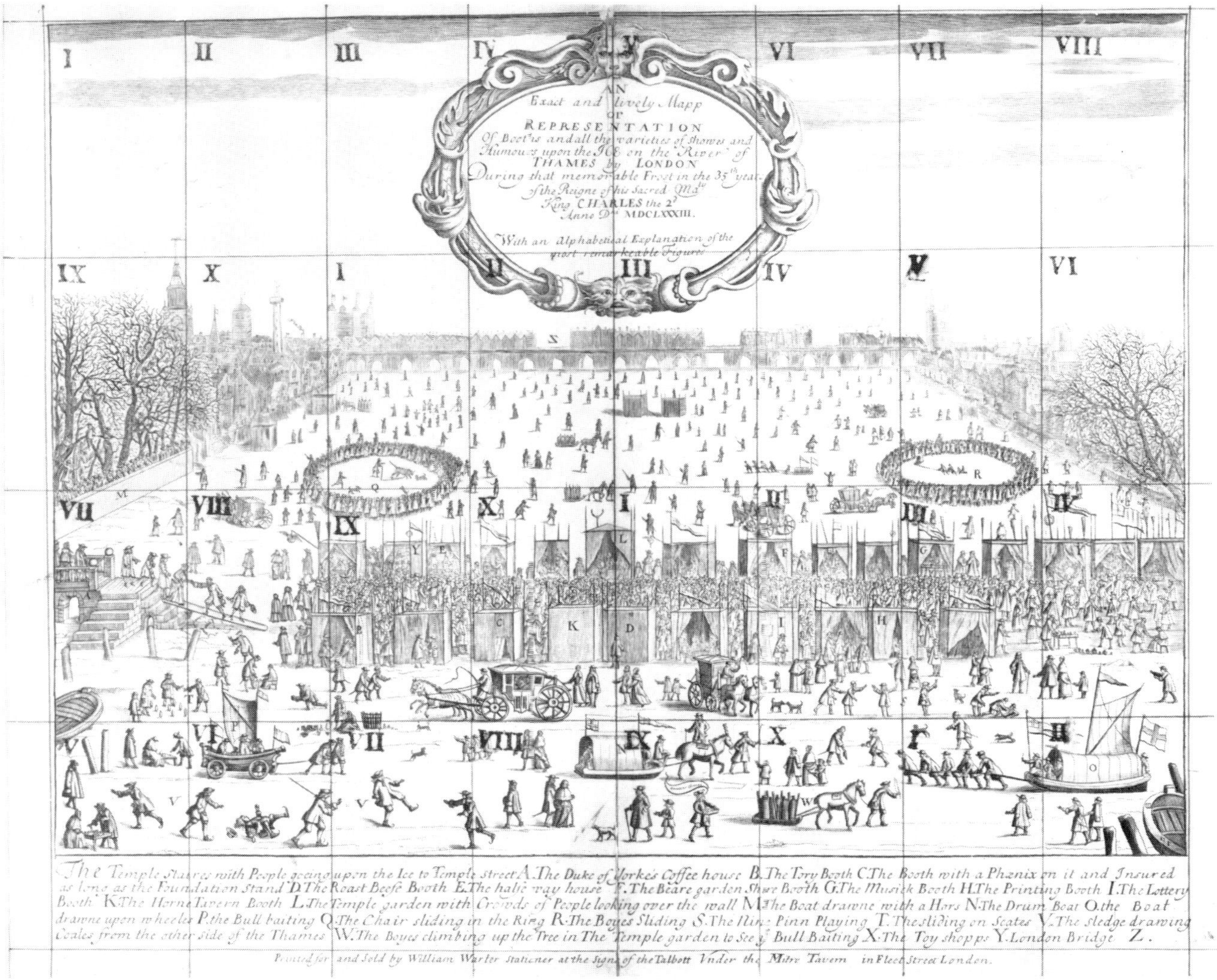

Plate 62. *British School.*
An Exact and lively Mapp... of Booths and all the varieties of Shows and Humours upon the Ice on the River Thames..., *1683. Engraving, 14 x 18ins. (35.5 x 45.5cm). During the reign of Charles II, bull and bear baiting were activities enjoyed by all classes of English society. This print depicts various activities on the frozen River Thames in 1683, including bull baiting in the upper left*

Private collection; photography Grant Taylor

The Bulldog

The Bulldog, rivalled only by the Mastiff as a contender for England's national breed, is also one of England's oldest and most beloved dogs. Bred originally as a guard dog and to bait bulls and bears, the pre-nineteenth century history of the Bulldog would rather be forgotten by most modern fanciers of the breed. As the eminent historian of the Bulldog, Edgar Farman, writing in 1899, has pointed out:

> The Bulldog has undoubtedly suffered considerably from its association with the lower classes of the community, especially from the time that bull-baiting ceased to be a fashionable pastime until the close of that still more degenerate period in the early years of the present century, when a lower depth of brutality than bull-baiting had been reached, and the 'bloodthirsty' sport of dog fighting was the entertainment provided for the lowest residuum of the canine fancy.

The antiquity of the Bulldog has long been a controversial subject, and the first mention of a Bulldog with its modern spelling was by Edward Jesse, in 1832,

Colour Plate 29. Abraham Cooper, R.A.
Crib and Rosa, *1817. Oil on panel, 9½ x 12ins. (24 x 30.5cm).*
Crib and Rosa were well known Bulldogs in the early nineteenth century. They are similar in type to the dog portrayed by Reinagle (Plate 64) about fifteen years before Collection The American Kennel Club; photography Dave King

Colour Plate 30.*Henry Alken, Snr.*
Bull Baiting. *Watercolour over pencil, 9¼ x 13ins. (23.5 x 33cm).*
Bull baiting was a barbarous practice whereby a staked bull was taunted by dogs, traditionally the Bulldog. The Bulldogs illustrated, having just attacked the bull, have been flung into the air
Photograph courtesy Guy Nevill Fine Paintings

when he wrote 'procure me two good Bulldogs'. The physical characteristics of the breed distinguish it from the Mastiff, for it was developed in order that it might perform its principal task — that of grasping the bull's nose, and not letting go. Again, Farman points out that:

> The under jaw projects beyond the upper, to enable the dog when running directly to the front to grasp the bull, and when fixed, to give him a firmer hold. The lower jaw being very thick and strong gives to the mouth an appearance of curving upwards across the middle of the face. The top of the nose inclines backwards, so as to allow free passage of air into the nostrils whilst 'holding' on to the bull.

While it seems bizarre indeed to modern sensibilities, the baiting of bulls was common from the reign of King John (1199-1216) onwards, though it is somewhat obscure how the practice originated. The training of bulls, bears, horses and other animals for the purpose of baiting them with dogs was, however, certainly practised by the jugglers who came to England with the Norman conquerors.

Colour Plate 31. *Henry Alken, Snr.*
Terriers Fighting. *Watercolour and pencil, 9½ x 13½ins. (24 x 34cm).*
While organised dog fighting for sport was outlawed in the mid-nineteenth century, it continues to the present day. Here an ancestor of the Manchester Terrier has managed to restrain an early Bulldog/Terrier cross Photograph courtesy Guy Nevill Fine Paintings

Plate 63. *Sydenham Edwards.*
The Bulldog, *from* Cynographia Britannica, *1799-1805.*
In 1800 the Bulldog was an intensely loyal and fierce fighting dog, known for its bravery in baiting the bull. Notice the slightly overshot jaw, which enabled the dog to continue breathing while holding on to the bull's nose Collection The American Kennel Club; photography Dave King

Plate 64. *Philip Reinagle, R.A.*
Bulldog, *c.1802. Oil on canvas, 14 x 19ins. (35.5 x 48cm).*
This painting of a Bulldog is one of the originals for the paintings which Reinagle completed to illustrate The Sportsman's Cabinet *of 1803. Looking at it, it is easy to discern the important role that the Bulldog played in the genetic backgrounds of such breeds as the Bull Terrier and the Boxer* Collection The Dog Museum, St. Louis, gift of Mr. and Mrs. Judson L. Streicher

Plate 65. *Henry Calvert.*
Bulldog, *1827. Oil on canvas, 24 x 30ins. (61 x 76cm).*
The breed of this dog is a matter of some conjecture — most probably it was a Bulldog and Terrier mix. It may well have been used for dog fighting, still a popular diversion around 1830

Photograph courtesy Arthur Ackermann & Son, Ltd.

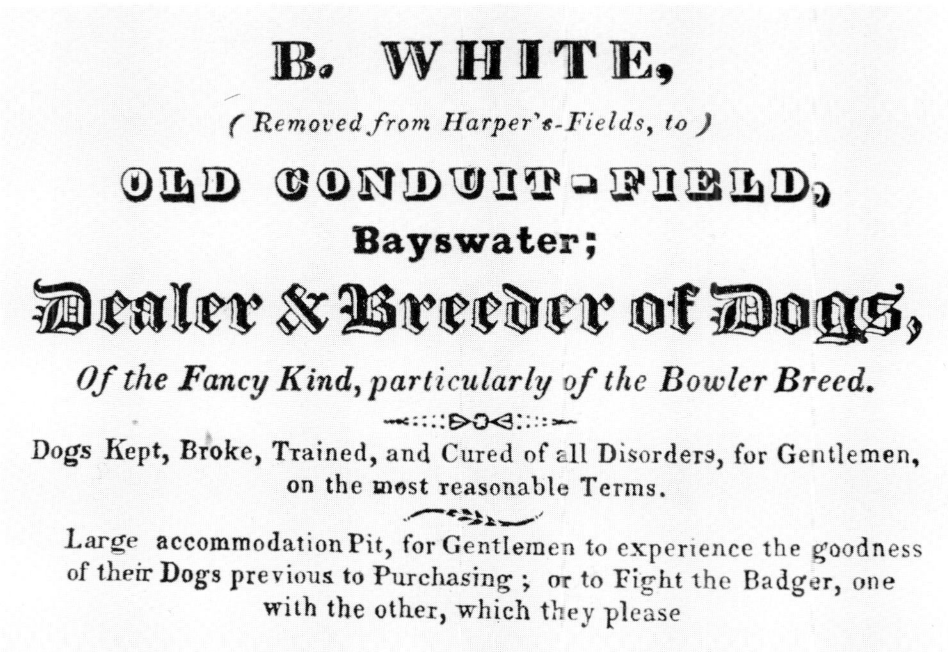

Plate 66. *Advertisement for B. White, a dog seller, c.1840.*
It was not uncommon for dog sellers also to provide facilities for dog fighting and ratting, both considered sports in 1840. This vendor offers to exhibit his dogs' abilities prior to purchase, in dog fighting or in baiting the badger

Colour Plate 32. *Thomas Clayton.*
Jem Burn's Four Pets, *c.1843. Oil on canvas, 20 x 24ins. (51 x 61cm).*
In 1843 these Bulldogs were thought to be fine examples of their breed, for they were engraved in Bulldog Pedigrees, *Volume II, and in* The Bulldog *by Edgar Farman, published in 1899. At the time, the Bulldog was a strong and very tenacious breed with much longer legs and a smaller head than present-day examples. The kennel boy, Ball, is the fourth 'pet'*

Photograph courtesy MacConnal-Mason Fine Paintings

Written during the reign of John, the *Survey of Stamford* credits the then Earl of Surrey, who was also Lord of Stamford, with introducing bull baiting into Stamford. Evidently the Earl, standing upon the castle walls of Stamford, saw two bulls fighting in an adjacent meadow, until a group of dogs belonging to the local butchers pursued one of the bulls. Much to the delight of the Earl, the furious bull ran through the entire town with the dogs yelping at his heels. The sight so pleased the Earl that he donated to the butchers of the town all the meadows where the duel between the bulls first began. But on one condition: the butchers were to find a mad bull six weeks before Christmas day for the continuance of the sport every year.

Over the years, the practice spread, as did the belief that if a bull were to be slaughtered, it should first be baited so that the meat would be more tender

Colour Plate 33. *Philippe Rousseau.*
Best of Friends. *Oil on panel, 10 x 14ins. (25.5 x 35.5cm).*
The French painter Rousseau was known for his still-lifes and paintings of animals. Almost a genre scene, this Bulldog and Bull Terrier-type were probably intended to remind us of the street urchins so popular in nineteenth century genre paintings
Collection Mr. and Mrs John H. Remer, Jnr; photography Dave King

and edible. Indeed, in some small towns, a butcher who sold the flesh of a bull in the market without having first produced the animal on the previous market day to be baited, was liable to a penalty. The flesh of a baited bull was universally considered to be not only much more tender but also more nutritious than that of animals slaughtered without being first submitted to the process.

In bull baiting, the objective for the dog was to 'pin and hold' the bull, that is to seize the bull by the nose and not let go.

So that he might turn around, the bull had a collar about his neck fastened to a rope some four or five yards long and attached to a stake. A circular low ditch was provided for additional sport — so that the bull could hide his nose from the dog. The dogs were held back by their masters, and usually let go one at a time on the bull, who would attempt to hide his nose in the small ditch. Inevitably, though, the bulldog would fiercely bite the bull's nose, and as this was the bull's most tender part, he was rendered helpless. The bull, in terrible

Plate 67. *John Frederick Herring, Snr.*
Bulldog, *1849. Oil on canvas, 21¼ x 30½ins. (54 x 77.5cm). Even at mid-century, one can see that the Bulldog was becoming shorter in the leg with a larger head. It was nevertheless still a strong, tenacious animal whose game qualities had not been suppressed for the show ring*

Photograph courtesy Arthur Ackermann & Son, Ltd.

Plate 68. *E. Aistrop.*
Mischief, *1890. Oil on canvas, 20 x 27ins. (51 x 68.5cm).*
This painting is typical of a pure-bred dog portrait: the dog faces right, in profile, to show how it conforms to the standard for the breed, while its head is turned slightly so that one can see its expression and head type

Photograph courtesy Iona Antiques

Plate 69. *Frank Paton.*
Salvo, *1892. Oil on canvas, 19½ x 23½ins. (49.5 x 59.5cm).*
Paton was an animal artist of considerable talent, painting in a tight, realistic style. Notice that even at this late date, the Bulldog has rather long legs, more characteristic of earlier examples of the breed Collection The American Kennel Club; photography Dave King

Plate 70. *Kole Sowerby.*
Don Leon, *1894. Oil on canvas, 20¼ x 25¼ inches (51.5 x 64cm).*
This Bulldog is more typical of the breed in 1894; the head has become much larger, the legs shorter and the body stockier. Selective breeding to a standard had transformed the Bulldog's appearance. Compare this dog, for instance, with Reinagle's portrayal of c. 1802, Plate 64 Collection The American Kennel Club; photography Dave King

Colour Plate 34. *George Earl.* Michael The Archangel, *c.1870. Oil on board, 14½ x 16ins. (37 x 40.5cm). This portrait of Michael, who was owned by R.T.L. Price, one of the founders of The Kennel Club, is from a series of head studies which Earl completed entitled* Champion Dogs of England Private collection; photography Dave King

pain, would try to throw the dog, and would often succeed, hence the many paintings which depict the Bulldog flying high in the air after being thrown by a bull (Colour Plate 30). Considered a sport at the time, many wagers were placed on which dog might hold on the longest, and dog after dog was let loose on the bull until he succumbed.

By the reign of Henry VII (1457-1509), bull and bear baiting had become popular diversions. In 1483 Richard III appointed a royal bear-ward named John Bronne and this office continued in the reigns of Elizabeth, James I and Charles I. The diversion was not just for the benefit of the lower classes, for as with dog fighting in the late eighteenth century, people of all classes enjoyed the spectacle. When Queen Mary visited her sister Princess Elizabeth, during her detention at Hatfield House, a grand exhibition of bear baiting was made for their amusement, with which, it is said, 'their highnesses were right well content.'

In the time of the Tudor sovereigns, London's Bankside was a thinly inhabited district. The celebrated Globe theatre, where many of Shakespeare's plays were performed, was later built here, and here it was that the first bull and bear baiting and similar amusements took place.

Both Charles I and Charles II patronised the sport, but with the latter's death, bull and bear baiting ceased to be fashionable amusements, although they were still immensely popular with the common people. Around 1800 there was a great resistance to this cruel sport, and in 1835 bull and bear baiting were both prohibited by law. Pitting one dog against another for 'sport', however,

Colour Plate 35. *Frances L. Fairman.*
The Boxer Rebellion, *1902. Oil on canvas, 48 x 36ins. (122 x 91.5cm).*
By 1902 the Bulldog had been a longstanding member of the dog show world. What once had been a strong and tenacious fighter had now become, through selective breeding, a show dog and a pampered pet, here pictured with a Japanese Chin
Collection Mario Buatta

had always been popular and although outlawed, its practice continued well into the nineteenth century. Terriers and Bulldogs were used, but a cross between the two seems to have been favoured.

There are many depictions of Bulldogs and Bulldog/Terrier crosses fighting, with men of many different social backgrounds cheering on the dogs (Colour Plate 31). Indeed, many prominent breeders and 'dog sellers' were prepared to offer facilities for the sport. Nor were such activities relegated to the lower classes, for it must be remembered that dog fighting was engaged in not only by the lower but also by the upper classes, and that such matches were an everyday occurrence; indeed dog dealers and breeders of reputation were prepared to offer facilities for the 'sport' for the private enjoyment of their patrons (Plate 66).

The eminent dog historian Jesse mentions Lord Camelford's renowned Bulldog Belcher, who fought 104 battles and never met defeat, and old volumes of *The Sporting Magazine* contain frequent accounts of contests between Bulldogs, such as this paragraph which appeared in an issue in 1825: 'Dog Fighting — The Westminster Pit was crowded on Tuesday evening, January 18, with all the dog fanciers in the metropolis to witness a battle between the celebrated dog Boney and a black novice called Gas, lately introduced to the fancy by Charley, to whom the dog belongs. The stakes were forty sovereigns, and everything was arranged to the satisfaction of the amateurs.'

Dog fighting declined after the passage of the act which prohibited it in 1835, and some nineteenth century authors feel that from that point onward the Bulldog began to go down hill. Edgar Farman, for instance, states that the breed began to deteriorate with the era of modern dog shows:

> [for the] appearance of an up-to-date specimen became a caricature of the active and plucky animal that baited the bull, and which was a dangerous customer at any time. For the show bench as an object lesson of what can be done by scientific breeding for 'points', the bulldog is an excellent example of the triumph of man over nature, but as an example of what the dog originally was he can hardly be considered a success.

The Terrier

Terriers had long been used for sports other than fighting. Traditionally when hunting, they had been the dog of choice to dig out the fox and the badger, and for centuries they had been used to control vermin.

In the early 1400s, for instance, *The Master of Game,* written by Edward, 2nd Duke of York, a grandson of Edward III, delineated the various types of game

Plate 71. *William Wissing.*
Mary of Modena, *c.1685. Oil on canvas, 47½ x 38½ ins. (120.5 x 98cm).*
One would be hard pressed to identify the breed of this dog, although it is undoubtedly a Terrier. Uncharacteristically for portraits of this type, the dog looks away from its mistress
Collection The National Portrait Gallery

Colour Plate 36. *Benjamin Marshall.*
Dustman, *1804. Oil on canvas, 11½ x 14ins. (29 x 35.5cm).*
Illustrated in The Sporting Magazine *in 1812, this painting depicts Dustman a well-known Bulldog/Terrier cross. Such dogs were prized for their fighting abilities and, according to the magazine, 'the Breed of dogs of this description has been encouraged of late'*
Collection Mr. and Mrs. John H. Remer, Jnr.; photography Dave King

which were hunted during the period, and describes several different types of dogs: running Hounds, Greyhounds, Alaunts, Spaniels and Mastiffs as well as Terrier-like dogs.

Dr. Caius spoke about Terriers in his famous letter:

> Another sorte there is which hunteth the fox and the badger or greye only, whom we call terriers: they creep into the ground, and by that means make afrayde, nyppe, and bite the fox and the badger in such sorte that they eyther teare them in pieces with theyr teeth, beying in the bosome of the earth, or else hayle and pull them perforce out of their lurking angles, dark dungeons and close caves.

In his *Rural Sports,* published in 1801, W.B. Daniels refers to Terriers, saying:

Plate 72. *Sydenham Edwards.* Terriers. *From* Cynographia Britannica, *1799-1805.*
Difficult as it is to believe, these dogs are the ancestors of many of our present-day Terriers. Prized for their alertness and tenacity, Terriers around 1800 were used to kill rats and dig out foxes and badgers Collection The American Kennel Club; photography Dave King

Plate 73. *Philip Reinagle, R.A.*
Terriers. *Detail from* The Sportsman's Cabinet, *1803.*
Reinagle, who did the original paintings for the illustrations in The Sportsman's Cabinet, *depicts the Terriers performing what they were bred for: to dig out the fox and the badger. Around this time such dogs were grouped together because of their function, rather than differentiated by breed*
Collection The American Kennel Club; photography Dave King

Plate 74. *Henry Bernard Chalon.*
Sportsman with a White English Terrier and a Toy Dog *(detail), 1804. Oil on canvas, 28 x 36ins. (71 x 91.5cm).*
The now extinct White English Terrier and other early Terriers were often used to catch foxes and badgers, the latter being seen in the left middleground of this painting. Notice the small size of the little dog at the sportsman's foot, a Terrier of unknown origins
Photograph courtesy Arthur Ackermann & Son, Ltd.

> No species of dog will fight the badger so resolutely and fairly as terriers, of which there are two kinds, the one is rough, short-legged, long-backed, very strong and most commonly of a black or yellowish colour mixt with white; the other is smooth-haired and beautifully formed, having a shorter body and more sprightly appearance; is generally of a reddish brown colour, or black with tanned legs; both these sorts are the determined foe of all the vermin kind.

In all probability, the Masters of the Hounds concentrated on breeding a Terrier that was principally white, so as not to be confused with a fox. Perhaps the Terrier was bred with a Beagle to achieve this, but in any case the result was what we know today as the Smooth-Haired Fox Terrier, which, with many of the other Terriers will be discussed in the following chapter.

Plate 75. *R. A. Gooch.* The Earl of Waldegrave's Terriers, *1842. Oil on canvas, 36 x 45ins. (91.5 x 114.5cm). By 1840, the various Terrier breeds were becoming differentiated, and while their functional attributes were still important, it is clear from this portrait that the Earl's Terriers were also his pets. Notice how by this time, the Black and Tan Terrier has been bred down to a toy, probably weighing no more than eight pounds* Photograph courtesy Arthur Ackermann & Son, Ltd.

Colour Plate 37. *George Earl.* Ch. Prince, *c.1870. Oil on canvas, 16 x 16ins. (40.5 x 40.5cm).*
The White English Terrier was very popular in the nineteenth century, and was actively shown in early dog shows. The anti-cropping law of 1895, however, discouraged breeders who did not like the appearance of an uncropped dog. The breed fell into disfavour, and eventually became extinct
Collection Mr. and Mrs. William Kendrick; photography Dave King

Colour Plate 38. *E. Mondy.*
White Terrier, *1875. Oil on canvas, 12 x 10ins. (30.5 x 25.4cm).*
While very little is known about this English artist, he has portrayed this dog — probably a White English Terrier — with great technical skill, creating an almost photographic quality. Note how beautifully the metal collar is painted Collection Mr. and Mrs. John H. Remer, Jnr.; photography Dave King

Plate 76. *Charles Towne.*
Bull Terrier, *1824. Oil on board, 4½ x 6ins. (11.5 x 15cm). Towne, who is best known for his small scale, highly detailed paintings, clearly delineates this Bull Terrier's cropped ears. They were cut as closely as possible, so that when fighting they would not be torn by the dog's opponent*
Photography courtesy Arthur Ackermann & Son, Ltd.

The Bull Terrier

Another breed which is closely associated with pre-Victorian England is the Bull Terrier. A breed native to England, it was developed in the later years of the eighteenth century. Although it is a matter of conjecture exactly which breeds it was created from, it is more than likely that they included the Bulldog, the early smooth coated Black and Tan Terrier and the White English Terrier (Plate 72).

The Bull Terrier of the early eighteenth century was a very strong and tenacious animal noted for its great bravery. The Bulldog-Terrier cross created

Plate 77. *George Cole.*
Bull Terrier with a Cat, *1843. Oil on board, 12 x 14ins. (30.5 x 35.5cm). This is a relatively early work of Cole's, a self-taught artist who, after studying the Old Masters in Holland, concentrated on landscapes. Note the dog's long straight front legs, typical of Bull Terriers at this time*
Collection Mr. and Mrs. John H. Remer, Jnr.; photography Dave King

Plate 78. *Frederick Hall.*
Ch. Gully the Great, *1894. Oil on canvas, 40 x 30ins (101.5 x 76cm).*
By 1894, the Bull Terrier was already taking on a more refined look, with more balance and symmetry. This example is all white, no doubt a descendant of Mr. Hinks's dogs. His sporting ancestry is implied by the boxing glove at lower right
Collection Mr. and Mrs. William Kendrick; photography Dave King

a dog which combined the alert agility of the Terrier with the strength and tenacity of the Bulldog. It was much leggier than the animal we know today and its head more closely resembled the early Bulldog. Of particular note were its ears (Plate 76) which were closely cropped so that in a fight they could not be bitten and torn by its opponent.

Now an affectionate pet, the Bull Terrier was originally bred for baiting bulls and other animals, as well as for the dog fighting contests which passed for 'sport' around the turn of the eighteenth century.

As with other Terriers of the period, the Bull Terrier was also sometimes used to kill rats, ratting contests being a popular diversion for the lower classes. As offensive as it seems to modern dog fanciers, rat killing was a very popular amusement during the first half of the nineteenth century, and individual dogs were timed to determine how many rats they could kill in a given period. Writing in *The New Book of the Dog,* Robert Leighton reports that Jimmy Shaw's Jacko could kill sixty rats in just three minutes!

With the advent of dog shows in the mid-nineteenth century, there was a desire on the part of certain breeders, most notably James Hinks of Birmingham, to improve the breed into something which would be more presentable for the show ring (Colour Plate 40). Hinks selectively bred the old fashioned Bull Terrier with other breeds, including the White English Terrier, to create a breed with a longer head and a more symmetrical body. The arched back, bent legs and undershot jaw of the Bulldog were eventually eliminated. Moreover, the 'Hinks breed', as it was first designated, was predominantly, if not all, white. Initially very controversial, it eventually became the accepted type and, once established, white dogs became so fashionable that the coloured variety was in danger of extinction. Dog fanciers continued to breed both types, however. Early members of The Kennel Club, including S.E. Shirley, (Colour Plate 41) and E.W. Jaquet, The Kennel Club's historian, were active in the breed. While its popularity decreased with the anti-cropping laws of 1895, it eventually became well established in the show ring and as a pet.

Colour Plate 39. *British School.* Bull Terriers, *c.1830. Oil on canvas, 17½ x 22ins. (44.5 x 56cm).*
These two early Bulldog/Terrier crosses were undoubtedly fighting dogs, normally tied up or confined in a kennel. By around 1860, an all white dog was the favoured colour variety of the Bull Terrier
Collection Mr. and Mrs. John H. Remer, Jnr.; photography Dave King

Colour Plate 40. *British School.* Champion Showdogs Belonging to James Hinks, *c.1860. Oil on canvas, 30 x 25½ins. (76 x 64.5cm). James Hinks, a prominent dog fancier from Birmingham, was the first to create what we know as the Bull Terrier. The animals depicted are reputed to have been portraits of his dogs, with the Bulldog prominently placed in the centre*
Collection Mrs. Elizabeth C. Clark; photography Grant Taylor

Colour Plate 41. *George Earl.*
Nelson, *c.1870. Oil on panel, 16 x 16ins. (40.5 x 40.5cm).*
This portrait of Mr. Shirley's miniature Bull Terrier Nelson is from a series of portraits by George Earl depicting the Champion Dogs of England. *Nelson was born in 1866 and was the winner of many first prizes at dog shows between 1868 and 1872*

Collection Mr. and Mrs William Kendrick; photography Dave King

Colour Plate 42. *Marmaduke C. William Flower.*
Reclining Bull Terrier with Scottish Terrier, *1892. Oil on canvas, 20 x 30ins. (51 x 76cm). While these are both pure-bred dogs, this painting is really a pet portrait, for it portrays the dogs in an anecdotal way. One can almost imagine the plight of the Scottish Terrier, unable to move for fear of waking his companion, who appears to sleep with a look of benign contentment on his face*

Collection Mr. and Mrs. William Kendrick; photography Dave King

The Foxhound

No other breed is more closely associated with the eighteenth century and the popular perception of the country life of the landed gentry than the Foxhound.

Much has been written about the political and social significance of foxhunting during this period, and it did indeed have an important social function. The source of eighteenth century political power lay with the landed gentry, and as new money developed as a result of trade and increased industrialisation, the newly rich sought to emulate the established order. One entrée into this world was through association with the sport of foxhunting, a tradition which was a direct descendant of the royal sport of stag hunting.

Foxhounds are mentioned during the reign of King John (1199-1216) and in Edward I's reign (1272-1307). During the reign of Edward II (1307-1327),

Plate 79. *George Stubbs, A.R.A.*
Brocklesby Hound, Ringwood, *1792. Oil on canvas, 39½ x 49½ ins. (100.5 x 125.5cm). George Stubbs was the pre-eminent animal artist in eighteenth century England. Known for his horse portraits, he also completed a large number of dog paintings, this example being much copied*
Photograph courtesy The Tryon Gallery

fox hunting started on the first day of September and ended on the last day of February, or from the eighth day of September to the twenty-fifth day of March.

While it would be inappropriate to attempt a detailed history of the Foxhound, it is interesting to note that as early as 1591, packs of Foxhounds were being kept for the exclusive use of foxhunting.

During the seventeenth century, many country squires had kept small packs of dogs which were used to hunt informally for hare or foxes. The aristocracy, who had inherited the royal privilege of hunting the stag, continued to do so, but as the eighteenth century wore on, so did demands on the land, and eventually stag hunting decreased in importance, with foxhunting taking over. The Duke of Rutland and the Marquis of Rockingham, for instance, changed to foxhunting in the 1750s.

Plate 80. *Philip Reinagle, R.A.*
Foxhounds. *Engraving from* The Sportsman's Cabinet, *1803.*
Foxhound fanciers were among the first to develop stud books, establishing the pedigrees of their hounds. While English Foxhounds have certainly changed since the painting for this engraving was completed some two hundred years ago, the breed has remained surprisingly consistent
Collection The American Kennel Club; photography Dave King

Colour Plate 43. *George Earl.*
On the Scent. *Oil on panel, 16 x 20ins. (40.5 x 51cm).*
While Earl is more often associated with the pure-bred dog portrait, this painting is a sporting picture, depicting the hounds in full cry Collection Mr. and Mrs. John Honig

Opposite top: Colour Plate 44. *John Emms.*
Two Foxhounds and a Fox Terrier on a Kennel Bench. *Oil on canvas, 19 x 29¾ins. (48 x 75.5cm).*
Emms is perhaps best known for his portrayals of Foxhounds and Fox Terriers, and this painting shows him at his best. Using a bold, expressive brushstroke, he captures the expression, anatomy and coat texture of animals resting after the hunt
Collection The American Kennel Club; photography Grant Taylor

Opposite: Colour Plate 45. *Edward Algernon Stuart Douglas.*
Foxhounds and a Terrier, *1884. Oil on canvas, 24 x 30ins. (61 x 76cm).*
While little is known about this artist, the quality of his work is very fine indeed. He exhibited some ten paintings at the Royal Academy, all of which were hunting scenes, and this highly detailed, soft technique is very typical of his style Photograph courtesy Richard Green

Plate 81. *Henry Bernard Chalon.* The Earl of Darlington's Kennels, *1813. Oil on canvas, 27¼ x 25ins. (69 x 63.5cm). This is a relatively rare depiction of Foxhounds being fed after coming in from the hunt. Notice the little Black and Tan Terrier in the foreground, a precursor of our present-day hunt Terriers*

Private collection; photography Grant Taylor

Plate 82. *E. Willis.*
Warefull, a Southern Hound *(detail). Oil on board, 8 x 11ins. (20.5 x 28cm). The Southern Hound was much slower than the Foxhound, and this animal, obviously a member of a pack, has been shaved with the initial 'S'. She was bred by Sir John Smyth*

Private Collection; photography Dave King

Plate 83. *Samuel John Carter.* Foxhound Bitch and Whelp, *1866. Oil on canvas, 34 x 45¼ ins. (86.5 x 115cm). Carter first exhibited at the Royal Academy at the age of twenty, and his highly finished soft style set him apart from other animal artists of the period. While the subject matter is Foxhounds, their playful, almost human expressions place this painting squarely in the tradition of the pet portrait*

Photograph courtesy Arthur Ackermann & Son, Ltd.

Plate 84. *Wright Barker, R.B.A.*
Recumbent Foxhound *(detail). Oil on canvas, 23 x 32ins. (58.5 x 81cm).*
Barker is known for his animal portraits, especially of dogs. Many include decorative elements in the background, such as the fireplace and fireplace equipment depicted here, conjuring up associations of hearth and home

Collection Mr. and Mrs. Michael Svirsky; photography Dave King

Colour Plate 46. *Charles Olivier de Penne.*
The Hunt Meeting. *Oil on canvas, 29 x 39½ins. (73.5 x 100.5cm).*
De Penne was a well known animal artist in nineteenth century France. This painting, once in the collection of Geraldine Rockefeller Dodge, depicts an early morning gathering of French Hounds and has a more formal feeling than many of its English counterparts

Private collection; photography Grant Taylor

Colour Plate 47. *Heywood Hardy, A.R.W.S., R.E., R.O.I.*
Quorn Foxhound Sunshine. *Oil on canvas, 11½ x 14ins. (29 x 35.5cm).*
An artist of great technical skill, this picture is typical of Hardy's work, for his oil paintings have a loose quality, reminiscent of transparent watercolour

Photograph courtesy Arthur Ackermann & Son, Ltd.

Plate 85. *Maud Earl.*
Foxhounds Giving Tongue, *c. 1905. Oil on canvas, 24 x 18ins. (61 x 45.5cm).*
This canvas is typical of Maud Earl's work around 1905, for while the main action is carefully depicted, the edges of the canvas are loosely sketched in. This is one of the paintings used to illustrate The Power of The Dog, *published in both a trade and limited edition in 1911*

Collection E.M. Hershey II; photography Grant Taylor

Colour Plate 48. *Thomas Blinks.*
Hounds at Full Cry. *Oil on canvas, 48½ x 32¾ ins. (123 x 83cm).*
This is one of Blinks's most dynamic compositions, completed by the artist at the height of his powers. Such a composition, however, was only possible after the advent of photography. The pose of the hound in mid-air on the right, for instance, was undoubtedly not perceived by the naked eye

Collection Mr. and Mrs. Robert Franzblau

Colour Plate 49. *Maud Earl.* A Check, *c.1905. Oil on canvas, 15 x 27ins. (38 x 68.5cm). This painting of Beagles is typical of Maud Earl's work around 1905, when she concentrated on the depiction of the dogs, and rendered the surrounding landscape with a loose, impressionistic brushstroke*

Collection Mrs. Damon Raike; photography Bill McLemore

The Beagle

Beagles had been used to hunt the hare in England for centuries, and by the time of Elizabeth I, nearly every nobleman in England kept a pack of hounds of some sort. By the mid-eighteenth century Foxhounds became popular with the younger generations, partly because they were faster than Beagles which were followed on foot.

Hunting with Beagles did continue as a sport, and even to the present day there are many active Beagle packs in both Great Britain and the United States.

Plate 86. *W. Murray.* The Beagles Gudger, Betsey and Tuner, *1808. Oil on panel, 6 x 10ins. (15 x 25.5cm). Around 1800, the Harrier was the preferred hound for hunting the hare. However, Beagles, which were low to the ground, and could sometimes catch the scent better than taller dogs, were also used. Notice how the two dogs on the right have been joined by a coupling collar* Photograph courtesy Arthur Ackermann & Son, Ltd

CHAPTER 3

Victorian England

The reign of Queen Victoria spanned some sixty-four years and saw tremendous changes within England and across the globe. Victoria ascended the throne during an expansionary and optimistic period; by the end of her reign, the Empire upon which 'the sun never set' was slowly receding into shadow and society, once based on the possession of land and the wealth of a privileged few, had changed to reflect a new order based in the cities rather than in the beautiful stately homes of rural England.

One can only speculate as to whether this population shift from the country to the city left in people a longing for nature and the gentler forms of human endeavour. There can be no doubt, however, that the English people, led by their much loved and respected Queen, found comfort from the daily toils of Victorian England by returning home to their favourite pet, the dog.

In addition to its role as a pet, the dog continued to be used in the sporting field, and in the latter half of the nineteenth century the pure-bred dog was exhibited in increasingly popular dog shows. Breeds which had been popular in eighteenth century Britain, such as the Foxhound, the Greyhound, and the Mastiff, continued to flourish. Pointers, Setters and Spaniels also continued to be popular in the field, but they were soon appropriated — as were the vast majority of breeds — by the quickly developing world of the dog show.

As we have seen, dog paintings may be divided into three general categories: the Hound and sporting dog paintings, the pure-bred dog portrait, and the pet portrait. The Hound and sporting dog paintings depicted dogs which were valued because of their performance: Foxhounds, Spaniels, Setters and Pointers. The pure-bred dog portrait, to become important in the late nineteenth century with the development of dog shows, stressed how a pure-bred dog conformed to the standard for the breed. The pet portrait, a category which includes almost all the paintings commissioned by Queen Victoria, was painted out of a simple affection for the dog as a loyal and loving companion. All three types are found throughout the Victorian era, but the last two were to take precedence.

While continuing to discuss how individual breeds came into existence, we shall see how in the 1860s the sporting tradition was continued and expanded upon with the development of organised field trials. In such events man and dog worked together as a team, testing the dog's ability to perform the function for which it was created.

The next section of this chapter is devoted to the origins and history of The Kennel Club. Many of the early dog fanciers commissioned portraits of their pure-bred dogs, reflecting not only a pride of ownership, but also an interest in salient breed characteristics.

The final sections of this chapter are given over to a discussion of Queen

Victoria and her patronage of Sir Edwin Landseer as well as the development of the pet portrait. Pet portraits reached a new and unprecedented popularity in the late nineteenth century, a development which was greatly influenced by the Queen.

Field Trials and the Sporting Dog Portrait

While sporting dogs had assisted in the hunt for centuries in England, organised field trials only came about in the third quarter of the nineteenth century. The first trial of field dogs took place on 18 April, 1865, at Southill, Bedfordshire, on the estate of Samuel Whitbread, M.P., when dogs were judged for nose, pace and range, temperament, staunchness before and behind, as well as style.

The second field trial was held in 1866 at Cannock Chase, Staffordshire, while in 1867 two meetings took place, the second national Pointer and Setter and Retriever trials at Stafford, and the first trials on partridge at Bala, North Wales, on the estate of Richard Lloyd Price.

Several other meetings were held in 1871 and 1872, but the first to be held under the rules of The Kennel Club, the regulatory body for pure-bred dogs in the United Kingdom, founded in 1873 (see page 162), took place at Orwell Park, Ipswich, on the estate of Colonel Tomline, M.P., in September 1873.

A painting by George Earl (fl.1856-1883), entitled *The Field Trial Meeting,* includes so many portraits of the people who were instrumental in early field trials and The Kennel Club, that it will serve as a starting point to illustrate the breeds and their history in the field (Colour Plate 50).

There can be little doubt that *The Field Trial Meeting* is one of Earl's most accomplished paintings, and includes virtually anyone who was of importance in the world of sporting dogs in the later part of the nineteenth century.

The painting is a composite picture of a mythical field trial, portraying over thirty Pointers and Setters and over eighty people: owners, handlers, trainers, dog show judges, breeders and writers about dogs. The site is probably the 64,000 acre estate of Lloyd Price in Bala, North Wales, for his wife — the only woman in the picture — is shown on a pony in the distance. Bala was the site where The Kennel Club Field Trials of Pointers and Setters took place in 1873.

As the late dog historian Gerald Massey has pointed out:

> The painting was composite in the sense that some of the portraits were evidently taken from photographs, for it would have been difficult to bring together such a gathering of personalities on amicable terms over a period of fifteen years. It was mythical in that Edward Laverack was dead when Romp's Baby was whelped in 1880, and Mr. J.H.

Whitehouse's famous pointer Hamlet would have been in his 19th year. All three, together with Mr. Whitehouse, appear in the engraving for the picture.

Practically every man depicted in George Earl's painting had an active role in developing sporting dogs and the sport of field trials, and at the time it was painted a print was published which provided a schema identifying the principal characters.

Colour Plate 50. *George Earl.*
The Field Trial Meeting, *c.1880. Oil on canvas, 51 x 75½ ins. (129.5 x 192cm).*
This painting, one of the most historic of all dog pictures, depicts a field trial meet at Bala in North Wales, and illustrates many of the important people connected with field trials and the early Kennel Club. In fact, the meet never took place, nor could it have, for several of the dogs pictured were not alive at the time it was painted Private collection; photography Grant Taylor

The Spaniel

The Spaniel is without a doubt one of the most important groups of dogs. With the exception of the Clumber and the Irish Water Spaniel, Spaniels have a common origin, although at a very early date they were divided into two distinct groups — Land and Water Spaniels — and bred to develop those points which were most essential for their different types of work.

The earliest mention of Spaniels in English literature is in the *Master of The Game* written by Edward Plantagenet, 2nd Duke of York, between 1406 and

Colour Plate 51. *Richard Ramsay Reinagle.*
Water Spaniel, *1815. Oil on canvas, 30 x 40ins. (76 x 101.5cm).*
While identified as a Water Spaniel, this dog is undoubtedly an ancestor of the Springer Spaniel, surprisingly similar in conformation to the Springer Spaniel depicted by Wardle some ninety years later (Colour Plate 56) Collection Mrs. Walter M. Jeffords

Plate 87. *Sydenham Edwards.* Spaniels. *From* Cynographia Britannica, *1799-1805. Although the dog on the left was probably an ancestor of the Springer Spaniel, one can see that around 1800 individual Spaniel breeds were virtually unidentifiable*

Collection The American Kennel Club; photography Dave King

Plate 88. *John Nost Sartorius.* Three Spaniels with a Woodcock, *1813. Oil on canvas, 10 x 12ins. (25.5 x 30.5cm). The son of the artist Francis Sartorius (1734-1804), John Nost was a prolific painter who specialised in horses and sporting dogs. While identified as Spaniels, these dogs have a strong similarity to Setters of the day*

Photograph courtesy Arthur Ackermann & Son, Ltd.

Plate 89. *James Ward, R.A.*
A Spaniel Frightening Ducks, *1821. Oil on canvas, 48 x 71ins. (122 x 180.5cm).*
Ward, predominantly a horse painter, was a romantic who often depicted animals in an individualistic style. Notice, for instance, how all the elements of the painting seem active, pointing to the anxiety of the flying ducks

Collection The Tate Gallery, London; photograph Art Resource, N.Y.

Plate 90. *John Frederick Herring, Snr.*
Spaniel With Mallard, *1849. Oil on canvas, 16 x 18ins. (40.5 x 45.5cm).*
Herring Snr. was a well known sporting artist of his day and has depicted this Spaniel with an extraordinary realism — one can even see the water dripping off the dog's coat

Photograph courtesy Arthur Ackermann & Son, Ltd.

Colour Plate 52. *Henry Bernard Chalon.*
Quaile, an English Water Spaniel, in a Wooded Landscape, *1797. Oil on canvas, 20 x 24ins. (51 x 61cm).*
Chalon was born in London of Dutch parents and during his lifetime enjoyed the patronage of the Duchess of York, the Prince Regent and William IV. Compare this dog, and its rather unlikely pose, to Reinagle's depiction of the breed in Colour Plate 51 Photograph courtesy Richard Green Gallery

1413, mainly a translation of the 1387 work *Livre de Chasse* by Gaston, Comte de Foix. It is safe to assume, therefore, that Spaniels were popular in France and England as early as the middle of the fourteenth century. Over the years, they have been used in hawking and to spring and retrieve fowl.

Eventually, the Spaniel evolved into several different breeds and by the early twentieth century, the English Cocker Spaniel, the English Springer Spaniel, the Field Spaniel, and the Sussex Spaniel were well established. The artist Arthur Wardle illustrated all of these breeds in his important multiple portrait, *Field Spaniels of the Twentieth Century* (Colour Plate 56).

Colour Plate 53. *George Garrard, A.R.A.* A Spaniel. *Oil on canvas, 28 x 36ins. (71 x 91.5cm).*
While Garrard is predominantly known for his horse paintings, he was also a sculptor of note, exhibiting at the Royal Academy. This painting has a monumental quality, similar to many of the dog portraits of George Stubbs
Collection Mrs. Vincent Astor; photography Dave King

Plate 91. *British School.*
Spaniel and Toy Terrier. *Oil on canvas.*
This Spaniel, of an indeterminate breed, is painted with a direct charm typical of many unsigned British dog paintings of the late nineteenth century. The little dog beside it may have been an early Yorkshire Terrier
Collection Mario Buatta

Plate 94. *George Armfield.*
Two Dogs in a Kitchen. *Oil on canvas, 14 x 12ins. (35.5 x 30.5cm).*
This painting is typical of the work of Armfield, who painted many Spaniels and Setters in rustic interiors as well as Terriers hunting for rats. The gun leaning against the wall probably means that these Spaniels have just returned from the hunt Private collection; photography Dave King

Opposite top: Plate 92. *William E. Turner.*
Spaniels, *1868. Oil on canvas, 23 x 29¾ins. (58.5 x 75.5cm).*
Turner was probably a self-taught artist, and there is a charming, awkward quality about this portrait of two early Spaniels that seems to bear this out. Note how the gun and the dead game have been formally posed in front of the dogs Collection The American Kennel Club; photography Dave King

Opposite: Plate 93. *George Earl.*
Bruce, *c.1870. Oil on canvas, 15½ x 16½ins. (39.5 x 42cm).*
Owned by the well-known dog fancier, R.T.L. Price, Bruce was a Clumber Spaniel, although somewhat different in type than the dog in Colour Plate 56 Private collection; photography Dave King

Colour Plate 54. *Edwin Frederick Holt.*
No. 5183. *Oil on canvas, 20 x 30ins. (51 x 76cm).*
Were it not completed by a different artist, this painting might well have been a pendant to Colour Plate 61. As in the painting by Bretland, the large dogs may be Irish Red and White Setters, while the smaller red and white dogs are undoubtedly Spaniels

Collection Mrs. Vincent Astor; photography Dave King

Colour Plate 55. *George Earl.*
Field Spaniel, *c.1870. Oil on canvas, 15½ x 15½ins. (39.5 x 39.5cm). Earl's work is characterised by a rich colour sense, and by the great attention he pays to the details which distinguish a breed, in particular the animal's expression* Private collection; photography Grant Taylor

Colour Plate 56. *Arthur Wardle, R.I., R.B.C., P.S.*
Field Spaniels of the Twentieth Century, *1906. Oil on canvas, 30 x 40ins. (76 x 101.5cm). This is a painting of great historical value to Spaniel fanciers because it depicts famous Spaniels of almost one hundred years ago. Each of the dogs is named on the frame of the painting: Ch. Preston Shot, Ch. Velox Powder, Ch. Bob Bowdler, Ch. Jetsam Bowdler, Ch. Shillington Rona, Ch. Druid, Ch. Bridford Bobs and Rosehill Rick*

Private collection; photography Dave King

Colour Plate 57. *George Earl.*
Nellie, *c.1870. Oil on canvas, 15½ x 16½ins. (39.5 x 42cm).*
Described as an English Cocker Spaniel by the artist, by today's standards it looks more like an English Springer Spaniel. It is from a series of portraits completed by Earl entitled Champion Dogs of England

Private collection; photography Grant Taylor

Plate 95. *Arthur Wardle, R.I., R.B.C., P.S.* Springer Spaniels. *Oil on canvas, 20 x 13ins. (51 x 33cm).*
Wardle did a series of paintings in this format which were subsequently reproduced on cigarette cards. Even with no background, it is a successful painting, for Wardle has captured the characteristic expression of the breed

Collection Mrs. Walter M. Jeffords; photography Grant Taylor

Plate 96. *Maud Earl.*
Ch. Lucknowe Crème de la Crème, *1931. Oil on board, 20 x 39ins. (51 x 99cm).*
By 1931 Maud Earl would have been sixty-seven years old, yet she continued to paint the pure-bred dogs which she had loved since her childhood in England. By 1931 she had been living in New York City for some fourteen years

Collection The American Kennel Club; photography Dave King

Colour Plate 58. *Thomas Earl.* Spaniels.
Little is known about Thomas Earl, although he is believed to have been related to George Earl. At first glance one might have ascribed this portrait to the latter artist, but it is somewhat more sentimental than is typical of George Earl's work

Collection Mrs. Damon Raike; photography Schopplein Studios

Colour Plate 59. *Maud Earl.* Sussex Spaniel, *c.1890. Oil on canvas, 24¼ x 29¼ ins. (61.5 x 74cm).*
This painting was undoubtedly of a show dog, for Earl was very active in Kennel Club circles and knew all the top breeders of the day. In an interview in 1898, the artist stated that she had painted virtually every known breed of dog Collection Mrs. Damon Raike; photography Schopplein Studios

The Setter

The Setter family is composed of English, Irish and Gordon Setters, and although their exact origins are uncertain, they undoubtedly derived from the same parent stock. Early sporting writers describe them as 'setting' or 'crouching' Spaniels, in contrast to the 'finding' or 'springing' Spaniels, which flushed game without pointing it. As time went on, the setting variety was evidently bred larger and larger with a view to increasing its speed. Most writers agree that as early as 1555, Robert Dudley, Duke of Northumberland, trained Setters to work with a net. Although the three Setter breeds are quite dissimilar, they all have common ancestors: on one side the Spaniel, while the other is a matter of conjecture, though most think it was the old Spanish Pointer, providing strong scenting power and staunchness in the field (Plate 116).

Much of the credit for the development of the English Setter as a distinct breed goes to Edward Laverack, who from about 1825 produced top English Setters. Laverack, with his English Setter Mike, can be seen to the left in George Earl's painting of *The Field Trial Meeting* (Colour Plate 50). Another noted English Setter breeder, R.L. Purcell Llewellin, can be seen to the right of the painting. At about the time that the Laverack strain was at its zenith in England, Llewellin purchased a number of Laverack's best show dogs, and crossed them with a strain from another part of England. The resultant dogs became well known, particularly at field trials, and the strain became known as the Llewellin Setter. Today, we simply refer to the breed as the English

Plate 97. *Benjamin Marshall.* Setter, *1801. Oil on canvas, 25 x 30ins. (63.5 x 76cm). Marshall was a very successful sporting artist, completing many horse portraits for the English aristocracy. His portraits of dogs, usually sporting dogs or Terriers, are rare. This dog's legs and feet seem very out of proportion with the rest of his body, although it is presumably how the dog appeared*

Photograph courtesy Arthur Ackermann & Son, Ltd.

Plate 98. *Charles Henry Schwanfelder.*
Shooting Scene in Cumberland. *Oil on canvas, 28 x 36ins. (71 x 91.5cm).*
Schwanfelder was born in Leeds of German descent and, while he visited London infrequently, he did exhibit at the Royal Academy. In 1816 he was appointed animal painter to the Prince Regent, a position he retained when the Prince Regent became George IV. While to the modern eye it seems incongruous for the hunters to be wearing top hats, this was the accepted hunting dress of the day
Photograph courtesy The Tryon Gallery

Setter, although most English Setter fanciers trace their dogs back to the Laverack or Llewellin types.

The Irish Setter is also well represented in Earl's painting, and the Rev. J.C. Macdona, important to the history of the breed, can be seen in the left middleground with his dog Plunket. The Irish Setter became popular in the eighteenth century in Ireland, the early dogs often being red and white, with white frequently predominating over red. The solid red first appeared in Ireland around 1810. As 'Stonehenge' has pointed out: 'The blood red or rich chestnut or mahogany colour is the colour of an Irish Setter of high mark. The colour must be unmixed with black; and studied in a strong light, there must not be black shadows or waves, much less black fringes to the ears, or to the profile of the form.'

Irish Setters did not become popular in England until about 1880, having acquired a reputation for 'unsteadiness' in the field, an accusation that 'Stonehenge' in his 1879 edition of *The Dogs of the British Islands* contested stoutly: 'I have seen several at work, and certainly have no reason to think them more unsteady than their English rivals, but neither will compare with the Pointer in that respect. They are slashing goers, with heads and flags well up, and the latter lashed merrily in most cases, though, like the English Dog, not invariably so. In endurance they are quite up to the best English form...'

The Gordon Setter comes from Scotland and can trace its origin at least as far back as 1665 when Markham, a writer of the time, praised a 'black and fallow setting dog...hardest to endure labour.' Its history as a breed started with a strain of Setters kennelled at Gordon Castle during the life of the 4th Duke of Gordon (1743-1827).

The Gordon Setter Kent (Colour Plate 62) was owned by S. Lang, an active Kennel Club member who had established the first stud book in 1874.

Colour Plate 60. *Philip Reinagle, R.A.*
The English Setter, *c.1800. Oil on canvas, 11½ x 13½ins. (29 x 34cm).*
Reinagle's dogs are meticulously drawn, and are often situated in extensive landscapes. An all white Setter such as this is rarely seen today Collection The American Kennel Club; photography Dave King

Plate 99. *Charles Henry Schwanfelder.*
Mons. *Oil on canvas.*
While the conformation of English Setters has not changed significantly over the last two hundred years, their style of pointing has. This dog, obviously highly prized in its time, is depicted with his tail down, unlike the present fashion for an erect tail
Photograph courtesy The Tryon Gallery

Colour Plate 61. *Thomas W. Bretland.*
Robert Masefield out Shooting. *Oil on canvas, 36 x 54ins. (91.5 x 137cm).*
An artist whose work varies in quality a great deal, Bretland was a painter of animals and shooting scenes, predominantly in oils. This gentleman is about to go hunting with what appear to be Irish Red and White Setters, a breed which has recently been reintroduced to Great Britain. Two sporting Spaniels appear on the left of the group Photograph courtesy MacConnal-Mason Fine Paintings

Plate 100. *Stephen Taylor.*
Red and White Setter, *1820. Oil on canvas, 18½ x 23ins. (45.5 x 58.5cm).*
This painting is characteristic of Taylor's work in that it is a shooting subject, painted with a characteristically soft, sensitive brushstroke. The dog, however, is very long in the leg, not typical of Setters around 1820
Collection The American Kennel Club; photography Dave King

Plate 101. *George Earl.*
Setters on the Moors, *1871. Oil on canvas.*
While a sporting painting, the bare-footed young ghillie introduces a sentimental quality to the painting, inviting the viewer to identify with this romantic scene. Such a painting would not have been possible without the precedent of Landseer, who often introduced a sentimental note into his pictures
Photograph courtesy The Tryon Gallery

Plate 102. *Richard Ansdell, R.A.*
A Young Ghillie with Setters and Game, *1871. Oil on canvas, 30 x 25ins. (76 x 63.5cm).*
This is typical of Ansdell's paintings of hunters in the Scottish Highlands. He often used a pyramidal composition, with great attention to the detail of the dogs' coats. The Setters are of a heavier, coarser type than most of today's examples
Photograph courtesy The Tryon Gallery

Plate 103. *Arthur Baker.*
Rover, Son of Beauty and Grouse, *1877. Pastel and water-colour on paper, 14 x 20ins. (35.5 x 51cm).*
The Irish Setter Rover was owned and exhibited by the prominent Setter fancier, the Rev. J.C. Macdona. According to the author Vero Shaw, Rover was sold to Mr. Purcell Llewellin for 150 guineas, only to be resold to America for £300, a very large amount in the 1870s
Private collection; photography Dave King

Colour Plate 62. *George Earl.*
Kent, *c.1870. Oil on canvas, 14 x 18ins. (35.5 x 45.5cm). Kent, owned by S. Lang, was a famous dog of his day. One should, however, be cautious when identifying specific dogs in nineteenth century paintings: Kent, for example, was a name used over and over again for Gordon Setters*

Collection Mrs. Gwynne G. McDevitt; photography Grant Taylor

Colour Plate 63. *Robert Nightingale.*
Rex, a Gordon Setter, *1881. Oil on canvas, 12 x 20ins. (30.5 x 51cm). Nightingale had an extraordinary ability to paint the texture of a dog's coat, in this case effectively standing out against a lightly painted landscape. While in conformation it differs strikingly from today's Gordon Setter of the show bench, it is quite similar to modern field trial examples*

Collection Mrs. Gwynne G. McDevitt; photography Grant Taylor

Colour Plate 64. *James Hardy, Jnr., R.I.*
A Good Day's Shooting, *1883. Oil on canvas, 14½ x 12ins. (37 x 30.5cm).*
This painting is very typical of Hardy's work, for he often grouped three sporting dogs together, lavishing a great deal of attention on the depiction of the dead game. Hardy was equally adept in watercolour Collection Mrs. Gwynne G. McDevitt; photograph courtesy MacConnal-Mason Fine Paintings

Plate 104. *Arthur Baker.*
Ranger II, *1877. Pastel and watercolour on paper, 14 x 20ins. (35.5 x 51cm).*
Owned by the well known Setter breeder, the Rev. J.C. Macdona, Ranger II was one of the first English Setters to succeed in the show ring as well as at field trials
Private collection; photography Dave King

Plate 105. *James Hardy, Jnr., R.I.*
Ned. *Oil on board, 6½ x 8½ins. (16.5 x 21.5cm).*
Ned was Sir John Rivett-Carnac's champion Black and Tan Setter, now known as a Gordon Setter. This picture is unusual, for it is a portrait of the dog at rest, without the spoils of the hunt Photograph courtesy Arthur Ackermann & Son, Ltd.

Plate 106. *Eugene Petit.*
On the Scent. *Oil on canvas.*
This painting is characteristic of the French artist's work, for he often depicted Pointers and Setters in the field. While the dogs are well painted, the landscape is too sketchy to give an adequate impression of the scene
Photograph courtesy The Tryon Gallery

Plate 107. *Robert Cleminson.*
English and Gordon Setter.
Oil on canvas, 14 x 18ins. (35.5 x 45.5cm).
This is typical of Cleminson's work, for he painted in a soft, diffuse style which sometimes masked a lack of anatomical knowledge. Compare, for example, the heads of these Setters with those in Colour Plate 66
Collection Mrs. Gwynne G. McDevitt; photography Grant Taylor

Colour Plate 65. *Edwin Armfield.*
English Setters on Point. *Oil on canvas, 10 x 18ins. (25.5 x 45.7cm).*
While Edwin Armfield was a relatively minor artist, he occasionally completed a picture which was far superior to his other paintings. Like George Armfield, he completed many portraits of Terriers and sporting dogs, here capturing the expressions of Setters on point
Collection Mr. and Mrs. Lawrence Kalstone; photography Dave King

Opposite above: Colour Plate 66. *Thomas Blinks.*
Three Gordon Setters in a Highland Landscape, *1895. Oil on canvas, 20 x 30ins. (51 x 76cm).*
Using a pyramidal composition to add tension to these Gordon Setters on point, Blinks has lowered his viewpoint to create a noble portrait of almost monumental scale. The rich coloration of the dogs and the attention to the details of the landscape are very typical of his work
Collection Mrs. Gwynne G. McDevitt; photography Grant Taylor

Opposite: Colour Plate 67. *Thomas Blinks.*
Setters on Point. *Oil on canvas, 14 x 18ins. (35.5 x 45.5cm).*
Blinks was extremely successful in his lifetime, for he had an uncanny ability to capture the expression, anatomy and coat texture of sporting dogs. These dogs are caught in a moment frozen in time, every muscle tensed in anticipation of their quarry
Collection Mrs. Gwynne G. McDevitt; photography Dave King

Plate 108. *Edwin Douglas.* Setters with Game, *1900. Oil on canvas.*
Although the subject matter is sporting dogs in a rugged landscape, Douglas nevertheless gives the dogs a soft, almost sweet expression, more typical of Victorian pet portraits
Photograph courtesy The Tryon Gallery

Plate 109. *Maud Earl.* Dear and Pabchick, *1912. Oil on canvas, 25 x 32ins. (63.5 x 81cm).*
This painting is finished in a loose, painterly style characteristic of many of the dog paintings completed by Earl after 1910. Seven years later she was to move to New York, where for a time she almost entirely abandoned dog portraits Photograph courtesy Arthur Ackermann & Son, Ltd.

Plate 110. *George Wright.*
On Point. *Oil on canvas, 8 x 12ins. (20.5 x 30.5cm).*
Primarily a painter of horses, Wright also completed costume or period pieces. The loose, painterly style of this picture is typical of his work, as is his strong, boldly painted signature

Photograph courtesy Christie's South Kensington

Plate 111. *F. Mabel Hollams, S.W.A.*
Sally and Susan. *Oil on panel.*
This picture is typical of the many dog portraits Hollams completed in the early years of the twentieth century. Often painted on a varnished board, they are usually inscribed with the names of the dogs. Note that each of these Irish Setters has a white blaze on its chest, today considered a fault in the show ring

Photograph courtesy Bonhams

Colour Plate 68. *William Arnold Woodhouse.*
English Setter and Gordon Setter with Dead Game. *Oil on canvas, 36 x 28ins. (91.5 x 71cm).*
While Woodhouse primarily painted sporting subjects, he also completed many portraits of animals and birds. Technically brilliant, he paid great attention to the textures of his subject matter
Photograph courtesy MacConnal-Mason Fine Paintings

Plate 112. *John Wootton.*
Spotted Pointer, *1738. Oil on canvas, 40 x 50ins. (101.5 x 127cm).*
Wootton, the first Englishman to paint horse portraits, studied in Rome and was very much influenced by classical precedents. He was for almost fifty years the primary sporting painter for the aristocracy Photograph courtesy Arthur Ackermann & Son, Ltd.

The Pointer

Pointers are also prominent in Earl's painting of *The Field Trial Meeting* (Colour Plate 50), and several are important to the history of the breed. The Pointer, the first dog to stand game in the sense which we use the term today, first appeared in England around 1650 when it was used to point hare for coursing Greyhounds. As soon as shooting game on the wing became popular, around 1711, the Pointer was used almost exclusively for pointing game birds. All authorities seem to agree that the breed came from the Iberian peninsula, assuming that the word 'Pointer' is derived from the Spanish *punta,* i.e. 'point'.

T. H. Whitehouse appears in *The Field Trial Meeting* with his famous lemon and white Pointer bitch Hamlet (Colour Plate 70), and Ch. Bang is depicted with the well known fancier Samuel Price. Perhaps none of the Pointer fanciers depicted is better known than the Pointer and sporting dog authority William Arkwright, author of *The Pointer and its Predecessors.* Illustrated by the artist

Colour Plate 69. *Charles Towne.* Pointers in a Stable. *Oil on canvas, 16½ x 20¾ ins. (42 x 52.5cm). Towne's work is usually on a small scale, executed in a very tight, meticulous style. This painting has a highly finished, almost porcelain-like surface. The Pointers have a more refined, attenuated look than was common during this period* Photograph courtesy Richard Green

Colour Plate 70. *George Earl.* Hamlet, *c.1870. Oil on canvas, 14 x 18ins. (35.5 x 45.5cm). This portrait of Hamlet, a Lemon and White Pointer owned by T.H. Whitehouse, was one in a series of paintings,* Champion Dogs of England, *done by Earl. The dog is depicted on point, tensely waiting for the bird to take flight*

Collection Mr. and Mrs. Lawrence Kalstone; photography Dave King

Colour Plate 71. *Richard Ansdell.*
Shooting Over Dogs, *1862. Oil on canvas, 12 x 22ins. (30.5 x 56cm).*
Ansdell was most accomplished at creating large, open air hunting scenes, this one depicting an English Pointer behind a Setter. His work is characterised by a meticulous attention to detail, with many of his paintings having the characteristic 'Ansdell blue' sky
Photograph courtesy MacConnal-Mason Fine Paintings

Maud Earl, his volume has become a standard reference on the breed. Arkwright was elected to The Kennel Club in 1876, and later joined its Committee, contributing occasionally to *The Kennel Club Gazette.*

Another prominent dog fancier and active field trial enthusiast illustrated in Earl's painting is Dr. J.H. Salter. Of him, C.H. Lane states:

> To give any list of the dogs owned by Mr. Salter or the many and important prizes they have won would take up more space that I am able to give them; but I hope I have said sufficient to show that he is one of the very best types of Doggy people we have; and his cheery and courteous manners and hearty good fellowship have made him universally popular with all who enjoy the pleasure of his acquaintance.

It is important to note that many of these early dog show and field trial enthusiasts were wealthy men who had the leisure time to pursue their interests. J.H. Salter, for instance, was an early member of The Kennel Club and, incredible as it may seem, during his lifetime he owned more than 1,000 Greyhounds, 300 Retrievers, 250 English Setters, 150 Field Spaniels, 1,000 Irish Setters, 50 Cockers, 12 Clumbers and nearly 100 Fox Terriers Showing dogs at this level was a very serious hobby indeed and, with the interest generated, some regulating body was soon needed to govern and give consistency to the sport.

Plate 113. *John Wootton.* Pointer. *Oil on canvas, 39½ x 49½ ins. (100.5 x 125.5cm). While the Pointer has changed over the last two hundred years, in the eighteenth century its conformation was surprisingly similar to that of today. Note how large the hare appears to be, in comparison with the dog*

Photograph courtesy Arthur Ackermann & Son, Ltd.

Plate 114. *Sawrey Gilpin, R.A., and George Barraud, Snr.* Colonel Thornton with his Celebrated Pointers Juno and Pluto. *Oil on canvas. Even in the eighteenth century, the English Pointer was a very staunch dog. According to Richardson, who was writing in 1847, Pluto and Juno, the dogs here depicted, stood on point for a full hour and a quarter while posing for Gilpin for this portrait* Photograph courtesy The Tryon Gallery

Plate 115. *Philip Reinagle, R.A.*
Pointer. *Engraving from* The Sportsman's Cabinet, *1803.*
Philip Reinagle painted a series of pictures to illustrate The Sportsman's Cabinet, *a two volume set with some fifty illustrations. His work shows the influence of the seventeenth century landscape artists, and he often included extensive backgrounds in his paintings*
Collection The American Kennel Club; photography Dave King

Plate 116. *Philip Reinagle, R.A.*
Spanish Pointer. *Engraving from* The Sportsman's Cabinet, *1803.*
The English Pointer is said to have been created by breeding the Spanish Pointer with the English Foxhound, the introduction of Foxhound blood being intended to give the slow Spanish Pointer greater speed. Notice the coarse, heavy set head and neck of the dog, very different from the Pointer in Plate 115
Collection The American Kennel Club; photography Dave King

Colour Plate 74. *John Charles Dollman, R.I., R.O.I., R.W.S.*
Pointers at Rest, *1874. Oil on canvas, 38 x 49ins. (96.5 x 124.5cm).*
Dollman was a painter of genre and animal scenes. Indeed, this painting, with the Pointers suspiciously eying the cat, has an anecdotal element which is essential to genre paintings
Collection Frances G. Scaife; photography Dave King

Opposite above: Colour Plate 72. *William Luker, Snr., R.B.A.*
Head of Brown and White Dog. *Oil on canvas, 18 x 16ins. (45.5 x 40.5cm).*
William Luker, Snr., who was a painter of dogs and horses in and around London, has here taken the perspective of the prey, portraying the Pointer head as it might have been seen by the startled game bird
Photograph courtesy MacConnal-Mason Fine Paintings

Opposite: Colour Plate 73. *Thomas Blinks.*
English Pointers in the Field. *Oil on canvas, 16 x 20ins. (40.5 x 51cm).*
Blinks, who completed many hunting and racing paintings, was a master at capturing the tense expression of hunting dogs in the field. He was a brilliant colourist, producing highly finished, expressive portraits
Private collection; photography Dave King

Plate 117. *John Nost Sartorius.* Sportsman with His Keeper and Pointers Pheasant Shooting. *Oil on canvas, 27½ x 36ins. (70 x 91.5cm).*
Black Pointers are today very rare indeed, but they played a great part in the history of the breed. Here they are acknowledging, or 'backing', the point of the leading dog Photograph courtesy Arthur Ackermann & Son, Ltd.

Plate 118. *Charles Towne.* Pointer, *1811. Oil on canvas, 13¾ x 17½ins. (35 x 44.5cm).*
This artist, one of the leading horse painters of the early eighteenth century, has taken a great deal of time to delineate the light on the trees, creating a rather mysterious effect. One wonders, however, whether the dog really looked like this, for it seems very out of proportion Photograph courtesy Ackermann & Son, Ltd.

Plate 119. *E.W. Gill.* Three Pointers With Dead Game, *1841. Oil on canvas, 24 x 28ins. (61 x 71cm). This portrait of Pointers, with an extensive landscape beyond, follows a formula for such pictures which had become established in the late eighteenth century: dogs portrayed at rest, with dead game proudly displayed at their feet*
Photograph courtesy Iona Antiques

Plate 120. *John Dalby.* Pointer Bitch, *1844. Oil on panel, 9 x 12ins. (23 x 30.5cm). This is a beautifully painted Pointer bitch on point, by a sporting artist about whom very little is known. He has, however, caught the expression of the dog, and the tense, expectant look of the moment* Photograph courtesy Arthur Ackermann & Son, Ltd.

Colour Plate 75. *Arthur Wardle, R.I., R.B.C., P.S.*
Two Pointers. *Oil on canvas, 21½ x 15½ins. (54.5 x 39.5cm).*
This painting, probably completed in the early years of the twentieth century, is characteristic of the best of Wardle's work, for it captures the particular expression of the dogs, ready to work. One is probably a dog, the other a bitch Photograph courtesy Richard Green

Colour Plate 76. *Maud Earl.*
Brace Work, *c.1905. Oil on canvas, 18 x 30ins. (45.5 x 76cm).*
Sub-titled September, *this painting is one from a series of twelve dog paintings which Maud Earl completed around 1905 to illustrate the months of the year. Although now rare, they were originally also published as colour prints. For another, see Plate 156*

Collection Mr. and Mrs. David Morris; photography Dave King

Early Dog Shows, The Kennel Club and the Pure-Bred Dog Portrait

By the mid-nineteenth century in Britain, the original function of the breeds was no longer as important as it had once been. Terriers during the Victorian period did continue to go to ground after the fox as well as the badger, but it was more for sport than out of necessity. Indeed, the majority of the breeds in Great Britain had come to be used for sport or simply as companion animals. Even the Bulldog, once a brave and incredibly tenacious animal, was almost in danger of extinction because of the outlawing of bull baiting and dog fighting.

Moreover, within the breeds which were used for sport and/or pets, there was no uniform body which regulated who did what, and the cross breeding of animals to improve their abilities was commonplace. While the official Foxhound stud book had been established in 1865 and the Greyhound equivalent in 1882, there was no registry for the vast majority of breeds. Indeed, for many the concept of keeping pure-bred lines pure was not thought to be particularly important.

This attitude was to change dramatically with the establishment of The Kennel Club and the advent of dog shows. As people brought their dogs together in competition it became very important that the dogs they were comparing were of the same breed. And while dog owners had for centuries compared their dogs, especially in terms of function, it was only in mid-nineteenth century Britain that more than one or two breeds were first gathered to compare the appearance of one dog with another.

Plate 121. *William Henry Davis.*
Five Prize Pigs, *1854. Oil on canvas, 11½ x 16ins. (29 x 40.5cm).*
Davis, who was born in Chelsea, specialised in portraits of prize farm animals. In the case of pigs, it was highly desirable that they be as fat as possible. Indeed, the animal on the far left looks as if it could hardly move
Photograph courtesy Iona Antiques

Concepts of breeding and animal husbandry had developed rapidly in the eighteenth century and a genre of art had developed around the breeding of cattle, pigs and farm animals. Cattle and pigs which by today's standards were overweight were highly prized (Plate 121) and some artists undoubtedly added a few extra pounds to the animal to please its owner.

Livestock shows and game fairs at mid-century were a form of popular entertainment, and the same could be said for the early nineteenth century bull baiting and dog fighting contests, until 1835 when an Act of Parliament prohibited these brutal sports. Like minded men still wanted to gather with their dogs as the focus of attention, and while blood sports continued for a time, especially in the provinces, they were eventually replaced by a more civilised form of competition: the dog show.

Early gatherings of dog fanciers were undoubtedly informal affairs which were often held in taverns or community gathering places. Called a 'match' or 'lead', they evolved out of dog fighting and rat killing contests where dog owners came together to compare the skills of their individual dogs. Little is known about these early canine meetings, though competitions for Foxhounds had been known from the early decades of the nineteenth century, with John Warde, for instance, holding small shows on his estate as early as 1800.

Larger shows for Foxhounds were organised almost as early as conformation shows for dogs, for it was in 1860 that one was held at Yarm, which was followed by a more important one the next year at Middlesbrough. These then became closely associated with the Great Yorkshire Agricultural Society under Tom Parrington, and other gatherings were seen at York, Malton, Redcar, Harrogate, Beverley, Hull, Doncaster, Leeds and Driffield. As Parrington was contemplating retirement from the managership of the Great Yorkshire, in 1877 he transferred the Hound Show to Peterborough where it eventually became a great national institution.

One of the earliest canine events for breeds other than Foxhounds and Greyhounds is depicted in a highly important painting by R. Marshall, *An Early Canine Meeting* (Colour Plate 77). Along with *The Field Trial Meeting* by George Earl (Colour Plate 50), it is one of the most historic of all dog pictures, for it depicts the origins of the dog shows of today. The painting shows a canine meeting at Jemmy Shaw's Queen's Head Tavern in 1855, almost twenty years before the founding of The Kennel Club. Located in Haymarket, London, the tavern was owned by the well-known Bulldog breeder Jim Beam.

This was not the first such meeting, for on the walls are various newspaper clippings showing that Shaw had managed another public house called The Blue Anchor where he ran a 'Toy Dog Club' as well as rat killing contests. One such advertisement announced a 'Grand Show next Sunday Evening, May 27, 1849,' where the principal attraction was a rat killing competition.

What is depicted in Marshall's painting, however, is a far more civilised crowd than that found at rat killing contests. Virtually a group portrait of the important dog personages of the day formally posing behind tavern tables, the painting shows some eighteen dog fanciers, each solemnly smoking a pipe, with refreshments placed before them. Clearly what is important in this painting, however, is the assemblage of some of the most interesting dogs of the day.

At least nine different breeds are depicted (with three varieties of King Charles Spaniel) each seated on the tables in front of their owners. Other breeds represented are the Bulldog, possibly a Toy Bulldog, two coloured Bull Terriers, a Skye Terrier-type on top of the table at the right, and the now extinct White English Terrier.

The uncertainty in identifying some of the breeds in this work is by no means out of the ordinary with early dog paintings. Gerald Massey, the noted English dog historian, for instance, identified the dog on the top of the table at the right as a 'so-called' Skye Terrier. He is quite correct to be uncertain, for many of the breeds had not yet been separated one from the other, nor were there any consistent rules for the breeding of pure-bred specimens. With regard to the Skye Terrier, for instance, one might think that so distinctive a breed would have great uniformity within it. This was not, however, the case. D.J. Thomson Gray, in his authoritative book, *Dogs of Scotland* (1891), for instance, states that before 1874:

> We have no authentic particulars regarding any of the terriers of Scotland, except the Dandi Dinmont and Skye, and for ten years previous to this date classes were given at our shows for these two breeds alone...The Skye classes, however, presented as a rule the heterogenous appearance of a variety class, and indeed might have been more than correctly catalogued rough-haired terriers, the plan adopted by our Aberdonian friends to cover a multitude of breeds.

The identification of breeds in paintings of this period is made even more perplexing by a change in nomenclature. The twentieth century dog fancier has more than likely not encountered the Poltalloch Terrier that existed in the mid-nineteenth century (now known as the West Highland White) or the Waterside or Bingley Terrier (now known as the Airedale). More important, however, is the fact that the breeds rarely looked like our modern day examples. This is, of course, to be expected, for dog breeders are continually improving their stock, and breeding to develop a more beautiful animal.

Moreover, the grooming techniques employed by modern-day exhibitors for the coated breeds such as the Poodle, have in some cases created animals with entirely different profiles.

Indeed, one of the principal attractions of nineteenth century paintings for dog breeders is that they establish a visual history, showing how the various breeds' physical appearance has changed over the years. It is fascinating to look at a group of paintings of one breed, arranged chronologically, and to see just how much — or how little — each has changed.

The large variety of breeds now recognised by The Kennel Club might well not have been established in the mid-nineteenth century, however, were it not for a group of individuals who saw a need for consistent breeding regulations, and the development of a stud book which would guarantee breed purity.

The Kennel Club was founded in April 1873 by Sewallis Evelyn Shirley of Ettington, its primary purpose being to provide a regulating body to legislate in canine matters. As we have seen, some twenty years before, the 'lead' or 'match' show was being held regularly on an informal, social basis. As such matches became more popular, there was a demand for bigger, more organised events.

The first dog show, more or less as we know it today, was held at the Town Hall at Newcastle upon Tyne on 28 and 29 June, 1859. Organised by John Shorthouse, R.W. Pape and Tom Reid, there were some sixty entries, with the breeds limited to Pointers and Setters, and with three judges appointed for each breed.

In spite of the organisational difficulties involved with the Newcastle Show, several others followed in quick succession and as dog shows became more and more popular, separate organisations were established to promote them, including the National Dog Club which held its first and only show in June 1869. The first dog show of greater significance and popularity was that held in June 1870 at the Crystal Palace. It was organised by a committee which had S.E. Shirley and J.H. Murchison (later both prominent Kennel Club members) at its head. While everyone agreed that it was a great success, it was financially a failure. A second show was held, however, with much less of a financial loss than the previous year's.

There can be little doubt that these early dog shows provided the impetus for the establishment of The Kennel Club, for the way in which dog shows were run had been the cause of considerable concern. As E.W. Jaquet, then Secretary of The Kennel Club, pointed out in his monumental work of 1905, *The Kennel Club: A History and Record of Its Work:*

> In the interval of fourteen years between the date of the first Dog Show and the foundation of The Kennel Club, many irregularities — not to say scandals — had arisen, and the need for legislation and guidance became an absolute necessity...No doubt Mr. Shirley's intimate knowledge of canine matters in those days had led him long before he took public action to perceive that unless a responsible authority took affairs in hand, dog showing and breeding must eventually become a pursuit in which no respectable person would care to engage.

Colour Plate 77. *R. Marshall.* An Early Canine Meeting, *1855. Oil on canvas, 29 x 37ins. (73.5 x 94cm).*
This is one of the most historic of all dog paintings, for it portrays an early canine meeting, or 'match', a predecessor of our present day dog shows, at Jemmy Shaw's Queen's Head Tavern. In the early nineteenth century, men came together at such gatherings to compare their dogs. Note that the walls are covered with prints depicting aspects of sporting life: cock fights, ratting and boxing
Collection The Kennel Club

Shirley and his associates took dogs seriously, and upon seeing a need for regulation and proper record keeping, Shirley quickly set about to establish a governing body for the sport of dogs. He held the first meeting in 1873. There were twelve other dog fanciers of diverse backgrounds in attendance, with sporting dog fanciers in the majority. They wasted no time in organising their first show which was held at the Crystal Palace on 17-20 June, 1873. The show had an astonishing entry of 975 dogs. As Brian Vesey-Fitzgerald says in *The Domestic Dog:* 'I think it may be said that this first Kennel Club Show was really the start of the modern show movement.'

Realising the importance of having pedigrees available, one of the earliest undertakings of The Kennel Club was a Stud Book. The Jockey Club had established an authoritative record of thoroughbred horses born each year, but there was no such authority in the dog world. The Stud Book was of crucial importance, for in effect it determined what was or was not a pure-bred dog in England. Great care was taken in the compilation of the first Stud Book in 1874, which also contained records of shows dating back to 1859. The prominent dog man C.S. Pearce was its editor and he tackled his job with great enthusiasm, contacting some 3,500 persons for pedigrees of their dogs, and carefully compiling the pedigrees of some 4,027 dogs, divided into forty breeds and varieties. As Pearce himself points out in the preface:

> This work, prepared by me for the Kennel Club, has been produced at a great and necessary expense, and is intended to fill up a blank in the history of the canine world...By rigidly excluding or pointing out all doubtful pedigrees, I have endeavoured to make it as much a record of fact and truth as possible, and if it is incomplete, I can only say that it must be borne in mind that a dog, unlike a horse, may have several lots of offspring in the year, and brings in some instances as many as fifteen or twenty puppies into the world at a time.

Also included in the first Stud Book, a work of some six hundred pages and of great importance to the civilised development of dog shows, was a 'Code of Rules for the Guidance of Dog Shows' as well as those for the 'Guidance of Field Trials for Sporting Dogs'. Whenever there is competition in a sport, there are those who would bend or break the rules in order to win, and the sport of dogs was certainly no exception.

In 1874, Kennel Club membership was limited to one hundred and was run by an elected committee of twelve. Needless to say, its members included some of the most prominent dog fanciers of the day, many of whom commissioned portraits of their dogs. In addition to S.E. Shirley, the names S. Lang, J.H. Murchison, and J.H. Whitehouse appear.

It is a testament to Shirley's foresight, that not only did dog shows become a pursuit of dedicated people, but also that the showing of dogs gained great popularity and enjoyed the active patronage of royalty. From its inception The Kennel Club was graced with royal patronage in the person of the then Prince of Wales, later Edward VII when he succeeded his mother Queen Victoria in 1901.

While no members of royalty helped to organise The Kennel Club, many of the members were sufficiently wealthy to have country estates and to lead a life devoted to their hobbies. Shirley, for instance, was a great lover of dogs and in comparison to modern fanciers — who more often than not are interested in only one breed — his interests were very wide-ranging indeed. He was a breeder and exhibitor of Retrievers, Wire Fox Terriers, Bulldogs and Bull Terriers. Moreover, while he was at Eton he kept a pack of Beagles and later in life maintained a pack of hounds in Ireland.

J.H. Murchison, with Shirley an organiser of the 1870 Crystal Palace show, also had wide ranging interests in dogs. Among the breeds which he owned were White English Terriers, Manchester Terriers, then known as Black and Tan English Terriers, and Fox Terriers.

The White English Terrier named Prince (Colour Plate 37), owned by Murchison was a fine example of the breed, but unfortunately a breed that has now become extinct. It had been a popular breed for most of the nineteenth century, but when the anti-cropping law was passed in 1895, breeders lost interest in maintaining the breed, for they did not like the look of a natural ear.

The Manchester Terrier

It is said that the Manchester was developed by a man named John Hulme who, trying to achieve an animal which would combine the strength and tenacity of the Terrier and the speed of the Whippet, crossed the two to produce the Manchester. The town of Manchester was the centre of breeding for this very fast and highly tenacious animal.

The Manchester, who received its name in 1874 when it was changed from the Black and Tan Terrier, was among those dogs which were highly skilled in killing rats, an important task when disease was spread by vermin.

With the advent of dog shows and The Kennel Club, the breed became more popular as a pet and was eventually bred down in size (Plate 123). By choosing the smallest examples from litters and breeding them with other small examples, fanciers created a new breed now known as the Toy Black and Tan, or in America as the Toy Manchester Terrier. Unfortunately, the craze for small dogs became so great that during the late 1880s they sometimes weighed only two or three pounds, a development which jeopardised their health.

Plate 122. *A.B.*
Two Dogs in a Landscape *(detail), c.1830. Oil on canvas, 11½ x 13½ ins. (29 x 34cm).*
Although undated, this painting was probably painted around 1830, based on the style of the painting as well as the dogs. Note that the little Manchester Terrier has closely cropped ears, the style at the time
Collection Mrs. Vincent Astor; photography Dave King

Colour Plate 78. *Briton Riviere, R.A., R.E.*
A Fleeting Encounter *(pair). Oil on canvas, each 12 x 10ins. (30.5 x 25.5cm).*
Riviere was known for his genre as well as his animal paintings, the latter often including an anecdotal element. He was a master of anatomy and facial expression, as seen in this brief encounter between a Fox Terrier and a Manchester Terrier Collection Ruth Havemeyer Norwood

Plate 123. *Arthur Wardle, R.I., R.B.C., P.S.*
Toy Manchester Terriers, *c.1890. Oil on canvas, 16 x 20ins. (40.5 x 57cm).*
During the nineteenth century, Toy Manchester Terriers were selectively bred until they weighed as little as three pounds. These dogs have a very light coat, in particular the one on the left, whose skin is clearly showing through
Collection Mr. and Mrs. William Kendrick; photography Dave King

Colour Plate 79. *Frances L. Fairman.*
Monkeyano, *1909. Oil on canvas, 26¼ x 20ins. (66.5 x 51cm).*
Fairman's paintings are characterised by a soft, loose brushstroke which creates an impressionistic quality. This dog resembles a Manchester Terrier, but may well have been a mixed breed

Photograph courtesy MacConnal-Mason Fine Paintings

Plate 124. *George Paice.*
Manchester Terrier, *1881. Oil on canvas, 15 x 21ins. (38 x 53.5cm).*
This is an archetypal pet portrait, the old Manchester Terrier obviously a favoured pet. The bell collar is very typical for toy dogs of the period, and the coat perhaps an indication that he was about to go out for a walk

Collection Mr. and Mrs. William Harman Jnr.; photography Grant Taylor

Plate 125. *John Boultbee.*
Smooth Fox Terrier, *c.1790. Oil on canvas, 24 x 30ins. (61 x 76cm).*
Reputed to be the first known painting of a Smooth Fox Terrier, this painting is typical of the work of Boultbee. Influenced by the paintings of George Stubbs, Boultbee was known as a horse and animal painter with a highly finished, precise style Private collection; photography Grant Taylor

The Fox Terrier and Jack Russell Terrier

Francis Redmond, elected to The Kennel Club in 1893, was associated perhaps more than any other with the Smooth Fox Terrier, a breed which he actively showed from at least the 1870s. His highly regarded Totteridge Kennel was prominent and successful (Colour Plate 83). Desmond O'Connell, writing on Terriers in *The New Book of The Dog,* says of him: 'To no one do we owe so much; no one has made such a study of the breed, reducing it to almost a science, with the result that even outside his kennels no dog has any chance of permanently holding his own unless he has an ample supply of the blood.' One of Redmond's dogs, Ch. Donna Fortuna (by Ch. Dominie ex Ch. Dame Fortuna) was considered at the time to be the best Fox Terrier specimen ever produced. Shown many times, she never knew defeat.

The Fox Terrier was one breed in a group of several Terriers whose original function was to go to ground after the fox, badger and other small vermin. Fox Terriers are believed to have derived from the old Rough Black and Tan

Plate 126. *Colin Graeme (Roe).*
A Wire Fox Terrier *and* An Irish Terrier *(pair). Oil on panel, each 8 x 6ins. (20.5 x 15cm).*
This artist painted many Terrier and sporting dog portraits. These are two of his better works, for he had an unnerving tendency to outline the eyes of the dog, sometimes making them look exaggerated and unnatural
Photograph courtesy Christie's South Kensington

Terriers of Wales, Derbyshire and Durham, but their exact origins are unknown. The history of the modern Fox Terrier dates back to about the 1860s, when three well-known dogs of the day, Jock, Trap and Tartar, became the ancestors of all of the great Smooth and Wire Fox Terriers. Early on the two types were bred together, regardless of coat.

In 1876, a tremendous stimulus was given the breed by the formation of The Fox Terrier Club. The idea originated at a dinner party at the London home of Harding Cox (a popular dog show judge who played a major role in popularising the Wire Fox Terrier). A committee was formed and a breed standard compiled. From this time onward, separate registers were kept for the different coated varieties, although cross-breeding between them was still allowed and practised. In the 1880s, The Fox Terrier Club became the strongest of all the specialty breed clubs. Fox Terriers were very popular until well into the twentieth century, and their popularity is reflected in the visual arts.

It would not be right to leave Fox Terriers, however, without discussing a strain which has become very popular today as a separate breed. The Jack Russell Terrier was named after the man who was responsible for developing the breed, the Rev. John (Jack) Russell. A native of Barnstaple, he joined The Kennel Club in 1873 and remained a member until his death in 1883, when he was considered the oldest Fox Terrier breeder in England. Today he is, of course, best known for starting the strain of Fox Terrier which bears his name.

Plate 127. *William Henry Hamilton Trood.*
Smooth Fox Terrier, *1884. Oil on canvas, 10 x 10ins. (25.5 x 25.5cm).*
Trood specialised in painting animals, in particular dogs. His work has a highly finished, sympathetic quality with great attention to detail, yet it is rarely sentimental
Collection Mrs. Eileen Weiler

Colour Plate 80. *William Henry Hamilton Trood.*
Family Cares, *1889. Oil on canvas, 15 x 19ins. (38 x 48cm).*
This painting is typical of the more sentimental side of Trood, in which he accentuates the emotional aspect of animals. Even the title pulls at the heartstrings!

Photograph courtesy MacConnal-Mason Fine Paintings

He started breeding a new type of Fox Terrier when he was eighteen, a type which is now known as the Jack Russell Terrier. Perhaps their most distinguishable feature at the time was their size, for most of them weighed no more than fifteen pounds and many less. Russell also insisted that they be good working Terriers.

There is some mystery behind the blood-lines of the Jack Russell Terrier. The first one, a bitch named Trump, was purchased from Russell's milkman. According to the Rev. E.W.L. Davis's biography, *A Memoir of the Rev. John Russell,* 1862, legend has it that young John Russell, an undergraduate at Oxford, was taking a walk in May 1819, when '...a milkman met him with a terrier — such an animal as Russell had only yet seen in his dreams; he halted, as Actaeon might have done when he caught sight of Diana disporting in her bath; but unlike the ill-fated hunter, he never budged from the spot till

Colour Plate 81. *John Emms.*
Vice Regal, *1893. Oil on canvas, 18 x 22ins. (45.5 x 56cm).*
This is one of Emms's finer dog portraits, for it incorporates elements which are typical of his better work, in particular the rich coloration and the broad, strong brushwork. Note how the broom and the brown bottle have been incorporated to show scale Collection Mr. and Mrs. David Morris; photography Grant Taylor

Colour Plate 82. *William Henry Hamilton Trood.*
A Hunt Terrier, *1894. Oil on canvas, 14 x 18ins. (35.5 x 45.5cm).*
It is likely that this is a working or hunt Terrier, for it does not have the breed refinements which were typical of the Smooth Fox Terriers of 1894. Although a standard pose, this is a beautifully painted and expressive portrait
Photograph courtesy Bellechasse Antiques

Plate 128. *Arthur Wardle, R.I., R.B.C., P.S.*
Look Out, *1885. Oil on canvas, 30 x 20ins. (76 x 51cm). The artist would have been twenty-one when he painted this picture, and his style here is almost photographic compared with some of his later, more painterly works*
Collection Frances G. Scaife; photography Dave King

he had won the prize and secured it for his own.'

Whatever Trump's rọle may have been as a progenitor of today's Terriers, her significance in the life of her master is indisputable. Following Russell's death in 1883, his estate either bequeathed or sold his favourite oil painting of the dog to the Prince of Wales. Ever since, Trump's portrait has hung in the tack room at Sandringham, for Russell had close personal ties with the Prince and Princess of Wales, visiting them often at Sandringham.

Russell stressed function over the form of a dog and, as the Terrier expert Rawdon Lee has stated, claimed that a 'dog with one short leg and three long

Plate 129. *Robert Morley, R.B.A.*
Not a Love Match, *1897. Oil on canvas, 34 x 44ins. (86.5 x 111.5cm).*
While Morley initially specialised in figural works, he soon turned to animal painting. Often exhibiting at the Royal Academy and elsewhere, his paintings have an anecdotal quality which gives them great charm
Collection Ruth Havemeyer Norwood; photography Grant Taylor

Plate 130. *Arthur Wardle, R.I., R.B.C., P.S.*
Wire Fox Terrier, *1897. Oil on canvas.*
This painting is typical of the pure-bred dog portrait, in that the dog is posed as if he were at a dog show in order to show off all the important ways in which he conforms to the standard for the breed. The Wire Fox Terrier had become a separate breed from the Smooth some eighteen years before, in 1879
Photograph courtesy Exclusively Dogs

ones was no eyesore — so long as it could work properly.'

From about 1860 the Fox Terrier had become a popular and important addition to the show ring, while at the same time being kept by fanciers for their working abilities with the badger, the otter, the fox and the water rat. According to one fancier, Reginald Bates, the working Terrier should 'stand on "short" legs, have a thick skin, good rough weather resisting coat, and last but not least, a big heart in a little body. A white dog is by far the best, especially when working with fox or otter hounds.'

Today's Jack Russells are said to descend directly from the original strain

Colour Plate 83. *Arthur Wardle, R.I., R.B.C., P.S.* The Totteridge XI, *1897. Oil on canvas, 28 x 35½ins. (71 x 90cm).*
There are at least two versions of this very famous dog picture of Francis Redmond's Fox Terriers, the earliest of which is in the collection of The Kennel Club in London. This later version is slightly smaller and does not include some of the pentimenti, or artist's changes, evident in The Kennel Club painting
Collection The American Kennel Club; photography Grant Taylor

propagated by Russell. Arthur Heineman, for instance, maintained a fine kennel of hunt Terriers whose pedigrees are traced back to Russell's original strain. In 1894 Heineman was the organiser of The Devon and Somerset Badger Club, subsequently The Parson Jack Russell Club, which remained active until after the founder's death in 1930. Other specialty clubs which stage 'digs' and shows have come into existence, generally being held with hunt Terrier events.

The Rev. Jack Russell was never a devotee of dog shows or show-type Terriers but he was a member of The Kennel Club from its founding in 1873 until his death. He also judged Fox Terriers and attended bench shows, but he always decried the stressing of 'fancy points' over working ability.

Colour Plate 84. *Maud Earl.* Wire Fox Terriers, *1893. Oil on canvas, 18 x 24ins. (45.5 x 61cm).*
During the 1890s, Maud Earl sometimes painted with very little paint on her brush, a technique which had a fresh, spontaneous effect. While these dogs are not named, they are clearly someone's favoured show dogs
The Richard D. Hammond Collection; photography Grant Taylor

Colour Plate 85. *Maud Earl.*
Totteridge Smooth Fox Terriers *(pair). Oil on canvas, each 48 x 24ins. (122 x 61cm). Redmond, also the breeder of* The Totteridge XI *dogs (Colour Plate 83), was the owner of these Smooth Fox Terriers from his famous Totteridge Kennels. The two panels are from a set of four*
Collection The American Kennel Club, gift of Richard D. Hammond; photography Grant Taylor

Plate 131. *Maud Earl.*
Ch. Cackler of Notts and Christopher of Notts, *1899. Oil on canvas, 14 x 18ins. (35.5 x 45.5cm).*
Both these dogs were owned by the Duchess of Newcastle. Cackler, on the left, was not only a top winner, but also a top sire, having a great influence on the breed. Private collection; photography Dave King

Plate 132. *F.W. Rogers.*
Terriers Rabbiting. *Oil on canvas.*
These dogs are more typical of the type which was promoted by the Rev. Jack Russell, who preferred a working Terrier with shorter legs. Russell was a well-known dog show judge, and was active in the early work of The Kennel Club Photograph courtesy The Tryon Gallery

Plate 133. *George Paice.* Bugler, *1894. Oil on canvas, 14 x 18ins. (35.5 x 45.5cm). This Terrier is a coarser dog than that which was winning at the shows in the 1890s, and may well have been a hunt or working Terrier not destined for the show ring* Private collection; photography Grant Taylor

Plate 134. *Alfred Duke.* The Inquisitive Terrier. *Oil on canvas. Victorian artists often played up the interrelationships between animals, and the image of the caged animal looking out at a dog occurs again and again* Private collection; photography Dave King

Colour Plate 86. *Arthur Wardle, R.I., R.B.C., P.S.* Reconnoitering. *Oil on canvas, 18 x 24ins. (45.5 x 61cm). While not dated, this work is typical of the many paintings of Fox Terriers which Wardle completed in the early years of the twentieth century. The dogs are alert and poised for action, waiting at a rabbit's burrow*

Collection Frances G. Scaife; photography Dave King

Colour Plate 88. *Arthur Wardle, R.I., R.B.C., P.S.* Realisation. *Oil on canvas, 20 x 16ins. (51 x 40.5cm). Here the proud champion shows off his catch. Notice how the dog's coat is far less developed than that of the Wire Fox Terriers of today*

Collection The Dog Museum, St. Louis, gift of The Lakeshore Kennel Club; photography Grant Taylor

Colour Plate 87. *Arthur Wardle, R.I., R.B.C., P.S.* Anticipation. *Oil on canvas, 20 x 16ins. (51 x 40.5cm). Along with Colour Plate 88, this is one of a pair of paintings of Terriers rabbiting. Compare the style of this later painting to that of Plate 128, one of the artist's earlier works*

The Richard D. Hammond Collection; photography Grant Taylor

Colour Plate 89. *Arthur Wardle, R.I., R.B.C., P.S.*
Wire Fox Terrier with Puppies. *Oil on canvas, 24½ x 19¼ ins. (62 x 49cm).*
Wardle did a series of paintings depicting various breeds either sitting in or around chairs, using them as props to show off the animals. The red coat is a very effective foil indeed for silhouetting the Fox Terrier

Photograph courtesy MacConnal-Mason Fine Paintings

Plate 135. *Frederick Thomas Daws.*
Wire Fox Terrier. *Oil on board, 10 x 14ins. (25.5 x 35.5cm).*
Daws was a minor dog artist, but in this little painting he has succeeded in capturing the feeling of dogs out on an autumn day
Private collection; photography Grant Taylor

Plate 136. *J. Fitz Marshall, R.B.A.*
Smooth Fox Terrier, *1909. Oil on canvas, 16 x 20ins. (40.5 x 51cm).*
While Marshall's works are relatively rare, he exhibited widely during his lifetime, including at the Royal Academy between 1883 and 1903. This Fox Terrier is very refined indeed, and one cannot help wonder whether or not the artist has stylised the animal
Private collection; photography Dave King

Plate 137. *Arthur Wardle, R.I., R.B.C., P.S.*
Chasing Butterflies. *Oil on canvas, 22 x 16ins. (56 x 40.5cm).*
While these are pure-bred dogs, this delightful portrait of Wire Fox Terriers at play is really a pet portrait, revelling in the 'dogginess' of its subjects. Wardle only rarely depicted dogs playing, favouring animals at work or in a show pose Private collection; photography Dave King

Colour Plate 90. *Marguerite Frobisher.*
In The Land of Dreams. *Oil on canvas, 15½ x 21ins. (39.5 x 53.5cm).*
Marguerite Frobisher was born in Leeds and studied under Lucy Kemp-Welch. While impressionistic in style, Frobisher has nevertheless captured the essence of the animals. Note in particular the left rear leg of the puppy characteristically jutting out from underneath Private collection; photography Grant Taylor

Colour Plate 91. *George Vernon Stokes.*
Winter Sports. *Oil on canvas, 16 x 20ins. (40.5 x 51cm).*
Stokes was an artist of considerable talent who was best known for his illustrations for books on the dog. This painting may well have been an experiment for him, as he only rarely worked in such an impressionistic style Private collection; photography Dave King

Colour Plate 92. *Arthur Wardle, R.I., R.B.C., P.S.*
Two Terriers and a Snake. *Watercolour on paper, 26 x 20ins. (66 x 51cm).*
While Wardle is today known for his oil paintings, he did a great number of watercolours and pastels, including many of African and Indian animals

The Richard D. Hammond Collection; photography Grant Taylor

Plate 138. *Frank Paton.* Rough and Ready, *1884. Oil on canvas, 21 x 27¼ ins. (53.5 x 69cm).*
Evidently waiting for his master, this dog is quite typical of Irish Terriers in the late nineteenth century. Although well painted it is not characteristic of the artist's work, who usually painted in a highly detailed style
Photograph courtesy Arthur Ackermann & Son, Ltd.

The Irish Terrier

Many writers claim that Irish Terriers have been around since the end of the eighteenth century, but until the mid-1880s the breed was virtually unknown in England. Even Idstone's book on dogs published in 1872 fails to mention the breed. Three years later, a group of fanciers in Ireland organised a show in Dublin for Irish Terriers, attracting around fifty entries for the event.

Plate 139. *Arthur Wardle, R.I., R.B.C., P.S.* Irish Terrier, *1897. Oil on canvas, 16 x 20ins. (40.5 x 51cm).*
This portrait is typical of many of the Terrier portraits Wardle did during his career. The dog is characteristically in profile, facing right and displaying all her Terrier alertness. Compare her uncropped ears to those of the Paton painting (Plate 138)
Photograph courtesy Exclusively Dogs

Plate 140. *Thomas Blinks.* Irish Terriers. *Oil on canvas, 14 x 18ins. (35.5 x 45.5cm). Blinks, along with Arthur Wardle, was a master at capturing a tense moment. These Terriers are alert and ready to move in a split second*

Photograph courtesy Richard Green

According to Rawdon Lee, the early volumes of The Kennel Club Stud Book did not contain special classes for Irish Terriers which were grouped with Wire Fox Terriers. However, the 1870s saw the breed become more popular, principally due to George R. Krehl, who presented several Irish Terriers to Queen Victoria.

The earliest dogs of any importance in the breed were George Jamison's Sport, Howard Waterhouse's Killiney Boy, W. Graham's Erin, G.R. Krehl's Sporter, and Mr. Pim's Play Boy.

The Welsh Terrier

Black-and-tan coloured Terriers have existed in Wales for centuries and were probably the progenitors of the modern Welsh Terrier. According to Walter Glynn, writing in Cassell's *Book of the Dog,* the Welsh Terrier 'is in reality identical with the old black-and-tan wire-haired dog which was England's first Terrier, and which has taken such a prominent part in the production and evolution of all the other varieties of sporting terrier.'

Indeed, in Carnarvonshire, there is evidence that a John Jones of Ynysfor, worked Black and Tan Terriers with a pack of Otterhounds around 1760. It was not until 1884, however, that specimens appeared on the show bench. About that year, several fanciers met to try to improve matters, the end result being the founding of The Welsh Terrier Club and the recognition of the breed by The Kennel Club.

Just after the Welsh Terrier made its début at shows, a rival, similar in size and colour, called the Old English Black and Tan Terrier, appeared on the scene. When The Kennel Club agreed to its entry in the Stud Book in 1886, the classification 'Welsh' or 'Old English Wire-Haired Black and Tan Terrier' was given. Within a short time, however, the 'Old English Black-and-Tan' more or less faded away, and it was in 1888 that the Welsh Terrier, as such, first appeared in the Stud Book.

Plate 141. *W. V. Longe.* Airedale Terriers in a Landscape, *1886. Oil on board, 12 x 16¾ ins. (30.5 x 42.5cm). These are clearly working Terriers, for a shovel is lying beside them, ready if necessary to dig out a rabbit. Moreover, they do not have the refinements of show dogs such as that in Colour Plate 93*

Photograph courtesy Bonham's

Colour Plate 93. *Arthur Wardle, R.I., R.B.C., P.S.* Ch. Dumbarton Lass, *1897. Oil on canvas, 16 x 20ins. (40.5 x 51cm).*

Ch. Dumbarton Lass was a well known Airedale in England who had an active show career in America. Notice how the artist has highlighted the area behind the dog, silhouetting her coat

Private collection; photography Dave King

The Airedale Terrier

The Airedale, the largest of the British Terriers, is not of ancient origin. It probably appeared around 1850 in Yorkshire, undoubtedly a cross between the Otter Hound and the Welsh or Old English Black and Tan Terrier, and was originally known as the Waterside Terrier or the Bingley Terrier. Later, partly at the suggestion of Dr. Gordon Stables and Hugh Dalziel, it was named the Airedale Terrier because of its popularity in the valley of the Aire.

Another group of Terriers which logically fits together with the Airedale includes those which were also earth dogs, but were bred in Scotland: the Scottish Terrier, the West Highland White Terrier, the Cairn Terrier, the Border Terrier and the Dandie Dinmont, all breeds which were quickly appropriated by the show ring.

Colour Plate 94. *Arthur Wardle, R.I., R.B.C., P.S.*
Airedale Head Studies. *Oil on canvas, 13 x 20ins. (33 x 51cm).*
Wardle was a master at capturing the expression of Terriers. This painting is from a series using a similar format, in which two head studies are silhouetted against a coloured background

Private collection; photography Dave King

The Scottish Terrier

The Scottish Terrier, once called the Aberdeen Terrier, had been popular in the Highlands for generations, wrote Rawdon Lee in the third edition of *Modern Dogs* (1903), 'where, strangely enough, he was known as the Skye Terrier, although he is so different from the long-coated, unsporting-like looking creature with which that name is now associated...I have seen an engraving of a picture at the close of 1700 in which there is a capital representation of a Scottish Terrier, one quite of the modern type.'

During the last half of the nineteenth century, many Cairns, Skyes, Dandie Dinmonts, and West Highland Whites were exhibited routinely under the title of 'Scottish Terriers' and, in the course of time, a great commotion arose over what was meant by breeders who described their dogs as the 'true' Scottish Terrier.

In the issues of the *Live Stock Journal* for January to May 1879, a heated controversy arose as to whether or not there actually was such a dog as a pure-bred 'Scottish Terrier'. Letters were published, written by various canine fanciers, prominent among whom were 'Strathbogie' (Captain Gordon Murray), 'The Badger' (Sir Paynton Piggott, M.V.O.), Sir John Everett Millais, Dr. Gordon Stables, and Thomas Gray. Murray and Piggott in particular wanted to tell the English all about the breed they knew to be real. Despite their many disappointments, the two men persevered and were eventually rewarded by S.E. Shirley, President of The Kennel Club, who established classes for Scottish Terriers at The Kennel Club show which was held at Alexandra Palace in 1879. They were called Hard-Haired Scotch Terriers at the time. In subsequent years, the 'Scottie' became one of the most popular Terriers in Britain and held that position for many years.

Plate 142. *Maud Earl.*
Taken by Surprise, *c.1900. Oil on canvas, 16 x 30ins. (40.5 x 76cm).*
Maud Earl believed that prints made from paintings such as this added to her popularity and allowed a wide range of people to enjoy her work. Someone has just startled this Scottie while he was eating, the ball caught in mid-air
Collection Mrs. Damon Raike; photography courtesy Schopplein Studio

Plate 143. *Lilian Cheviot.*
Black and White. *Oil on canvas, 22 x 26ins. (56 x 66cm).*
The dogs in many of Cheviot's portraits have soft, sympathetic expressions, with somewhat stylised coats. This painting is very similar in style to that in Plate 144 The Richard D. Hammond Collection; photography Grant Taylor

Plate 144. *Lilian Cheviot.*
A West Highland White and a Scottish Terrier in a Landscape, *c.1930. Oil on canvas, 25 x 30ins. (40.5 x 76cm).*
This portrait is typical of many of the dog paintings of Lilian Cheviot, with the landscape idealised and the sky a characteristic blue-mauve. The artist often depicted these breeds in the Scottish Highlands Photograph courtesy Iona Antiques

Plate 145. *Arthur Wardle, R.I., R.B.C., P.S.*
Scottish Terriers, *c.1935. Oil on panel, 11 x 11ins. (28 x 28cm).*
One of a series of dog paintings on this scale, this example is characteristic of Wardle's Terrier paintings, for the dogs are at work, in typical poses. Notice how Wardle includes very little of the sky, stressing the dogs as the primary subject matter
Private collection

The West Highland White Terrier

The West Highland White Terrier is descended from white and pale cream Cairn Terriers which, according to Clifford Hubbard in *Dogs in Britain,* had usually been destroyed at birth for reasons based mostly on superstition. The Malcolm family, of Poltalloch in Argyllshire, thought differently. They believed that a white dog used to destroy vermin in the rocky crags of the Highlands was easier to see. Known as the Poltalloch Terrier or the Roseneath Terrier, Colonel Malcolm said that prior to their appearance at dog shows they had been bred and maintained by his family for more than a hundred years. So while most Cairn breeders were eliminating the whites from their strains, the Malcolm family were working the opposite way and rejecting all the coloured dogs. By the time West Highland White Terriers were introduced at dog shows by Colonel E.D. Malcolm at the beginning of the twentieth century, they were firmly established.

The Cairn Terrier

Scotland was the birthplace of many of the rough-coated, short-legged Terrier breeds which are closely associated with one another, such as the Cairn, the Scottish, the Skye, the Clydesdale or Paisley, and the West Highland White Terrier. Which of them was the primary type is difficult to say, although many experts suggest it was the Cairn. These small Terriers — bred to bolt and destroy foxes, otters, badgers, and other small vermin from the cairns and

Colour Plate 95. *George W. Horlor.*
Give a Poor Dog a Bone, *1856. Oil on canvas, 17½ x 22¼ ins. (44.5 x 56.5cm). Horlor's individual portraits are often brilliantly painted, with details of the dog's anatomy just loosely sketched in. These dogs, a West Highland White, a King Charles Spaniel and a Cairn Terrier, are obviously pets, anxious to please their owners*

Photograph courtesy MacConnal-Mason Fine Paintings

Plate 146. *Thomas Earl.* Terriers, *1881. Oil on canvas, 24 x 30ins. (61 x 76cm). Thomas Earl specialised in painting dogs and rabbits, exhibiting at the Royal Academy between 1840 and 1880. While the dog on the left is an early Cairn, that on the right is probably an early West Highland White Terrier* Collection Frances G. Scaife; photography Dave King

Colour Plate 96. *Maud Earl.* Come Play With Me, *1900. Oil on canvas, 30 x 40ins. (76 x 101.5cm). Maud Earl painted several Cairn Terrier paintings around this time, but this is perhaps the most charming — the image of the happy pet ready to play. Notice how little coat the dog has, compared with the Cairn Terrier of today* Private collection; photography Dave King

Plate 147. *Edwin Douglas.*
A Cairn Terrier in a Red Armchair *(detail). Oil on canvas, 28 x 21¾ ins. (71 x 55cm). Douglas excelled at capturing the coat texture and expression of dogs, the one seen here performing a trick for her master*
Photograph courtesy Christie's South Kensington

Plate 148. *George Armfield.*
King Charles Spaniels with Terriers and a Parrot in a Parkland Landscape. *Oil on canvas, 44 x 34ins. (111.5 x 86.5cm).*
This is one of the largest and most accomplished of Armfield's paintings, incorporating a bird, several breeds of dog and a garden landscape. Armfield's paintings are usually small, depicting two or three dogs at most
Photograph courtesy Christie's South Kensington

crags of the Highlands — had been kept for generations both by owners of large estates and the farmers of the small crofts.

There is no doubt that the Cairn originated centuries ago, for many early authorities mention such a Terrier. Dr. Caius makes reference to these vermin-killing dogs in 1576, and there are depictions of dogs resembling Cairns as we know them today in paintings of the period.

The history of the breed was closely associated with the Isle of Skye, so it seems fitting that when it first appeared at the Inverness Dog Show in 1909, it should be classified as a 'Shorthaired Skye'. There were scores of complaints by Skye Terrier enthusiasts and the controversy raged up until 1910 when the name of this hardy little dog was changed to the Cairn Terrier, a designation chosen because of the nature of its work. Two years later, the Cairn was granted official breed status by The Kennel Club.

Plate 149. *W.J. Stevenson.* Border Terrier, *1879. Oil on canvas, 19 x 23ins. (48 x 58.5cm).*
Border Terriers were bred to chase the fox to ground, and dig him out if necessary. This dog's rather sharp expression would suggest that he is ready for business Photograph courtesy Christie's

Plate 150. *Alfred Duke.* Border Terrier with Rabbit. *Oil on canvas, 18 x 24ins. (45.5 x 61cm).*
The Border Terrier had its origins on either side of the Cheviot Hills which form the Border country, and was very much a working Terrier. While this dog has a somewhat dishevelled appearance, he is clearly proud of his catch
Photograph courtesy Tryon Gallery

The Border Terrier

As its name implies, the Border Terrier originated along the border between England and Scotland. It was used by local farmers and shepherds to hunt and kill foxes which often depleted the farmer's livestock and worried the shepherd's flocks. Unlike some of the other earlier Terriers it was bred with legs long enough to keep up with a horse, a distinct advantage.

A persistent and tireless little dog, the Border Terrier was used as a working Terrier until the early twentieth century, when it was appropiated by the show ring. Perhaps because of its late introduction to the world of conformation shows, there are very few nineteenth century paintings that can with any certainty be identified as Border Terriers.

Colour Plate 97. *Richard Ansdell, R.A.*
Highland Tod, Fox Hunter, *1859. Oil on canvas, 29 x 63½ins. (73.5 x 161.5cm).*
This painting is typical of the work of Ansdell, who often painted scenes in the Scottish Highlands. Notice the two early Dandie Dinmonts at the front.
Collection The American Kennel Club; photography Dave King

The Dandie Dinmont Terrier

The origins of the Dandie Dinmont are unknown and it is difficult to decide where legend ends and reality begins. Some say that the Dandie's long body and short legs resulted by crossing strains of rough coated Terriers with Dachshunds; others say that rough coated Terriers were crossed with Otter Hounds. The most probable interpretation of the Dandie Dinmont's origin is that it was developed from the native rough-haired Terrier breeds that worked in the hill country along the border between Scotland and England.

What is known is that as far back as the seventeenth century these dogs were owned by farmers of the Border counties and were used to kill the badger, fox

Plate 151. *George W. Horlor.*
What Will He Do With It?, *1882. Oil on canvas, 17 x 21ins. (43 x 53.5cm).*
Horlor was an animal and sporting painter whose style is characterised by a soft, painterly brushstroke. While he specialised in shooting scenes in the Scottish Highlands, this example of his work might be considered an archetypal pet portrait
Private collection; photography Dave King

and otter. One early owner of the breed was Willy 'Piper' Allan, of Holystone, a man who is also credited with developing the Bedlington Terrier. One of Allan's pack of rough-coated, short-legged Terriers, a dog named Hitchem, excited the interest of the Duke of Northumberland who wished to purchase the animal. In spite of the Duke's generous offer of a life rent lease of a farm, Allan refused to sell. 'Na, na, ma Lord,' he said, 'keep yer ferum. What wud a piper do wi' a ferum?' After Piper's death in 1704, his sons and grandsons carried on the strain.

These courageous Terriers were unknown outside the border area until 1814, when Sir Walter Scott published his novel *Guy Mannering*. Scott

Colour Plate 98. *John Emms.* Dandie Dinmont Terriers, *1889. Oil on canvas, 24 x 47ins. (61 x 119.5cm).*
This is an extraordinary picture of Dandie Dinmonts. Although the dogs are not identified, it was obviously a group portrait of someone's prize-winning Dandies
Photograph courtesy Burlington Gallery

Colour Plate 99. *Margaret Collyer.*
Dandie Dinmont Terrier, *1899. Oil on canvas, 28 x 37ins. (71 x 94cm).*
Margaret Collyer was a Nottingham artist, and exhibited regularly at the Royal Academy between 1893 and 1910. This Dandie Dinmont is set up in a standard show pose. Notice how little coat the dog has compared with examples of today Photograph courtesy Iona Antiques

patterned one of the characters after James Davidson of Hyndlea, a farmer who maintained a pack of the Terriers. Scott called him 'Dandie Dinmont' and, like Davidson, Dinmont kept a pack of Terriers, which were named Auld Pepper, Auld Mustard, Young Pepper, Young Mustard, Little Pepper, and Little Mustard. Scott wrote of them: 'They fear naething that ever cam we' a hairy skin on't.'

The breed, then called the Pepper and Mustard, was soon regarded with favour. Rawdon Lee in the third edition of *Modern Dogs* (Terriers) writes that: 'The original Dandie Dinmont Terrier stood higher on legs and was shorter in body than the modern article. This may be observed by reference to early pictures of this dog, notably that by Landseer in his well-known portrait of Sir Walter Scott. Here a "mustard" dog is introduced, said to have been painted from a Terrier then at Abbotsford, and which originally came from James Davidson.'

By the time of Davidson's death in 1820, the breed had been renamed the Dandie Dinmont. Although classes were provided for Dandies at dog shows as early as 1861, little excitement was generated until the Birmingham Show of 1867. There, the judge refused to award any prizes to Dandies on the grounds that they were 'nothing but a bunch of mongrels.' Countless letters appeared in *The Field* elaborating on this theme. Much confusion prevailed as to correct breed points until 1876, when The Dandie Dinmont Terrier Club was formed and a breed standard drawn up and adopted.

Plate 152. *Helen Cridland.*
Dandie Dinmont and Puppy, *1891. Oil on canvas, 20 x 30ins. (51 x 76cm).*
Known as a painter of domestic scenes, Cridland has very sympathetically painted this portrait of a bitch with her puppy Photograph courtesy Christie's South Kensington

Plate 153. *F. Bailey.*
Boy, Three Dogs and Dead Game, *1884. Oil on canvas, 47 x 38ins. (119.5 x 96.5cm). This portrait of a young man with his Terriers captures the alert, quick nature of the Norwich Terrier, somewhat larger than today's breed* Collection The Dog Museum, St. Louis, gift of Richard D. Hammond

Plate 154. Gourlay Steell.
Sketch of Brandy, *1870. Oil on board, 10 x 10ins. (25.5 x 25.5cm).*
In just a few short strokes, Steell has created a memorable portrait of a little Norwich Terrier type dog, full of expression. Steell succeeded Landseer as Queen Victoria's animal painter in Scotland, and one can see a similarity between the two artists' work Collection Gilbert S. Kahn; photograph courtesy Carlos Domenech

The Norwich and the Norfolk Terrier

Until recently these were recognised as one and the same breed. In 1964 The Kennel Club recognised what was up until then known as a drop-eared Norwich Terrier as a Norfolk Terrier. In 1979 The American Kennel Club followed suit. Developed in Britain as a small sporting Terrier, the breed evidently got its start as a ratting Terrier in East Anglia, and by the 1880s it had become a fashionable pet among the undergraduates of Cambridge University.

The progenitors of the Norwich Terrier as we know it today developed near the city of Norwich. It was in Market Harborough, however, that Frank 'Roughrider' Jones developed a dog to be used as a ratter and to bolt foxes. In 1914, one of his breeding was the first Norwich Terrier to be imported to America, where it was known as the Jones Terrier. While known by most today as loyal and affectionate pets, the Norwich and Norfolk Terriers have not lost their working abilities, going to ground whenever given the chance.

Plate 155. *Philip Eustace Stretton.*
Terrier, *1884. Oil on canvas, 10 x 8ins. (25.5 x 20.5cm).*
This is a fine example of Stretton's work, a simple, direct portrait of a Norfolk Terrier type executed with an almost photographic realism. There is, however, a hint of sadness in the dog's face, for during the nineteenth century artists often imbued their portraits of dogs with human emotions
Photograph courtesy MacConnal-Mason Fine Paintings

Plate 156. *J. Beard.*
The Otter Hunt. *Oil on canvas, 27 x 36ins. (68.5 x 91.5cm). Otter hunting was first practised in Britain when otter were found to be preying on fish in the streams and rivers. In the late nineteenth century, it became a fashionable sport*

Collection Frances G. Scaife; photography Dave King

The Otter Hound

As its name implies, the Otter Hound was bred to hunt otters, considered at one time in England to be a great nuisance, for they preyed on fish in rivers and streams.

While some believe that the Otter Hound developed from a cross between the Southern Hound and the Welsh Harrier or the Bloodhound, its exact origins are still a matter of debate. It did, however, originate in France, and is very similar in appearance to the old 'Vendée' hound.

The breed's origins in England are very early indeed, for Henry II was the

Plate 157. *Walter Hunt, Jnr.*
On the Scent, *1900. Oil on canvas, 28 x 40ins. (71 x 101.5cm). Hunt was a well known animal painter who in this portrait captures all the excitement of the hunt. Compare this to the relatively calm composition of Plate 156*

Private collection; photography Grant Taylor

Plate 158. *Maud Earl.*
Near the Holt, *c.1905. Oil on canvas, 18 x 30ins. (45.5 x 76cm).*
This painting of Otter Hounds is typical of Earl's work around 1905. It is one in a series of twelve paintings entitled The Sportsman's Year *which were reproduced in a portfolio of prints. This painting corresponds to the month of July* Collection Mrs. Walter M. Jeffords; photography Grant Taylor

earliest known Master of the Otterhounds, and Queen Elizabeth the first lady Master. Described as early as the fourteenth century to be 'a rough sort of dog, between a hound and a terrier', the dogs were first used to hunt otter out of necessity, and then as a sport, for it was the only kind of hunting possible between April and September. Otter Hounds were kept in packs, and by the nineteenth century many famous packs had been developed, including the Hawkstone Pack which was reputed to have killed some 704 otters between 1870 and 1890. The heyday for the Otter Hound was from mid- to late nineteenth century in England, when eighteen to twenty packs hunted regularly.

Plate 159. *Arthur Wardle, R.I., R.B.C., P.S.*
Otter Hounds. *Oil on board, 6½ x 7¾ins. (16.5 x 19.5cm).*
This little sketch captures all the excitement and anticipation of Otter Hounds waiting to go on the hunt Photograph courtesy Sara Davenport Fine Paintings

Plate 160. *Sydenham Edwards.* The Bloodhound. *From* Cynographia Britannica, *1799-1805.*
In the late eighteenth century the Bloodhound was used to pursue deer which had been shot and injured, but not killed. Were this illustration not named, one would hardly imagine them to be ancestors of our present-day breed
Collection The American Kennel Club; photography Dave King

The Bloodhound

Once known as the St. Hubert's Hound, this is a very old breed, its progenitors known in parts of Europe from before the Crusades. Esteemed for its great scenting powers, it is still used today to track criminals or missing persons.

The breed as we know it today, however, became popular in England in the nineteenth century, and although Bloodhound packs were certainly kept before that time, the advent of dog shows ensured their preservation and increased popularity. Classes for Bloodhounds were first put on at the Birmingham Show in 1860, when the famous Druid was shown. Among others Edwin Brough of Wyndyate near Scarborough was instrumental in keeping interest in the breed alive.

Plate 161. *Philip Reinagle, R.A.*
Bloodhound *(detail). Engraving from* The Sportsman's Cabinet, *1803.*
Evidently the early Bloodhound was only one colour in contrast to the black and tan which predominates today. This and the absence of a heavy head and prominent dewlap make it virtually unrecognisable as a Bloodhound
Collection The American Kennel Club; photography Dave King

Above: Plate 162. *John Sargent Noble, R.B.A.*
On the Scent. *Oil on canvas, 53 x 43ins. (134.5 x 109cm).*
In the nineteenth century Bloodhounds were often used to track criminals or people who had lost their way. The artist has given these dogs a noble and almost monumental quality as they give voice at the discovery of a hat Private collection; photography Grant Taylor

Left: Plate 163. *John Sargent Noble, R.B.A.*
The Captive. *Oil on panel, 24 x 18ins. (61 x 45.5cm).*
Noble was a pupil of Landseer and exhibited at the Royal Academy between 1871 and 1895. His animals exhibit a strong understanding of anatomy, the Bloodhound being a particularly difficult subject Collection Mr. and Mrs. Robert Raife; photography Dave King

Opposite: Plate 165. *Reuben Ward Binks.*
Brigadier, *1935. Watercolour, 12½ x 15¾ins. (31.5 x 40cm).*
This is one of the Bloodhounds from the Giralda Kennels in New Jersey, owned by Mrs. Geraldine Rockefeller Dodge. She commissioned over two hundred portraits by Binks and, unlike many of them, this one has a loose, sketch-like quality Private collection; photography Dave King

Plate 164. *Charles Burton Barber.*
Ch. Don, *c.1880. Watercolour, 6 x 8ins. (15 x 20.5cm).*
Mrs. Humphries owned the Bloodhound Don, a dog who won many prizes on the show bench, including first prize at Alexandra Palace in 1877. In addition to his fine physical characteristics, Don was known for his obedience and gentle disposition
Photograph courtesy Arthur Ackermann & Son, Ltd.

Plate 166. *Sydenham Edwards.*
Newfoundlands. *From* Cynographia Britannica, *1799-1805.*
The early Newfoundland had less bone and substance than our present-day dog, looking more like a retriever. Note also that at the time he painted it, the now standard black variety was not even included in Edwards's portrait Collection The American Kennel Club; photography Dave King

The Newfoundland

Another breed closely associated with the nineteenth century was the Newfoundland. As with many of the breeds, its exact origins are uncertain, but it is thought to have originated in Newfoundland, Canada, and that its ancestors were brought there by fishermen from Europe.

Known in popular legend as a life-saving dog, there are several eighteenth century accounts which indicate that the distinction was well earned, including one of a child who fell into the River Tyne and was rescued by a Newfoundland. Accounts of the breed's life-saving activities continued until well into the nineteenth century and the Newfoundland is now forever fixed in the popular imagination as a dog who saves lives. Indeed, the majority of paintings of Newfoundlands which survive from the nineteenth century somehow allude to this. Landseer's portrait of *A Distinguished Member of the Humane Society* (Plate 169), shows a black and white Newfoundland on a wharf, looking out confidently at the viewer. Landseer was so fond of the black and white variety of the breed that it eventually became known as the Landseer Newfoundland.

Plate 167. *Philip Reinagle, R.A.* Newfoundland Dog. *Engraving from* The Sportsman's Cabinet, *1803*
This portrait of a Landseer Newfoundland named Bell, seems to indicate that the Husky may have been one of the breed's ancestors. Most agree that the dog originated in Newfoundland
Collection The American Kennel Club; photography Dave King

Plate 168. *Samuel John Egbert Jones.*
Bay Hack with Newfoundland, *1829. Oil on canvas, 17 x 29ins. (43 x 73.5cm).*
Horses and dogs were often depicted together in eighteenth and nineteenth century British pictures, as if waiting for their master. The black and white variety of Newfoundland, known as the Landseer, was prevalent in the early nineteenth century
Photograph courtesy Arthur Ackermann & Son, Ltd.

Plate 169. *Sir Edwin Landseer, R.A.*
A Distinguished Member of the Humane Society — a Landseer Newfoundland, *c.1838. Oil on canvas, 43¾ x 56ins. (111 x 142cm).*
This was one of Landseer's most popular subjects; engraved by his brother Thomas, it sold innumerable copies Photograph courtesy The Tryon Gallery

Plate 170. *Horatio Henry Couldery.*
The President, *1868. Oil on canvas, 20 x 24ins. (51 x 61cm).*
While Couldery only rarely anthropomorphised his dogs to such an extent, one can see that his choice of breed was very appropriate. This Newfoundland was chosen in order to depict a rather forlorn, worried look Collection The Dog Museum, St. Louis, gift of Frank T. Sabella

Plate 171. *Sir Edwin Landseer, R.A.*
Princess Mary and Nelson, *c.1839. Oil on canvas, 56⅛ x 44⅛ ins. (142.5 x 112cm). Exhibited at the Royal Academy, this painting illustrates a then popular trick for dogs: the Newfoundland was intended to toss the biscuit up in the air and catch it in his mouth*
Collection Her Majesty the Queen

The St. Bernard

The origins of the St. Bernard are uncertain, and their history surrounded by romance. We do know that the breed has been associated for centuries with the Great St. Bernard Hospice in the Swiss Alps, at the summit of the St. Bernard Pass which links Switzerland to Italy. Oliver Goldsmith (1730-1774) writes: 'They have a breed of noble dogs, whose extraordinary sagacity often enables them to rescue the traveller. Though the perishing man lie ten or even twenty feet beneath the snow, the delicacy of smell with which they can trace him offers a chance of escape.'

The perils of crossing the Alps have long interested writers and artists and many legends have flourished about the rescue work done by the Hospice's Alpine Mastiffs, or St. Bernards as they later became known. The most famous concerns Barry, the gallant dog credited with saving forty-one lives, including that of an unconscious child trapped on an icy ledge. According to the story,

Plate 172. *Sir Edwin Landseer, R.A.*
Alpine Mastiffs Reanimating a Distressed Traveller, *1820. Oil on canvas, 74 x 93ins. (188 x 236cm).*
Landseer has chosen the exciting moment when the St. Bernards have found the fallen traveller, no doubt caught in the Alps by an avalanche. This breed was known for its uncanny ability to find lost people in the Alps, even if buried twenty or thirty feet below the snow
Collection The Warner Collection of Gulf States Paper Corporation, Tuscaloosa, Alabama

though no human could reach the youngster, Barry inched down the ledge and revived the boy by licking his face.

Lion, a dog that lived about the same time as Barry, appears in a portrait painted in 1815 by Landseer. Lion is believed to have been the first St. Bernard to arrive in England. Originally from the Hospice, he came into the possession of a Mrs. Boode who lived at Leasowe Castle, Cheshire. He sired many offspring, among them a dog named Caesar, which is thought to be portrayed in Landseer's large painting *Alpine Mastiffs Reanimating a Distressed Traveller* (Plate 172).

Except for a few names, until the organisation of dog shows, there is little to record of the St. Bernard in Britain; then known as the Mount St. Bernard Dog — the breed was officially named the St. Bernard in 1865. Some early dogs of the 1830s and 1840s include Sir Thomas Lauder's Barry, Mr. Lukey's

Plate 173. *Horatio Henry Couldery.*
Recumbent St. Bernard, *c.1890. Oil on canvas, 13 x 18ins. (33 x 45.5cm).*
Couldery, who is known for his depictions of cats as well as dogs, had a highly finished, tight style which was particularly successful on a small scale. This painting of a smooth-coated St. Bernard probably dates from the time when there was a great fascination for the breed in Britain
Collection Mr. and Mrs. Michael Svirsky; photography Dave King

Plate 175. *R.S. Moseley.*
Sandringham Count. *Oil on canvas, 24 x 18ins. (61 x 45.5cm).*
Sandringham, the Norfolk home of Edward VII and Queen Alexandra, had very extensive kennels, with accommodation for well over one hundred dogs. This portrait is typical of Moseley's style, for he often painted with a heavy impasto Photograph courtesy Christie's South Kensington

Plate 174. *John Emms.*
Recumbent St. Bernard, *1893. Oil on canvas.*
Even if this painting were not signed, one would easily recognise the characteristic style of John Emms, the rich colour and strong brushstroke creating an almost sketch-like quality
Photograph courtesy Burlington Galleries

Lion (it has been written that the number of Barrys and Lions in early St. Bernard history rivals that of the number of French kings named Charles and Louis), and Queen Victoria's Alp and Glory.

Even though there was enormous early interest in the breed, the St. Bernard's true renown began only when the Rev. J.C. Macdona dazzled the show world with his dog Tell. Macdona, who is called the father of the St. Bernard fancy in England, purchased Tell from Switzerland for the express purpose of breeding in England. Wherever he appeared with Tell, an enthusiastic crowd gathered. 'Stonehenge' wrote that 'the first prize was invariably awarded to him by acclamation;' indeed to encourage Macdona to enter Tell in a show, the rules, if need be, were modified. We read how the dog was brought to the show at his convenience 'and resigned himself to being chained up, submitting with heroic resignation to the various trials of patience and affront to his dignity...' One of Tell's sons was presented to the Prince of Wales (later King Edward VII).

The breed club was formed in London in 1880, and in 1887 at the International Congress in Zurich, Switzerland, a breed standard was drafted which was accepted internationally.

The Poodle

The Poodle was very popular indeed in the late nineteenth century, with many fanciers owning this breed exclusively. Mrs. Claude Hay (Plate 181), for instance, was one of the members of The Ladies' Kennel Association who enjoyed the breed: 'Words can never express what our doggies are to myself and my husband — I think were it a case of one meal only to be got, the doggies would have it. They are consulted in everything, and always give an answer, sometimes the wag of a tail or a forlorn look, this mostly when friends, not lovers of dogs, have sent them no invitation to accompany "Father and Mother".'

Given their ancient history and popularity, it is surprising that Poodles were not more often depicted in art. While known today primarily as pets, they were originally water dogs trained to retrieve waterfowl.

Although the Poodle is thought of as a French dog, there is little doubt that it originated in Germany, under the name *Pudel.* It was, of course, very popular in France, in particular during the reign of Louis XVI, and while there were certainly Poodles in England during the eighteenth century, they were first exhibited at dog shows only in 1875. Miss Quain's *Zulu* was the first English champion, soon followed by many others.

The Poodle quickly became very popular at dog shows, and while most around this time had an early version of our present day show clip, there was a brief fashion for the corded coat. Very difficult to care for, the hair was oiled so that it would not break, and the natural curl of the hair made to fall into corkscrew-like locks of hair (Colour Plate 102). The sight of a corded Poodle was very impressive indeed, and great crowds would gather when they were shown. Unfortunately, as the corded coat could not be brushed or easily cleaned, the fashion soon fell out of favour.

Plate 176. *John Wootton.* The Dancing Dogs. *Oil on canvas, 44 x 54ins. (111.5 x 137cm).*
One can only assume that these performing dogs were the favoured pets of one of Wootton's aristocratic clients. They are, however, given great distinction by their classical surroundings Collection Wallington House: The National Trust

Plate 177. Richard Ramsey Reinagle.
Poodle and Wildcat, *1793. Oil on canvas, 60 x 48ins. (152.5 x 122cm).*
Richard Ramsay was the son of the artist Philip Reinagle, R.A., and like his father often placed his animals in extensive landscapes. The composition, although vertical, is curiously similar to a Fox Terrier painting by Boultbee (Plate 125) Photograph courtesy Arthur Ackermann & Son, Ltd

Plate 178. *John Watkins Chapman.*
White Poodles with a Bird, *1858. Oil on canvas, 24½ x 29½ins. (62 x 75cm).*
This is the archetypal pet portrait, the beribboned dogs relaxing on the sofa. Even the family parrot was included, as it was in Landseer's portrait of Queen Victoria's pets, Plate 200

Photograph courtesy Iona Antiques

Plate 179. *Charles Hancock.*
A Pet Dog, *1875. Oil on panel, 8½ x 10¼ins. (21.5 x 26cm). It is sometimes very difficult to identify the breed in early dog paintings. Is this a an unclipped Poodle or an early Bichon Frisé?*

Photograph courtesy Arthur Ackermann & Son, Ltd

Colour Plate 100. *James Ward, R.A.*
Buff, *1812. Oil on wood panel, 27¼ x 36ins. (69 x 91.5cm).. Ward, who had an individualistic, almost romantic style, was known primarily for his horse portraits, although this portrait of the black Poodle Buff indicates that he would have been an equally good dog painter*
Photograph courtesy The Tryon Gallery

Colour Plate 101. *J. Jack.*
Parti-Coloured Poodle on the Beach with a Man's Hat, *1867. Oil on canvas, 18½ x 24ins. (47 x 61cm).*
While little is known about this artist, the message of the painting is clear; the dog, dripping with water, has picked up the hat of someone lost at sea. Compare this dog with that in Plate 177, painted some seventy-five years before Collection Mrs. Vincent Astor; photography Grant Taylor

Plate 180. *Nevison Arthur Loraine, R.B.A.*
Mouton, *c.1890. Oil on canvas, 24 x 28ins. (61 x 71cm). The practice of inscribing the dog's name on the canvas is more a French than British convention. In any case, this Poodle is clearly a pampered pet* Collection The Dog Museum, St. Louis, gift of Frank T. Sabella; photography Grant Taylor

Plate 181. *Mrs. Claude Hay, active in The Ladies' Kennel Association, here proudly poses with two of her Poodles and their assorted dog show trophies. Reproduced from* The Ladies' Kennel Journal, *c.1895*

Plate 182. *Maud Earl.* Black Standard Poodle, *1906. Oil on canvas, 24 x 20ins. (61 x 51cm).*
Maud Earl did a series of paintings around 1905 which silhouetted the dog against a simple, pale background, often a mauve-grey. This particular example is given an anthropomorphic twist by the addition of an open book Private collection; photography Dave King

Plate 183. *Maud Earl.* Ch. Nunsoe Duc de la Terrace of Blakeen, *1935. Oil on board, 36 x 60ins. (91.5 x 152.5cm).*
This portrait of a white Standard Poodle owned by the American dog fancier Mrs. Sherman Hoyt was painted when Earl was about sixty-seven years old. The dramatic water setting was appropriate, for while most are now pets, Standard Poodles were originally water dogs who retrieved game Collection The American Kennel Club; photography Dave King

Colour Plate 102. *Lucy Waller.*
Ch. Joe II. *Oil on canvas, 26 x 32ins. (66 x 81cm).*
Corded Poodles, popular in the 1890s, created quite a sensation in the show ring, with members of the public queuing just to catch a glimpse of one. The style for the corded coat, however, quickly dropped in popularity because it was so difficult to care for Collection The American Kennel Club; photography Dave King

Colour Plate 103. *Maud Earl.*
Distinguished Foreigners, *c.1900. Oil on canvas, 26 x 30ins. (66 x 76cm).*
While these are probably portraits of individual dogs, Maud Earl gave the painting a title which was more universal, conjuring up images of foreign dogs landing on British soil
Collection The Dog Museum, St. Louis, gift of Frank T. Sabella; photography Grant Taylor

Colour Plate 104. *Lilian Cheviot.*
Circus Dogs, *c.1894. Oil on canvas, 24 x 30ins. (61 x 76cm).*
This endearing portrait of circus dogs is somewhat ambiguous for we are uncertain if they are about to start or have just finished their tricks. There can be no doubt however, that the little Westie, eager to please, continues to perform

Collection Ruth Havemeyer Norwood; photography Grant Taylor

Colour Plate 105. *Florence Jay.*
Recumbent Poodle. *Oil on canvas, 21 x 27ins. (53.5 x 68.5cm).*
While a portrait of a pure-bred dog, this painting falls squarely in the tradition of the pet portrait: a beloved member of the family, he relaxes languidly on the family sofa

Collection Dr. Jacklyn E. Hungerland; photography Grant Taylor

Plate 184. *Sir Joshua Reynolds, P.R.A.*
Nelly O'Brien. *Oil on canvas, 50¼ x 40ins. (127.5 x 101.5cm).*
The Maltese claims an ancient history as a companion to royalty and the landed gentry. The sitter, although not a member of royalty, was a famous beauty of her time
By permission of the Trustees of the Wallace Collection, London

The Maltese

The Maltese is one of the oldest toy breeds and its likeness has appeared on art objects dating back some three thousand years. Before the birth of Christ, the breed was described under the name *Canis melitaeus,* from which its modern name derived. Where it originated is a mystery, for in the ancient world there were at least three locations to which the name Melita was given: the island of Malta (then called Melita), the Adriatic island of Melita, and the town of Melita in Sicily.

From the earliest times, however, the Maltese appears to have been known throughout the European continent where it was enjoyed for its beauty and

Plate 185. *J.F. Maggs.*
Maltese with a Blue Bow, *1863. Oil on board, 19 x 24ins. (48 x 61cm).*
This dog, by a little known artist, might well have been a Poodle, or simply a mixed breed Whatever its lineage, it was clearly a much loved pet Collection Mrs. Vincent Astor; photography Dave King

companionship, especially by women. George Jennison, in *Animals for Show and Pleasure in Ancient Rome,* describes small pet dogs (*catelli, catellae*) which were common in Imperial Italy. They were probably of the Maltese kind, which had been popular in Egypt and Greece for centuries, with a long-haired silky coat and a curly feathered tail.

It is believed one reason this charming little dog became so popular was because it was used by the Dutch, Portuguese and Spanish traders as an object of barter, and was introduced to the many cities along their trade routes. Virginia Leach writes in her monumental breed study, *The Maltese Dog,* that by the thirteenth century the Maltese was in evidence throughout Europe.

Exactly when and how the Maltese was first introduced into England is a mystery. One theory is that it was brought by the Roman soldiers during their occupation of England. Another is that the returning Crusaders carried them home as gifts for their ladies. What is known is that the breed was well established by the reign of Elizabeth I (1558-1603). Dr. Caius described them

Colour Plate 106. *English School.*
Maltese on a Table. *Oil on canvas, 20 x 24ins. (51 x 61cm). This painting is typical of the many unsigned dog paintings which one finds from the mid- to late nineteenth century. While the painting is rather naïve, the artist has clearly enjoyed capturing all the details of this small dog*

Collection Mrs. Vincent Astor; photography Dave King

Colour Plate 107. *B.A. Hyland.*
Maltese Terrier, *1881. Oil on canvas, 18 x 24ins. (45.5 x 61cm).*
This pure-bred dog portrait shows how Maltese were groomed for the show bench in the late nineteenth century: note how the feet have been clipped, in contrast to today's more natural look

Collection Gilbert S. Kahn; photography Dave King

Colour Plate 108. *Arthur Wardle, R.I., R.B.C., P.S.*
Maltese Terriers, *c.1910. Oil on canvas, 22 x 14ins. (56 x 35.5cm).*
This painting is from a series which Wardle completed in this format and which were later illustrated on cigarette cards. Notice how the decorative hair brush is included, possibly to establish scale

Photograph courtesy Iona Antiques

as being distinct from the 'spaniel gentle or comforter...There is, besides those which we have already delivered,' he wrote, 'another sort of gentle dogges in this our English style, but exempted from the order of ther residue. The dogges of this kinde doth Callimachus call Melitaers, of the Iseland Melita, in the sea of Sicily (which at this day is named Malta, an iseland indeede famous and renouned).'

Queen Victoria owned a Maltese dog and a watercolour by Alfred Edward Chalon depicts her holding the dog in her arms. It has also been speculated that the Maltese portrayed in Sir Edwin Landseer's *The Lion Dog from Malta — The Last of his Tribe* was the Queen's dog. The Maltese first appeared at dog shows in England in 1862 when twenty dogs were entered in the Holborn show in London.

Plate 186. *R. Dinmont.*
Maltese Terrier with King Charles Spaniel. *Oil on Board, 13½ x 17½ ins. (34 x 44.5cm). Early paintings of Maltese are very rare, and this has a naïve quality which adds to its value. Notice how the coat of the little King Charles Spaniel is treated, creating an almost abstract pattern of curls across the floor*
Collection Mrs. Eileen Weiler; photography Grant Taylor

Plate 187. *Philip Reinagle, R.A.*
Italian Greyhounds. *Engraving from* The Sportsman's Cabinet, 1803.
If these dogs were not identified, one might easily call them Greyhounds, for they look very similar. The Italian Greyhound is a very old breed, claiming a Mediterranean ancestry of some two thousand years
Collection The American Kennel Club; photography Dave King

The Italian Greyhound

This graceful and smallest member of the Greyhound family is of ancient lineage, its history dating back at least two thousand years. Although the name of the breed might suggest its origin was Italy, cynologists believe this charming little dog originated in Egypt as the result of breedings between small Greyhounds. Eventually, the breed was taken from Egypt to other Mediterranean areas by Roman soldiers where they soon became the favourite companions of Roman ladies.

Throughout the centuries Italian Greyhounds have been favoured as pets by royalty: Catherine the Great of Russia, Mary Queen of Scots, Charles I of England, Frederick the Great of Prussia, Queen Anne of Denmark, and Queen Victoria were but a few of the regal owners. By the nineteenth century, the breed had become a favourite throughout Europe with society in general and ladies in particular. In Britain the breed club was founded in 1900, the dog's popularity eventually rivalling that of the King Charles Spaniel and the Maltese.

Colour Plate 109. *English School (initialled W.H.).*
Grey Italian Greyhound on a Red Cushion, *c.1870. Oil on panel, 12 x 8½ ins. (30.5 x 21.5cm).*
This charming pet obviously comes from a doggy family for an oil painting depicting a group of dogs hangs on the wall behind her Collection Mrs. Vincent Astor; photography Dave King

Colour Plate 110. *English School (initialled C.D.).*
A Yorkshire Terrier, *1877. Oil on canvas, 21 x 25ins. (53.5 x 63.5cm).*
Yorkshire Terriers were very popular in England in the latter part of the nineteenth century, when they were adopted by the dog show world. Before that, they were traditionally the dogs of Scottish weavers
Photograph courtesy Bellechasse Antiques

Colour Plate 111. *English School.*
Yorkshire Terrier. *Oil on canvas, 20 x 24ins. (51 x 61cm). Nineteenth century dog fanciers, as those of today, were very interested in developing a lush coat on the Yorkshire Terrier. Indeed, some early book illustrations of Yorkies show them with a coat so long that it trails along the ground behind them*
The Richard D. Hammond Collection; photography Grant Taylor

The Yorkshire Terrier

The Yorkshire Terrier has for over a century been a fashionable pet, but its origins are among the industrial classes of England, who bred the dog as a ratter. Evidently the Yorkshire Terrier was first bred in Scotland, a mixture of a variety of Terriers brought to Yorkshire by Scotch weavers around the mid-nineteenth century. The original breed was much heavier than today's specimens, weighing up to 12 or 14lbs. Today's American standard for the breed calls for a dog not to exceed 7lbs.

Known by a number of different names, this charming little dog was first

Plate 188. *Walter Harrowing.* Yorkshire Terriers, *1891. Oil on canvas, 22 x 26ins. (56 x 66cm).*
Although he also painted horses and farm animals, Harrowing's dog portraits are among his best pictures. Here he has lavished great attention on the dogs, while the classical architecture is very loosely sketched in
The Richard D. Hammond Collection; photography Grant Taylor

called a Yorkshire Terrier around 1870. After a dog named Mozart won First Prize in the Variety Class at Westmorland, a writer for *The Field* magazine commented that 'they ought no longer to be called Scotch Terriers, but Yorkshire Terriers.' The breed quickly established itself in dog shows around the turn of the century, becoming known for its glorious long coat, sometimes so long that it trailed on the ground behind the dog.

Plate 189. *Maud Earl.* Yorkshire Terrier, *c.1900. Oil on canvas, 13½ x 15½ins. (34 x 39.5cm).*
The paintings of Maud Earl often tell a story, typically linked to the nature of the dog depicted. This mischievous little Yorkie has been caught in the act of tearing up a letter, perhaps unopened
Collection The American Kennel Club; photography Dave King

Plate 190. *John Watkins Chapman.*
Yorkshire Terrier. *Oil on canvas, 17½ x 25¼ins. (44.5 x 64cm).*
Chapman was an accomplished genre painter, painting portraits of animals, flowers and still-lifes. This portrait may be of an early Yorkshire Terrier, although it is more likely a mixed breed
Photograph courtesy Iona Antiques

Plate 191. *English School (initialled B).*
Gee Gee, a Yorkshire Terrier. *Oil on canvas, 20 x 16ins. (51 x 40.5cm).*
It seems hard to imagine a more endearing portrait of a pampered pet, beribboned with a huge pink bow, ready to respond to her master's voice
Collection Pat Beresford

Colour Plate 112. *Maud Earl.* Charge of the Light Brigade, *c.1900. Oil on canvas, 26½ x 32¼ins. (67.5 x 82cm).*
This is one of a series of paintings which was commissioned by the Buchanan Distiller's Company for their collection. While somewhat coarser than today's Yorkie, these dogs from around the turn of the century more or less conform to today's standard for the breed
The Richard D. Hammond Collection; photography Dave King

Plate 192. *Maud Earl.* Brussels Griffon, *1899. Oil on canvas, 18 x 24ins. (45.5 x 61cm).*
The Brussels Griffon, a native of Belgium, is known for his mischievous good nature. Here he is playing with a huge rose
Private collection; photography Grant Taylor

Plate 193. *Léon Paul Pierre Glaize.*
'Pomm a sa Mère', *c.1860. Oil on canvas, 16 x 13ins. (40.5 x 33cm).*
This is a charming portrait of a pet, done by an artist who was better known for his human portraits. Evidently this Brussels Griffon was the 'apple of his mother's eye' Collection Gilbert S. Kahn; photography Carlos Domenech

The Brussels Griffon

As its name implies, the Brussels Griffon originated in Belgium, evidently a cross between a German Affenpinscher and a Belgian street dog. In the late nineteenth century it was crossed with a Pug, which explains why we have the two distinct types of coat in the Brussels Griffon, the rough and the smooth, the smooth being known as a Brabancon.

By 1880, the Brussels Griffon, then known as a Griffon Bruxellois, was well established in the show dog world, the parent club in England being established just before the turn of the century. The breed is, of course, most at home in Belgium, but breeders in both Britain and America have added to the popularity of the little dog.

The Papillon

So named because of the resemblance of its ears to the outspread wings of a butterfly, the Papillon is reputed to have originated from the Toy Spaniel of Belgium, although its exact origins are uncertain. The eighteenth century examples of this breed often had drop ears, and today the drop-eared variety is known as the Phalene Papillon.

The Papillon, or a breed very similar to it, is seen in many sixteenth and seventeenth century paintings. It was popular in France during the first half of the eighteenth century, evidently having been bred for no other reason than to be a favoured pet.

Plate 194. *Malcolm S. Tucker.*
Papillon, *1893. Oil on canvas, 20 x 24ins. (51 x 61cm).*
Surprisingly, very little is known about this artist. The dog, which appears much more like today's Papillon than that in Plate 195, is placed in a landscape in a manner reminiscent of the dog paintings of George Stubbs. The dog is silhouetted against a dark background, with a clearing sky just perceptible to the right Collection The Dog Museum, St. Louis, gift of Mrs. Catharine D. Gauss

Plate 195. *Maud Earl.*
Papillon, *1880. Oil on canvas.*
Maud Earl began painting dogs at a very early age. This portrait, for instance, would have been painted when she was only sixteen years old Collection Mrs. Darron Raike; photography Schopplein Studios

The Chihuahua

While the exact origins of the Chihuahua are actively debated, it is one of the few dogs that was first more popular in America than Britain. Renowned for their diminutive size, they were first known in the States around 1888, and first registered by The American Kennel Club in 1903. The Chihuahua Club of America was established in 1923, and since then it has become a very popular dog indeed.

The breed was known in England from around the mid-nineteenth century, but the first example was not shown until 1897 at The Ladies' Kennel Association Show, and the first dog registered by The Kennel Club in 1907. The breed club was formed in May 1949.

Plate 196. *British School.* Chihuahua on a Red Footstool. *Oil on canvas, 13 x 17ins. (33 x 43cm).*
Paintings of Chihuahua's are very rare, and this one is a good representation of the breed. Notice that the ears appear to be cropped, indicating that it was probably painted before 1895 when the anti-cropping law was passed in England
The Richard D. Hammond Collection; photography Grant Taylor

Plate 197. *R.A. Venables.* Vic, *1881. Oil on canvas, 20 x 16ins. (51 x 40.5cm).*
The inscription with this painting adds to its interest, for we learn that this portrait of the well-fed Chihuahua Vic was given to Mr. and Mrs. Butt, on Christmas Day, 1881 The Richard D. Hammond Collection; photography Grant Taylor

Queen Victoria and Sir Edwin Landseer

Queen Victoria's love of dogs is legendary, as was her regard for all dumb creatures. This sentiment was directly translated to patronage of the animal artists of the day, and her retinue of dog artists was most impressive. Gourlay Steell, Charles Burton Barber and Maud Earl are but a few of the artists who painted portraits of her faithful pets.

The artist Edwin Landseer, however, was to stand head and shoulders above the rest, and when his work came to her attention, Queen Victoria and Prince Albert commissioned a stream of paintings depicting court life at Windsor, as well as life at Balmoral in the Scottish Highlands. While fascinating in herself, the influence which the Queen had on her subjects cannot be underestimated. Her love of animals, her active support of animal causes and her great love of animal portraits, can only have served to instil similar interests in her subjects. Queen Victoria had loved animals from childhood, and this simple, direct affection became in her adult life a devotion which encompassed all breeds of dogs, and a compassion for animals which might well serve as a model for the general public today. As she was to say in one of her speeches to the public: 'No civilisation is complete when it does not include the dumb and defenceless of God's creatures within the sphere of charity and mercy.'

Victoria came to the throne in 1837 at the age of eighteen, when she was still almost a child and ill-prepared to rule the vast empire then under British rule. William IV's reign had been short lived (1830-1837) and Victoria, born in 1819, had been the only child of William's brother Edward, the Duke of Kent, the fourth son of George III. Edward remained single until the age of fifty when, on 29 May, 1818, he married the dowager Princess of Leiningen who gave birth to little Victoria on 24 May. While some in the royal family had reason to believe that she would never come to the throne, from the very beginning her father had no doubt. She was virtually brought up by her governess, the beloved Baroness Lehzen, and her childhood was ordered and disciplined in a manner befitting a future queen.

As a child, she lived by a timetable: she did her lessons from 9:30 to 11:30, then played and went for a walk, after which she had dinner at 1 o'clock, did more lessons from 3 to 5, and learned poetry by heart (English, French and German) from 5 to 6. Her instruction was very regulated, with lessons in foreign languages, music and strict religious training in the Church of England.

In private life, Victoria's affection for animals soon became obvious, and as a child she sketched many of the household pets. At the age of eleven she was portrayed by her early art teacher, Richard Westall, with her favourite Black and Tan Terrier, the little Nellie, frolicking by her side (Plate 198).

The artist most closely associated with the Queen, however, was Landseer (1802-1873), whose youthful output alone outshone the life's work of many of his contemporaries. By the age of sixteen Landseer was a regular exhibitor at the Royal Academy, and he quickly became established among an aristocratic set from whom he was to receive patronage for the rest of his life.

Plate 198. *Richard Westall.*
Young Victoria with Nellie, her Black and Tan Terrier, *1830. Oil on canvas.*
Westall was predominantly a watercolourist and book illustrator, exhibiting actively at the Royal Academy. In later life he was the drawing master to Princess Victoria. Nellie was one of Victoria's first dogs, and one which was her constant companion Collection Her Majesty the Queen

Landseer was not from the aristocracy himself, however, and his acceptance among them was a reflection not only of his talent, but also of his attractive wit and great ambition. The artist was born of a family of modest means, but one to which the importance of education and the arts was always stressed. His father, John, was a well-known engraver who for years fought to have engraving promoted to the status of a primary art form.

The art of engraving, or in effect copying an artist's image on to a plate from which prints were then pulled, was well established in early nineteenth century England. Such prints were sold for modest sums and in many cases established the reputation of artists. Landseer, whose paintings of animals and little children had an emotional appeal for a wide audience, was popular from very early on in his career. His paintings, and in particular his dog pictures, told a story or expressed a feeling which made them immediately accessible to the public, and he quickly became one of the most published artists of the period.

The artist himself, however, had very ambivalent feelings about the popularisation of fine paintings, for he felt that they had little to do with art, and were merely a means of making money. It must have been with mixed feelings, then, that he regarded his father, who strove to establish print-making as an art form, and his brother, Thomas, who engraved the vast majority of the prints of Landseer's work. Edwin was, however, very fond of his family and in several cases supported them financially.

He was the youngest boy in a family of seven children and his talent as well as his good looks made him a favourite. Nor was he the only artist in the family, for his sisters Jessica and Emma were painters of miniatures, his elder brother Charles was a painter and his brother Thomas followed in his father's footsteps to become an engraver.

The early years of Landseer's life were marked by one extraordinary accomplishment after another. He was a precocious child and created competent drawings at the age of four. Even at this early age he was very fond of animals. His earliest drawings were actually done under his mother's supervision, but when his father recognised the child's talent, he took over his instruction in art.

In 1815, at the age of twelve, Landseer was awarded a silver medal by the Society of Arts for his drawing of a hunter, the same year in which he made his first contributions to the annual exhibitions at the Royal Academy.

After working under B.R. Haydon, who encouraged him to study anatomy, in 1816 Landseer was formally admitted to the Royal Academy schools, where he stayed for about three years. By 1817, at the age of fourteen, he was a regular exhibitor at the Royal Academy's annual exhibitions as well as at the Society of Painters in Oil and Watercolour. At the young age of twenty-four he was elected as an Associate of the Royal Academy. In 1831 he was elected to full membership.

By his early twenties Landseer was an established artist with a quickly developing roster of patrons. And while he is most closely associated with Queen Victoria, by the 1820s he had already become well-known among a small but important group of aristocratic patrons.

It was in 1836 that the first breed most closely associated with the Queen was painted by the young Edwin Landseer. Dash (Plate 199) depicts the young Princess's favourite pet, a King Charles Spaniel. Dash was a black and white dog with tan eyebrows, or what is now known as the tricolour or Prince Charles, as distinct from the black and tan King Charles, red and white or lemon and white Blenheim or the all red Ruby, which were all recognised varieties in 1839.

The painting of Dash had been commissioned by the Princess's mother the Duchess of Kent for Victoria's seventeenth birthday — just a year before she ascended the throne. The young Princess was very taken with the little painting

Plate 199. *Sir Edwin Landseer, R.A.*
Dash, *1836. Oil on panel, 12 x 11¼ins. (30.5 x 28.5cm).*
Dash was given to Queen Victoria in 1833, when she was only a child, and it soon became her favourite dog. This little portrait is one of the most widely copied in the history of dog painting
Collection Her Majesty the Queen

and for Landseer it was to mark the beginning of his long and happy relationship with the royal family.

The history of the King Charles Spaniel (see Chapter 2) is rather confusing, in no small part due to the nomenclature for the breed. In Britain today, the dog which looks most like the portrait of Dash is known as the Cavalier King Charles Spaniel, yet this is a relatively new breed. As discussed in Chapter 2, the Cavalier was developed as a separate breed some seventy years ago. The King Charles Spaniel (in America the English Toy Spaniel), which today is a much smaller dog with a flatter muzzle, is actually the elder breed of the two. It derives its name from the dog's favoured status in the court of Charles II.

The breed known in England as the King Charles Spaniel is an old and venerable one, tracing its ancestry back for at least three hundred years. What was originally a small pet Spaniel with a definite muzzle (see Plate 199) was, in the nineteenth century, selectively bred to become a much smaller dog. There are several references to Dash in the Queen's journals, and when the pet died in 1840, she wrote: 'I was so fond of the poor little fellow and he was so attached to me; I had him since the beginning of February 1833.'

Dash was buried in the gardens of Adelaide Lodge with the following

Plate 200. *Sir Edwin Landseer, R.A.*
Queen Victoria's Favourite Pets, *1837-1838. Oil on canvas, 47½ x 59⅛ ins. (120.5 x 150cm).*
After Queen Victoria received Landseer's little portrait of Dash, as a present, she commissioned him to complete a more ambitious work. Dash is now ensconced in the lap of luxury, with the other favourite pets equally comfortable. Compare this composition with Plate 204
Collection Her Majesty the Queen

touching epitaph: 'Here lies DASH, The Favourite Spaniel of Her Majesty, Queen Victoria, By whose command this Memorial was Erected. He died on the 20th December, 1840, in his 9th year.

His attachment was without selfishness,
His playfulness without malice,
His fidelity without deceit.

READER, if you would live beloved and die regretted, profit by the example of DASH.'

The Queen became very fond of the artist who depicted the little Dash, and Landseer soon became a frequent guest at court. Indeed he was to tutor the Queen in etching, and in effect helped to teach her drawing.

Landseer's early years at court are perhaps best epitomised by the portrait *Queen Victoria's Favourite Pets,* completed just two years after she had ascended the throne (Plate 200). The painting is the quintessential pet portrait, creating a rich domestic scene reflecting the Queen's affection for her charges. The beloved Dash is seen recumbent on a rich velvet stool, the picture of canine elegance, while before him the impish parrot Lory has scattered the floor with nut shells. Majestically posed behind him is the Prince Consort's favorite Greyhound, Eos, and a noble Deerhound, echoing a pose which the artist again used in a composition completed shortly after (Plate 204).

Except perhaps for the court pet portraits by the eighteenth century French painters Oudry and Greuze, the dog had never before been depicted in such a luxurious domestic interior. The pets are surrounded with symbols of wealth and luxury: the rich silk curtains, the velvet footstool upon which Dash is so languidly posed, and the gold-tasselled pillow against which the head of Eos is silhouetted.

Plate 201. *Sir Edwin Landseer, R.A.*
Eos, *1841. Oil on canvas, 44 x 56ins. (117.5 x 142cm).*
This portrait of Prince Albert's favourite Greyhound, Eos, is one of Landseer's most successful dog portraits. Brilliantly painted without sentimentality, it is a noble portrait of a faithful pet
Collection Her Majesty the Queen

This regal canine domesticity is taken yet a step further in a painting which reflects the happiest times of Queen Victoria and Prince Albert's too short life together. *Windsor Castle in Modern Times* (Plate 202) was completed between 1841 and 1845 and, in addition to its success as a pictorial composition, it brilliantly portrays an imaginary moment in the daily routine of the Queen.

The Queen and the young Prince Consort, seated on an upholstered bench, are surrounded by symbols of domestic happiness, while the viewer's eye is drawn to the beautifully ordered landscape of the Windsor gardens beyond. The young Princess Victoria holds a dead kingfisher, and on the green upholstered stool and floor are more spoils of the day's hunt: pheasants, mallards and a jay. Of more interest to the dog fancier, however, are the four dogs which appear in the scene.

Eos, the black and white greyhound bitch which was Prince Albert's favourite, looks fondly into her master's eyes, as does the Terrier Dandie, who sits to Albert's right. It should be noted that the name Dandie is somewhat of a misnomer, for the dog was clearly an early Skye Terrier, a breed which the Queen was to have for many years and which continued to be a favourite throughout her life. Considering that the painting was started in 1841, it is a very early depiction of a Skye.

The dog sitting on its hind legs and posing in a begging position is another Skye Terrier, Islay, as is the Terrier seen beyond, looking up at the young Princess.

Landseer himself did portraits of many individual royal dogs. Typical of his

Plate 202. *Sir Edwin Landseer, R.A.*
Windsor Castle in Modern Times, *1841-1845. Oil on canvas, 44⅝ x 56⅞ins. (113.5 x 144.5cm).*
One can hardly imagine a more endearing portrait of domestic happiness: Prince Albert has just returned from hunting and his beloved Victoria greets him, attended by all their adoring pets. It is somewhat incongruous, however, to see dead game lying around the room and the little Princess Victoria holding a dead kingfisher Collection Her Majesty the Queen

style is the extraordinary portrait of Eos (Plate 201). One of the artist's most successful dog portraits, the painting was commissioned as a gift for Prince Albert.

Landseer has chosen a composition which complemented the dog's large scale, and while some of the props — the top hat, gloves and cane — are ambiguous clues to the scene which Landseer has set, there is nothing ambiguous about the noble dog's love and devotion for her master. Standing at attention, her black coat glistening against the rich red ground of the tablecloth, she is the picture of canine grace and devotion.

Prince Albert was himself very fond of dogs and excelled in the hunting field, and his fondness for outdoor sports undoubtedly contributed to the royal couple's interest in the Scottish Highlands.

The royal family paid their first visit to Scotland in 1842, some eighteen years after Landseer's first visit, and one can imagine that it must have had a strong effect on them. Following the advice of the Queen's physician, Sir James Clark, who recommended the Highlands for their bracing, pure mountain air, the couple stayed at Taymouth Castle for their first visit, and they were both enchanted. 'Scotland has made the most favourable impression on us both,' wrote Prince Albert. ' The country is full of beauty, of a severe and grand character; perfect for sport of all kinds, and the air remarkably pure and light in comparison with what we have here.'

Plate 203. *Sir Edwin Landseer, R.A.*
The Connoisseurs, *1867. Engraving by H. Graves, 16 x 12ins. (40.5 x 30.5cm).*
From an early age Landseer was very fond of animals, dogs in particular. Here he has asked them to engage in perhaps the most personal act of all, that of commenting on his work
Collection The Dog Museum, St. Louis, gift of Helen Hunt

By this time the castle at Windsor, which had once been a country retreat for the royal family, had become too accessible from London. It had evolved into an extension of the court life in town and did not provide any real privacy or break for the Queen and her family. The couple was looking for a place which might provide a respite from the whirl of court activities and political intrigues which were for them a daily routine. It was a fortuitous turn of events when, in 1847, Sir Robert Gordon, tenant of Balmoral, died. The Prince took the lease on the house, first visiting on 8 September, 1848. Balmoral was, wrote the Prince, 'a complete mountain solitude, where one rarely sees a human face, where the snow already covers the mountain tops and the wild deer come creeping around the house.'

Balmoral, which itself became too small as the royal family grew, was bought with its 1,700 acres from the Earl of Fife in 1852. The new, enlarged castle, designed by the Prince, was started in September 1853.

It was in the Scottish Highlands that many of Landseer's most popular scenes were painted. The artist had been visiting Scotland since 1824 when at a young age he had gone to visit Sir Walter Scott. The artist continued to visit Scotland, going virtually every year thereafter. Inspired by the breathtaking landscape and the vigorous lifestyle of the Scottish Highlands, his sojourns must have provided a much needed relief from the hurried pace of London. He depicted the hunt in all its aspects in great detail, as well as completing several dog portraits. He also painted many watercolours depicting royal life in the Highlands, and these were often brought back to Windsor Castle to be fitted into large albums.

Plate 204. *Sir Edwin Landseer, R.A.*
Deerhound and Recumbent Foxhound, *1839. Oil on canvas, 45 x 48ins. (114.5 x 122cm).*
The pose of this Scottish Deerhound is virtually identical to that in the royal commission (Plate 200), completed the year before. Notice, however, that in this painting the Deerhound is affectionately licking the Foxhound's head Private collection

The Scottish Deerhound

Most of the dog portraits done by Landseer and other dog artists in the Highlands were of hunting dogs, and perhaps none is more typical than the indigenous Scottish Deerhound. An old and noble breed, the Scottish Deerhound was known by at least the sixteenth century when it was acknowledged to be best suited for the pursuit of deer.

Some believe that the early Scottish Deerhound was the same breed as the Irish Wolfhound, for the early names given both breeds are very confusing. Indeed, the early names refer more to the function of the dog rather than the breed, hence the 'Irish Wolf Dog', the 'Scotch Greyhound' or the 'Rough Greyhound'.

Dr. Caius, writing in 1576, adds further confusion to the issue when describing Greyhounds: 'Some are of the greater sorte, some of a lesser; some are smooth skynned and some curled, the bigger therefore are appointed to hunt the bigger beastes, the duck, the hart, the doe.'

Dogs which are clearly Deerhounds, however, are identifiable as early as the seventeenth century, being those considered the most suitable to hunt deer. From early on, great value was set on the breed; indeed a desire for exclusive ownership on the part of Highland chieftains caused the breed to dwindle in number, reaching a low in the late eighteenth century. The restoration of the breed was subsequently undertaken by Archibald and Duncan McNeill who, about 1825, established an extensive breeding programme.

The Scottish Deerhound appears in nineteenth century dog shows, but its true home remained in the Scottish Highlands where its pre-eminence as a hunter could come to the fore. Its great speed and keen nose made it a perfect companion for the Victorians, Prince Albert among them, who fled from London to breathe the fresh mountain air.

Plate 205. *James William Giles, R.S.A.*
Scottish Deerhounds in a Highland Landscape, *1845. Oil on panel, 10 x 13ins. (25.5 x 33cm).*
Giles was an Aberdeen landscape and sporting painter who specialised in portraying fish as well as deer in the Highland landscape. One can almost see a similarity between those dogs and the deer he was accustomed to painting Private collection; photography Dave King

Plate 206. *Conradijn Cunaeus.* Scottish Deerhounds in an Interior. *Oil on panel, 15¾ x 22½ins. (40 x 57cm). This is typical of the style of Cunaeus, who has here included the trappings meant to denote the noble ancestry of the Scottish Deerhound. Note in particular the armour which is casually placed around the room, an indication not only of the stately home in which the Deerhounds live but also of their ancient heritage* Collection The American Kennel Club; photography Dave King

Plate 207. *George Earl.* Warrior, *c.1870. Oil on board, 20 x 18½ins. (51 x 47cm). Warrior, a Scottish Deerhound who belonged to Joshua Dawes, was a well known dog at dog shows in the late nineteenth century* Collection The American Kennel Club; photography Dave King

Plate 208. *Gourlay Steell, R.S.A.*
Ghillie with Scottish Deerhounds. *Oil on canvas, 24 x 30ins. (61 x 76cm).*
While Steell is best known for his watercolours, he completed a number of fine oil paintings, such as this and Plate 209. Scottish Deerhounds were often depicted in pairs, or braces, as they hunted in this way
Collection Mr. and Mrs. Lawrence Kalstone; photography Dave King

Plate 209. *Gourlay Steell, R.S.A.*
Bran, a Favourite Deerhound, *c.1880. Oil on canvas, 57 x 73ins. (144.5 x 185.5cm). This portrait of Bran, commissioned by Dr. Alexander and exhibited at the Royal Academy in 1880, presents a very noble dog indeed. He remains unperturbed by the activities of the churlish Terrier under the stool, who seems about to attack*
Photograph courtesy The Morgan and Allen Gallery

Colour Plate 113. *James Hardy, Jnr., R.I.*
Deerhounds with a Ghillie in a Highland Landscape, *1872. Pencil and watercolour heightened with white, 10 x 14½ins. (25.5 x 37cm).*
Hardy, who painted in oils as well as watercolour, was a brilliant technician. In this work, all the detail is lavished on the dogs and the ghillie, while the background fades away in a wash of pale lavender Photography courtesy Christie's South Kensington

Queen Victoria and Pet Portraits

The age of Victoria was the age of the pet portrait, though there was a precedent for the genre in eighteenth century France (Plates 210 and 211). Probably the most important influence on the popularity of pet portraits was Queen Victoria herself.

The Queen's dogs were a great solace to her and she wished to be surrounded by visual reminders of her favourite pets. Moreover, she took a great interest in their well-being and visited her kennels often. While she was not active in the exhibiting of pure-bred dogs, the list of breeds which she owned was extensive. Another volume might easily be dedicated to a study of the Queen's affection for the dog, her kennels and the many dog portraits which she commissioned. Her position as the sovereign of a country already enamoured of the dog established her supreme importance as a model to be emulated by the rest of her people. Queen Victoria was, in some sense, the archetypical pet lover, and the majority of the paintings commissioned by her

Plate 210. *Paul Lamerie.*
Lowchen on a Table with Quill. *Oil on canvas, 9½ x 12¾ ins. (24 x 32.5cm).*
This toy dog is reputed to have been a favourite of the famous Madame de Pompadour. The diminutive size of the little dog is suggested by the accompanying quill and ink pot
Collection Mrs Vincent Astor; photography Dave King

Plate 211. *Anne Vallayer-Costus.*
Les Petits Favoris, *c.1775/80. Oil on canvas, 16 11/16 x 20 9/16 ins. (42.5 x 52.5cm).*
This painting of two obviously much-loved dogs is a precedent for the nineteenth century English portraits of pampered pets Collection Mr and Mrs John Pomerantz; photography Grant Taylor

Plate 212. *Philip Reinagle, R.A.*
Portrait of an Extraordinary Musical Dog, *c.1805. Oil on canvas, 28¼ x 36½ ins. (72 x 93cm).*
This is an early example of the pet portrait, although it must have been somewhat of a curiosity when exhibited at the Royal Academy in 1805. It is not typical of Philip Reinagle's work, whose dog portraits were usually in the tradition of the sporting picture
The Virginia Museum of Fine Arts, Richmond, The Paul Mellon Collection

Plate 213. *Sir Edwin Landseer, R.A.*
Islay, *1840. Oil on board, 16 x 12⅛ ins. (40.5 x 31cm).*
This charming little dog, one of the Queen's Skye Terriers, also appears in Windsor Castle in Modern Times *(Plate 202). This painting may have been a preliminary study for the larger composition*
Collection Her Majesty the Queen

Plate 214. *Sir Edwin Landseer, R.A.*
Princess Alice, *1843. Oil on canvas, 11⅜ x 9⅝ ins. (29 x 24.5cm).*
This small portrait was a birthday present to Queen Victoria, depicting the royal couple's third child, Princess Alice, and Dandie, the Skye Terrier. One can hardly imagine a more touching image of the canine/human bond
Collection Her Majesty the Queen

Colour Plate 114. *Richard Ansdell.*
Buy a Dog Ma'am?, *1860. Oil on canvas, 35½ x 29ins. (90 x 73.5cm).*
The attachment of the middle class to dogs was such that by mid-century there were approximately twenty thousand London street dealers who dealt in live animals. Both the vendor and the dogs, however, have a somewhat forlorn, uncomfortable look Collection The Kennel Club

Colour Plate 115. *Lucy A. Leavers.*
Barn Yard Friends. *Oil on canvas, 35 x 40ins. (89 x 101.5cm).*
This is typical of the work of Lucy Leavers who produced highly finished, anecdotal paintings of dogs, often with other animals Private collection; photography Grant Taylor

are pet portraits, as opposed to pure-bred dog portraits. She had little concern for how her dogs conformed to the standard for the breed, but loved them for the companionship they provided.

The Queen's kennels at Windsor Castle were of necessity extensive, for her favourites included many breeds: the Toy Spaniel, the rough-coated Scotch Terrier, the Skye Terrier, the Collie, the Dachshund and the Pug, to name but a few. And of course there were the many foreign breeds for, as *The Ladies' Kennel Journal* of January-February 1901 pointed out: 'Then as to foreign breeds, I think I am right in saying that at one time or another every sort of dog has found its way to Windsor and that many years in advance of its appearance elsewhere in England.' As we have seen, Queen Victoria adored dogs and in 1835, two years before she came to the throne, she became the patron of the Society for the Prevention of Cruelty to Animals, and in 1840 directed that it should enjoy the distinction of the prefix 'Royal', a support which, of course, encouraged many others.

In a letter to address the R.S.P.C.A. and to celebrate its jubilee, her secretary wrote to '...give expression publicly of Her Majesty's warm interest in the success of the efforts which are being made here and abroad for the purpose

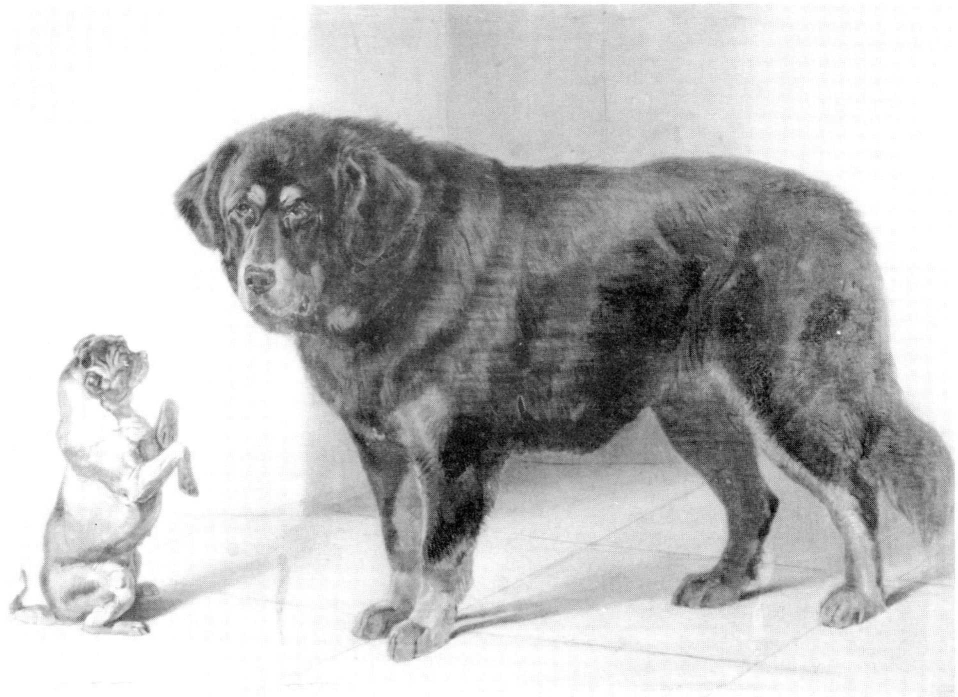

Plate 215. *Friedrich Wilhelm Keyl.*
Minka and Bout, *c.1850. Oil on board, 11⅞ x 15⅞ins. (30 x 40cm).*
Queen Victoria was often the first in England to have a new and exotic breed. This must have been the case with the Tibetan Mastiff, named Bout, an animal whose massive size is accentuated by the little Pug, Minka Collection Her Majesty the Queen

Plate 216. *Friedrich Wilhelm Keyl.*
Boz, *1861. Oil on canvas, 13 x 15ins. (33 x 38cm).*
Queen Victoria kept Skye Terriers from the early 1840s. She did, however, have her favourites, and Boz was one of them. Frogmore House can be seen on the opposite side of the lake Collection Her Majesty the Queen

Plate 217. *Queen Victoria's cottage by the kennels in Windsor Park, reproduced from* The Ladies' Kennel Journal. *The Queen's Window, where she looked out to see her dogs playing, can just be seen on the right*

of diminishing the cruelty practised on dumb animals. The Queen read with horror of the sufferings which the brute creation often undergo from the thoughtlessness of the ignorant, and she fears also sometimes from experiments in pursuit of science.'

The Queen's support of the Society was heartfelt and her interest a personal one. At her own kennels, for instance, she would not allow any puppy to be destroyed, and each puppy was given the same care. On the issues of cropping ears and docking tails, she also stood firm and refused to have what she would have seen as a mutilated dog appear in her presence. Nor were her dogs ever allowed to be muzzled.

She took a very personal interest in her dogs, and in turn they provided a welcome diversion for her. Pure-bred or mongrel, domestic or foreign, she

Plate 218. *Queen Victoria's room at the cottage in Windsor Park, reproduced from* The Ladies' Kennel Journal. *The room is literally covered floor to ceiling with portraits of some of her favourite dogs, all of which are still in the Royal Collection*

Colour Plate 116. *Henry Garland.*
Saint Bernard and Friend, *1892. Oil on canvas, 19¾ x 29ins. (50 x 73.5cm).*
Anecdotal paintings such as this, where dogs are given human emotions, were quite common in Victorian England. Dogs were a part of the household and, as such, were thought to have feelings
Photograph courtesy MacConnal-Mason Fine Paintings

loved all dogs and had no particular interest in exhibiting them at dog shows. She did, however, win several prizes for her entries — a silver cup won by her Collie Darnley for the best local exhibit at the Cruft's show, and another prize for Fluffy, a Spitz. In 1873 she won a medal for her Pomeranians bred at Windsor. Just when she seemed disposed to enter more of her dogs in championship events, she was discouraged by an outbreak of distemper which she blamed on her dogs' attendance at a show a few weeks before.

Her principal kennels, built in 1841, were situated in the centre of the beautiful Home Park at Windsor Castle. In addition to the main kennel buildings, the puppy kennels and the Home Park Cottage where the kennelman lived, the Queen had a little house of her own (Plate 217) known as The Queen's Cottage, from which she could comfortably see her dogs. Sitting at one window, which became known as the Queen's Window, she would view her dogs as they were brought out to play. Later, she might drive in her pony carriage to see the head kennelman who would present various dogs for her inspection.

As *The Ladies' Kennel Journal* wrote in a description of the kennels: 'Singly or in couples, the animals which she wished to see are brought out and are either handed up into the carriage to be patted or let loose in groups, in the

Colour Plate 117. *Maud Earl.*
White Terriers, *c.1895. Oil on canvas, 16 x 20ins. (40.5 x 51cm).*
Although the breed of these dogs is uncertain, Earl has captured an expectant expression which is very characteristic of Terriers. The dog on the right appears to be a Fox Terrier, with a Toy Terrier on the left
Collection Mrs. Walter M. Jeffords; photography Grant Taylor

paddock to which the don gives admission, so that the Queen may see them play together.'

The Queen took a keen interest in all the details surrounding her dogs, and went so far as to name each one of the newborn pups, no name being allowed until she had thus christened them. Another reflection of her true love of her dogs is in her repetition of certain names, Sharp I, II, and III for example, and a whole series of Nobles. Her loyalty to her dogs continued even after they had died.

Of all the breeds which she owned, there is little doubt that the Skye Terrier and the Collie continued to be her favourites. In 1842 the Prince Consort presented her with the Skye Terrier Dandie Dinmont, and during the 1840s a number of the breed entered the royal kennels. Dandie was a prick-eared Skye, and for the time was an unusually long-coated Terrier. He was to become the Queen's favourite Skye, travelling with the court wherever it went. Dandie died on 3 January, 1858, at the age of nineteen.

Around this time, the Windsor register referred to Skye Terriers as Scotch

Plate 219. *George Horlor.* The Gatekeeper's Cottage. *Oil on canvas, 18 x 24ins. (45.5 x 61cm). While the table is laden with dead game, this warm, glowing picture accentuates the values of hearth and home*

Collection Mr. and Mrs. Lawrence Kalstone; photography Dave King

Plate 220. *Arthur Charles Dodd.* Hide and Seek. *Oil on canvas, 18 x 24ins. (45.5 x 61cm). Anecdotal paintings such as this were very popular in the late Victorian period, where the emotion, rather than the appearance of the dog, was the message*

Photography courtesy Bonhams

Plate 221. *Karl Reichert.*
Toy Terrier, *1872. Oil on panel, 10 x 8ins. (25.5 x 20.5cm).*
Reichert is known for his small-scale, highly detailed portraits of dogs. Notice how meticulously he has delineated the dog's coat as well as his heavy metal collar

Collection Mr. and Mrs. Dennis Sprung; photography Grant Taylor

Terriers, and indeed the nomenclature for dogs during this period was very confusing. What are now known as the Skye Terrier, the Dandie Dinmont Terrier and the Scotch Terrier were somewhat jumbled together, and the Queen's portrait commissions of her dogs provide a valuable visual record of early examples of each breed.

Colour Plate 118. *Josef Smitzberger.*
Inseparable. *Oil on canvas, 16 x 18ins. (40.5 x 45.5cm).*
One could almost establish a separate category for puppy pictures, for no matter what breed, they are always endearing. Smitzberger seems to have specialised in them
Photograph courtesy Bellechasse Antiques

Colour Plate 119. *Philip Eustace Stretton.*
The Foster Mother. *Oil on canvas, 10 x 14ins. (25.5 x 35.5cm).*
Stretton often depicted dogs seated or lying down by a fireplace, creating inviting domestic scenes
Photograph courtesy Bellechasse Antiques

Opposite: Colour Plate 120. *Maud Earl.*
Playmates, *1902. Oil on canvas, 40 x 28ins. (101.5 x 71cm).*
Maud Earl was fond of depicting dogs in a natural environment, often putting them in the garden of a country house. Compare this painting with Plate 192
The Richard D. Hammond Collection; photography Dave King

Plate 222. *Philip Eustace Stretton.*
Peeping Tom, *1895. Oil on canvas, 11 x 15ins. (28 x 38cm). It seems that Stretton did a series of such paintings, with dogs waiting for their master, in this case in a changing cabin at the beach. Notice how the dog has a worried, slightly anxious look*

Photograph courtesy Michel Fine Art

Plate 223. *Philip Eustace Stretton.*
The Best of Friends, *1918. Oil on canvas, 25 x 30ins. (63.5 x 76cm). One rarely sees such an incongruous group of dogs which look so right together. Obviously, they are someone's beloved pets, painted in a style very similar to Plate 51*

Photograph courtesy Michel Fine Art

The Skye Terrier

As early as 1845 Queen Victoria was presented with a couple of old working Scotch Terriers by two country gentlemen of Argyllshire, one of them from the Duke of Argyllshire's kennels and the other from Donald Ferguson, the Lochgilpead foxhunter. The Queen seems to have taken to the breed immediately and over the years she continued to enjoy their company. With the Terriers was Caernach, a sandy-coloured Skye who, along with Eos the Greyhound, accompanied the Queen on her first visit to Scotland. Islay was for five years her favourite dog, while Corran, brought from Balmoral to Windsor in 1863, was the favourite Skye of Prince Albert. There were many more Skye Terriers who, along with other breeds, were to provide canine companionship for Queen Victoria.

Plate 224. *Gourlay Steell, R.S.A.*
Dandy, *1869. Pastel and oil, 18½ x 14½ ins. (47 x 37cm).*
Steell, who painted many commissions for Queen Victoria in the Scottish Highlands, is a very underrated painter, for his work includes some of the best dog portraits completed in the Victorian period. This Skye was owned by Lady Dunfermline Collection Walter F. Goodman

Plate 225. *Sir Edwin Landseer, R.A.*
Box. *Oil on canvas, 25⅛ x 30⅛ ins. (64 x 76.5cm).*
Box was just one of the many Skye Terriers which Queen Victoria had in her kennels. Overall, the Skye and the Collie were undoubtedly her favourite breeds Collection Her Majesty the Queen

Plate 226. *George Earl.*
Rook, *c.1870. Oil on canvas, 16 x 17ins. (40.5 x 43cm).*
Rook was a well-known Skye Terrier of his day, belonging to the Rev. J.C. Macdona. This portrait is one in the series of paintings completed by George Earl entitled Champion Dogs of England

Collection Walter F. Goodman

Plate 227. *Thomas Hold.*
Wheaten Skye Terrier, *1872. Oil on canvas, 25 x 30ins. (63.5 x 76cm).*
Hold is one of the many Victorian animal artists about whom little is known. This Wheaten Skye Terrier, however, is a finely executed portrait of a pure-bred dog, but sparse of coat indeed compared with modern Skye Terriers

Collection Walter F. Goodman; photography Wallace Heaton Ltd.

Plate 228. *Attributed to Arthur Wardle, R.I., R.B.C., P.S.* Blue-Grey Skye Terrier with Red-Wheaten Companion, *c.1890. Oil on canvas, 12 x 20ins. (30.5 x 51cm). Although unsigned, this little painting is beautifully worked and may well have been done around 1890 by Arthur Wardle. Unsigned paintings by Wardle are known but they are the exception rather than the rule*

Collection Walter F. Goodman

Plate 229. *Robert L. Alexander, R.S.A., R.S.W.* Rabbit Fanciers. *Oil on canvas, 37 x 31ins. (94 x 78.5cm). From about 1868, Alexander devoted himself to the painting of dogs and other animals. Compare this painting with Plate 134, also of a dog looking up at a caged animal*

The Richard D. Hammond Collection; photography Grant Taylor

Plate 230. *Sydenham Edwards.* The Collie. *From* Cynographia Britannica, *1799-1805.* *Around 1800, when this illustration was completed, Collies were strictly working dogs, used to guard and herd sheep and cattle. Once Queen Victoria took an interest in the breed, however, it quickly became fashionable among dog fanciers. Note that the dog in the right foreground is a smooth-coated Collie*

Collection The American Kennel Club; photography Dave King

The Collie

Long considered a humble shepherd's dog, the Collie received a great boost in popularity when Queen Victoria accepted an example of the breed named Sharp. She fell in love with the animal, and thereafter, the breed increased in popularity, reaching a peak around 1900.

Perhaps because the Collie was once considered a plain working dog, few authors have written in any depth about it. Of Scottish ancestry, it was originally introduced to England by shepherds bringing their flocks over the borders (Plate 230). Once taken up by the Victorian show fancy, it became a fashionable breed and by 1895 there were seven separate breed clubs, many of which sponsored all-Collie shows. As a result the conformation of the Collie changed substantially in a matter of fifty years. What once had been a rough and ready working dog was, by 1896, an elegant, refined show dog (Plate 234).

This transformation was perhaps best illustrated in 1895 when Maud Earl was invited to Windsor where she was to paint Snowball, one of the Queen's Collies. Miss Earl was allowed to use one of the Queen's private rooms near the kennels, appropriately hung with portraits of the Queen's dogs (Plate 218).

Plate 231. *Friedrich Wilhelm Keyl.*
Gypsy. *Oil on canvas, 11¾ x 14⅞ ins. (30 x 37.5cm).*
Keyl was born in Frankfurt-am-Main and studied art under the animal artist Eugene Verboeckhoven. He moved to London in 1845, where he completed many commissions for Queen Victoria and Prince Albert, including this one of Gypsy, probably a Border Collie

Collection Her Majesty the Queen

Plate 232. *Frank Paton.*
Eclipse, *1887. Oil on canvas, 27⅛ x 22⅝ ins. (69 x 57.5cm).*
Paton was primarily a painter of dog and cat portraits. His work is characterised by a highly detailed, finished quality. Look, for instance, at the finely detailed hair around the head

Photograph courtesy Christie's South Kensington

Plate 233. *Maud Earl.* Nicholas, *c.1890. Oil on canvas, 42½ x 52ins. (108 x 132cm). While heavier than today's dogs, this is undoubtedly an early smooth-coated Collie. Except for the shorter coat, it very closely resembles its long-coated relatives*

Photograph courtesy Bonhams

Plate 234. *Maud Earl.* Collie, *1896. Oil on canvas, 30 x 40ins. (76 x 101.5cm). Although the identity of this dog is unknown, it is a sensitive and touching portrait, typical of Maud Earl's work at this time. Earl did similar portraits of Collies for Queen Victoria*

Collection Mr. and Mrs. William Kendrick; photography Dave King

Plate 235. *Mr. Panmure Gordon, President of The Scottish Kennel Club, c.1900. The dog at his feet appears to be an early Bearded Collie. Reproduced from* Dog Shows and Doggy People

Plate 236. *John Emms.*
Nell, a Collie, *1899. Oil on canvas, 20 x 25ins. (51 x 63.5cm).*
While Emms is best known for his portrayals of English Foxhounds and Fox Terriers, he completed many sympathetic portraits of household pets. Notice the characteristic heavy brushstroke, delineating the dog's coat
Photograph courtesy Bellechasse Antiques

Plate 237. *The Princesse de Montglyon, one of the most enthusiastic Collie breeders in Europe around the turn of the nineteenth century, surrounded by some of her favourite Collies. Reproduced from* The Ladies' Kennel Journal

Plate 238. *Edwin J. Douglas.* Waiting for Master. *Oil on canvas, 41 x 31¾ins. (104 x 80.5cm).*
Douglas produced several versions of Collies sensitively painted, with soft, sympathetic expressions. Notice how he, like Landseer before him, has included a top hat, glove and cane, to remind us of the absent master (Plate 201)
Collection MacConnal-Mason Fine Paintings

Plate 239. *Maud Earl.*
Four by Honours, *c.1899. Oil on canvas, 20 x 38ins. (51 x 96.5cm).*
This multiple portrait depicts Ch. Barwell Masterpiece, Lilly Rightaway, Ch. Old Hall Beatrice and Old Hall Shamrock, all owned by the prominent Collie fancier, the Princesse de Montglyon (Plate 237) Private collection; photography Grant Taylor

Plate 240. *F. Sinet.*
International Ch. Seedling Sterling, *1916. Oil on canvas, 26 x 29ins. (66 x 73.5cm).*
The practice of showing dogs other than in their country of origin is rather new. This is hardly surprising when one considers the long process of quarantine one must go through when bringing a dog into the United Kingdom
Collection The Dog Museum, St. Louis, gift of Mr. and Mrs. Royal Peterson II; photography Grant Taylor

Plate 241. *George Morley.*
Waldmann, *1841. Oil on canvas, 10 x 12⅛ ins. (25.5 x 30.5cm).*
Many of the Dachshunds in the royal household were gifts from relatives in Germany. While this is certainly not a show specimen, Morley has caught the characteristic expression of a Dachshund looking up at his master. Note the crooked front legs, evidently more the rule than the exception around 1850
Collection Her Majesty the Queen

Plate 242. *Walter Harrowing.*
Dachshund, *1875. Oil on canvas, 14 x 12ins. (35.5 x 30.5cm).*
In this early work by Harrowing, the artist has captured the mischievous look so typical of the breed. While the bell collar was often seen on Pugs, it is rare to see one on a Dachshund
Collection Mr. and Mrs. Michael Svirsky; photography Dave King

Plate 243. *Friedrich Wilhelm Keyl.*
Dacko, *1871. Oil on canvas, 22½ x 18¾ ins. (57 x 47.5cm).*
Notice how different Waldmann (Plate 241), painted by Morley some thirty years before, looks from Dacko. This dog is much stockier, and its front legs have improved a great deal
Collection Her Majesty the Queen

The Dachshund

Another favourite breed of the Queen and the Prince Consort was the Dachshund, in the mid-nineteenth century known as the Dachs dog. The Dachshund is the smallest member of the Hound family. Its name translates as 'badger-dog' and reflects the fact that the breed was for centuries used in Germany and Austria for going to earth after vermin.

The origins of the Dachshund are not known. Some authorities believe it descended from the short-legged, long-backed dogs which existed in ancient

Colour Plate 121. Maud Earl.
Black and Tan Dachshund, *1890. Oil on canvas, 30 x 22ins. (76 x 56cm).*
Earl has succeeded in capturing the expression and glistening coat of this dog, accentuated by the pink curtain in the background. This Dachshund of 1890 has much more of a 'hound' expression than do Dachshunds of today Collection Mr. and Mrs. David Morris; photography Grant Taylor

Egypt. Others trace it to the French Basset Hound, and still others believe it is related to the old Turnspit dog, long of body and short of leg, of whom Dr. Caius wrote: 'When any meat is to be roasted they go into a wheel, where they, turning about with the weight of their bodies, so diligently look to their business that no drudge nor scullion can do the feat more cunningly, whom the popular sort hereupon term Turnspits.' Whatever its history, through the centuries there have been references in European history to small hounds, from which the Dachshund probably evolved.

*Plate 244. *John Sargent Noble, R.B.A.*
Dachshunds and a Pug. *Oil on canvas, 37 x 34ins. (94 x 86.5cm).*
Noble, a pupil of Landseer, was a London animal painter known for his depictions of Bloodhounds and Otter Hounds. Compare the characteristic expression of the Dachshund on the left with that in Plate 242 Collection Frances G Scaife; photography Grant Taylor

Dachshunds were certainly at Windsor since at least 1841, for the artist George Morley painted Waldmann during that year (Plate 241). Another dog, Deckel, was brought over from Coburg by the Prince Consort and seems to have been the first of this breed to find favour, for on the slopes of Home Park there stands a monument — a solid pillar, broken at about six feet in height — on which is inscribed:

Here is Buried
DECKEL
The faithful German
Dachshund of Queen Victoria,
Who brought him from Coburg
in 1845
Died August 10, 1859
Aged 15 years

Evidently the best, if not the only, early Dachshunds were from Germany. *The Ladies' Kennel Journal,* for instance, mentions that 'That country held then, as indeed for many years later, the monopoly of first class dachshunds, and moreover, the monopoly was in the hands of the nobility who did not care to part with even a puppy, except perhaps as a present occasionally to a relative or friend in their own sphere of life.'

Of the dogs donated to the Queen the *Journal* continues: 'This imposing list of donors, including the Prince Consort, the Prince of Wales, the Crown Princess of Germany, Princess Christian, Princess Frederica of Hanover, Prince Edward of Saxe-Weimar et.al...fully bears out what we said at the beginning, of the noble sources and all German, from which the best of the breed were derived.'

The Pomeranian

The Pomeranian, despite its small size, is a member of the Spitz family of breeds, all of which originated in the Arctic Circle and all of which have certain characteristics in common: prick ears, a mane of hair around the neck, and a high-set plumed tail carried over the back.

The exact origin of the breed is obscure, but there is no doubt it is an ancient one. The Hon. Mrs. Neville Lytton, in *Toy Dogs and their Ancestors*, claims to have traced the Pomeranian's history back to Greece around 400 B.C., and from there to the Roman empire, through Italy to France, Germany and England.

The name of the breed is taken from Pomerania, a former province of northern Germany on the Baltic Sea. The original Pomeranians were a good deal larger than the dogs of the present day, weighing up to thirty pounds or more; some were so large that they were even used to herd sheep or pull carts.

The first imports that arrived in England from Pomerania early in the nineteenth century failed to excite the interest of the public or dog authorities of the day. Indeed, little attention was paid to a breed that had no sporting background and one that compared unfavourably with British sheep dogs. Breeders soon discovered, however, that undersized puppies appeared occasionally in otherwise normal litters, and while most considered these small puppies to be runts and immediately put them to sleep, a few raised them to discover that they matured into perfectly normal, tiny replicas of their littermates. Called 'Toy Pomeranians,' these little miniatures quickly attracted a great deal of attention.

The Pomeranian was officially recognised by The Kennel Club in 1870 and classes were first offered for the breed at The Kennel Club show in June of 1871.

As with so many different breeds in the last half of the nineteenth century, public attention became focused on Pomeranians as a result of Queen Victoria's interest, for after a visit to Florence in 1888 the Queen acquired several. Edward Ash writes that her Pomeranian line was started by Sasha, a dog presented to her by one of her many granddaughters. Also in the royal kennels were Marco, a rich deep buff colour, and Beppo, a white with a lemon patch on one eye.

It is known that Queen Victoria exhibited at The Kennel Club show in April of 1891 and won all the prizes in her class, with Windsor Marco winning first place. She preferred dogs in the twelve to sixteen pound range, which made the old style Pomeranian appear gigantic, and within a short time the style set

Colour Plate 122. *Frances L. Fairman.*
Pomeranians, *1895. Watercolour, 24 x 18ins. (61 x 45.5cm).*
Fairman was equally as comfortable working in watercolours as she was in oils, maintaining a soft, atmospheric style in both media. While rarely seen today, the black Pomeranian was very popular in England around 1890
The Richard D. Hammond Collection; photography Grant Taylor

by the Queen became the norm.

Even this smaller Pomeranian was soon to be considered large as breeders discovered they could reduce size even further, and that they could accomplish this feat without endangering the dog's health or losing its coat. The early specimens were white and black, and later a wide range of vivid colours was introduced. As one writer noted in *Hutchinson's Dog Encyclopedia:* 'The smaller size, the wonderful coat and the brilliant colours made the breed yet more fashionable, and when, later, sables were evolved, the breed forged yet further ahead in that particular direction, which meant high prices: a dog of fashion which no well-dressed lady could be without.'

One Victorian fancier who was associated with The Ladies' Kennel Association and who took a great interest in Pomeranians was a Miss Chell (Plate 246). She kept a substantial kennel, mostly of the medium size but with some toys. Commenting on her dogs she stated:

> 'Pomeranians have been for years my favourite dogs, and as I have never kept any other kind perhaps I may be rather bigoted, for I think that they are the most affectionate, faithful and knowing dogs of any...My father

began to breed them over twenty years ago, and of course I helped him with them to the best of my ability…I am pleased to say that I have bred some very good whites, blacks, browns, and one blue; but whites are still my particular favourites, as there is more certainty and satisfaction with them than any other colour.'

Colour Plate 123. *Henry Crowther.*
Pomeranian, *1916. Oil on canvas, 14 x 18ins. (35.5 x 45.5cm).*
This example of the breed is quite close to today's standard in the sable colour that one most often sees at dog shows
The Richard D. Hammond Collection, photography Grant Taylor

Plate 245. *Thomas Gainsborough.*
Pomeranian Bitch and Puppy, *c.1777. Oil on canvas, 32¾ x 44ins. (83 x 111.5cm).*
Gainsborough, a landscape and portrait painter, often treated his portraits of dogs with the same seriousness as his human sitters. While it is difficult to establish the scale of this painting, the Pomeranian is clearly much larger than today's examples
The Tate Gallery Collection, photograph Art Resources, N.Y.

Plate 246. *Miss Chell with her Toy Pomeranians Dot, Dainty and Topsy. From a photo by J.W. Wayne, Belper, c.1900. Reproduced from* The Ladies' Kennel Journal

Plate 247. *Sydenham Edwards.*
Pomeranians and Dingo. *From* Cynographia Britannica, *1799-1805.*
Around 1800 Pomeranians in England were much larger than they are today. A smaller dog was developed through selective breeding in the late nineteenth century

Collection The American Kennel Club; photograph Dave King.

Plate 248. *British School.*
Best of Friends, *c.1870. Oil on canvas, 8 x 10ins. (20.5 x 25.5cm).*
There are many well painted nineteenth century paintings of dogs which are not signed yet have great charm

Photograph courtesy Bonhams

Plate 249. *Wright Barker, R.B.A.*
Roy, *1910. Oil on canvas, 18 x 24ins. (45.5 x 61cm).*
When Pomeranians were first introduced into England, the larger varieties were more usual. Queen Victoria's interest in the toy variety meant that small dogs such as Roy, a chocolate brown example, quickly became popular
Private collection; photography Dave King

The Ladies' Kennel Association

In the third quarter of the nineteenth century more and more women became active in the dog show world. Queen Victoria and the Princess of Wales were both very active, as were a large number of the aristocracy. In the 1890s a group of ladies got together to create The Ladies' Kennel Association. A show-giving group, it made its début as an organised and recognised club at the Crystal Palace in October 1894.

Its objectives were 'To promote and protect the interests of lady-exhibitors of dogs; to discountenance the many dishonest practices rampant in dog shows; to put a stop to the cruelty and maiming certain breeds of dogs by exhibitors and professional breeders, and, generally, to improve the conditions under which dogs are shown, and by example and influence, to raise the tone of dog showing.'

Among the most popular breeds shown by the ladies of the day were the Pomeranian, the Poodle, the Italian Greyhound, the Maltese and the Yorkshire Terrier. Less popular, but nevertheless a presence in the show ring were the Papillon and the Chihuahua. Nor were the dogs which were shown by women restricted to the smaller breeds, for St. Bernards also enjoyed a degree of popularity around 1900.

The Ladies' Kennel Association grew very quickly and became very successful. In 1895 the Princess of Wales agreed to be its patron, and in 1900 Her Royal Highness the Duchess of Connaught accepted the post of President, while Her Serene Highness Princess Victoria of Schleswig-Holstein, granddaughter of Queen Victoria, sat on the Grand Council. At the three-day show in 1900 held at Alexandra Palace over £4,000 in cash prizes and trophies were offered, with more than six thousand dogs entered. It was three times larger than any previously held dog show.

CHAPTER 4

Between Victoria and World War II

Edward VII came to the throne in 1901, at a time when the dog had reached an unprecedented popularity. With the establishment of The Kennel Club and organised dog shows, vast numbers of people came into contact with pure-bred dogs, and it became socially *de rigueur* to be accompanied by a highly bred canine. Many new breeds were imported from around the world and, with the support of Queen Victoria and the titled classes, interest in dogs at the turn of the century had reached a new height.

In a country which was, during the nineteenth century as today, fascinated by its royal family, Queen Victoria's humane attitude toward animals, her love of dogs, and her interest in dog shows all had a great influence on the popularity of pure-bred dogs. Queen Victoria loved dogs as pets. They were all loved alike by her, fine specimens or not, and it took a man of extraordinary skills to convince her that she should exhibit her dogs in public.

Charles Cruft, the founder of the now world-famous Crufts dog show, was born in 1852. He was the son of a London jeweller and had for years worked for the James Spratt Company, makers of biscuits for dogs. Specialised food for dogs was a great novelty at the time. In an era when dog shows were rapidly expanding in size and number, Cruft travelled the country, successfully increasing Mr. Spratt's business. In 1878 he introduced Spratt's biscuits to France.

Recognising an increasing demand for dog shows, Charles Cruft put on his first show in London at the Royal Aquarium in 1886. For the next fifty years he organised dog shows, culminating in his jubilee show in 1936 which attracted 10,000 dogs.

This young entrepreneur somehow convinced Queen Victoria that her public deserved a glimpse of some of her many pure-bred dogs, and in 1891 she agreed to exhibit her Collie, and six of her Pomeranians: Fluffy, Nino, Mino, Beppo, Gilda and Lulu. All of them won prizes. The Queen exhibited her dogs again, but an outbreak of distemper in her kennels a few weeks after they had been shown convinced her not to exhibit any more, for she was certain they had caught the illness at the dog show. She nevertheless maintained an active interest in show activities, often visiting dog shows with her son, the Prince of Wales (later Edward VII) and his wife Alexandra, but was never again to have her own animals entered in a show.

Queen Victoria had remained to the end a great symbol of the era, but in her later years she was increasingly hidden from the public eye. After the death of Prince Albert in 1861, she had entered a long period of mourning. By the time of her death, the Prince and Princess of Wales had taken over the public appearances and ceremonial functions which the Queen had found so onerous.

In contrast to his mother, the Prince of Wales was very sociable and spent

Colour Plate 124. *Maud Earl.*
Luska, A Siberian Sledge Dog in a Snowy Landscape, *c.1908. Oil on canvas, 30½ x 40¼ ins. (77.5 x 102cm).*
This painting, reproduced in de Bylandt's two-volume edition of Dogs of All Nations, *was owned and exhibited by Edward VII. Luska was a magnificent animal, clearly an ancestor of a present day Siberian Husky*
Collection Mrs. Damon Raike; photography Bill McLemore

a great deal of his time travelling around Europe and visiting friends in the great country houses of rural Britain. When he came to the throne at the age of sixty, he was a well known figure both at home and around the world, as was his Danish-born wife Alexandra.

The Prince and Princess of Wales had always shown very active support for pure-bred dogs and dog shows, and both loved animals dearly. Edward had been a patron of The Kennel Club since 1875, and he continued his patronage when he came to the throne. Throughout his life the Prince of Wales was an active breeder and exhibitor of dogs as well as an avid sportsman.

Alexandra, however, was interested in more than just winning at dog shows, for she cared deeply for animals. One story, for instance, tells of Luska, a sled dog and no doubt the ancestor of our present day Siberian Husky, which had been presented to the King in 1908. As a newcomer to the kennels, Luska was treated with the same care as all the dogs, but he would not eat meat. Alexandra, apprised of the situation, took the matter in hand and went to the kennels where she learned that the dog had never before been fed meat, but preferred a diet of fish and rice. Upon receiving his new diet, the dog settled in and was shown extensively, eventually having his portrait painted by Maud Earl (Colour Plate 124).

In the 1870s Edward and Alexandra moved to Sandringham, an estate in Norfolk. Here at last was an appropriate place for the Prince to raise his family with his young wife, and to enjoy the pleasures of a great country house on their own.

Sandringham was bought for the young couple in 1863, and with the purchase of additional lands there were some 7,000 acres. The Prince of Wales extensively rebuilt the house to his own arrangement and construction; by the time he had finished there were some three hundred rooms, gardens, stables, and, of course, extensive kennels.

Sandringham was to become one of the principal residences of the Prince and Princess and upon his ascension to the throne Edward established it, not Windsor, as his country home; indeed he had only been on the throne for two years when in 1903 he closed the vast kennels at Windsor and moved all his late mother's dogs to Sandringham. There were over seventy, including Harriers, Setters, Pointers, Deerhounds, Spaniels, Pomeranians, Retrievers, Bulldogs, Borzois, Terriers, Collies, St. Bernards and many other breeds. The move suited Queen Alexandra, for in her own words, she was 'mad about animals.'

As a writer in *The Ladies' Kennel Journal* of 1897 pointed out:

> At Windsor there are some sixty dogs and at Sandringham (not counting those kept purely for sporting purposes) about seventy, and it would be impossible to say which of the kennels, the Queen's or the Prince's, afford a better model and example for lovers of dogs, for in each the arrangements are not only perfect, but under the direct supervision of their illustrious owners.

By the turn of the century, dog shows and dog people had become a topic of public interest and the journals responded with articles on 'doggy' people, with accompanying photographic essays on their dogs and kennels. With the advent of illustrated newspapers the public also could have immediate access to images of royalty with their dogs. *The British Annual Fancier's Review,* for instance, ran a series of articles on important kennels like those of the Prince of Wales at Sandringham and the Duchess of Newcastle at Clumber House. In the last few years of the nineteenth century, *The Ladies' Kennel Journal* ran a series of very flattering articles on Queen Victoria's dogs and her kennels at Windsor, following it later with a series of similar articles on Sandringham. It was a reflection not only of the public's interest in the royal family, but also an indication of just how popular dogs had become. At the turn of the century it was commonplace for popular celebrities such as actors and actresses to be photographed in the company of their dogs. This, along with the royal family's interest in dogs, undoubtedly led to a fashion for certain breeds of dogs, which in turn led to an interest in dog portraits painted by the fashionable artists of the day.

Queen Victoria had created a flurry of interest in the Pomeranian when she had exhibited hers in 1891, a time when the Collie (also a royal favourite), the Fox Terrier, St. Bernard, Pug, Newfoundland and Great Dane were among the most popular breeds. By the end of the century, perhaps because of the movement of families to smaller houses, the Smooth Fox Terrier was the favourite, followed by the Irish, Scottish and Wire Fox Terriers, along with Dachshunds.

The Borzoi

No individual dog, however, could have created more public interest than one owned by Queen Alexandra. Alex (Plates 250 and 254), the Borzoi (known till 1936 as the Russian Wolfhound), had been given to her by her brother-in-law, Tsar Alexander II of Russia.

Alexandra was much loved by her subjects. Born the daughter of Prince Christian of Gluecksburg, who later became Christian IX of Denmark, and Louise, the daughter of the Landgrave William of Hesse, Alexandra had been born in Copenhagen. As a young girl she was very fond of animals, even bringing a pair of turtle doves with her when she travelled to England to marry her prince in 1863, a fact which undoubtedly endeared her to the British people. She hated cruelty to animals, and supported the R.S.P.C.A., as did her mother-in-law before her. She publicly disapproved of the wanton killing of animals. Indeed, when it came to hunting, she often sided with the prey, hoping for instance that the fox would escape the hounds.

Plate 250. Princess Alexandra with her Pekingese Little Billie and Borzoi Alex, at Sandringham, c.1895.
Alexandra, the Danish-born wife of the Prince of Wales, was a great animal lover, a fact which endeared her to the British people

Her sport was found in the show ring, with the public exhibition of dogs. Alex had been imported with another Borzoi, Gatchina, from Prince Galitzin's kennels, and perhaps no other dog of hers was more exhibited than Alex. He won over one hundred awards, including the famous 500 Guinea Dohlpur Gold Cup in 1910. People would queue at dog shows by the hundreds just to catch a glimpse of this most famous of royal dogs.

The Borzoi had a relatively short history in England, first being mentioned in English literature around 1812. The eminent historian 'Stonehenge', for instance, in 1859 commented that 'I am not aware of this breed having been imported into this country, nor of a correct portrait having been painted; so my readers must depend upon description alone.'

The Borzoi is a sight hound which had been bred by the aristocracy in Russia for hundreds of years before it was first imported to Britain. In pre-revolutionary Russia, ownership of the Borzoi had been the privilege of the imperial court and the grand dukes. Tsar Nicholas II, for instance, kept fourteen men to train his Borzois, and it was not unusual for his kennels to house forty to sixty adult dogs, with as many puppies.

The Borzoi was used to hunt wolves and, in a show of lavish expenditure rivalled only by the eighteenth century kings of France, the Russian royal hunting parties would often set off to hunt in a train with as many as forty cars. People, horses, dogs, tents, kitchens and carriages, were all transported to a location where wolves might be found. There would be as many as one hundred Borzois in the hunting party with an equal number of Foxhounds,

Colour Plate 125. *Maud Earl.* On Leash, Korotai, Zeneitra and Piolla *(detail), 1892. Oil on canvas.*
This painting was completed when the artist was in her thirties and at the height of her powers as a dog portraitist. Her mastery in depicting the Borzois, named Korotai, Zeneitra and Piolla, is extraordinary. Earl's ability to capture their anatomy, coat texture, but most of all their expressions, established her as one of Britain's finest animal painters
Collection Mr. and Mrs. N.J. Reese

and as many attendants.

The first example of the breed to be exhibited at a dog show in Britain was Katae, shown at Birmingham in 1863 by the Duchess of Manchester. Eight years later, at the Crystal Palace, there was an entire class for the breed. The Prince of Wales showed Molodetez at Laycock's Yard, Islington, shortly thereafter.

It was the Duchess of Newcastle (Plate 255), a prominent dog fancier who had several breeds including Wire Fox Terriers, who became renowned for her support of the Borzoi, and in 1890 she imported a dog named Spain. She owned many important dogs, and in 1892 bought Ouslasd, Kaissack and Malodka from Mr. Blees, who had imported them from Russia. The famous portrait of her Borzois Tsaritsa, Milka and Vikhra dates from 1896 (Colour Plate 126).

Since the Russian royal family was directly related to the British royal family, it is not surprising that a considerable number of dogs were imported from Russia, and that the Russian royal family exhibited dogs in Britain. In 1892, for instance, the Imperial Kennels entered a team of Borzois, some of which were owned by the Tsar and some by the Grand Duke Nicholas.

Colour Plate 126. *John Emms.*
Champion Tsaritsa, Milka and Vikhra Rabbiting, *1896. Oil on canvas, 77 x 64ins. (195.5 x 162.5cm).*
This is an extraordinary painting, for it depicts, on a very large scale, three of the Borzois who helped establish the breed in England. Note that these Borzois are hunting rabbits, although they were originally trained to chase down wolves Collection The Kennel Club

Plate 251. *Arthur Wardle, R.I., R.B.C., P.S.*
Prominent Dogs, *c.1895. Gouache on paper, 16½ x 10½ins. (42 x 26.5cm).*
The dogs depicted in this composite picture have obviously been chosen for their excellence, as well as for the social prominence of their owners. The Borzoi, for instance, belonged to Princess Dhuleep Singh, and the Basset Hound to the Princess of Wales

Photograph courtesy Sara Davenport Fine Paintings

Plate 252. *Arthur Wardle, R.I., R.B.C., P.S.*
Borzoi and Skye Terrier, *c.1895. Oil on panel, 11½ x 15ins. (29 x 38cm).*
While the dogs in this portrait are unidentified, they could easily be portrayals of dogs belonging to Prince Edward and Princess Alexandra, for they had both breeds at their kennels at Sandringham. Notice that the Skye Terrier is of the drop-eared variety

Collection Walter F. Goodman

Plate 253. *Arthur Wardle, R.I., R.B.C., P.S.*
Borzois on Lead, *c.1895. Oil on canvas.*
While Wardle was known for straightforward portraits of dogs, he occasionally included people in his compositions (see Colour Plate 8)
Photograph courtesy Exclusively Dogs

Plate 254. *Benjamin Firth, Jnr.*
Alex, *1896. Oil on canvas, 17 x 19½ins. (43 x 49.5cm).*
Alex, who belonged to the Princess of Wales, was one of the best known dogs in late nineteenth century Britain. People queued by the hundreds when he was shown, just to catch a glimpse of him
Collection Her Majesty the Queen

Plate 255. Her Grace The Duchess of Newcastle, the first President of the Borzoi Club, with one of her Champion Borzoi, *c.1895.*
The Duchess of Newcastle, along with Queen Alexandra, was one of the most prominent and successful Borzoi fanciers in the early part of the twentieth century

Plate 256. *Arthur Wardle, R.I., R.B.C., P.S.*
Pair of Borzois *(detail), c.1935. Oil on board, 11 x 11ins. (28 x 28cm).*
This portrait is one of a series in the same format which had once belonged to the prominent dog writer Theo Marples. Completed about 1935, the Borzois appear more stylised than in Wardle's earlier work such as Plate 253
Private collection; photography Dave King

Colour Plate 127. *Friedrich Wilhelm Keyl.*
Lootie, *1861. Oil on canvas, 13⅛ x 15ins. (33.5 x 38cm). Keyl was predominantly a painter of animals and completed many commissions for Queen Victoria, including this little portrait of Lootie, one of the first Pekingese to have been imported into England*

Collection Her Majesty the Queen

Colour Plate 128. *Arthur Wardle, R.I., R.B.C., P.S.*
Pobbles, *c.1900. Oil on canvas, 16 x 22ins. (40.5 x 56cm). Although the date of this portrait is uncertain, it was probably completed around 1900, at a time when Pekingese had much less coat than they do today. Modern top winning Pekingese routinely have coats which easily overflow to the floor*

Photograph courtesy Richard Green

Plate 257. *Edith A. Simkins.* Two Pekingese with a Black Pug, *1917. Oil on canvas, 12 x 15½ ins. (30.5 x 39.5cm). Edith Simkins has produced an almost perfect example of a pet portrait: the dogs are posed elegantly in luxurious surroundings, each looking out attentively at their mistress. The Black Pug is barely perceptible in the shadows to the right*

The Richard D. Hammond Collection; photography Grant Taylor

The Pekingese

Just as during the reign of Victoria, many foreign and exotic dogs continued to be imported under Edward VII. As we have seen, the King and Queen's affection for dogs was well known, and the animals were assured a warm reception. However, one breed which is closely associated with Queen Alexandra had been imported during the reign of another sovereign: the Pekingese.

Billie, pictured with the Borzoi, Alex (Plate 250), was a constant companion of Alexandra, sleeping on a cushion at the foot of her bed. She is said to have travelled everywhere with her mistress, going as far as Russia on one occasion.

The history of the Pekingese is full of romance and intrigue, for in China, its country of origin, ownership was thought to have been the privilege of the royal family. These little dogs were kept by the eunuchs of the Imperial Palace, and its beautiful, secret corridors are said to have echoed with the playful barking of the little 'lion dog of Peking'. Indeed, the dog held a special place because of its likeness to the lion. As Edward C. Ash has pointed out in *Dogs: Their History and Development:* 'The Pekingese dog represented to the Chinese mind a symbol of the great protector of the faith — the Buddha's lions, which when the necessity arose, were produced by stretching forward his hand, his fingers changing into five of these lions, which, roaring with a voice that shook the heavens, brought enemies into subjection.'

In China, the earliest of the Pekingese can be traced to the eighth century and they are depicted throughout Chinese art on tapestries, vases and screens. However, it was not till the nineteenth century that they were first imported to England. The Empress Dowager Tzu Hsi had been very fond of Pekingese, having taken great care in her breeding programme to achieve desirable colours and markings. Unfortunately, when the British invaded the Imperial

Plate 258. H.R.H. The Princess of Wales with Plumpie, Punch, and Little Billie, *c.1895.*

The Princess of Wales, later Queen Alexandra, was a lover of all animals, but especially dogs. Here we see her with her Japanese Chin, her Chow, and her favourite Pekingese Chow, Little Billie

Plate 259. *Maud Earl.*
From The Temple of Heaven — Champion Yen Chu of Newnham, *1910. Oil on canvas, 30 x 32ins. (76 x 81cm).*
This grey brindle Champion Pekingese was very well known as a fine example of the breed, belonging to the prominent Pekingese fancier, Mrs. Herbert. Maud Earl frequently included accessories in her dog paintings, such as this Han dynasty vase. These were intended to conjure up the origins of the dog portrayed
Private collection; photography Dave King

Plate 260. *Lilian Cheviot.*
Jane. *Oil on canvas, 14 x 18ins. (35.5 x 45.5cm).*
Little is known about Lilian Cheviot, but she was a highly accomplished artist who in this portrait portrays a Pekingese with a luxuriant coat posing proudly for the artist. Compare, for instance, this dog with that by Arthur Wardle in Colour Plate 128 Collection Mrs. Walter M. Jeffords

Plate 261. *Bessie Bamber.* Pekingese on a Pillow, *c.1910. Oil on glass, 7 x 10ins. (17.5 x 25.5cm).*
Bessie Bamber is known for her endearing portraits of cats and kittens, usually on a small scale. Her soft, diffuse style is evident in this little study of a Pekingese
Collection Gilbert S. Kahn; photography Carlos Domenech

Palace in 1860, many of the dogs were found lying dead, for the Chinese did not want them to fall into the hands of the infidels.

Five living dogs were found, however, evidently protecting the body of the Emperor's aunt. Admiral Lord John Hay, captain of *H.M.S. Oding* procured one pair, while a second pair, later to be named Guh and Meh, was presented to the Duchess of Richmond and Gordon (who founded the well-known Goodwood strain of Pekingese) by a relative of her husband who was in Peking at the time. The last of this group of five — the charming little Lootie — was presented to Queen Victoria by General Dunne.

If we are to judge by the portrait by Keyl (Colour Plate 127), Lootie was a sleeve Pekingese, or one of the smaller varieties, so named because they would fit in one of the voluminous sleeves of the robes worn at the Imperial

Plate 262. *Maud Earl.* Two Pekingese with an African Grey Parrot, *c.1920. Oil on silk, 24 x 48ins. (61 x 122cm).*
This painting was completed in the 1920s after Maud Earl had, in 1917, moved to New York. While she continued to paint dogs, she also completed a great number of large bird paintings done in a decorative, oriental style
Collection Mr. and Mrs. William Kendrick; photography Dave King

Plate 263. *Henry Crowther.* Pekingese *(detail), 1929. Oil on canvas, 11 x 14ins. (28 x 35.5cm).*
The work of Crowther, who often painted single dogs in a landscape, sometimes has an abstract, rather stiff quality. Notice how the tail seems almost separate from the rest of the dog's coat
Private collection; photography Grant Taylor

court of China. In Keyl's portrait he is carefully posed by an oriental vase and a bouquet of pansies, placed for their decorative qualities but also to establish scale. Lootie lived out the rest of his life at Windsor in the Home Park Kennels.

During the 1860s several more Pekingese were imported from China and the breed quickly established itself. The Pekingese Club was founded in 1902 and the Peking Palace Dog Association in 1908. Indeed, the breed became very popular, and perhaps because of its mysterious origins and exotic appearance it became a favourite with artists. F.W. Keyl, Lilian Cheviot, Arthur Wardle and Frances Fairman all depicted the Pekingese, but perhaps none was more suited to the task than Maud Earl.

In a beautiful example of her work dated 1910, *From The Temple of Heaven,* Earl depicts Mrs. Herbert's Yen Chu of Newnham, surrounded by the symbols of her country of origin (Plate 259). A rich blue brocade is casually draped in the background and a large Han dynasty bronze vase silhouettes the dog's tail. Artists often included some of the dog's favourite things when painting a dog portrait, but in this painting Earl includes accessories which represent the breed itself, and its origin in China, the implication being that Yen Chu was a fine enough specimen to represent the entire breed.

An equally decorative painting by Maud Earl from approximately ten years later depicts two Pekingese, an African Grey parrot and an ikebana flower arrangement (Plate 262). Although the identity of the dogs is unknown, they were probably American, for in 1917 Miss Earl had moved to the United States. For a period of several years around 1920 she virtually abandoned her portraits of dogs and painted large decorative panels depicting birds. She stated that these were influenced by Chinese art, and went so far as to sign her name in a stylised, oriental manner. Plate 262 as well as Plate 264 are undoubtedly from this period.

Above left: Plate 264.
Maud Earl.
Pekingese, *c.1920. Oil on canvas, 48 x 24ins. (122 x 61cm).*
Completed in a style similar to Plate 262, Maud Earl considered these paintings to be in what she referred to as her 'Oriental Style', citing the influence of Chinese art. Note that even her signature has been stylised to complement the painting

Collection Mrs. Walter M. Jeffords; photography Grant Taylor

Above: Plate 265. *Maud Earl.*
Head Study of a Pekingese *(detail), c.1930. Oil on board, 15½ x 13¾ins. (39.5 x 35cm).*
This painting was probably completed in the 1930s when Maud Earl worked on a range of dog paintings executed on panel. A portrait of someone's pet, the background has been left a solid colour

Photograph courtesy Bonhams

Plate 266. *Harry Rountree.*
Cream Puff. *Oil on canvas, 14 x 18ins. (35.5 x 45.5cm).*
This portrait, while stylised and somewhat abstract, has caught the almost haughty expression of this rather pampered Pekingese

Private collection; photography Dave King

Plate 267. *Florence Mabel Hollams.*
Pekingese. *Oil on board, 12 x 17ins. (30.5 x 43cm).*
Mabel Hollams, an artist who is known for horse as well as dog portraits, often painted single animals on varnished wood with the grain showing through. This Pekingese has a very luxuriant coat indeed — notice the length of the feathering on the feet
Photograph courtesy Bonhams

Plate 268. *Frederick Thomas Daws.*
A Pekingese and a Pomeranian. *Oil on canvas, 20 x 14ins. (51 x 35.5cm).*
Daws, a painter and sculptor, specialised in painting pure-bred dogs, often working for prominent members of the dog fancy. The books on the right were probably introduced to establish scale
Collection Mrs. Walter M. Jeffords

Plate 269. *Sir Samuel Luke Fildes.*
Queen Alexandra when Princess of Wales, *1893. Oil on canvas, 57 x 41ins. (145 x 104cm).*
Princess Alexandra is here portrayed with one of her favourite Japanese Chin
Collection Her Majesty the Queen

The Japanese Chin

Another of Queen Alexandra's favourite breeds was the Japanese Chin, known as the Japanese Spaniel. Punch and Facey were two of which she was particularly fond and they travelled widely with her. Writing in *The Ladies' Kennel Journal* one author noted that 'Facey is a pretty dog, but is rather large and slightly undershot. Punch is a better example, being under four pounds in weight. The feeding of the Japs is attended to "at the house", but all other privileged pets are fed by Brunsdon on the same fare as the dogs in the kennels.'

The artist Frances Fairman, herself a member of the Ladies' Kennel Association, seems to have made somewhat of a specialty of painting the Japanese Chin. Plate 270, for instance, depicts a group of dogs belonging to Queen Alexandra. The pair of red and white Japanese Spaniels, Haru and Togo, the latter a gift from the Mikado, are depicted in Plate 272.

An artist of considerable merit, Fairman was one of the first dog artists from the turn of the century to have developed a loose, somewhat impressionistic style which was extremely effective in depicting the coat texture of these little dogs. A less well known artist, Janet Archer continued in Fairman's tradition.

Plate 270. *Frances L. Fairman.* Queen Alexandra's Japanese Chin, *1894. Oil on canvas, 30 x 40ins. (76 x 101.5cm).*
While more loosely painted than Plate 271, this portrait of the Queen's Japanese Chin is typical of Fairman's work Photography courtesy Sara Davenport Fine Paintings

Plate 271. *Frances L. Fairman.* Three Japanese Chin, *1909. Oil on canvas, 28 x 35¾ins. (71 x 91cm).*
Fairman, like Maud Earl, often put appropriate accessories in her dog portraits. The oriental stand and the floral arrangement are meant to remind us of the dogs' country of origin. Fairman has included both the accepted colour varieties for the breed, the black and white and the red and white Collection Gilbert S. Kahn; photography Carlos Domenech

Plate 272. *Frances L. Fairman.* Haru and Togo *(detail), 1910. Oil on canvas, 20⅛ x 24⅛ ins. (51 x 61cm). These Japanese Chin, both favourites of Queen Alexandra, seem startled. Perhaps they have been caught in the act of playing with the chrysanthemum blossoms strewn at their feet*

Collection Her Majesty the Queen

Plate 273. *Frances L. Fairman.* Lady Onslow's Japanese Chin, Danshi. *Oil on canvas, 27 x 22ins. (68.5 x 56cm). While not signed, this painting is clearly a fine example of the work of Frances Fairman. Her typical style as well as the inclusion of the chrysanthemum make the attribution of this painting certain*

Collection Gilbert S. Kahn; photography Carlos Domenech

Colour Plate 129. *Janet Archer.*
Japanese Chin. *Oil on canvas, 16 x 22ins. (40.5 x 56cm).*
Miss Archer exhibited extensively between 1881 and 1916, painting with a style which, although more precise than Fairman's, nevertheless has a similar atmospheric quality

Private collection; photography Dave King

The Tibetan Spaniel

The Pekingese and the Japanese Chin were not the only dogs imported during the early years of the twentieth century. The Tibetan Spaniel, for instance, was first imported to England in the late 1800s by the Hon. Mrs. McLaren Morrison. Subsequent travellers to Tibet brought back other examples of the breed, as was the case with Llassa (Colour Plate 130), who was brought back by Colonel Bailey in 1905 after he accompanied Sir Francis Younghusband on his expedition to Mount Everest.

A native of Tibet, the breed, which is undoubtedly related to the Pekingese, was kept in monasteries by monks, and, like the Pekingese, was called a lion dog.

Colour Plate 130. *Florence Jay.* The Tibetan Spaniel, Llassa, Lying on a Stool *(detail), 1915. Oil on canvas, 16¼ x 20ins. (41 x 51cm).*

Florence Jay's style is characterised by a loose brushstroke and the inclusion of bright, decorative accents, such as the stool in this portrait. Compare this painting with Colour Plate 105

Photograph courtesy Richard Green

Colour Plate 131. *Maud Earl.* Tibetan Spaniels, *1898. Oil on canvas, 24 x 30ins. (61 x 76cm).*

This painting is from Miss Earl's best period. It is perhaps the archetypal pet portrait, depicting three colour varities of the rare Tibetan Spaniel in a luxurious, domestic environment

Collection Mr. and Mrs. David Morris; photography Dave King

Plate 274. *Thomas Blinks and Fred Morgan.*
Queen Alexandra with Her Grandchildren and Her Favourite Pets, *1902. Oil on canvas, 49 x 64½ins. (124.5 x 164cm).*
This is a rare collaboration between a portrait artist, Fred Morgan, and an artist who excelled in the depiction of dogs, Thomas Blinks. Although it is not known how this came about, both artists have signed the painting depicting the Queen with her grandchildren and favourite dogs by her kennels at Sandringham. The small black dog on the right is a Schipperke Collection Her Majesty the Queen

The Schipperke

Another import, although somewhat earlier, was the Schipperke, well known in England since about 1902. It is illustrated in Thomas Blinks's and Fred Morgan's portrait of Queen Alexandra with her grandchildren and some of her dogs (Plate 274) — a little Schipperke is on the right, jumping up for attention. The Queen is surrounded by some of her favourite breeds and is feeding them treats while the children gather around her. In the background a kennel helper is releasing another of her Collies.

The Schipperke originated in the Flemish provinces of Belgium, developing from a small black sheep dog called a Leauvenaar, which was often seen following behind wagons. The breed was for the most part associated with the working classes until 1885, when Queen Henriette, wife of Leopold II, acquired one. Overnight, the breed became fashionable as a pet.

Plate 275. *John Henry Frederick Bacon.*
Colonel Temple's Daughter Maud, with Her Two Schipperkes. *Oil on canvas, 34 x 26ins. (86.5 x 66cm).*
While the Schipperke continues to be a relatively rare breed, it was well known around the turn of the century when this portrait was painted. Bacon, a portrait and genre painter, has successfully captured the character of these old, much-loved pets
Collection The Dog Museum, St. Louis, gift of Mrs. Paul R. Willemsen.

The Afghan Hound

Another rather more exotic import was the Afghan Hound, first brought to the attention of the western world during the nineteenth century. In their native land, the dogs were used for hunting, for the Afghan was a coursing hound which pursued its quarry by sight often being followed by sportsmen on horseback.

Specimens of the breed had been brought to England in the late 1800s (Plate 276). In the latter part of the nineteenth century British officers brought back Afghans from the wars along the Indian-Afghanistan border, some of which were exhibited at dog shows. They attracted no serious attention until 1907 when Captain John Barff brought his dog Zardin back from Persia

Afghans virtually disappeared during World War I. The breed as we know it today was really started when Major and Mrs. G. Bell Murray and Miss Jean C. Manson brought a group of Afghans to Scotland in 1920. They had acquired or bred the dogs during an eight year stay in Baluchistan, then an independent state south of Afghanistan.

Plate 276. *B.A. Hyland.*
Afghan Hounds, *1886. Oil on canvas, 22 x 27ins. (51 x 68.5cm).*
The Afghan was relatively rare at dog shows, even in the early twentieth century. Although painted in England, this portrait depicts the dogs against a backdrop of the mountains of Afghanistan
Collection Roger Rechler; photography Dave King

Colour Plate 132. *Charles Hamilton.*
Zillah, a Persian Greyhound, *1837. Oil on canvas, 16½ x 20ins. (42 x 51cm).*
This portrait, published in The New Sporting Magazine *in 1837, is of Zillah, a two year old black and tan Saluki bitch who was bred at London Zoo. At the time the breed was known as the Persian Greyhound, as the first examples to be imported to England were brought from that country* Private collection

Colour Plate 133. *James Ward.* Persian Greyhounds, *1807. Oil on canvas, 40 x 50ins. (101.5 x 127cm).*

This life-size portrait of Salukis was exhibited at the British Institution in 1807. Note the growling dogs at top right: while now known as an elegant pet, the Saluki was a sight hound whose incredible speed made it well-suited to pursue the gazelle, one of the fastest of antelope

Private collection

The Saluki

The Saluki, another exotic import brought into England during the nineteenth century, was for centuries a highly prized hunting dog. As the Hon. Florence Amherst stated around the turn of the century:

> Eastern records show that these swift hounds of the desert have been prized for remote ages. Salukis are most carefully pedigree bred by the great Sheikhs of the Bedouin tribes, and they are very refined, with splendid attributes. They are principally used for hunting gazelle, and the fact of them being true today to the type thousands of years ago makes them a valuable addition to the study of heredity and dog lore.

The breed was evidently first imported into Britain during the eighteenth century, and was most certainly there by 1807 when James Ward painted *Persian Greyhounds* (Colour Plate 133) which was exhibited at the British Institution and reproduced in *The Sporting Magazine.* The first record of a Saluki being a prize-winner at a dog show appears in 1878. Again referred to as a Persian Greyhound, the bitch Tierma belonged to H. Allen of London. She was registered by The Kennel Club in 1877 as a 'foreign' dog.

Around the turn of the century the breed attracted the interest of the Hon. Florence Amherst of Hackney. She had been given a brace of Salukis in 1895 by W. Jennings-Bramley, and it was largely as a result of her efforts as well as those of Brigadier and Mrs. F.F. Lance that the breed was officially recognised by The Kennel Club and the breed club founded in 1923.

Plate 277. *Arthur Wardle, R.I., R.B.C., P.S.*
Prominent Dogs, *c.1895. Gouache on paper, 16½ x 10½ins. (42 x 26.5cm).*
This may well have been an illustration for a dog-related periodical, with the King's Clumber Spaniel and the Queen's Basset Hound prominently displayed in the upper right
Photograph courtesy Sara Davenport Fine Paintings

Plate 278. *Arthur Wardle, R.I., R.B.C., P.S.*
Basset Hounds. *Oil on canvas, 22 x 14ins. (56 x 35.5cm).*
This is one in a series of paintings by Arthur Wardle which were reproduced as cigarette cards, now themselves collectables
Photograph courtesy Sara Davenport Fine Paintings

Other 'Royal' Breeds

Edward VII was a great animal lover, and was very active in exhibiting dogs and breeding them at Sandringham. As Prince of Wales, he was the first patron of The Kennel Club, and continued his support after his ascension to the throne. He first showed at the Royal Agricultural Hall Show in 1864 when he exhibited a Newfoundland, an Indian Mastiff, a Russian Retriever and a Harrier, all of which won prizes.

Like his mother, he was an active supporter of the R.S.P.C.A., once visiting an annual meeting in London in 1880 with Princess Alexandra, Prince Albert Victor and Prince George (afterwards George V). Moreover, soon after he ascended the throne, he abolished the pack of royal Bloodhounds because he

Plate 279. H.R.H. the Princess of Wales, with the Duke of York, the Duchess of Fife, and the Princesses Maud and Victoria, *1893*. *The royal family often posed for portraits with some of their favourite pets, in this case, Jack a Fox Terrier, Flypie a Persian cat, and Plumpie a Chow*

so disliked the then-accepted practice of hunting tame deer with hounds.

He was equally unsympathetic towards the practice of cropping dogs' ears and tails. The practice had evolved during the period when dogs were used to fight one another, and cutting off an animal's ears meant that the dog's opponent would have one less appendage to grasp. The matter of ear cropping was even controversial within The Kennel Club, with the Club's membership divided on the issue.

The matter was brought before the general public, however, at the instigation of the R.S.P.C.A. which brought a legal action against a London couple for cropping a dog's ears. The man was sent to jail for having 'caused to be tortured and ill-treated by cutting its ears, a certain dog.' The public, who had not realised that ear cropping was still widely practised, was outraged.

In 1895, perhaps at Victoria's request, Edward wrote a letter to The Kennel Club expressing his strong disapproval of ear cropping:

> Sir, — I am desired by the Prince of Wales to acknowledge the receipt of your communication, and to inform you in reply that he has kept dogs for many years, and frequently sends some of them to exhibitions, but that he has never allowed any dog belonging to him to be 'mutilated'. His Royal Highness has always been opposed to the practice, which he considers causes unnecessary suffering, and it would give him great pleasure to hear that owners of dogs had agreed to abandon such an objectionable fashion.

Such a letter from the Prince of Wales as the royal patron of The Kennel Club was virtually a royal command, and The Kennel Club moved quickly to outlaw the cropping of dogs' ears. It is still practised in some countries, including America, mostly for aesthetic reasons.

Edward, as Prince of Wales and later as King, had many dogs, including

Colour Plate 134. *R.S. Moseley.* Chow-Chow in a Forest, *1897. Oil on canvas, 24 x 20ins. (61 x 51cm). Moseley, a genre and animal painter, exhibited several of his works at the Royal Academy and is known to have completed commissions for King Edward and Queen Alexandra. This Chow-Chow, whose ear set gives him a somewhat comical appearance, seems to be smiling at the viewer*
Private collection; photography Grant Taylor

Basset Hounds, Clumber Spaniels, Chow Chows, and French Bulldogs and, as *The Ladies' Kennel Journal* pointed out: 'There is no known breed of dog that has not been found at some time or another in either the Royal Kennels at Windsor or those at Sandringham.'

No dog, however is more closely associated with Edward VII than the Wire Fox Terrier Caesar, who was bred by the Duchess of Newcastle and was the son of Ch. Cackler of Notts (Plate 131), one of the best Wire Fox Terriers that ever lived. Caesar was to become the King's constant companion, at times even protecting him, whether he needed it or not, from houseguests and employees who might have come too close.

Maud Earl painted two portraits of Caesar. For the first, the artist was summoned to Buckingham Palace to execute the commission. Such was the King's affection for the dog, that Earl was installed within the palace, in close proximity to the King's own quarters. As she pointed out: 'I painted the picture of Caesar at Buckingham Palace. The work was under the direct and constant supervision of King Edward and Queen Alexandra. I was given a

Colour Plate 135. *Reuben Ward Binks.*
George V's Clumber Spaniels at Sandringham, *1930. Gouache on paper, 13½ x 17½ ins. (34 x 44.5cm).*
With the encouragement of the Countess of Howe, Ward Binks specialised in the depiction of gun dogs. In this commission, the King's favourite Clumber, Sandringham Susan, is lying down in the centre of the composition Collection Dr. and Mrs. Richard Rothman; photography Dave King

room between the private apartments of the monarch and his consort.' She called the painting *Caesar: I belong to the King* and it was engraved, as were many of Earl's paintings from this period, by the Berlin Photographic Company.

The last painting which the artist completed of one of the King's dogs was *Silent Sorrow,* a portrait of Caesar, leaning his head on his master's chair (Plate 282). Edward VII died in 1910, and his faithful dog Caesar was mourning his passing. The portrait was reproduced in *The London Illustrated News* of May 21, 1910.

George V, the first sovereign of the House of Windsor, was by comparison to Edward a shy, quiet man. He nevertheless had inherited from his parents a great liking for dogs. In addition to the gun dogs which he used for pheasant and woodcock, he owned five personal pets whose lives spanned some forty years.

The Collie, Heather (d.1904), the mixed breed Terrier, Happy (d.1913), the Sealyham Terrier, Jack (d.1928), the Cairn Terrier, Snip (d.1931) and

Plate 280. Edward VII with his French Bulldog, *c.1901.* *The French Bulldog pictured here is probably Paul, who won first prize at a Bulldog show in 1901. He was the son of Peter, an excitable dog who was almost killed when he was run over by a butcher's cart*

Plate 281. *Maud Earl.*
Ch. Peter Amos and Ch. Nimon de l'Enclos, *c.1903. Photogravure, 14 x 18ins. (35.5 x 45.5cm).*
This print, from Earl's Terrier and Toys *portfolio, depicts what she refers to as Toy Bulldogs. It is believed that these dogs, many of which were imported from France in the mid-nineteenth century, were the ancestors of our modern-day French Bulldogs* Private Collection; photography Dave King

another Cairn named Bob were his personal pets, but he also exhibited pure-bred dogs. As Prince of Wales he had exhibited Labradors at Crufts, taking the prefix Wolferton, from one of the villages on the Sandringham estate. George V's mother, Queen Alexandra, was still actively interested in breeding dogs at the time of his ascension to the throne, so the Sandringham kennels were left at her disposal. Indeed, it was not until his mother's death in 1925 that the King assumed the Sandringham prefix, abandoning the name Wolferton.

Among the breeds King George V kept at his kennels were Black Labrador Retrievers and Flat-Coated Retrievers, but perhaps the most well-known were the Clumber Spaniels, used for covert shooting. The Clumbers were worked in packs of four or six with as many as eighty beaters in the field. One of the King's favourites was Sandringham Susan, a lemon and white bitch (Colour Plate 135).

Edward VIII was a great lover of the Pug dog as was George VI, who was an active supporter of the R.S.P.C.A. When one thinks of the royal family today, however, one cannot help but think of a dog which has become a symbol of canine affection, the Corgi.

Princess Elizabeth and Princess Margaret Rose were evidently first introduced to the Corgi when, after seeing one which belonged to the children of Viscount Weymouth, they were presented with Rozavel Golden Eagle, a Welsh Corgi puppy, nicknamed Dookie. It was to be the first of a long succession of Corgis over the years to come, a breed which has become forever linked with Elizabeth II and her family.

Plate 282. *Maud Earl.*
Silent Sorrow *(detail), 1910. Oil on canvas, 35½ x 27½ins. (90 x 70cm).*
The painting depicts George V's Wire Fox Terrier, Caesar, mourning at his master's chair. Caesar, who was bred by the Duchess of Newcastle, never left his master's side and even walked in the King's funeral procession
Collection The American Kennel Club photography Grant Taylor

Plate 283. *Arthur Wardle, R.I., R.B.C., P.S.*
Pembroke Welsh Corgi. *Oil on canvas, 20 x 13ins. (51 x 33cm).*
Paintings of Corgis are very rare, although the breed is reputed to have been brought into England by Flemish weavers in A.D. 1107. This example is from a series by Arthur Wardle which was reproduced as cigarette cards
Photography courtesy Exclusively Dogs

Plate 284. *William Barraud.*
Black Retriever with a Pheasant. *Oil on canvas, 42 x 60ins. (106.5 x 152.5cm).*
At the time this painting was completed, around the mid-nineteenth century, Flat-Coated and Curly-Coated Retrievers were not separate breeds
Collection The American Kennel Club; photography Dave King

Colour Plate 136. *English School.*
Recumbent Labrador Retriever, *c.1890. Oil on canvas, 24 x 36ins. (61 x 91.5cm).*
By an unknown artist, this portrait, perhaps of an early Labrador, is surrounded by symbols reflecting his station in life: the ornate collar, the riding crop, and his master's hat. Compare this with Plate 201 Collection Mrs. Vincent Astor; photography Dave King

Colour Plate 137. *Florence Mabel Hollams.*
Mr. Tod. *Oil on panel, 12 x 16ins. (30.5 x 40.5cm).*
This portrait is very typical of Hollams's style, in which the dog is straightforwardly presented with no background. The grain of the wood panel was clearly intended to be part of the overall design Photograph courtesy MacConnal-Mason Fine Paintings

CHAPTER 5

Dog Painting in America

The history of pure-bred dogs, dog shows and field trials in America to a certain extent parallels that in Great Britain. There are very few breeds, however, which can be considered native to the United States, the vast majority having been imported from Great Britain and Europe. Relatively few breeds existed in eighteenth century America, and while some were imported to the United States around the same time that they were brought to England, the majority were first established in England before being brought to America.

Moreover, one cannot compare the popularity of pure-bred dogs in America with the great fashion for dogs which consumed the British public in the late nineteenth century. Perhaps because of this, there was no group of artists to emerge in nineteenth century America which specialised in painting dogs; rather, a handful of artists specialised in portraying sporting dogs. Only at the beginning of the twentieth century do we see artists emigrate to America to continue a tradition of painting all breeds.

Colour Plate 138. *D. G. Stouter.* On Point, *c.1840. Oil on canvas, 18½ x 21½ins. (47 x 54.5cm).*

This portrait has become an icon of American folk art; the Pointer looming ominously over the bob-white for whom it has become too late to flee

Collection Mrs. Gwynne G. McDevitt, photography Grant Taylor

Perhaps none of the nineteenth century painters is better known than Arthur Fitzwilliam Tait, an artist who was born in Liverpool, England, and emigrated in 1819 to America where he became best known for his many paintings of the sporting life in the Adirondacks, a vast forested area in upstate New York. Although less well known, artists such as J.M. Tracy and Thomas H. Hinckley, continued this sporting tradition, painting predominantly Pointers and Setters. Later in the century, the artists Gustav Muss-Arnolt, Edmund Henry Osthaus and Percival Leonard Rosseau were to become well-known for their depictions of dogs in the field, as well as the occasional pet.

One further important difference greatly influenced how pure-bred dogs developed in America. The United States lacked a monarchy, and the established social structure which supported it. Dog fanciers in England were greatly influenced by the tastes and preferences of the royal family, made public by the many newspaper and periodical articles which profiled them. Because America did not have a monarchy or an aristocracy, individuals who had amassed great fortunes became the American 'royalty' of the popular imagination. In the dog world, one individual personified this stratum of society: Geraldine Rockefeller Dodge. Her dog world activities, which included the sponsorship of a lavish dog show in the middle of a serious economic depression, could be said to rival those of the British royal family. Unlike the royal family, however, her life was very much protected from the public eye, and as a result she did not have a great influence on the popularity of individual breeds.

Because nineteenth century American dog paintings were primarily of sporting dogs; because dog shows and field trials developed differently in America; and because of the absence of a single great influence like Queen Victoria, this chapter will be organised along different lines than the preceding chapters on dogs in Great Britain.

Divided into three sections, we shall look at early dog shows and field trials, the development of The American Kennel Club, and study in depth one great American collector and dog fancier, Geraldine Rockefeller Dodge. Because we have discussed in Chapters 3 and 4 most of the breeds which the American artists depicted, the illustrations of American dog paintings will be loosely grouped into two sections: sporting dogs in the section on field trials, and early twentieth century paintings of dogs included in the section on Mrs. Geraldine Rockefeller Dodge.

Early Dog Shows and Field Trials

The nature of early dog shows in America was somewhat similar to those in England, as these early gatherings were rather informal affairs and were held predominantly for sporting dogs. Hounds were also in evidence, with wealthy landowners maintaining packs of Foxhounds. Indeed, George Washington himself had Foxhounds. He maintained written records of individual dogs from as early as 1758, and was very careful to maintain strict bloodlines. His interest in the breed was well known to his contemporaries, for after the

Plate 285. *Henry Rankin Poore.*
Foxhounds, *1888. Oil on canvas, 26 x 36ins. (58.5 x 91.5cm).*
Henry Rankin Poore was a painter, writer and teacher who studied at the Pennsylvania Academy of Fine Arts in Philadelphia as well as in New York and Paris. He often used a sombre rich palette, similar to that of this painting
Photograph courtesy Red Fox Fine Art

Revolution in 1785 the French General Lafayette gave Washington a gift of seven French Hounds.

While America established its economic independence in 1776, the wealthy landowners nevertheless still looked to Great Britain as the origin of their American traditions. As late as 1829, for instance, *The American Turf Register* reported both American and British field sport information, and to this day there is a close link between the sporting traditions of the two countries.

The precursors of organised shows for pure-bred dogs were also similar to those in England. Bull baiting and dog fighting events were routinely held and, of course, there was the agricultural fair or livestock show.

While the identity of the first dog show in America is somewhat controversial, it is generally agreed that one of the first was the Illinois State Sportsman's Association of Chicago held on 2 June, 1874. No award was given, however, and a second attempt was held under the auspices of the New York State Sportsmen's Association at Oswego, New York, on 22 June, 1874. A third show was held, this time under the rules of The English Kennel Club on 7 October, 1874 in Mineola, New York. It had a satisfactory entry of Pointers and what were called 'Setters of any breed'. Just one day later, on 8 October, 1874, The Tennessee Sportsman's Association held a combined dog show and field trial event in Memphis, Tennessee. In January 1875, Detroit held the first all breed dog show in America, open to dogs 'besides those devoted to field sports'.

One feature which distinguished the showing of pure-bred dogs in America was the great distance between shows. While English shows were held comparatively close together, allowing for a greater number of dogs to be

Plate 286. *Marguerite Kirmse.*
The Hound. *Etching, 19½ x 15ins. (49.5 x 38cm).*
Marguerite Kirmse was born in England but moved to America where she became well known for her many etchings of dogs and horses. This is one of a pair, the other being a fox
Photograph courtesy Red Fox Fine Art

Plate 287. *Benjamin West.*
Heads of Two Dogs *(detail). Oil on canvas laid down on board, 10¼ x 5¾ ins. (26 x 14.5cm). West was a prominent portrait and history painter. He was born in Pennsylvania, but travelled to England where he became historical painter to George III. These portraits appear to be early Terriers*
Collection Mrs. Vincent Astor; photography Dave King

Plate 288. *William Jacob Hays, Snr.*
Terrier Head Study, *1859. Oil on canvas, 9 x 8ins. (23 x 20.5cm). Hays had an ability to capture the particular expression of a dog, in this case the alert attention of an early Norwich Terrier*
Private collection; photography Dave King

shown, the early American shows were held hundreds of miles apart. The Memphis Show of October 1874, for instance, was held some one thousand miles from the Mineola show the day before.

Such vast distances undoubtedly made very difficult the organisation of a body which might supervise the sport and keep an appropriate stud record of the pure-bred dogs in America.

The first comprehensive attempt at a stud record in America was developed in 1867 by Arnold Burgess, published in New York under the title *The American Kennel and Sporting Field.* He included the particulars on 327 dogs, all sporting breeds, and provided a listing of the first pure-bred dog competitions in America.

Some six years later Burgess published a revised edition of his book. Commenting in the preface on the increased number of field events and dog shows, he stated that 'In a country where field sports have but recently come into general recognition, and where but a few years since, canine breeding and selling was confined to a disreputable class, a short time naturally produces great alterations, and the writer who honestly tries to keep up with the

Plate 289. *William Jacob Hays, Snr.*
A Pointer Honouring a Setter, *1853. Oil on canvas, 50 x 60ins. (127 x 152.5cm).*
Hays, born in Catskill, New York, was a student at the National Academy of Design in New York. His dog paintings are characterised by an attention to detail and soft facial expressions
Photograph courtesy Red Fox Fine Art

development of the day, will find himself compelled to retract assertions made upon authority of different circumstances.'

The number of field trials and dog shows had indeed increased rapidly in the 1870s. The National American Kennel Club had been founded in 1876, one of its primary purposes being the development of a stud book. Burgess decided that he did not want to compete with it, and The National American Kennel Club rapidly grew in importance. It had been founded at a Chicago show in 1876, with headquarters in St. Louis, and the majority of its members were field trial oriented and not active in dog shows.

It was this orientation which caused the organisation to change its name to the National Field Trial Club in 1884 and drop all interest in dog shows. The American Kennel Club had been organised in 1884, and it assumed jurisdiction over conformation shows. Dr. Rowe, originally of The National American Kennel Club, had continued his activities with regard to a stud record, and in 1886 he gave his first three volumes to the then fledgling American Kennel Club.

Before looking at the early development of The American Kennel Club, however, one dog club deserves attention. The Westminster Kennel Club had been formed in 1877 and it was to have a lasting influence on the sport of pure-bred dogs. The first show of the club was held at Gilmore's Garden, formerly a railway depot on Madison Avenue and 26th Street, in May 1877. It was evidently a great success, for some 1,201 dogs were entered.

From the beginning, Westminster was much more than just a dog club whose main purpose was to put on shows. The certificate of incorporation, filed in 1878, states that the purpose of the club was to breed and improve the breeds of dogs, maintain a club and to exhibit dogs. The club initially maintained a club house, kennels and pigeon shooting grounds on Long Island, New York, where it had purchased over sixty acres of land. When pigeon shooting was made illegal in New York, the club moved to Tenafly, New Jersey, but New Jersey followed New York's lead, and the club eventually made its headquarters in New York City.

The Westminster Kennel Club Show, held in early February in New York City, has become a great institution on the dog show scene. Today, while Westminster is not the largest American show, it is still the most prestigious and holds the enviable world record of more than one hundred consecutive shows (Crufts was suspended during both World Wars). *The National Geographic* magazine once commented that 'in the United States only the Kentucky Derby and two other Churchill Downs races first run in 1875 have a sporting record as long and unbroken. But even the Derby has not always had its present prominence, while Westminster has always been Queen of American dog shows, with a win there prized above all others.' It was not until the twentieth century and the emergence of the prominent dog fancier, Geraldine Rockefeller Dodge, that another club was founded to rival Westminster's prestige.

Plate 290. *Gustav Muss-Arnolt.*
On Point. *Oil on canvas, 16 x 20ins. (40.5 x 51cm).*
Muss-Arnolt was a sportsman and an avid follower of upland game. While he specialised in sporting dogs, he also painted many pet breeds. This painting of a Setter and a Pointer is very typical of his work, with the landscape painted in rich, autumnal colours

Private collection; photography Grant Taylor

Plate 291. *Percival Leonard Rosseau.*
On Point, *1909. Oil on canvas, 32 x 40ins. (81 x 101.5cm).*
Rosseau often placed his sporting dogs in an extensive landscape, creating effects of light and shadow which accentuated the dogs

Photograph courtesy Gerold Wunderlich & Co

Plate 292. *James Henry Beard.*
English Setter, *1877. Oil on canvas, 28 x 36ins. (71 x 91.5cm).*
Beard devoted the first part of his life almost entirely to portrait painting. After moving to New York in 1846, however, he concentrated on animal pictures in his later years. This English Setter takes on an almost monumental quality, on point in the field

Private collection; photography Dave King

Plate 293. *Thomas B. Griffin.*
On the Scent. *Oil on canvas, 24 x 36ins. (61 x 91.5cm).*
Little is known about the work of Griffin. Although he was known as a landscape painter, this portrayal of sporting dogs is very accomplished. The red Setter in front is probably an early Irish Setter Photograph courtesy P.C. Trisdonn Gallery

Plate 294. *Arthur Fitzwilliam Tait.*
Ruffled Grouse Shooting, *1875. Oil on canvas, 20¼ x 29¾ins. (51.5 x 75.5cm).*
Most Americans would know Tait's compositions from the prints produced by Currier and Ives in the late nineteenth century. Notice how the viewpoint of this composition is from below the Setters, making them seem to loom over the ruffled grouse Private collection; photography Grant Taylor

Plate 295. *John M. Tracy.*
English Setters. *Oil on canvas, 24 x 44ins. (61 x 111.5cm).*
Tracy was well known for his depictions of sporting dogs, often working in a small scale. This is one of his most successful compositions, highlighting the dogs, yet including the hunters in the background
Photography courtesy Meredith Long & Co.

Plate 296. *Alexander Pope.*
English Setters, *1891. Oil on canvas, 36 x 48ins. (91.5 x 122cm).*
Pope was born in Boston, and while he is remembered largely for his animal paintings, he was chiefly a portrait painter. These two Setters wait expectantly to start work in the field
Collection Frances G. Scaife; photograph Dave King

Plate 297. *Percival Leonard Rosseau.*
English Setter in The Field, *1908. Oil on canvas, 36 x 50ins. (91.5 x 127cm).*
The work of Rosseau is characterised by a loose, painterly style which was influenced by the French Barbizon school of painting. This Setter has an almost monumental quality, posed boldly against a background of grass and trees

Collection The Dog Museum, St. Louis, gift of The Westminster Kennel Foundation; photography Grant Taylor

Plate 298. *Edmund Henry Osthaus.*
Toledo Blade. *Oil on canvas, 15¾ x 23¼ins. (40 x 59cm).*
Toledo Blade, owned by J.E. Dager of Toledo, Ohio, was renowned for combining the best of both bench and field trial qualities. This was and continues to be rare, as most Setters are suited either to conformation shows or field trials, but not both

Collection The American Kennel Club; photography Dave King

Colour Plate 139. *Arthur Fitzwilliam Tait.*
A Surprise, *1888. Oil on canvas, 14½ x 22½ins. (37 x 57cm).*
This painting is typical of many of Tait's compositions, in that he has used the diagonal of a fallen tree to draw the viewer into the composition. The tree also effectively separates the English and Irish Setters from a quail which has just taken flight Private collection; photography Dave King

Colour Plate 140. *Arthur Fitzwilliam Tait.*
Daisy, *1882. Oil on canvas, 20¼ x 32ins. (51.5 x 81cm).*
Tait was born in England, coming to America in 1850 where he became very successful at painting animals, as this painting of a Pointer attests Private collection; photography Grant Taylor

Plate 299. *Gustav Muss-Arnolt.*
Pointer, English Setter and Gordon Setter. *Oil on canvas, 24 x 26ins. (61 x 66cm).*
Muss-Arnolt is best known for his dogs, on point, in the field. Here he has used an unorthodox composition to accentuate the dogs' tense anticipation. The Gordon Setter has become almost a silhouette, directing the viewer's eye to the English Setter and Pointer
Collection The American Kennel Club; photography Dave King

Plate 300. *Percival Leonard Rosseau.*
Gordon Setter, *1904. Oil on canvas, 14 x 18ins. (35.5 x 45.5cm).*
Depictions of Gordon Setters are rare in American art, for during the late nineteenth and early twentieth centuries they were supplanted in popularity by the English Setter. This painting is more typical of Rosseau's later work, for the background is very impressionistic
Collection Mrs. Gwynne G. McDevitt; photography Grant Taylor

Plate 301. *Gustav Muss-Arnolt.* Irish Water Spaniel. *Oil on canvas, 9 x 12ins. (23 x 30.5cm). The Irish Water Spaniel, long established in southern Ireland, was relatively popular in late nineteenth century America. As early as 1877, for example, there were four Irish Water Spaniels entered at The Westminster Kennel Club Show* Collection Nick Waters

Plate 302. *Henry Rankin Poore.* Bloodhound. *Oil on canvas, 14 x 12ins. (35.5 x 30.5cm). This is typical of Poore's work, for he often used rich, sombre colours. Compare with Plate 285.* Collection Mrs. Walter M. Jeffords

Colour Plate 141. *Edmund Henry Osthaus.*
Setters on Point. *Oil on canvas, 30 x 40ins. (76 x 101.5cm). Many of Osthaus's paintings, such as this one, are highly coloured. Look, for instance, at the intensity of the blue sky*
Collection Mrs. Gwynne G. McDevitt; photography Grant Taylor

Colour Plate 142. *Edmund Henry Osthaus.*
Portrait of Count Noble. *Oil on canvas, 45 x 60ins. (114.5 x 152.5cm). Count Noble, whose remains have been preserved by taxidermy at the Carnegie Museum in Pittsburgh, was brought to the United States from England. He was one of the most famous of all English Setters, siring some twenty-eight field trial champions*
Collection The Dusquene Club

Colour Plate 143. *Thomas Hewes Hinckley.*
Setters in the Field. Oil on canvas, 14 x 20ins. (35.5 x 51cm).
Hinckley devoted himself to animal painting, in 1851 going to London to study the work of Landseer and the Flemish masters. Note how the Gordon Setter on the right is lowering its head and tail to point, in a manner very different from today's field trial Gordon Setters
Collection Mrs. Gwynne G. McDevitt; photography Dave King

Colour Plate 144. *Herman G. Simon.*
Resting, *1888. Oil on canvas, 24 x 40ins. (61 x 101.5cm).*
This is a fine example of the American pet portrait, the dogs depicted resting on the lawn after playing with the ball: a Bull Terrier, an Old English Mastiff, and what appears to be a drop-eared Skye Terrier
Collection The Dog Museum, St. Louis, gift of Marie A. Moore

The American Kennel Club

When the National American Kennel Club changed its name and direction in 1884, dog shows suffered, for there was no longer a central governing body for pure-bred dogs and dog shows. Major James Taylor, a prominent dog show judge, and Elliott Smith of The Westminster Kennel Club made an attempt to create such an organisation. It failed, but in an 1884 issue of *The American Kennel Register,* they were encouraged to try again. A meeting was scheduled for September 1884, in Philadelphia, and delegates from across the United States and Canada attended.

Initially called the National Bench Show Organization, the group met again in October 1884 and approved the newly drafted by-laws and a constitution. The name was changed to The American Kennel Club, thus marking the origins of what has become the principal registry organisation for pure-bred dogs in America.

The American Kennel Club differed from its British counterpart in that individuals were not members. Rather, kennel clubs from across the country were to send delegates to act on the member clubs' behalf, and in this way more appropriately reflect the wishes of the pure-bred dog fancy at large. Moreover, The American Kennel Club was not to be a show-giving organisation, but was to provide guidance and supervision for the burgeoning number of dog shows that were emerging across America. The American Kennel Club marked its one hundredth anniversary when, in 1984, it held a dog show in Philadelphia.

American 'Royalty': Geraldine Rockefeller Dodge

The American dog fancy did not look to Queen Victoria to establish the fashion for certain breeds, nor to represent a lifestyle which might be emulated by prominent dog fanciers. There were a number of American dog fanciers in the early years of the twentieth century, however, whose activities in the dog world reflected not only a life of wealth and privilege, but also a serious attitude towards the breeding of dogs. While to name a few of them is to leave out many, kennels such as The Squirrel Run belonging to Mr. and Mrs. S. Hallock du Pont, and the Irish Setter kennels belonging to Mrs. Cheever Porter, were more interested in improving breed type than in winning at any cost.

Of all the prominent Americans who were involved with pure-bred dogs in the late nineteenth and early twentieth centuries, however, perhaps none is better known or more fondly remembered than Geraldine Rockefeller Dodge. Born into a family of great wealth, she dedicated her life to animals, and in particular to the dog.

Ethel Geraldine Rockefeller was born in New York City on 3 April, 1882, to William Rockefeller and Almire Geraldine Goodsell Rockefeller. The niece of John D. Rockefeller — founder of Standard Oil and the father of a dynasty which is to this day synonymous with great wealth and privilege — her upbringing was characterised by a curious combination of Protestant ethics and extreme wealth.

There were six Rockefeller children, of which Ethel Geraldine was the youngest. The family was headed by William Rockefeller, brother of John D. Rockefeller, arguably the prime mover in the business life of late nineteenth and early twentieth century America.

William's family divided their time primarily between their New York City home and the then still-developing estate of Rockwood Hall in Pocantico Hills, the family retreat which exists to this day, located in the beautiful Hudson River valley in upstate New York. Like many of his generation, however, William maintained several homes: in addition to the house in the city and the estate in Pocantico Hills, there was a house in the rugged Adirondack wilderness and a winter retreat on Jekyll Island off the coast of Georgia.

Ethel Geraldine Rockefeller's interest in animals developed very early on, and she was known to have brought stray dogs home from her frequent walks in Central Park. While her father raised Beagles, she had Spaniels on which she doted. Her first love was horses, however, and the stables at Pocantico Hills could accommodate up to two hundred. In 1902, for instance, she persuaded her father to allow her to enter twenty-nine horses in the Westchester Horse Show. At the young age of twenty, she was an accomplished horsewoman and won a blue ribbon with her horse Tendresse.

Plate 303. Geraldine Rockefeller Dodge, with her son Marcellus Hartley Dodge, Jnr. and German Shepherds. *Mrs. Dodge doted on her son Marcellus Hartley, going into mourning for years when he was tragically killed in a car crash in Europe*

It was with her marriage to Marcellus Hartley Dodge in 1907, however, that Ethel came into her own. The young couple had probably met at the original Waldorf Astoria, where eligible people of their class met to socialise at 'proper' teas and dances.

The subdued setting created at the Waldorf was no doubt considered appropriate by their respective families, for neither was part of the glittering social set which reigned in New York around the turn of the century. Indeed, the couple shunned publicity, as they did for the rest of their lives.

While not as wealthy as his bride's family, young Marcellus was no pauper: with an estimated wealth of some $60 million, he was president and director of the Remington Arms Company, vice president of the Union Metallic Cartridge Company, president of Bridgeport Gun Implement Company and held directorships on the boards of several major American companies.

After the requisite honeymoon in Europe, Ethel Geraldine and Marcellus moved to Morris County, New Jersey, then an enclave of the very rich. Their new estate, originally 240 acres and later added to, gave them enough room to indulge in horse-breeding activities. Later, the estate was to become a truly national centre for the dog world, with extensive kennels and a world class dog show. Mrs. Dodge renamed her estate Giralda, with reference to St. Giralda, the Spanish patron saint of orphans. When she later created an animal shelter on her estate, it was named St. Hubert's, after the patron saint of animals.

It was shortly after her marriage that Mrs. Dodge (she was to drop the Rockefeller from her name, preferring to be called Geraldine R. Dodge) bought her first German Shepherd, a breed which along with the English Cocker Spaniel was to figure very prominently in her life at Giralda.

During her lifetime she was to raise more than eighty-five different breeds,

Colour Plate 145. *Percival Rosseau.*
Pekingese, *1910. Oil on canvas. 22 x 18ins. (56 x 45.5cm). Rosseau only rarely depicted toy dogs, preferring instead to paint Pointers and Setters. Nevertheless, this Pekingese is beautifully painted and clearly a pampered pet*
Collection Mrs. Walter M. Jeffords

among them: American and English Cocker Spaniels, Beagles, Belgian Sheepdogs, Bloodhounds, Bull Terriers, Dalmatians, Dobermans, Foxhounds, German Shepherds, Golden Retrievers, Greyhounds, Old English Sheepdogs, Pointers, Rottweilers, Schipperkes and Scottish Terriers. She produced innumerable champions of the show ring and more than two hundred 'Best in Show' dogs.

Before Mrs. Dodge became involved with German Shepherds, the breed was known primarily in the world of obedience trials; she changed that. She imported from Germany the very best dogs she could find, paying particular attention to soundness and temperament. When asked about the training of her dogs, she replied with an answer reflecting her serious approach: 'I feel that

Colour Plate 146. *Edmund Osthaus.*
Ready to Go, *c.1900. Oil on canvas, 28 x 28ins. (71 x 71cm).*
These English Setters are undoubtedly waiting impatiently to go off hunting. Note that the horse-drawn wagon holds an oak and metal dog kennel, the typical transportation for dogs around 1900
Private collection; photography Dave King

I have the right idea... My dogs are trained to be alert companions, with plenty of affection for the family, yet game to a marked degree. I strive for brains in my dogs to fit them to be companions; yet they must also be thorough watch-dogs.'

Unlike today, transportation to dog shows in the 1920s and 1930s meant hours and days of car or train travel. For Mrs. Dodge, however, the comfort of her dogs was paramount, so she commissioned a custom-designed maroon Cadillac touring car. The car, which could hold up to a dozen dogs comfortably, had eight doors so that the animals could climb in and out easily (Plate 304). The vehicle was built in Madison, New Jersey, taking three men over three years to construct!

Mrs. Dodge's kennels were equipped with every convenience. Built of brick and oak with many windows, the kennels could comfortably accommodate 150 dogs. They had areas for each dog to run free, were provided with plenty of fresh water and were, of course, scrupulously clean. Each dog run averaged two hundred feet in length, was ten feet wide, and was surrounded with fencing

Plate 304. *The custom-built cadillac made to transport Mrs. Dodge's dogs to shows in comfort. During the 1930s dogs would normally have been transported to shows in wooden crates, shuttled on and off various trains as they travelled long distances from show to show*

ten feet high. The dogs were treated with great care, and each kennel dog had his day in the house with Mrs. Dodge, where he was treated as a pet.

Nor were the dogs' diets neglected; steam kettles were used to prepare the food which came out of large refrigerators — meat, eggs, milk and vegetables were used to create each special diet. Grown dogs, for instance, were fed a breakfast of specially prepared oatmeal, slowly steamed in the double kettles. Raw eggs, produced on the farm, were added to the oatmeal along with milk from the Giralda herd of Jerseys.

Lunch consisted of chopped steak flavoured with onion and garlic. Dinner was equally tasty and consisted of chopped steak, vegetables and a base of shredded wheat or toasted rye bread. In lieu of this mixture, stud dogs were given a meal of chopped steak with the fat removed and additional raw eggs.

The nursery was composed of seven separate buildings enclosed with a run of half an acre. Trees shaded the area so that the dogs would be cool during the summer months. Perhaps the most interesting aspect of the nursery area was a special glass-enclosed, octagonal structure. This contained large turntables which could be rotated to give the older puppies as much sun as

Plate 305. *Mrs. Dodge with Captain von Stephanitz at The Morris and Essex Kennel Club Show, 1930. Von Stephanitz was the most respected German Shepherd Dog Judge in the world, and it was a great coup when Mrs. Dodge convinced him to judge at Morris and Essex* *(see pages 334-335)*

Plate 306. *The Morris and Essex Dog Show Grounds, 1947. During the 1930s and 1940s the Show was the social event of the dog world*

possible. One can only guess at how many staff (which numbered well over sixty for the entire estate) were required to run such an operation.

In addition to the kennels in Madison, Mrs. Dodge maintained a training centre for dogs at nearby Princeton, New Jersey, which she visited once a week to check each dog's progress. The Princeton facility was under the direction of John Simson and was used exclusively for breeding and training dogs.

While Mrs. Dodge's dogs were shown by her staff, her own personal entry into the dog world came as a conformation dog show judge, when in 1924 she adjudicated German Shepherds in Newark, New Jersey. Less than ten years later she was chosen as the first woman to judge 'Best in Show' in America's most prestigious dog show competition, The Westminster Kennel Club Dog Show, in New York City. Over the next few years, she was to officiate at dog shows in many countries around the world including Canada, Great Britain, Ireland and Germany.

Mrs. Dodge continued to be interested in many different breeds, but it was around 1934 that she focused her attention on the Cocker Spaniel. Her first was the American Cocker, Amber of Giralda. During one of her visits to Britain in 1935, however, her eye was caught by the English Cocker and she purchased three: Defanotis of Ware, Erna of Silverlands and Surmise of Ware. It was the beginning of a love affair with the breed, and between 1935 and 1939 she imported twenty-three English Cocker Spaniels as her interest in them grew.

The American Kennel Club had made the English Cocker a separate variety of Cocker Spaniel in 1936, but much to the frustration of breeders, the interbreeding of English and American Cockers continued. This diluted the English Cocker and made its breeding and showing much more problematic. It was felt that the only solution was to make the English Cocker a separate breed; Mrs. Dodge agreed, and came to the rescue.

At the annual meeting of The English Cocker Spaniel Club of America in

Colour Plate 147. *Edwin Megargee.*
Ch. Lancelot of Rowanoaks and Ch. Taraleeds of Rowanoaks, *c.1941. Oil on canvas, 18 x 24ins. (45.5 x 61cm). The Bedlington Terrier, one of the more rare breeds in America today, is carefully groomed to achieve its distinctive profile. Note the little tufts of hair which are left at the end of the ears*
Collection The Dog Museum, St. Louis, gift of Elsie McMillan, F. Rockefeller and William Rockefeller; photography Grant Taylor

1941, Mrs. Dodge was appointed president, and at the same time authorised to secure material for a book on the English Cocker, a book which would define the breed, record its history, and present the claim that it was once and for all a breed separate from the American Cocker and, as such, a breed which should be registered separately by The American Kennel Club.

This was a huge undertaking, not only because The American Kennel Club was loathe to move quickly on such a significant step, but also because it represented the great task of unravelling years of interbreeding in the United States, Britain and Canada. Mrs. Dodge embarked on the project, with Josephine Z. Rine doing the research.

The end result was worth the effort, for as a direct result of the publication in 1942 of *The English Cocker Spaniel in America* a new breed standard for the English Cocker was written. With the co-operation of The American Cocker Spaniel Club and The English Cocker Spaniel Club of America, the English Cocker was declared a separate breed in 1946.

Mrs. Dodge remained active in the breed, both importing dogs and buying American-bred examples. She also continued to write, publishing with the artist Enno Myer the *Descriptive Standard of the English Cocker*, and later in the 1950s the article 'The English Cocker Spaniel at Home and Abroad', published in the 1952 issue of *The American Kennel Club Gazette.*

Her affection for dogs — and animals in general — was not limited, however, to living specimens, for very early on Mrs. Dodge began collecting

examples of animal art. Unlike other great collectors of her time, such as J.P. Morgan who put together a world-class collection of carefully selected incunabula, rare editions and art works, Mrs. Dodge's collection was more of an accumulation. She collected animal images and she collected in great numbers.

During the period which she was amassing her immense art collection — when she died she owned more than six thousand items — nineteenth century academic art was not favoured by collectors, and she was able to purchase great examples for what now appear to be bargain-basement prices. In most cases she bought works of art because of their subject matter, rather than their artistic merit. Even the curator of her collections, Josephine Z. Rine, for example, was as much an expert on dogs as she was on art.

Nor did she seem to take any pleasure in the hunt. While she might easily have visited the living artists she collected, or patronised a variety of dealers in Europe and America, she chose instead to purchase the majority of her collection through one dealer — John Graham of Madison Avenue. Commenting on her vast collection, the dealer stated when she died, in 1973,

Colour Plate 148. *Edwin Megargee.*
Ch. Merridip Ethel Ann and Ch. Downberry Volunteer.
Oil on canvas, 28 x 32ins. (71 x 81cm).
These Old English Sheepdogs were among the first imported to the United States by Mrs. Edward Renner. They helped to establish the breed in America

Private collection; photography Dave King

Plate 307. *Many of Mrs. Dodge's showdogs were also her pets, and she doted over them. Her favourites were commemorated by red granite grave markers, neatly lined up at Giralda Farms*

that 'even with $100 million no one these days could collect half of what she had because it isn't available. She was the only one buying this type of art. . . Mrs. Dodge was unhappy if we had nothing to show her on her weekly shopping trips.'

Her taste was eclectic to say the least. In addition to her collections of porcelains, American bronzes, bronze hands, bells, and household furnishings, the great bulk of her art works were of animals. She had vast numbers of nineteenth century animalier bronzes, including virtually

Plate 308. *Reuben Ward Binks.* Ch. Giralda's Geisha, *1936. Gouache on paper, 12 x 15½ ins. (30.5 x 39.5cm). The German Shepherd, along with the English Cocker Spaniel, was one of Mrs. Dodge's favourite breeds and she published a book on it with Josephine Z. Rine*

Private collection; photography Dave King

Plate 309. *Reuben Ward Binks.* Ch. Ferry Von Rauhfelson of Giralda, *c.1940. Gouache on paper, 10 x 14ins. (25.5 x 35.5cm).*
This Doberman was one of the most famous in the history of the breed. Imported from Germany, it actually stepped off the boat to win at The Westminster Kennel Club Collection St. Hubert's Giralda Animal Welfare and Humane Education Center

everything produced by the great Antoine-Louis Barye, perhaps best known for his muscular depictions of animals in combat. She owned forty works by the American Malvina Hoffman, fifty-two works by Rosa Bonheur, major examples of the work of Edwin Landseer, and literally hundreds of nineteenth century animal paintings.

This vast collection of dog and animal paintings seems to have evolved, not from an interest in the aesthetics of the nineteenth century or even in the merits of individual artists, but out of a desire to create a historical record of the animals which were depicted.

It was this impulse to chronicle the history of dogs which was also at play when she invited the English animal artist Reuben Ward Binks to paint portraits of her Giralda dogs. He came to New Jersey in 1931 and stayed for almost a decade, painting over two hundred portraits of Mrs. Dodge's favourite dogs. Binks was known in England to a select few and it was his link with the royal family that may have convinced Mrs. Dodge he was the one to paint portraits of her dogs.

Reuben Ward Binks was born in 1880 in Bolton, and early on exhibited a great talent for painting. Although first interested in painting portraits, he was soon attracted to animals, and in particular, to dogs. 'I was always a natural dog lover,' said Binks, 'and so I leaned toward and graduated into dogs. And here I've been ever since. . . My motto is "a dog is a dog for all that," by which I mean that all kinds of dogs — mongrels or otherwise — are the same to me. I'd lief paint a dog for a gamekeeper as for his master. You see I respect everybody — every man. But I do love and admire dogs.'

As a young boy of ten, Binks won a Raphael Tuck open art competition for boys with a four panelled painting of chrysanthemums. Soon after, he went to study with George Perkins of Manchester. A few years later, on the advice of the great sporting dog enthusiast, Lorna, Countess of Howe, he decided to devote most of his time to the depiction of gun dogs.

As Binks commented during an interview with the writer Freeman Lloyd in 1931:

Colour Plate 149. *Edwin Megargee.*
Royaline White Foam, *1944. Oil on canvas, 24 x 26ins. (61 x 66cm).*
Compare this dog of some fifty years ago with the Clumber Spaniels of today, and one can see that even with a relatively rare breed, the conformation changes over time Collection The American Kennel Club; photography Dave King

Plate 310. *Reuben Ward Binks.*
Ch. Clarion Trumpet, *1936. Gouache on paper, 11½ x 13¼ins. (29 x 33.5cm).*
This Spaniel is one of the many different breeds of dog Mrs. Dodge had in her extensive kennels at Madison, New Jersey, which were capable of housing as many as one hundred animals.
Private collection; photography Dave King

Plate 311. *Gustav Muss-Arnolt.* Wan Lung. *Oil on canvas, 17 x 14ins. (43 x 35.5cm). Notice how the breed has changed in the ninety years or so since this was painted. Today's Chow-Chow, for instance, has much more coat* Collection The American Kennel Club; photography Dave King

> Nearly all the prominent dog owners of England have given me commissions. . . Dr. Turton-Price of Dundee, Scotland, whose 'Crombie' pointers and setters are so popular over here in America as well as elsewhere in the shooting and dog show worlds, has a large collection of my pictures. The Countess of Howe's Labrador and Springer Spaniels are her prime favourites. I must have painted scores and scores of portraits of that great sportswoman's dogs.

In the early years of the twentieth century Binks became well known among dog fanciers in England, often working for the royal family, including Edward VII and Queen Alexandra, George V and his sister Princess Victoria. For George V, for instance, Binks completed portraits of the royal Labrador Retrievers and Clumber Spaniels (Colour Plate 135).

Travelling to visit his clients as the need arose, Binks went to India, staying in Patiala, a Sikh state in the Punjab, for eight months. It was there that he painted the sporting dogs of the Maharaja Dhiraj of Patiala, a great sportsman. Among other breeds, the Maharaja owned Labradors, Springer Spaniels and Cocker Spaniels, Terriers and Chow-Chows. Binks painted approximately one hundred of his dogs.

At a time when Mrs. Dodge might just as easily have commissioned photographs of her dogs, one can only assume that the work of Binks particularly appealed to her, and she perhaps imagined herself linked with British royalty and Binks's other illustrious clients. The Dodges lived in a world completely apart from the vast majority of American society; they were members of a select economic and social group who made their fortunes before the advent of income tax, a group which may best be described as American 'royalty'.

While Mrs. Dodge's interest remained the breeding and exhibiting of dogs, she eventually became dedicated to the promotion of the sport in general, and wanted to promote good breeding and competition on a larger scale than was possible in her kennels, however extensive. In the 1920s she had allowed the German Shepherd Dog Club of America to hold their specialty shows at Giralda Farms. Her interest in German Shepherds was well known, and it was logical that she would support the breed club to this extent. Nonetheless, if she were to further advance the case for the serious breeding of all pure-bred dogs, it seemed appropriate that she should become more involved.

The early German Shepherd specialty shows were perhaps the impetus for the now legendary Morris and Essex Dog Show, a world-class dog show which Mrs. Dodge created and ran on and off from its inception in 1927 until the last show was held in 1953. It was to become one of the most lavish and widely attended dog shows in the world.

The first Morris and Essex was held at Giralda in 1927, with 595 dogs entered representing seventeen breeds. Mrs. Dodge's original idea was that it be restricted to some of the more popular breeds, and the first show excluded hounds and toys. In the following years, however, more breeds were added. In 1932 thirty-six different breeds were shown. In 1936 it was opened up to represent sixty, and in that year it was the largest bench show in the United States. In 1939 it attracted a total of 4,456 dogs, a large number even by modern American standards.

Called the finest outdoor dog show in the world and 'a model of its kind', the show continued to grow, but Mrs. Dodge did not allow its burgeoning size to affect its quality. It was first and foremost a dog show created for the comfort and convenience of the exhibitors, with all possible amenities. It was a marvellous show all-round, with the best judges enlisted, no doubt attracted by the prestige of the show and the $150 judging fee, an unheard of amount during the depression. The prizes — both cash and sterling silver — were lavish and, of course, all supplied by Mrs. Dodge.

As the writer Freeman Lloyd commented, 'Everything at Morris was done on a grand scale, even to the cards of welcome and florists' boxes of choice blooms left for the wives of the judges and other guests staying at the hotels. What a charming little town is Madison with its lush meadows, highly bred dairy kine, lovely lawns, seas of learning, and wealth of foliage at its greenest and brightest towards the end of May.'

The show ground itself was a model for all dog shows to emulate: Mrs. Dodge's private polo field was rolled smooth, and additional fields were

Plate 312. *G. Muss-Arnolt.*
Ch. Windholme's Roadster, *1903. Oil on canvas, 22 x 30ins. (56 x 76cm)*
The Dalmatian is only rarely depicted in art, and even then in conjunction with a coach scene or horse. Here the artist has presented it in a standard show pose, showing off the animal's best features
Collection The Dog Museum, St. Louis, gift of The Westminster Kennel Foundation

prepared for parking the 10,000 or so passenger cars, trucks and trailers which came to the show. If the weather was fine, the dogs were judged in the open air, but as a contingency, mammoth maroon and gold circus tents were constructed along the edges of the field. Some 160,000 square feet of awning were required, a huge amount considering that the famous Barnum and Bailey circus needed only 70,000. Luncheons were provided for both judges and exhibitors (an unheard of luxury) and a cafeteria provided for the public.

The show grew in size in the 1930s and 1940s until, during its heyday, it required as many as eight hundred people to run on the day itself. The local police and state troopers were enlisted to control the exhibitors, dogs and the public alike, for by 1939 it had attracted a record number of exhibitors and up to 50,000 spectators, all of whom paid the entry fee. It was a social event that was not to be missed. Thousands came from all around to witness the festivities, and it was widely covered by the press.

The Morris and Essex Show was tremendously successful, and continued to be held except for a few interruptions; in deference to the war effort, no shows were held between 1942 and 1945, and there was no show in 1954. Mrs. Dodge had requested a date for that year's show, which The American Kennel Club did not grant, having approved it for another dog show. The only date available was the Memorial Day weekend. Mrs. Dodge could not possibly hold the dog show at that time because the local off-duty policemen she required to handle traffic and the large crowds in attendance would not be available

Plate 313. *Louis Contoit.*
Queensbury White Bird, *c.1940. Oil on canvas, 14 x 18ins. (35.5 x 45.5cm).*
Queensbury White Bird, a top winning Bull Terrier of his day, is much more of the 'Terrier' type rather than the 'Bully' dogs which are winning in the show ring today
Collection Mr. and Mrs. William Kendrick; photography Dave King

Plate 314. *Mildred Megargee.*
Ch. Hollycourt Silverado and Ch. Belle Isle. *Oil on panel, 7 x 9ins. (17.5 x 23cm).*
Mildred Megargee, the sister of Edwin, was an artist of considerable achievement, preferring to work on a small, intimate scale. She often executed portraits on glass similar in scale to this small painting
Collection The Dog Museum, St. Louis, gift of the Sara C. Chisholm Estate

Plate 315. *Edwin Megargee.*
Great Pyrenees, *1930. Oil on canvas, 32 x 38ins. (81 x 96.5cm)*
The most impressive in a series of Edwin Megargee paintings which were commissioned by the late Mary Crane, these dogs are portrayed with the Pyrenees in the background, from which the breed derived its name

Collection The Dog Museum, St. Louis, gift of The Estate of Mary Crane; photography Grant Taylor

because of traffic duties in their own communities, so she cancelled the show and Morris and Essex was never held again.

Mrs. Dodge's love of animals and a concern for their welfare went back to her childhood days in New York City when she would pick up stray dogs in Central Park and take them back to her Fifth Avenue home. This background, along with her continuing interest in horses and pure-bred dogs, led in a natural way to the development of St. Hubert's Giralda, an animal shelter which she founded in 1939. Named after the famous patron saint of animals, the shelter was to be set up to care for stray cats and dogs, and eventually to find them good homes. Because of the war, however, and various administrative problems, the shelter did not function as Mrs. Dodge had hoped until 1958, when it offered dog warden services to the surrounding community and cared for strays.

The shelter exists to this day, and has become a model of its kind. St. Hubert's Giralda responds to animals in trouble, and provides an adoption service as well as educational programmes on how to take care of a pet once it is adopted. Educational programmes on animals, their care and treatment, are provided on a regular basis for school children as well as adults.

The shelter is also a repository for a small portion of Mrs. Dodge's collection, the vast majority of which was sold by Sotheby's in a record-breaking series of auctions in 1976, the work of Reuben Ward Binks being by far the best represented.

Plate 316. *Edwin Megargee.*
Kerry Blue Terriers. *Oil on canvas, 21 x 27½ins. (53.5 x 69cm).*
These rather stiffly posed Kerry Blue Terriers, were clearly show dogs. This breed has only rarely been depicted in the visual arts, perhaps because it only became popular in the 1920s
Collection The American Kennel Club; photography Dave King

Plate 317. *Gustav Muss-Arnolt.*
Old English Sheepdog. *Oil on canvas, 9 x 12ins. (23 x 30.5cm).*
This painting is a rare departure for Gustav Muss-Arnolt, who more often depicted Setters and Pointers. Depictions of Old English Sheepdogs are rare in the history of art
Private collection; photography Dave King

APPENDIX

Selected Dog Artists

A.B.
Plate 122.

E. AISTROP, English, fl.1890
Plate 68.

Cecil Charles Windsor ALDIN, R.B.A., English 1870-1935

While not a dog painter per se, Aldin's many drawings, pastels and prints of dogs call for his inclusion here. Born in Slough, Aldin studied art at South Kensington under Frank Calderon and at Midhurst, Sussex, where Calderon took his pupils from London for the summer. It was there that Aldin began his hunting career, and also where he developed rheumatic fever, which curtailed his stay in Sussex, and troubled him intermittently for the rest of his life.

Shortly after his return to London, his first picture was published in the *Building News,* 1890. In 1904 Aldin moved to Henley-on-Thames, and continued to hunt as much as possible, making sketches from the saddle. He developed arthritis in his hands which considerably slowed his drawing and painting, and finally forced him to give up hunting and move to a warmer climate.

Aldin worked mainly in pastel or watercolour. He is perhaps best known for his delightful pictures of dogs, as well as the many books which he illustrated.

Robert L. ALEXANDER, R.S.A., R.S.W., Scottish 1840-1923

Born at Dolgaren, Ayrshire, Alexander was first apprenticed to a Kilmarnock house painter who also painted landscape. From 1868 he devoted himself to painting dogs and horses. Alexander often painted in a loose style with a quick active brushstroke. Many of his paintings of dogs show animals interacting — Skye Terriers looking at rabbits in a pen, or a mother with her puppies. During his lifetime he exhibited at many different exhibitions, but primarily at the R.S.A.
Plate 229.

Henry ALKEN, Snr., English, 1785-1851
Colour Plates 30, 31.

Richard ANSDELL, R.A., English, 1815-1885

Born and educated in Liverpool, Ansdell is known for his many dog and animal portraits executed in a tight, academic style. He studied under W.C. Smith, a Chatham portrait painter, and collaborated occasionally with Thomas Creswick, R.A.

Ansdell must certainly be considered one of the finest of all nineteenth century animal artists and by some is compared favourably with Sir Edwin Landseer. While Landseer often imbued his animals with an almost human quality, Ansdell's pictures are much more matter-of-fact, with a great attention to the details of anatomy and coat texture.

He spent much time in the Scottish Highlands where he had a lodge on Loch Laggan. A sportsman, he particularly enjoyed shooting.

Ansdell was very successful during his lifetime. He was a member of the Liverpool Academy and President from 1837 to 1852. He also exhibited 149 paintings at the R.A. between 1840 and 1885.
Plates 38, 102; Colour Plates 21, 71, 97, 114.

Janet ARCHER, English, exh. 1881-1961
Colour Plate 129.

Edwin ARMFIELD, English, 19th century
Colour Plate 65.

George ARMFIELD, English, c.1820-1893

George Armfield Smith (better known as George Armfield) was born, and lived most of his life in London, but was an avid sportsman. He was a prolific and popular painter, and exhibited under the family name 'Smith' from 1830 to 1839. He exhibited thirty-two paintings at the R.A. between 1840 and 1862 and exhibited regularly at both the British Institute and at Suffolk Street until 1875.

His work should not be confused with the less accomplished E. Armfield. They both evidently had a tremendous output, with George in particular known for his small paintings of Terriers ratting, or Spaniels flushing ducks.

At his best, Armfield's paintings are technically very fine, with a quick, painterly brushstroke which enlivens his subject matter. His output was so prodigious, however, that many of his paintings repeat a standard pictorial formula.

Plates 94, 148.

B, 19th century

Plate 191.

John Henry Frederick BACON, English, 1866-1914

Plate 275.

F. BAILEY, English, fl.1884

Plate 153.

Arthur BAKER, English, 1864-1889

Baker produced many well-executed sporting and animal compositions in both oil and watercolour. He lived in London and Tunbridge Wells. Between 1885 and 1889 he painted in Essex, northern France, and Scotland. He exhibited two works at the R.A.

Plates 103, 104.

Bessie BAMBER, English, fl.1910

Plate 261.

Charles Burton BARBER, English, 1845-1894

Born in Great Yarmouth, Barber is perhaps best known because of Queen Victoria's patronage of his work. Primarily a painter of sporting scenes and animals, he seems to have been influenced by the work of Sir Edwin Landseer, for his paintings often have a rather sentimental turn. Technically, he was a highly accomplished artist and produced very finished paintings of dogs.

Barber exhibited thirty-two works at the R.A. from 1866.

Plates 58, 164.

Wright BARKER, R.B.A., English, 1848-1941

Sometimes known as John Wright Barker, Barker always signed with a bold signature in full, and frequently dated his work. Many of his paintings of dogs include very decorative backgrounds, establishing the dog in a domestic interior.

Barker painted hunting scenes, horses, and highland cattle, and more occasionally, landscapes. He executed some fairly large portraits, and frequently worked on large canvases, (50 x 70ins. not being uncommon). Twenty-one of his paintings were exhibited at the R.A.

Plates 84, 249.

Francis C. BARLOW, English, 1626-1704

Francis Barlow, who painted birds, fish and animals, came to London from Lincolnshire and was apprenticed to William Shepherd the court portrait painter. His style was based on close observation, and had little in common, other than subject matter, with his exotic contemporaries such as Bogdani and Hondius.

Barlow's earliest known work, dated 1648, is a drawing of 'David Slaying the Lion', now in the British Museum; the following year his engraving of 'Princess Elizabeth' was published in

The Hague.

The quality of Barlow's paintings, showing so vividly the rural life of his age, place him far above his contemporaries. The writer Walter Shaw Sparrow called him the 'Father of Sport in Art'.

Plates 23, 24.

George BARRAUD, English, 18th century

Plate 114.

Henry BARRAUD, English, 1811-1874

Younger by a year than his brother, the artist William Barraud, Henry and he shared a studio and worked in collaboration. They exhibited sporting scenes and portraits both singly and jointly, and achieved a wide popularity with owners of horses, hounds and dogs. The *Old Sporting Magazine* published seven prints of his work. He exhibited seventeen of his own works at the R.A. and fifteen executed with William.

William BARRAUD, English, 1810-1850

William Barraud, a pupil of Abraham Cooper, shared a studio with his younger brother Henry, with whom he collaborated, exhibiting sporting scenes and portraits both singly and jointly. At the R.A., where he first showed when he was eighteen, he exhibited forty-four of his own paintings and fifteen in collaboration with Henry.

William was considered the more talented of the brothers, but his career was cut short by his untimely death. Among his engravings published in the *Old Sporting Magazine* was a portrait of the racehorse 'British Volunteer' and four prints of greyhounds.

Plate 284.

Antoine-Louis BARYE, French, 1796-1875.

Plate 22.

Arthur J. BATT, English, fl.1875-1897

Born in Hampshire, Batt lived variously at Romsey, Lyndhurst and Brockenhurst. He painted small pictures, sometimes on panel, of domestic animals and birds. Batt's paintings of dogs, although often small, are usually highly expressive and beautifully finished. He exhibited four works at the R.A.

J. BEARD, English, 19th century

Plate 156.

James Henry BEARD, American, b.1812-c.1880

Plate 292.

Reuben Ward BINKS, English, 1880-1950

Reuben Ward Binks was born in Bolton, Lancashire, and from an early age showed a great aptitude for the visual arts. He studied under George Perkins, and while little is known about his early artistic training, he soon became known for his depictions of animals, and dogs in particular.

The artist's talent soon gained him the recognition of the animal-loving landed gentry and, with the support of Lorna, Countess of Howe, Binks established himself as a fine animal artist. Working mostly in watercolour, he completed commissions for the Prince of Wales, the Duke of York and King George V. Binks travelled extensively, including to India where he worked for the Marahaja Dhiraj of Patiala. In America, he worked for a number of clients, including Mr. and Mrs. S. Hallock du Pont as well as Mrs. Geraldine R. Dodge who commissioned over 200 watercolour portraits of her dogs.

Binks, who worked almost exclusively in transparent watercolour and gouache, held his most extensive exhibition at New York's Harlow and Macdonald Galleries in 1931.

Plates 165, 308, 309, 310; Colour Plate 135.

Thomas BLINKS, English 1853-1910

Blinks is among the best known and most highly regarded of those who painted sporting dogs in the late nineteenth century. His paintings, executed in a highly finished style, often depict sporting dogs in the field, characteristically posed on point or, in the case of Foxhounds, running over fields and fences in pursuit of the fox.

Born in Mardston, his family soon moved to Ticehurst where the young Blinks went to school. He was sketching by the age of ten, and although he wanted to study art he was, at his father's insistence, apprenticed to a tailor. Although he was to receive no formal training, his keen observation and natural talent soon had him producing paintings of the sporting life with an almost photographic quality.

Blinks worked in both oil and watercolour, although he is certainly best remembered for his oil paintings. He first exhibited at the Dudley Gallery in 1881, and at the R.B.A. in 1882. He exhibited twenty-nine works at the R.A. from 1833 to 1910.

Plates 140, 274; Colour Plates 48, 66, 67, 73.

John BOULTBEE, English, 1753-1812

Boultbee, whose work is for the most part confined to equestrian and animal portraiture, was an artist of considerable standing, executing highly detailed portraits, often set in a classical landscape.

The twin brother of painter Thomas Boultbee, John was raised and lived at Stordon Grange, Leicester, then moved with the family to London in the 1770s where Thomas was enrolled in the Academy Schools. In the 1780s John worked in the Loughborough area where he painted several pictures for the well-known Robert Blakewell (1726-95). He exhibited six paintings at the R.A.

Boultbee's paintings are characterised by a great attention to detail and anatomical precision. No action or hunting pictures are recorded by him, and his paintings often have a serene, peaceful quality, an impression which is often strengthened by the inclusion of classical buildings or ruins in the distant landscape.

Plate 125.

Thomas W. BRETLAND, English, 1802-1874
Colour Plate 61.

C.D., English, fl.1877
Colour Plate 110.

Henry CALVERT, English, 1798-c.1869
Plate 65.

Samuel John CARTER, English, 1835-1892
Plate 83.

Henry Bernard CHALON, English, 1770-1849

While known as a painter of horses, Chalon did many small scale portraits of dogs. He studied at the R.A. Schools and enjoyed success as a painter during his lifetime. In 1795 he was appointed animal painter to the Duchess of York and later to the Prince Regent and William IV. He had many important patrons, exhibiting almost two hundred paintings at the R.A.

Page 17; Plates 74, 81; Colour Plates 16, 62.

John Watkins CHAPMAN, English, fl.1853-1903
Plates 178, 190.

Lilian CHEVIOT, English, exh.1894-1902
Plates 143, 144, 260; Colour Plate 104.

Thomas CLAYTON, English, fl.1843
Colour Plate 32.

Robert CLEMINSON, English, fl.1865-1868

Little is known about Cleminson who was both a landscape and animal painter, executing many paintings of Setters. His work, sometimes deficient in an understanding of anatomy, is often very expressive, especially when depicting Highland game.

Plate 107.

George COLE, English, 1810-1883

Early in his career Cole was a painter of horses and dogs, turning to landscape later in his life. One of his first commissions was to paint a series of posters for a travelling circus. He then studied animal painting more seriously, going to Holland to study the Dutch Masters. Returning to London, he exhibited portraits, landscapes and animal subjects from about 1840, including nineteen paintings at the R.A.

Plate 77.

Margaret COLLYER, English, fl.1897-1910

Colour Plate 99.

Louis CONTOIT, American, fl.1940

Plate 313.

Abraham COOPER, R.A., English, 1787-1868

One of the best known of English sporting artists from the first half of the nineteenth century, Abraham Cooper was largely self-taught. He received encouragement and a number of lessons from the well-known sporting artist, Benjamin Marshall.

Cooper was predominantly a painter of horses but executed several dog portraits. His work is characterised by a high finish and rich, naturalistic colouring, as well as a strict attention to anatomy. Several important artists studied under him, including John Frederick Herring and William Barraud. He was elected to the R.A. in 1817, becoming known as 'Horse' Cooper. He exhibited 332 paintings there between 1812 and 1869

Plate 45; Colour Plate 34.

Alexander Davis COOPER, English, fl.1837-1888

The son of the sporting painter Abraham Cooper, Alexander followed in his father's footsteps, executing many equine and canine portraits. He exhibited some sixty-seven works at the R.A., the majority of which were landscapes. Cooper was a fine painter but he did not achieve the renown of his father who was truly a major sporting artist.

Horatio Henry COULDERY, English, 1832-1893

Born the son of a painter and apprenticed to a cabinetmaker, Couldery soon realised his true vocation when, at the age of twenty-five, he entered the R.A. Schools.

Known predominantly as a painter of cats and dogs, his work is tightly painted with great attention to detail. Indeed, in 1875 he attracted the attention of the art critic John Ruskin, who in his *Academy Notes* commented that one of his paintings was 'quite the most skilful piece of minute and Dureresque painting in the exhibition.'

Couldery exhibited some twenty works at the R.A., and although many know him for his very sensitive portrayals of cats, his dogs are painted equally well, with a great attention to expression and coat texture.

Plates 170, 173.

Helen CRIDLAND, English, fl.1886-1901

Plate 152.

Henry CROWTHER, English, fl.1905

Plates 33, 263; Colour Plate 123.

Conradijn CUNAEUS, Dutch, 1828-1895

Born in Dendermonde, Cunaeus trained at the Academy of Amsterdam (1844-49) and studied under Nicolas Pieneman, a Dutch landscapist and portraitist. In 1850 he became a member of 'Arti et Amicitiae' in Amsterdam.

Cunaeus was a painter of genre scenes with dogs rather than a dog or animal painter. His canvases are well executed although his palette is rather flat, with more white added to the colours than that of his British contemporaries.

Plate 206.

Albert CUYP, Dutch, 1620-1691
Plate 15.

John DALBY, English, c.1810-c.1865
Plates 46, 120.

Sir William Henry DAVIS, English, 1783-1864
Plate 121.

Frederick Thomas DAWS, English, b.1878
Plates 135, 268.

R. DINMONT, English, 19th century
Plate 186.

Arthur Charles DODD, English, fl.1878-1890
Plate 220.

John Charles DOLLMAN, R.I., R.O.I., R.W.S., English, 1831-1934
Colour Plate 74.

Edward Algernon Stuart DOUGLAS, English, fl. 1860-1918

Little is known about Douglas who painted in oil and watercolours. He exhibited ten pictures at the R.A. between 1880 and 1892, all of which were hunting scenes. He also painted portraits of horses, dogs and group portraits, such as *Lord Portman's Hounds: The East Dorset,* which was exhibited at the R.A. in 1890. He often produced pictures in sets of four, and occasionally worked in miniature. His works exhibit a detailed and delicate finish.

Colour Plate 45.

Edwin DOUGLAS, Scottish, 1848-1914

Douglas, who studied at the R.A. Schools, was an animal artist in the tradition of Sir Edwin Landseer. A painter of both horses and dogs, his animals have soft, sympathetic expressions and often lustrous coats. He exhibited forty-three paintings at the R.A. between 1869 and 1900.

Plates 108, 147, 238.

Alfred DUKE, English, fl.1890-1910
Plates 134, 150.

Albrecht DÜRER, German, 1471-1528
Plate 13.

George EARL, English, fl. 1856-1883

The father of the better known animal artist, Maud Earl, George Earl was an active sportsman who excelled in the depiction of dogs. Little is known of his background and training or his early work.

Earl exhibited nineteen paintings at the R.A. between 1857 and 1882, although only two were of dogs (a Maltese and an Old English Mastiff). He is remembered primarily as a sporting dog painter. His most important work was undoubtedly *The Field Trial Meeting* which depicted a mythical field trial in Bala, North Wales, in which almost all the important field trial personalities of the day were depicted with their dogs (Colour Plate 50). Another important project for which he is often remembered was an important series of portrait head studies of dogs. This series, entitled *Champion Dogs of England,* was painted in the 1870s and is illustrated in a now rare volume of the same name.

Plates 93, 100, 207, 226; Colour Plates 34, 37, 41, 43, 50, 55, 57, 62, 70.

Maud EARL, English, 1864-1943

Perhaps more than any artist born in the nineteenth century, Maud Earl is associated with the painting of pure-bred dogs. Born into an artistic family — her father was the well-known animal artist, George Earl, and her uncle, Thomas Earl, painted horses and other animals — Maud was taught by her father and quickly developed her natural talent for capturing the true character of her canine subjects.

Maud Earl exhibited regularly in England and Europe. She was a prolific and much sought after artist who painted many of the important dogs of her day, including those belonging to famous dog fanciers such as Edward VII and the Duchess of Newcastle. By 1916, she had received international recognition, with several solo exhibitions, and her work was widely reproduced, both in books and in print form.

Her *oeuvre* may be loosely divided into four styles: the naturalistic, richly painted portraits of dogs from around 1880 to 1900; a looser, more sketchy style from about 1900 to 1915; what she referred to as her oriental style from about 1916 into the 1920s after she emigrated to New York; and her late, rather stylised portraits of dogs painted during the 1930s in America. It was during her early years in America when she painted her little known but elegant paintings of birds which she considered some of her best work.

Plates 50, 59, 85, 96, 109, 131, 142, 158, 182, 183, 189, 192, 195, 233, 234, 239, 259, 262, 264, 265, 281, 282; Colour Plates 1, 7, 49, 59, 76, 84, 85, 96, 103, 112, 117, 120, 121, 124, 125, 131.

Thomas EARL, English, fl.1836-1855

Plate 146; Colour Plate 58.

John EMMS, English, 1813-1912

Emms is predominantly known for his paintings of horses, Hounds and Terriers, but he painted many portraits of other pure-bred dogs as well.

Born in Norfolk, he was the son of the artist Henry William Emms. He worked in London as a studio assistant to the successful Lord Frederick Leighton, but soon went on his own.

Emms was a very prolific artist and while his early portraits were highly finished he later developed a very distinctive style in which he created expressive animal portraits with a bold, almost calligraphic brush stroke. Because of his deep understanding of animal anatomy and his painterly skills, this often resulted in loose, painterly portraits that have a fresh, immediate quality.

He exhibited 290 works at the R.A. from 1866 on, and in 1875 three of his paintings were exhibited at the London exhibition, 'The Beauties of the New Forest'.

Plates 174, 236; Colour Plates 28, 44, 81, 98, 126.

Charles van den EYCKEN, Belgian, 1839-c.1925

Frontispiece.

Frances L. FAIRMAN, English, 1836-1923

Frances Fairman, perhaps more than any artist, is associated with the oriental breeds and, in particular, the Japanese Chin. She was very active in the Ladies' Kennel Association and enjoyed the patronage of many prominent dog fanciers, including Queen Alexandra. She exhibited twice at the R.A.

Fairman worked in a soft, impressionistic style, often including a flower in her compositions. As one interviewer from *The Ladies' Kennel Journal* pointed out: 'What Miss Fairman feels about flowers and fruits she feels about dogs, she loves to have them around her. The walls of her studio are lined with studies of tropical vegetation, portraits of dogs, studies of her own dogs, studies of heads of famous dogs, and her own pet spaniels lie in their cages in the middle of the studio and repose in her visitors' laps.'

Plates 270, 271, 272, 273; Colour Plates 35, 79, 122.

Sir Samuel Luke FILDES, English, 1843-1927
Plate 269.

Benjamin FIRTH, Jnr., English, fl.1896
Plate 254.

Marmaduke C. William FLOWER, English, fl.1873-1910
Colour Plate 42.

Jean-Honoré FRAGONARD, French, 1732-1806
Plate 20.

Marguerite FROBISHER, English, fl.1916-1940
Colour Plate 90.

Thomas GAINSBOROUGH, English, 1727-1788
Plate 245.

Henry GARLAND, English, fl.1854-1890
Colour Plate 116.

Valentine Thomas GARLAND, English, fl.1868-1903

The son of Henry Thomas Garland of Winchester, Garland worked in oils and watercolour, painting animals and genre. He exhibited twenty-four works at the R.A. His paintings have a very finished, if sometimes sentimental quality about them and he was quite successful during his lifetime.

George GARRARD, A.R.A., English, 1760-1826
Colour Plate 53.

James William GILES, R.S.A., Scottish, 1801-1870
Plate 205.

E.W. GILL, English, 19th century
Plate 119.

Sawrey GILPIN, R.A., English, 1733-1807
Plate 114.

Léon Paul Pierre GLAIZE, French, 1842-1932
Plate 193.

R.A. GOOCH, English, c.1790-1860
Plate 75.

Colin GRAEME, English, 1859-1910

One of the sons of R.H. Roe, Colin dropped the surname Roe to distinguish himself from other members of his family. Graeme was a very prolific animal artist, painting many portraits of horses, sporting dogs, and Terriers. He had a good understanding of anatomy and a painterly technique, but an unfortunate habit of sometimes outlining the eyes of the animals which he depicted, giving them an exaggerated, almost 'made-up' appearance.
Plate 126.

Thomas B. GRIFFIN, American, 19th century
Plate 293.

Frederick HALL, English, 1860-1948
Plate 78; Colour Plate 22.

Charles HAMILTON, English, fl.1831-1867
Colour Plate 132.

Charles HANCOCK, English, 1802-1877
Plate 179.

Heywood HARDY, A.R.W.S., R.E., R.O.I., R.P., English, 1843-1933

Heywood Hardy was the youngest son of the distinguished artist James Hardy, Snr. He painted equestrian, hunting, coaching and genre scenes. Following his initial failure as an animal artist, he joined the 7th Somerset Volunteers.

In 1864 Hardy went to Paris and entered the Ecole des Beaux-Arts, and studied under Pielse (a painter of battle scenes). He later visited Antwerp, and returned to England just before 1868.

In 1870 he settled in London, where he shared a studio with Briton Riviere, the animal artist. His career flourished almost immediately. Forty-six of his paintings were exhibited at the R.A. He also worked as an illustrator for the *Illustrated London News* and *Graphic*.

Hardy's style is characterised by painterly application of what appears to be thin layers of paint. His oil paintings have a luminescent, almost transparent quality similar to watercolours.
Colour Plate 47.

James HARDY, Jnr., R.I., English, 1832-1889

The son of the landscape painter, James Hardy, Snr., two of James Jnr.'s brothers were also artists. Hardy worked in both watercolour and oils and was perhaps best known for his paintings of rustic landscapes and hunting scenes. His portrayals of sporting dogs were often accompanied by dead game. Hardy became a member of the New Watercolour Society in 1877, and exhibited some nine works at the R.A.
Plate 105; Colour Plates 64, 113.

Walter HARROWING, fl. 1877-1904

Very little is known about Harrowing. He specialised in animal paintings, in particular farm animals and dogs. Many of his paintings have a naïve quality about them which adds to their charm.

Harrowing was obviously fond of dogs, and usually painted them in a domestic interior.
Plates 57, 188, 242.

William Jacob HAYS, Snr., American, 1830-1875
Plates 288, 289.

Wilson HEPPLE, English, 1854-1937
Plate 32.

John Frederick HERRING, Snr., English, 1795-1865
Plates 28, 67, 90; Colour Plate 6.

Thomas Hewes HINCKLEY, American, 1813-1896

Born in Boston, Hinckley specialised in painting animals, in particular sporting dogs. In 1851 he travelled to England where he studied the work of, among others, Sir Edwin Landseer and the Flemish Masters. While in England two of his paintings were exhibited at the R.A. in 1858.

Upon returning to America, Hinckley excelled in the depiction of sporting dogs. Although influenced by Landseer, his mature style is more reminiscent of Landseer's contemporary Richard Ansdell, who painted in a tightly controlled manner.
Colour Plate 143.

William HOGARTH, English, 1697-1764
Plate 52.

Thomas HOLD, English, fl.1872
Plate 227.

Florence Mabel HOLLAMS, S.W.A., English, 1877-1963
Plates 111, 267; Colour Plate 137.

Edwin Frederick HOLT, English, fl. 1854-1897

Holt painted mythological, biblical, historical and genre subjects. He studied at the R.A. Schools, and won a silver medal in 1854. He exhibited seven works at the R.A. and was a regular exhibitor at the British Institution and Suffolk Street Gallery.

Later in his career, he devoted his attention to animals and painted many sporting subjects, farm animals and domestic pets. Much of his later work is characterised by a bold painterly style. Many of his portraits of dogs, however, are rather weak anatomically, and sometimes have rather exaggerated expressions.

Plates 40, 47; Colour Plate 54.

Abraham HONDIUS, Dutch, c.1638-1695

The Dutch-born Hondius moved to London from Rotterdam about 1666, and remained there for the rest of his life, painting animals. One of the first foreigners to influence British artists in this field, he brought with him a realism and sound knowledge of anatomy. The critic George Vertue praised his paintings of bull-baiting and his famous *The Dog Market* which showed dogs of thirty different breeds.

Colour Plates 3, 9.

George W. HORLOR, English, fl. 1849-1891

Noted for his landscapes, in which animals predominate, as well as portraits of animals and sporting scenes, Horlor's best work was done in a soft, detailed style. This was ideally suited to depicting the expressions of various animals, and especially those of dogs.

He worked at Cheltenham, Birmingham and Brentford, and exhibited a total of nineteen works at the R.A.

Plates 151, 162; Colour Plate 95.

B.A. HOWE, English, fl.1844-1857
Colour Plate 25.

Walter HUNT, Jnr., English, 1861-1931

The son of Walter Snr., and father of Edgar Hunt. All three were animal painters who lived in Warwickshire. Walter Jnr. went further afield for his subjects than Edgar, to include many sporting scenes. He exhibited some nineteen paintings at the R.A.

Plate 157.

B.A. HYLAND, English, fl.1886
Plate 276; Colour Plate 107.

J. JACK, English fl.1867
Colour Plate 101.

Florence JAY, English, fl. 1905-1920

This artist lived in Peterborough and Liverpool. She painted portraits, genre scenes and sporting subjects, showing a special talent for depicting dogs. Her paintings are often worked rather loosely, with emphasis on the dog's expression and coat texture.

She exhibited five paintings at the R.A. from 1905 to 1908, and at the Liverpool Autumn Exhibitions held at the Walker Art Gallery, Liverpool, in 1915 and 1920.

Colour Plates 105, 130.

Paul JONES, English, fl. 1856-1879

The son of Samuel John Egbert Jones, the better known sporting artist of the two, Paul Jones specialised in dogs and horses and particularly liked Terriers either ratting or rabbit hunting. His works are primarily known for their small dimensions and are executed with great care and detail.

Samuel John Egbert JONES, English, c.1795-c.1855
Plate 168.

Lucy KEMP-WELCH, English, 1869-1958
Plate 34.

Friedrich Wilhelm KEYL, English, 1823-1871
Plates 215, 216, 231, 243; Colour Plate 127.

Marguerite KIRMSE, American, 1885-1954
Plate 286.

James LAMBERT, Snr., English, 1725-1788
Plate 36.

Paul de LAMERIE, French, eighteenth century
Plate 210.

Sir Edwin Henry LANDSEER, R.A., English, 1802-1873

The third and youngest son of the engraver John Landseer, A.R.A., Edwin's precocious talent made him one of the most famous animal painters of all time. From a very early age he was drawn to sketching animals, sometimes in company with the young artist J.F. Lewis. He received encouragement from the artist Benjamin Robert Haydon and was influenced by James Ward and Stubbs, whose drawings for *The Anatomy of A Horse* Landseer eventually acquired. He first exhibited at the R.A. when he was twelve years old When he exhibited *Fighting Dogs Getting Wind* at the R.A., it established his reputation, and he exhibited regularly from then on.
In 1824, he went to the Highlands with C.R. Leslie and returned there year after year to paint its scenery and life. He achieved quick success both in his profession and society. He was elected A.R.A. in 1826 and R.A. in 1831 and became one of Queen Victoria's favourite artists, further establishing his reputation and the demand for his paintings.

Landseer was a superb draughtsman and anatomist, capable of painting animals with vigour and true insight.

In 1865 he was elected P.R.A. but refused the honour due to ill health. He exhibited 179 works at the R.A.

Plates 44, 169, 171, 172, 199, 200, 201, 202, 203, 204, 213, 214, 225.

Lucy A. LEAVERS, English, fl. 1887-1898

Lucy Leavers, from Nottingham, specialised in painting pictures of dogs and cats. Often painting in a large scale, her work is characterised by a highly finished style and her choice of compositions, which often put animals in amusing situations. She exhibited seven works at the R.A.

Colour Plate 115.

Mary Lascelles LEESMITH, English, fl.1893-1897
Colour Plate 23.

Sir Peter LELY, English, 1618-1680
Colour Plate 10.

W.V. LONGE, English, nineteenth century
Plate 141.

Nevison Arthur LORAINE, R.B.A., English, fl.1889-1903
Plate 180.

William LUKER, R.B.A., English, c.1820-1892
Colour Plate 72.

J.F. MAGGS, English, 19th century
Plate 185.

Benjamin MARSHALL, English, 1768-1834
Plates 25, 97; Colour Plate 36.

J. Fitz MARSHALL, R.B.A., English, 1859-1932
Plate 136.

R. MARSHALL, English, 19th century
Colour Plate 77.

Edwin MEGARGEE, American, 1883-1958

Born in Philadelphia, the son of a well-known lawyer and sportsman, Megargee studied at Drexel Institute in Philadelphia and the Art Student League in New York.

Although Megargee painted animals of all kinds — dogs, horses and cattle — he is best known for his many depictions of pure-bred dogs. An active American Kennel Club judge, he painted many portrait commissions and participated in several projects such as the completion of a series of circular portraits of pure-bred dogs commissioned for the kennels of the ship, the S.S. *America.* His paintings illustrated many publications including *Field and Stream* and *Country Life* as well as several Derrydale Press books.

Because of his active involvement in pure-bred dogs, almost his entire output of dog paintings falls into the pure-bred dog portrait category. Most were portrait commissions.
Plates 315, 316; Colour Plates 147, 148, 149.

Mildred MEGARGEE, American, 20th century
Plate 314.

Gabriel METSU, Dutch, 1630-1667
Plate 18.

E. MONDY, English, fl. 1875
Colour Plate 38.

George Charles MORLAND, English, 1763-1804

George Morland was the son of the painter Henry Morland; he was apprenticed to his father at the age of fourteen. His first painting was accepted by the R.A. in 1781, and he soon established a reputation for rustic scenes which often included animals.

Morland was particularly adept at painting dogs and horses, although his proclivity for painting pigs saw him dubbed a pig painter. His best work was executed in a quick, painterly style, which captured the anatomy and expressions of the animals he depicted. Unfortunately, the artist suffered from a drinking problem which resulted in his premature death. He exhibited thirty-eight works at the R.A.
Colour Plate 11.

George MORLEY, English, fl.1832-1863
Plates 30, 241.

Robert MORLEY, R.B.A. English, 1857-1941

Morley studied art at the Slade School, later attending classes in Munich and Rome. Around

1888 he turned to landscape and animal painting, often depicting dogs in domestic surroundings. He was appointed the Hon. Secretary of the R.B.A. in 1890. He exhibited some five works at the R.A.

Plate 129.

Antonio MORO, Spanish, 1517-1575

Plate 12.

R.S. MOSELEY, English, fl.1860-1893

Plates 39, 175; Colour Plate 134.

W. MURRAY, c.1780-c.1820

Plate 86.

Gustav MUSS-ARNOLT, American, 1858-1927

Muss-Arnolt was one of a small group of American painters, among them Percival Rosseau and Edmund Osthaus, who specialised in the depiction of sporting dogs.

He lived and worked in New York City and Tuckahoe, New York for most of his life. In the early 1890s he wrote and illustrated several articles for *Harper's Weekly* and between May of 1895 and December of 1909 he did over 170 illustrations for *The American Kennel Club Gazette.* Between 1880 and 1894, Muss-Arnolt was a frequent contributor to the National Academy of Design annual exhibitions.

Little is known about his life, though it is known he was involved with conformation dogs as well as field trial dogs. He was on the board of directors of The American Kennel Club between 1906 and 1909.

Page 15; Plates 290, 299, 301, 311, 312, 317.

William NEDHAM, English, fl.1823-1849

Plate 48.

Robert NIGHTINGALE, English, 1815-1895

Colour Plate 63.

John Sargent NOBLE, R.B.A., English, 1848-1896

Little is known about this artist. He was noted for painting sporting scenes, especially gun-dogs and Otter Hounds, painting with a quick, sure hand and a rich palette.

He was a pupil of Sir Edwin Landseer and studied at the Royal Academy Schools. Noble exhibited forty-eight paintings at the R.A. from 1871 to 1895. Member R.B.A. 1872.

Plates 162, 163, 244; Colour Plate 27.

Edmund Henry OSTHAUS, German-American, 1858-1928

Born in Hildesheim, Germany, Osthaus studied at the Royal Academy of Arts in Dusseldorf between 1874 and 1882, immigrating to the United States in 1883. He was the director of the Toledo Academy of Fine Arts between 1886 and 1893, when he left to devote himself full-time to painting, shooting and following field trials. He was a charter member of the National Field Trial Association formed at Newton, North Carolina, in November 1895.

Working in both watercolour and oils, Osthaus's portrayal of sporting dogs became well known.

Plate 298; Colour Plates 141, 142, 146.

Jean-Baptiste OUDRY, French, 1686-1755

Plate 21; Colour Plate 4.

George PAICE, English, fl.1878-1900

Plates 124, 133.

Frank PATON, English, 1856-1909

Paton worked in London and Gravesend, painting animals and genre in a tight, detailed style. His work is characterised by the inclusion of myriad details depicted with an almost photographic realism.

He painted in both oils and watercolour, with subject matter varying from straightforward portraits of dogs to hunting scenes of dogs after game. He exhibited some twenty works at the R.A.

Plates 69, 138, 232.

John PAUL, English, 1820-1890
Plate 56.

Charles Olivier de PENNE, French, 1831-1897
Colour Plate 46.

Eugene PETIT, French, 19th century
Plate 106.

PISANELLO (Antonio Pisano), Italian, c.1395-c.1455
Plate 8.

Henry Rankin POORE, American, 1859-1940
Plates 285, 302.

Alexander POPE, American, 1849-1924
Plate 296.

Samuel RAVEN, English, 1775-1847
Colour Plate 17.

Karl REICHERT, Austrian, 1836-1919
Plate 221.

Philip REINAGLE, R.A., Scottish, 1749-1833

Of Hungarian parentage, Philip Reinagle was one of the best of the sporting artists who depicted dogs in late nineteenth century Britain. In 1769 he travelled to England where he enrolled at the Royal Academy Schools. Early in his career he painted portraits, but soon came to specialise in depicting birds, dogs and horses, often presented in an extensive landscape.

Reinagle is perhaps best known in the world of dog painting for the series of twenty-four paintings executed by him which were engraved by J. Scott for *The Sportsman's Cabinet* completed between 1803 and 1804. His interest in landscape is evident in these portrayals, a genre which he subsequently concentrated on to the exclusion of animal paintings.

Reinagle exhibited extensively at the R.A., showing some 114 works.

Plates 26, 27, 37, 53, 64, 73, 80, 115, 116, 161, 167, 187, 212; Colour Plate 60.

Richard Ramsey REINAGLE, English, 1775-1862
Plate 177; Colour Plates 26, 51.

Sir Joshua REYNOLDS, P.R.A., English, 1723-1792
Plate 184.

Briton RIVIERE, R.A., R.E., English, 1840-1920

Riviere received his artistic training at Cheltenham College under J. Pettie and W. Orchardson. The majority of his work is of historical or genre subject matter, but he often introduced animals into his scenes. Riviere's depictions of single dogs are rare (most were somewhat anecdotal in nature), his reputation being established by the many prints which were taken from them.

Riviere was popular during his lifetime, exhibiting some 108 works at the R.A.
Colour Plate 78.

F.W. ROGERS, English, late 19th century
Plate 132.

Percival Leonard ROSSEAU, American, 1859-1937

Born about thirty miles north of Baton Rouge, Louisiana, Rosseau's early adulthood was spent in developing a business which provided him with a financial base. Once established, he enrolled at the Académie Julien in Paris where he stayed for three years.

Influenced by friends who painted in the tradition of the Barbizon School, he exhibited a painting of Setters at the Salon of 1904. From that point on he devoted himself entirely to the painting of dogs, including a picture of a panther hunt which was awarded a Gold Medal at the Salon of 1906.

Rosseau's best pictures exhibit a loose painting style which captured the tense action of the sporting dogs which he painted. More than his contemporaries Muss-Arnolt and Edmund Osthaus, he was very concerned about the quality of light in a painting, and many are enhanced by the subtle depiction of its changing qualities.
Plates 291, 297, 300; Colour Plate 145.

Harry ROUNTREE, English, 1878-1950
Plate 266.

Philippe ROUSSEAU, French, 1816-1887
Colour Plate 33.

Peter Paul RUBENS, Flemish, 1577-1640
Plate 17.

J.R. RYOTT
Plate 29.

John Nost SARTORIUS, English, 1759-1828
Plates 88, 117.

Charles Henry SCHWANFELDER, English, 1773/4-1837
Plates 98, 99.

Edith A. SIMKINS, English, exh. 1896-1913
Plate 257.

Herbert G. SIMON, American, 1846-1893
Colour Plate 144.

H. Hardy SIMPSON, English, fl.1882
Colour Plate 14.

F. SINET, English, fl. 1907
Plate 240.

Josef SMITZBERGER, German, b. 1851
Colour Plate 118.

Kole SOWERBY, English, 19th century
Plate 70.

Samuel SPODE, English, fl.1825-1858
Colour Plate 18.

Arthur James STARK, English, 1831-1902
Plate 49.

Gourlay STEELL, R.S.A., Scottish, 1819-1894

Currently an underrated artist, Gourlay Steell was born in Edinburgh where he trained at the Edinburgh Galleries and the Board of Manufacturers. Steel was a brilliant technician, especially in watercolour, and his talent was recognised by Queen Victoria who, in 1874, after the death of Sir Edwin Landseer, appointed him Animal Painter for Scotland. He was also appointed painter of the Highland and Agricultural Society.

While now remembered primarily for his royal connections, Steell was a highly accomplished artist who, although he did complete some historical and genre subjects, was best known for his depictions of dogs. He exhibited some 22 works at the R.A.

Plates 154, 208, 209, 224; Colour Plate 20.

Carl STEFFECK, German, fl. 19th century
Plate 55.

W.J. STEVENSON, English, 19th century
Plate 149.

George Vernon STOKES, English, 1873-1954
Colour Plate 91.

D.G. STOUTER, American, fl.1840
Colour Plate 138.

Philip Eustace STRETTON, English, fl. 1884-1919

Born in London, Stretton was an accomplished animal artist who painted chiefly dogs and sporting subjects. His paintings, often exhibiting a sentimental side, were executed with a loose painterly style during a period when most of his contemporaries were painting in a much more finished way. He exhibited some eighteen works at the R.A.

Plates 51, 155, 222, 223; Colour Plate 119.

George STUBBS, A.R.A., English, 1724-1806

Recognised as the best horse painter in England during a period when horse and sporting artists abounded, Stubbs's work was not exclusively of horses. He also painted exotic animals, and his dog portraits make up a substantial body of work.

The son of a Liverpool tanner, Stubbs received little academic training but from an early age showed an interest in anatomy. Indeed, he lectured on human anatomy to students at York Hospital, and after visiting Italy in 1754, spent four years working on one of his most successful projects: *The Anatomy of the Horse.*

This understanding of anatomy is evident throughout Stubbs's work, and his many depictions of the horses and dogs of the English gentry established him as the premier animal painter of his time. His portraits of animals, although realistically portrayed, are highly finished and have a monumental almost timeless quality. He exhibited 53 works at the R.A. between 1775 and 1803.

Plate 79.

Arthur Fitzwilliam TAIT, English, 1819-1905

Tait, one of the best known of America's early sporting artists, was born in Liverpool. He studied at The Manchester Royal Institute and completed a number of animal paintings in England before emigrating to the United States in 1850.

In America he became best known for his paintings of the sporting life of the Adirondacks, a vast and largely unsettled sportsman's paradise in northern New York. Like many of his contemporaries in England, his reputation was established by prints of his work, in his case being produced by Currier and Ives. He was elected an associate of the National Academy in 1853.

While Tait did paint a few pet dogs, the bulk of his canine work was of Pointers and Setters working in the field.

Plate 294; Colour Plates 139, 140.

Stephen TAYLOR, English, fl.1817-1837
Plate 100.

TITIAN (Tiziano Vecellio), Italian, c.1487-1576
Plate 9.

O.A. TOMPKINS, fl. 1860
Plate 31.

Charles TOWNE, English, 1763-1840

While Charles Towne is known predominantly as a horse painter, he did execute several portraits of sporting dogs. Born in Wigan, he worked briefly with the landscapist John Rathbone before working in Manchester as a coach painter and japanner.

Towne established himself on his own as a painter at the age of seventeen and worked in London and Essex before settling in Liverpool where he added the 'e' to his name. He was a meticulous painter, depicting in great detail all the aspects of his subject. Unlike many of his contemporaries, he also paid a great deal of attention to the landscapes around his subject matter. Greatly influenced by Dutch landscape painters, the trees and surrounding landscape in Towne's paintings are rendered with a tight almost obsessive attention to detail. He showed seven paintings at the R.A.

Plates 54, 76, 118; Colour Plates 12, 69.

John M. TRACY, American, 1843-1893

Tracy was one of a handful of American artists who, in the late nineteenth century, specialised in sporting dogs. Like Rosseau and Osthaus, he often painted sporting dogs working in the field, often within an extensive landscape.

He attended Oberlin College and Northwestern University of Chicago, but between 1867 and 1868 studied at the Ecole des Beaux Arts in Paris. Initially a painter of landscapes, he also exhibited a full-length portrait of his wife at the Salon of 1874.

In 1881 Tracy moved to Greenwich, Connecticut, where he painted the majority of the sporting dog paintings for which he became known. He later moved to Ocean Springs, Mississippi.

Plate 295.

William Hamilton Henry TROOD, English, 1850-1889
Plate 127; Colour Plates 13, 80, 82.

Malcolm S. TUCKER, English, fl.1893
Plate 194.

William E. TURNER, English, c.1820-1885
Plate 92.

Anne VALLAYER-COSTUS, French, 1844-1818
Plate 211.

Sir Anthony VAN DYCK, Flemish, 1599-1641
Plates 35, 41.

Jan VAN EYCK, Flemish, 1390-1441
Plate 14.

Diego VELAZQUEZ, Spanish, 1599-1660
Plate 11.

R.A. VENABLES, English, fl.1844-1846
Plate 197.

Paulo VERONESE, Italian, 1528-1588
Plate 10.

Paul de VOS, Flemish, 1596-1678
Plate 16.

W.H., English, fl.1870
Colour Plate 109.

Lucy WALLER, English, late 19th century
Colour Plate 102.

James WARD, R.A., English, 1769-1859

Ward was an artist of great skill whose individual style distinguished him from his contemporaries. While capable of more directly realistic work, many of his depictions of animals are executed in a linear style which echoes the overall mood of the painting.

A pupil of his brother William, Ward was later apprenticed to Raphael Smith, the engraver. He was influenced by his brother-in-law, George Morland, but eventually developed his own particular style. In 1794 he was appointed Painter and Mezzotint Engraver to the Prince of Wales. He was also commissioned by the Agriculture Society to paint some 200 portraits of native breeds of livestock, although, due to no fault of his own, the project was never completed.

Ward was made an A.R.A. in 1807 and a full member of the R.A. in 1811; he exhibited 287 works of art at the R.A.

Plate 89; Colour Plates 100, 133.

Arthur WARDLE, R.I., R.B.C., P.S., English, 1864-1949

Wardle is best known for his paintings of dogs, and in particular, Terriers, but throughout his life he painted a great variety of wild and domestic animals. He evidently had very little formal training, but he studied live animals at the London Zoo and became an animal artist of considerable talent.

He was equally proficient in oils, watercolour and pastel, and became Member P.S. 1911 and R.I. 1922. He exhibited at the R.A. from 1880 to 1938, showing some 113 works.

Plates 95, 123, 127, 130, 137, 139, 145, 159, 228, 251, 252, 253, 256, 277, 278, 283; Colour Plates 28, 15, 56, 75, 83, 86, 87, 88, 89, 92, 93, 94, 108, 128.

Benjamin WEST, American, 1738-1820
Plate 287.

Richard WESTALL, English, 1766-1836
Plate 198.

E. WILLIS, English, 1808-1899
Plate 82.

William WISSING, Dutch, 1656-1687
Plate 71.

William Arnold WOODHOUSE, English, 1857-1935

A Lancashire artist born near Morecambe, Woodhouse rarely left the area where he was born. He developed a soft realistic style which was well suited to the depiction of animals. He

contributed many works to the Lancashire Art Exhibitions, and entered two at the R.A.
Colour Plate 68.

John WOOTTON, English, c.1682-1764

Wootton was a pupil, and later assistant, to Jan Wyck, the painter of battle and hunting scenes. After Wyck's death in 1702, Wootton established himself at Newmarket where by 1714 he had made a great reputation with the nobility as a painter of horse portraits and racing scenes on the Heath.

In 1721 Wootton travelled to Rome, a trip which was to influence his painting. The artist was exposed to the great classical art of Rome and, upon his return, he in effect became the founder of a school of sporting art. He did more than merely portray the anatomy of a horse or dog, for he often ennobled them by placing them in a classical landscape.

Plates 112, 113, 176; Colour Plate 5.

George WRIGHT, English, 1860-1942

Plate 110.

Selected Bibliography

Arkwright, William, ***The Pointer and his Predecessors: An Illustrated History of the Pointing Dog from the Earliest Times,*** London 1902.

This book, lavishly illustrated with paintings by Maud Earl, represents a collaboration between the artist and the noted Pointer authority William Arkwright. A trade edition was also produced. This book is of importance both for information on the breed and as a visual record of many of Earl's paintings.

Ash, Edward C., ***Dogs: Their History and Development,*** 2 vols., London 1927.

This set provides some of the most authoritative information on the history of various breeds. It is illustrated with hundreds of reproductions of old engravings and provides an introduction to the visual history of each breed.

Barnes, Duncan and the staff of The American Kennel Club (eds.), ***The AKC's World of the Pure Bred Dog,*** New York 1983.

Published to coincide with the Centennial of The American Kennel Club in 1984, this volume offers a variety of information to those interested in the pure-bred dog. More importantly, however, it includes a concise survey of the dog in art by Shirlee Kalstone, as well as illustrations of several dog paintings in the collection of The American Kennel Club.

Bylandt, Comte Henri de, ***Dogs of all Nations: their varieties, characteristics, points, etc.,*** Vol.1: Sporting Dogs, Vol.2: Non-Sporting Dogs, first published Brussels 1897. Text in English, German and Dutch.

This is one of the most comprehensive dog books to be published and was produced in several editions. Its two volumes are written in several languages and present information on some 316 breeds. Extensively illustrated in black and white, it reproduces many dog paintings by English and continental artists, sometimes identifying the specific dog depicted.

Caius, Johannes, ***Joannis Caii Britanni de Canibus Britannicis, Liber Unus. De Rariorum Animalium, et Stirpium Historia, Liber Unus. De Libris Propiis, Liber Unus. Iam Priumu Excusi,*** London 1570.

This is the first dog book ever to be printed. Printed throughout in Latin, it was not until six years later, in 1576, that Abraham Fleming published his famous translation *On Englishe Dogges.*

Caius, Johannes, ***Of Englishe Dogges, the Diversities, the Names, the Natures, and the Properties:*** *A Short Treatise written in Latin by Johannes Caius of late memory, Doctor of Physicke in the Universitie of Cambridge, and newly drawne into Englishe by Abraham Fleming, Student.*

Published London 1880, this is the second edition, originally published in 1576, by Abraham Fleming, of the English language version of Doctor Caius's important work.

Collier, V.W.F., ***Dogs of China and Japan in Nature and Art,*** London 1921.

This work is beautifully illustrated with black and white and colour reproductions of art works of oriental breeds. Even after some seventy years it still provides some of the most authoritative information on the Pekingese, the Japanese Chin and the Chow-Chow.

Cox, Harding (ed.), ***Dogs: by Well-Known Authorities,*** London 1906-1908.

Published in a series of ten parts, the series makes up two of the four volumes which were originally planned. While unfinished, these over-sized volumes on Terriers, Hounds and Coursing dogs were edited by the eminent dog historian Harding Cox, and represent a great visual resource. Each instalment is lavishly illustrated in colour and black and white by such artists as Thomas Blinks, Margaret Collyer, Maud Earl, John Emms, Frances C. Fairman and Arthur Wardle.

Edwards, Sydenham, ***Cynographia Britannica:*** *consisting of coloured engravings of the various breeds of dogs existing in Great Britain; drawn from the life, with observations on their Properties and Uses,* London 1800-1805.

One of the most important of all dog books, this volume was originally published in parts between 1800 and 1805 but never completed. It is beautifully illustrated with hand-coloured engravings of dogs from 1799, which in some cases provide the earliest identified depiction of the breed.

Farman, Edgar, ***The Bulldog,*** London 1899.

Although published in 1899, this volume is a model which modern monographs might well imitate. Beautifully illustrated with photographs of the breed as well as reproductions of early paintings and prints, it leaves no stone unturned in its study of the origins and development of this, perhaps the most English of all breeds. It includes important sections on the history of the breed, early dog shows and the early history of the English Bulldog Club.

Fountain, Robert and Gates, Alfred, ***Stubbs' Dogs,*** London 1984.

In addition to a discussion of the artist and his many dog paintings, this book includes a fascinating series of essays on the dog in eighteenth century England.

Hutchinson, Walter (ed.), ***Hutchinson's Dog Encyclopaedia,*** 3 vols., London 1934-1935.

This three-volume work has information on breeds of dogs from many countries, including advice on their care and treatment by some of the most eminent authorities of the day. The volumes are extensively illustrated with many dog paintings reproduced to illustrate the development of the various breeds.

Jackson (Frank), ***Crufts, The Official History,*** London 1990.

This very thorough volume traces the origins of Crufts, one of the most famous of all dog shows. Published to coincide with the centennial of Crufts Dog Show, it offers specialised information for the serious student of dog show history.

Jaquet, Edward William, ***The Kennel Club: A History and Record of its Work.*** London 1905.

A specialised history, this volume is invaluable to the student of early dogs and dog show history. Many early dog paintings were commissioned by prominent nineteenth century dog fanciers, and Jacquet discusses these fanciers as well as their place in the early history of dog shows and the development of The Kennel Club. It includes numerous portraits and illustrations.

Jesse, Edward, ***Anecdotes of Dogs,*** London 1846.

The work is important because the some twenty engravings, mainly by W.R. Smith, give an exact representation of breeds as they were in 1846. This is the last dog book to be illustrated by copper or steel engravings.

Kennel Club, ***The Kennel Club's Illustrated Breed Standards,*** London 1989.

Unlike its American counterpart, this volume illustrates the breeds in full colour, a feature which enhances the overall appeal of the book. Each breed recognised by The Kennel Club is briefly discussed, and the official standard for each breed described.

Ladies' Kennel Journal, The, London, 1896-1898.

This series, produced in the late nineteenth century, includes fascinating essays on dog shows and 'doggy' people, including reports about important dog shows and news of importance to lady exhibitors. The series on Queen Victoria's Kennels at Windsor, as well as those of the Prince of Wales at Sandringham, give many clues to the important role which dogs played in the life of the royal family.

Lane, C.H., ***Dog Shows and Doggy People,*** London 1902.

This fascinating little book is a compendium of sketches or essays on 'doggy' people of some social standing. Illustrated with photographs of the owners and/or their dogs, it provides great insight into dogs, dog shows and 'doggy people' around the turn of the century.

Lee, Rawdon B., ***A History and Description of the Modern Dogs of Great Britain and Ireland:*** Vol.1 Sporting Division; Vol. 2 Non-Sporting; Vol. 3 Terriers, illustrations by Arthur Wardle and R.H. Moore, London 1893 and 1894.

This is considered by most to be the last really important work on dogs published in the nineteenth century, the author's classification of breeds being subsequently adopted by The Kennel Club. While giving his own opinion on the history of the various breeds, Lee went to a great deal of trouble in verifying facts, and his book goes into detail about important breeders.

Leighton, Robert (ed.), ***The New Book of the Dog,*** London 1907.

This beautifully produced and authoritative book offers a comprehensive natural history of British and foreign dogs. It provides chapters on law, breeding, kennel management and veterinary treatment and includes many illustrations of famous dogs, paintings and prints.

Lytton, Judith Anne, Baroness Wentworth, ***Toy Dogs and Their Ancestors,*** London 1911.

Includes reproductions of early paintings and prints placing the English Toy Spaniel, Japanese Chin, Pekingese and Pomeranian in a historical context. Most of the volume is dedicated to the author's breed, the English Toy Spaniel, and it is particularly rich in paintings which illustrate it.

Mandeville, John and Sidewater, Ab (ed.), ***The Complete Dog Book,*** New York 1985, 17th edition.

The standard reference for breeds recognised by The American Kennel Club, this volume illustrates each breed, briefly describes its history, and provides the official standard for each breed admitted to AKC registration. The chapters on the selection, training, care and feeding of pure-bred dogs are helpful, especially for the novice. However, the histories of the breeds which are provided along with the official standard are somewhat impressionistic at best. While some are better than others, many must be read with a good deal of healthy scepticism.

O'Neill, Charles A.T. and the Staff of The American Kennel Club (eds.), ***The American Kennel Club, 1884-1984, A Source Book,*** New York 1985.

The date in the title of this book clearly indicates its nature, for it is a history of The American Kennel Club, from its early activities in the 1880s through to the modern dog shows of the 1970s and beyond. While it does have an interesting essay on The Dog Museum of America, its most valuable section is that on the American Kennel Club Art Collection, listing each work of art with dates and sizes.

Opperman, Hal, ***J.B. Oudry, 1686-1755,*** Fort Worth 1983.

A catalogue for the exhibition at the Kimbell Art Museum in Fort Worth and travelling to the Nelson-Atkins Museum of Art in Kansas City, it is the best appraisal of an artist who set an important precedent for animal painting in the nineteenth century. It is well illustrated in black and white, with twenty-two works reproduced in full colour.

Ormond, Richard, ***Sir Edwin Landseer*** (with contributions by Joseph Rischel and Robin Hamlyn), London 1982.

A catalogue for the exhibition which originated at The Tate and travelled to Philadelphia, this is a key text for understanding not only the work of Sir Edwin Landseer, which was important in itself, but also his influence on other nineteenth century artists. Long considered by art historians to epitomise the sentimental aspects of nineteenth century painting, Landseer's work has here achieved serious academic consideration.

Ritvo, Harriet, ***The Animal Estate: The English and other Creatures in The Victorian Age,*** Cambridge, Massachusetts, 1987.

This is a fascinating study of the role of the animal in Victorian England. Of particular interest is the section on 'Prize Pets' in which the author looks at the evolution of the pure-bred dog in England from the viewpoint of a social historian.

Rosenblum, Robert, ***The Dog in Art from Rococo to Post-Modernism,*** New York 1988.

A delightful book by the noted art historian Robert Rosenblum. Images of the dog abound, painted in every style, from the refined realism of Oudry to the schematic renderings of the twentieth century artist Keith Haring. While tracing the history of the dog in art over three centuries, Rosenblum's thoughtful insights point the reader in new and unexpected directions.

Shaw, Vero, ***The Illustrated Book of the Dog,*** London 1881.

This encyclopaedia of dogs covers some sixty-nine breeds with sections on canine medicine and surgery. However, its well-deserved reputation is based on its illustrations: twenty-eight full colour illustrations of celebrated dogs as well as numerous woodcut engravings. Originally published in parts 1879-1881.

Smith, A. Croxton, ***The Power of the Dog,*** London 1911.

This lavishly produced volume includes essays by Harding Cox on twenty different breeds, each of which is accompanied by a tipped-in colour reproduction of one of Maud Earl's paintings.

Taplin, W., ***The Sportsman's Cabinet: or, A Correct Delineation of Various Dogs Used in the Sports of the Field; including the Canine Race in General. Consisting of a Series of Engravings of Every Distinct Breed, from Original Paintings, taken from Life,*** London 1803-1804.

This book is a landmark in the history of dog books, for, in addition to discussing the various breeds which existed around the turn of the nineteenth century, it includes twenty-four fine copperplate engravings by John Scott after the animal artist Philip Reinagle, R.A., as well as numerous vignettes by Thomas Bewick. Reproductions of these engravings appear again and again in subsequent books on the dog.

Vesey-Fitzgerald, Brian (ed.), ***The Book of the Dog,*** London 1948.

This was the first general dog book of any importance to be published after the Second World War. It includes essays by many leading authorities of the day, including a well illustrated section on the history of the dog by A. Croxton Smith.

Walsh, John Henry, ***The Dog in Health and Disease: Comprising the Various Modes of Breaking him for Hunting, Coursing, Shooting, etc., and including the Points and Characteristics of Toy Dogs,*** London 1859.

This is one of the most famous of the Victorian dog books, and one of the first on dogs to give points of the breeds and portraits of dogs at the time.

Walsh, John Henry (ed.), ***The Dogs of the British Islands,*** a series of articles and letters by various contributors, reprinted from *The Field,* London 1867.

The earliest book on dogs to contain the opinions of numerous breeders on their respective breeds. It includes twenty-nine woodcut engravings of important dogs. Edited by 'Stonehenge', a pseudonym for John Henry Walsh.

Watson, James, ***The Dog Book: A Popular History of the Dog, with Practical Information as to Care and Management of House, Kennel, and Exhibition Dogs: and Descriptions of All the Important Breeds,*** 2 vols., London 1906.

First published in America in 1905, this book provides extensive historical information on the various breeds, and reproduces many early depictions of the dog in art.

Index

Page numbers in italics indicate paintings of dogs.